SAME OLD SONG

American Made Music Series

Advisory Board

David Evans, General Editor
Barry Jean Ancelet
Edward A. Berlin
Joyce J. Bolden
Rob Bowman
Curtis Ellison
William Ferris
John Edward Hasse
Kip Lornell
Bill Malone
Eddie S. Meadows
Manuel H. Peña
Wayne D. Shirley
Robert Walser

SAME OLD SONG

The Enduring Past in Popular Music

John Paul Meyers

University Press of Mississippi / Jackson

The University Press of Mississippi is the scholarly publishing agency of
the Mississippi Institutions of Higher Learning: Alcorn State University,
Delta State University, Jackson State University, Mississippi State University,
Mississippi University for Women, Mississippi Valley State University,
University of Mississippi, and University of Southern Mississippi.

www.upress.state.ms.us

Portions of chapter 3 were originally published as "Standards and Signification between Jazz and Fusion: Miles Davis and 'I Fall in Love Too Easily,' 1963–1970" in *Jazz Perspectives* 9, no. 2 (2015). My thanks to Taylor & Francis Ltd, http://www.tandfonline.com, for allowing me to reuse this work.

Portions of the introduction and chapter 1 were originally published in *Ethnomusicology* 59, no. 1 (Winter 2015). My thanks to the Society for Ethnomusicology for allowing me to reuse this work.

The University Press of Mississippi is a member
of the Association of University Presses.

Copyright © 2024 by University Press of Mississippi
All rights reserved

∞

Library of Congress Cataloging-in-Publication Data

Names: Meyers, John Paul, author.
Title: Same old song : the enduring past in popular music / John Paul
  Meyers.
Other titles: American made music series.
Description: Jackson : University Press of Mississippi, 2024. | Series:
  American made music series | Includes bibliographical references and
  index.
Identifiers: LCCN 2023054133 (print) | LCCN 2023054134 (ebook) | ISBN
  9781496850867 (hardback) | ISBN 9781496850874 (trade paperback) | ISBN
  9781496850881 (epub) | ISBN 9781496850898 (epub) | ISBN 9781496850904
  (pdf) | ISBN 9781496850911 (pdf)
Subjects: LCSH: Popular music—United States—History and criticism. |
  African Americans—Music—History and criticism. | Rap (Music)—History
  and criticism. | Davis, Miles—Criticism and interpretation. | Tribute
  bands (Musical groups) | Nostalgia in music.
Classification: LCC ML3477 .M507 2024 (print) | LCC ML3477 (ebook) |
  DDC
  782.421642092/2—dc23/eng/20231207
LC record available at https://lccn.loc.gov/2023054133
LC ebook record available at https://lccn.loc.gov/2023054134

British Library Cataloging-in-Publication Data available

CONTENTS

vii   Acknowledgments
3   Introduction

21   **CHAPTER 1**
Twenty Years Ago Today: Tribute Bands and Historical Consciousness in Popular Music

49   **CHAPTER 2**
Yesterdays: Performing the Past Through the Great American Songbook from Ella Fitzgerald to Bob Dylan

89   **CHAPTER 3**
Memories and Standards: Miles Davis and "I Fall in Love Too Easily," 1963–1970

117   **CHAPTER 4**
Old School: Sampling, Re-Playing, and Re-Hearing the 1970s in Hip-Hop

145   **CHAPTER 5**
"I Just Wanna Go Back, Baby, Back to the Way It Was": The Past, Activism, and Recent Black Popular Music

179   Conclusion
189   Notes
217   Bibliography
231   Index

ACKNOWLEDGMENTS

This is a long book about many different genres and decades of American popular music. Writing it drew on twenty-five years of playing, listening to, and talking about music with just about everyone in my life. Parts of that time have been stressful, no doubt, but it has also been an incredible luxury to live a life in thinking, teaching, and writing about music.

I want to first thank my parents, Paul Meyers and Deborah Holzwarth, for their love and support—and for footing the bill for music lessons and instruments. My sisters Elizabeth, Rachel, and Becky have provided hospitality, baked goods, and rides from the airport. Their homes have also been amazing places to rest and recharge on breaks from academic life. Myra Swanger has been an absolute delight to get to know and is a brilliant pianist. Clark Holzwarth grills the best steaks in Arizona. I acquired a second family in the Fairbairn clan. Many thanks to Hannah, Neil, Madeleine, and Robbie Guertin for taking good care of us when we go to California. As an ethnomusicologist, I had no idea that I would be in a tight three-way race with a former indie rock star and a professional bassoonist for "weirdest musical interest" in the family.

Thanks to the music teachers who got me started and encouraged me to think about and experiment with music, Brian Tessmann and Diane Townsend, especially. My thanks to everyone I played with and talked obsessively about music with back in North Dakota, including Josh Cushing, Daniel Gillispie, and Sarah Legowski.

My professors at Columbia opened up my ears and shook me out of my preconceptions; I owe a large debt of gratitude to Sebastian Currier, Aaron Fox, George Lewis, Robert O'Meally, Peter Susser, and Chris Washburne. When I was a student at Columbia, the Louis Armstrong Educational Foundation provided funds to have a visiting professor of jazz studies. I was lucky to study with three very different but all brilliant jazz scholars: Stanley Crouch, John Szwed, and Sherrie Tucker. Michael Skelly taught me a ton about music in one-hour increments every week for four years. I also met the woman I would marry at an informal piano recital he arranged in Dodge Hall.

The best times that I had at Columbia were with the people I met. Nicole Bryant, Lauren Mancia, and Pat Young were my friends from the beginning and have stayed my friends for twenty years. I gained a lot of practical experience in music with Rocky Jones, Mike Kraft, Averill Leslie, Liz Maynes-Aminzade, Claire Snyder, and Mahesh Somashekhar. More importantly, I had a blast writing songs, playing gigs, and hauling our equipment between cramped dorm rooms and rehearsal spaces.

In graduate school at the University of Pennsylvania, I was fortunate to benefit from an amazing group of mentors and teachers. I especially want to thank my main advisor, Carol Muller, and my two committee members, Guthrie Ramsey and Timothy Rommen. Most of my best ideas were worked out in close consultation with Carol, but maybe the best testimony to her influence is that I find myself repeating advice that she gave to me fifteen years ago to my own students now. Guy and Tim provided incredible examples of people doing sharp, thoughtful, and open-hearted research into music of the Americas.

Equally as important as my professors were my fellow graduate students who formed part of a very supportive intellectual community, including Charles Carson, Jessamyn Doan Ewing, Roger Grant, Monique Ingalls, Jennifer Kyker, Deirdre Loughridge, Evelyn Malone, Elizabeth Mellon, Peter Mondelli, Jennie Noakes, Greg Robinson, Jennifer Ryan, and Emily Zazulia. I especially would not have made it through seminars, fieldwork, and exams without the friendship and insights from my ethnomusicology cohort: Darien Lamen, Ian MacMillen, and Gavin Steingo.

In Pittsburgh, while my wife was in graduate school, I taught piano lessons, ran marathons, and played in a samba band. It was a nice way to spend a few years. And I got to meet some great people, including all of my friends in Timbeleza, Carrie Gibson, Mike Sayers, Andrea Weinstein, and Tim Verstynen.

I spent the 2014–2015 year at Michigan State University. My thanks to Ken Prouty for his mentorship and to Joanna Bosse and Chris Scales for showing me the ropes around RCAH and driving with me to a Stevie Wonder concert in Detroit on a cold night in November.

Since 2015, I have been at the University of Illinois at Urbana-Champaign and I have benefitted from a tremendous amount of resources, intellectual community, and incredible friends. Some of the ideas for this book first percolated during a First Book Writing Group workshop organized by the Office of the Vice Chancellor for Research. Thanks to Maria Gillombardo for facilitating that group and to some of the faculty members who gave their time and mentorship, including

Carol Symes and Craig Koslofsky. Through that group I also met a dear friend, Glen Goodman, who hosted the best dinner parties in town before he departed for the warmer climate of his native Arizona. Luckily, his culinary skills and treasure trove of 1960s and 1970s LPs have relocated within a reasonable driving distance of my mother's home and the Musical Instrument Museum in Phoenix.

The African American Studies department at Illinois has been my home, and I have to particularly thank my former department head Ronald Bailey for seeing potential in me as a scholar and a teacher. I also want to express my gratitude for conversations, guidance, and camaraderie to Merle Bowen, Eddie O'Byrn, Faye Harrison, Irvin Hunt, Candice Jenkins, Erik McDuffie, Bobby J. Smith, and Alexia Williams. And I cannot thank Desirée McMillion enough for her friendship, support, and knowledge. Thanks also to my colleagues across the street in the School of Music: Donna Buchanan, Gayle Magee, Michael Silvers, and Gabriel Solis (now of the University of Washington).

Working with University Press of Mississippi has been fantastic. Craig Gill deftly navigated this manuscript through pandemic delays and disruptions. Amy Atwood, Joey Brown, Todd Lape, and Laura Strong have all shown great care and professionalism with this book. Will Rigby did an excellent and thorough job as a copyeditor. I also want to thank a couple of scholars whom I called on late in the process for their expertise: Jeff Magee, Tracie McMullen, Thomas Patteson, and Nate Sloan. Of course, any errors or misconceptions in the text remain my responsibility.

In Illinois, we have been fortunate to find a great group of friends, and I highly doubt I would have finished this book without going on bike rides with Chadly Stern and Nigel Bosch, watching *Star Trek* episodes and Minnesota Twins games with Andrea Miller and Aleks Ksiazkiewicz, or drinking fancy cocktails and eating desserts with our neighbors Diane Beck and Steve Drake. Eric Calderwood and Jamie Jones have been our traveling companions and dear friends—and also helped me navigate the book publication process at the exact same time that they did. Avital Livny and Ben Miller are our concert-going buddies and conspired to help throw the most overwhelming surprise birthday celebration a music scholar could ask for.

Matt Valnes has been my friend for a very long time, will be my friend for a long time in the future, and is the best person I know to talk about funk, live performance, and all things Prince with.

Of course, my last words of gratitude go to my wife Catharine Fairbairn. There is no way I could have written this book without her incredible love and support over the years. She provided a model of a graceful writer, deep thinker, and conscientious scholar. I hope that she will keep coming with me to concerts and research trips for the next book.

SAME
OLD
SONG

INTRODUCTION

Popular music in the United States is made and listened to by people from a variety of racial groups, ages, genders, sexualities, and regions, but it is often dominated by an ideology of newness. Since the early 2000s, some of the most popular television shows have been devoted to discovering young new artists ready to make a mark on the popular music world, including *American Idol*, *The Sing-Off*, *The Voice*, and *Rhythm and Flow*.[1] The Grammys give out an award for "Best New Artist" every year. And the most vibrant forms of popular music culture seem to be produced by and for the young: those with the facility for creating and consuming music using the latest technology, the free time to follow the latest trends, and the energy to stay out at night dancing to the latest hits. This description could apply to the popular music and youth culture of any decade from 1900 to the present day; the propensity toward newness is, itself, a quite old and persistent feature of popular music. As Elijah Wald summarizes:

> The pop music world that began with ragtime is fiercely democratic. Whatever its underlying commercial foundations, it claims to be the music of all America, rich and poor, country and city, black and white (and yellow, red, and brown, when it bothers to acknowledge such subtleties). The only gap it does not strive to bridge is that of age: Each shift of genre blazons the arrival of a new generation and threatens all doubters with the ignominy of hunching over their canes and mumbling impotent imprecations as youth dances by.[2]

Examples of this emphasis on newness, youth, and an uneasiness about aging or being old abound in the practices and discourses of various popular music genres. Hip-hop culture produces a new crop of very young stars seemingly every year, a trend that might be most dramatically apparent in the fact that "Young," "Baby," and especially "Lil" are ubiquitous parts of rap nicknames.[3] The tension between established, older (or old-at-heart) artists and their "Young" and "Lil" counterparts can be easily viewed in dueling social media posts on Instagram and Twitter, diss tracks, and interviews with self-appointed guardians of hip-hop culture like Pete Rock, J. Cole, and Joe Budden criticizing newer artists like Lil Yachty, Lil Pump, and Migos.[4] According to the genre's establishment gatekeepers, the sins of these younger artists are many. They use similar rap flows, their production styles deviate from classic hip-hop techniques (techniques which themselves are based on sampling soul and funk from the past), their lyrics address a narrow range of topics, and—perhaps most tellingly—they have limited knowledge of and fail to pay appropriate homage to the earlier acknowledged greats of the genre. Still, these musicians have taken on leading roles in hip-hop culture as best-selling artists and concert headliners, and older artists who release new albums can only rarely count on the kind of popular and critical attention routinely given to the new sounds created by younger artists.

Jay-Z's album 4:44 is probably the work of hip-hop culture most associated with getting older, reflecting on what he has learned as a middle-aged husband and father, and offering advice to his imagined younger self and to younger listeners and artists. The record was released in the summer of 2017, when Jay-Z was forty-seven, and entirely produced by the veteran hip-hop producer No I.D., who constructed the album's beats from the canon of African American music: "classic" R&B and gospel samples, including Stevie Wonder, Donny Hathaway, the Clark Sisters, and two songs that borrow from the music of Nina Simone.[5] The album was received fairly well by writers, critics, and those with established influential platforms to broadcast their thoughts about hip-hop culture—including college professors, such as myself.[6] As a longtime fan of Jay-Z and of No I.D.'s boom-bap, sample-based production style, I was excited to share 4:44 with the undergraduates in my history of hip-hop class in the fall of 2017.[7] My course was structured chronologically, so I saved this album until the final week, when I highlighted how Jay-Z's lyrics explored topics such as financial security over immediate gratification, emotional maturity, and thinking about one's family and legacy. The album also challenged some of the dominant ideas about Black masculinity in hip-hop—ideas that Jay-Z himself had been integral in creating in his earlier work, in songs like his notorious 1999 hit "Big Pimpin.'"[8] The teenagers and twenty-somethings in my class, however, were unimpressed by 4:44's aesthetically conservative production featuring samples from the 1960s and 1970s and did not think the lyrics about overcoming challenges in marriage, investing in expensive artwork, and passing money on to your children related to their lives. Instead, they much preferred releases by younger artists with more contemporary production styles and lyrics more concerned with dancing and partying. Their lack of interest mirrors the chart performance of *4:44*, which languished at #36 on the *Billboard* year-end list of Top 200 albums of 2017, behind a variety of younger hip-hop artists including Migos, Future, Post Malone, Travis Scott, Logic, Rae Sremmurd, Childish Gambino, and two different albums by Drake. If *4:44* was an attempt by Jay-Z and No I.D. to challenge the dominance of youth and newness in hip-hop, it was largely unsuccessful.

Hip-hop is far from the only genre of popular music to feature a bias toward newness and youth. One of rock's most well-known and genre-defining tracks, the Who's 1965 song "My Generation," triumphantly declares, "Hope I die before I get old!" In the Who's recorded version of the song, singer Roger Daltrey stutters through every other line in the verses *except* this one, giving it special emphasis as the only clearly pronounced lyric, the sentiment of which he (or at least, the song's protagonist) is apparently most confident. In the first decade of the 2000s, while I was doing fieldwork for my dissertation, I often heard this song performed live—perhaps with some irony—by middle-aged tribute band musicians for middle-aged audiences. Daltrey and Pete Townshend themselves—the only surviving original members of the Who—are in their late seventies now, and they still play this song on their sold-out, high-priced tours across the United States, Europe, and the rest of the world, more than fifty years after its original release.[9]

The ideology of newness is indeed alive and well in rock, hip-hop, and in other areas of popular music, but this is an ideology with a long history, dating back far longer than the 1960s and the rise of the baby boomer generation. Originality is one of the main defining aesthetic values of music in the West: a set of values that began as part of the discourse around Western classical music but has been adopted—sometimes skeptically, sometimes uncritically—by various genres of popular music culture, including jazz, rock, and hip-hop. This shift away from imitation toward an emphasis on originality occurred about two hundred years ago, but it is a shift whose ramifications remain influential today. Indeed, this emphasis on originality can be seen as one of the most enduring effects of the Enlightenment and political liberalism. Nascent versions of copyright law date from around this time period and are inextricably linked to the idea that one should be able to profit from one's individuality and creativity—thereby giving a financial incentive to the creation of identifiably "new" works, as opposed to the recycling of old ideas.[10] Starting around the mid-eighteenth century, as J. Peter Burkholder explains,

> originality and genius were considered central to the creative process . . . and by the early 19th century the invention of new melodies and new effects had

replaced the skillful manipulation of given material as the sign of a great composer. Only in the training of young composers did overt imitation still meet approval. Romanticism has no more profound source than this change in emphasis from the continuity and collectivity of a tradition sustained through imitation of exemplary models to the individualism of an artistic culture that prized genius, inspiration and innovation.[11]

As Burkholder's description suggests, it is easy to find this prizing of originality in discourse about both popular and classical music. The most respected musicians of the last two hundred years, classical or popular, whatever their genre, are typically written and talked about in very similar tones: as great artists breaking down the boundaries of what was acceptable in order to create new, original works of genius. Depending on their particular aesthetic disposition, scholars, critics, and ordinary listers may find originality either present or lacking in the music under discussion, but a general consensus exists in both the Western classical music world and the American popular music realm that originality is something to be valued. Copying and reuse exist in both the classical and popular music realms, of course, but ideologically speaking, they hold a very circumscribed place: apprenticeship and development. Indeed, this progression from imitation to originality is one that Burkholder finds when he notes that, in our postclassical era, imitation of earlier models or reworkings of earlier compositions is only acceptable for "the training of young composers."

Musicians, critics, and popular music listeners might not use the exact same words, but the process Burkholder is describing in Western classical music is the same in the popular music world, whether a young musician is copying the dance moves and vocal flourishes of a pop star, learning to duplicate every word and inflection from a favorite MC, or meticulously re-creating a rock guitar solo with friends in a garage band. Roy Shuker describes the hierarchy of prestige given to various types of musicians in popular music culture, with "auteurs and stars" ranked most highly—those who, accurately or inaccurately, are viewed as the authors or sole creators of their performances. They are followed, in turn, by "session musicians and house bands," "tribute bands," and then "cover bands."[12] In Shuker's analysis, creativity and control are the metrics in which success and importance can be viewed, with session musicians and house bands being directed on what they play by their employers (Shuker's "auteurs and stars"). Tribute bands and cover bands are even lower on Shuker's hierarchy because they not only do not create their own new music but also re-create and re-perform music from the past. Shuker's success continuum implicitly assumes that popular musicians will move from cover and tribute groups to being "auteurs and stars" as their artistic ability develops; that is, they will move from just copying and imitating the past to creating their own new music.

Even as they themselves age, critics and writers on popular music still exhibit this ideology of newness, fetishizing the new and the novel and criticizing artists they view as having fallen down the path of repeating themselves or offering nostalgia, instead of artistic innovation, to their audiences. While musicians who fail to progress to a stage of originality are largely ignored or given low prestige in the popular music world analyzed by Shuker, special scorn is reserved for musicians who were once deemed original, perhaps even revolutionary, but who have now regressed to endlessly repeating and copying themselves. As part of a spirited attack against what he calls "the decline from rebellion to nostalgia" in rock music, John Strausbaugh singles out Mick Jagger—and his audiences—for special criticism:

> If Mick Jagger wants to sit on a stool at the Blue Note and croak de blooz [sic] with Keith on an acoustic guitar, I wouldn't say a word. It's Mick butt-shaking and pretending to be really into "Satisfaction" for the millionth time that's unseemly. And it's what buying into this pretense does for us in the audience, we middle-aged boomers "recapturing the magic" of our teen years, that unsettles me.[13]

In Strausbaugh's formulation, there is a clear sense that some genres of music, like the acoustic blues (perhaps belonging to a static and mythical "folk" past), are a more natural fit for aging musicians, suitable to be endlessly replayed for nostalgic listeners. To recall Wald's definition of popular music culture, the blues is no longer a type of popular music; Mick and Keith might not be "hunching over their canes" in this imagined scenario, but they are comfortably perched on stools as "youth dances by." In this vision, the blues is an out-of-time, ahistorical style played by musicians who function as a kind of folk bard, with no greater ambition than enough whiskey to tide them over to their next performance.[14] Rock music, on the other hand, is viewed as inherently linked to youth, rebellion, change, revolution, and agency. There is also clearly a racial undercurrent in this discussion as well. While both the blues and rock are rooted in African American culture, rock has been "whitened," with its Black beginnings largely erased in contemporary critical discourse and popular imagination, in favor of a focus on whiteness and youth. The disapproval expressed by Strausbaugh at the idea that an aging Jagger would continue to "pretend to be really into 'Satisfaction' for the millionth time" is a common feature in the contemporary reception of older white rock musicians from the 1960s and 1970s who, more than fifty years later, are still performing their old hits on tours across the world, such as the Who, Paul McCartney, the Eagles, and Roger Waters.

Ironically, this idea that popular music should be new and revolutionary shares much in common with conservative critiques of popular music, which were, and are, often threatened by what they perceive as the music's newness and its break with prior musical and social conventions—particularly those conventions relating to hierarchies and roles of race and gender. This idea that popular music can be socially disruptive is a longstanding criticism of various genres of popular music over the last hundred years, including negative reaction to ragtime in the 1910s, jazz in the 1920s, rock 'n' roll in the 1950s, disco in the 1970s, and hip-hop in the 1980s.[15] All of these styles originated in African American culture and there was often a thinly veiled (or not-so-thinly veiled) racist fear of this music—and its accompanying dancing and sexualized or violent bodies—threatening society's established order and the "purity" of the white youth population. These critiques are not just a feature of some benighted past; they are a durable characteristic of how popular music is understood in the United States, and popular music's accepted associations with youth, newness, and revolutionary ideas is still an attitude that animates rejection of some popular music today. Consider, for example, the antifeminist denunciation of Janelle Monáe's 2018 song "Pynk" by the conservative media provocateur Ben Shapiro. Titled with the inflammatory language typical of social media clickbait— "Shapiro RIPS Obscene Feminist Music Video"—Shapiro is particularly troubled by the fact that the lyrics and music video for "Pynk" signal a new acceptance and celebration of the female body, female pleasure in sexuality, and relationships other than the accepted model of patriarchal heterosexuality.[16] (And I cannot blame Shapiro's criticism of Monáe solely on his age, since he is exactly a year and a day younger than I am.) For both its supporters and detractors, then, popular music has long been a setting on which both fantasies and fears about newness, youth, and artistic and societal change can be staged.

Yet despite this ideology of newness, this shared understanding that newness is a key defining trait of popular music, I have discovered a challenge to this idea in a variety of popular music scenes. I call this *historical consciousness in popular music*: a fundamental shift in the understanding of popular music that treats the events and artifacts of the popular music past as properly historical phenomena, not as trivial minutiae, obsolete, or irrelevant, as the ideology of newness would seem to dictate. In this book, I illuminate this important but little-understood aspect of popular music culture: a sense that the past in popular music is worth knowing about, remembering, celebrating, and, in various ways, re-playing. In the chapters that follow, I will trace this historical consciousness in many different genres of American popular music, across decades and demographics.

While my specific focus on historical consciousness in popular music is a new contribution, scholars in many different fields have been interested in the usage of the past not as a neutral record but as something that is invoked for different purposes by later subjects. In a discussion of cultural productions and their relationships to the past, the folklorist Barbara Kirshenblatt-Gimblett analyzes the idea of "heritage," emphasizing its construction in the present day by contemporary actors. She makes this intervention to counter the notion of heritage existing as a natural or universal consequence of the passage of time; for Kirshenblatt-Gimblett, artifacts or events do not become "heritage" merely because they gain chronological age. While she focuses on "heritage," one could productively substitute the related concepts of memory, history, and tradition into her analysis to understand how various uses of the past depend on agency and action in the present: "Heritage is not lost and found, stolen and reclaimed. Despite a discourse of conservation, preservation, restoration, reclamation, recovery, recreation, recuperation, revitalization, and regeneration, heritage produces something new in the present that has recourse to the past."[17] Kirshenblatt-Gimblett's notion of heritage has strong resonances with what in this book I explore as historical consciousness in popular music, something which, to borrow the definition quoted above, certainly qualifies as "something new in the present that has recourse to the past." Historical consciousness refers to the sense that, rather than being trivial or ephemeral, the popular music past is worth taking seriously, worth remembering, and worth celebrating.

At popular music museums, in magazines, and on television specials, "history" is being made from a specific subset of previous events that are only now being recognized as "historical" by people who have not been typically viewed as historians. The anthropologist Michel-Rolph Trouillot argued that historical narratives are produced by:

> not only professional historians, but ethnic and religious leaders, political appointees, journalists, and various associations within civil society as well as independent citizens.... This variety of narrators is one of many indications that theories of history have a rather limited view of the field of historical production. They grossly underestimate the size, the relevance, and the complexity of the overlapping sites where history is produced, notably outside of academia.[18]

Historical narratives in this sense refers not only to written and published books and articles, but also performances, commodities, souvenirs, discourse, and mental understandings of the meaning and importance of past events.

We can see historical consciousness in many areas of popular music culture, including the actions of sales and marketing executives in the record industry, ordinary listeners, and pop stars themselves. CD reissues or box sets chronicling an artist's career reflect a desire to memorialize popular culture and are consistent sellers for the industry at a time when sales of new music are in a digitally induced flux.[19] Impersonators and karaoke singers attempt to copy the nuances of the performances of beloved figures from the past.[20] A holographic appearance at the Coachella music festival in 2012 by the rapper Tupac Shakur was perhaps the most infamous "live" performance of the 2010s, despite the fact that Shakur had died nearly sixteen years prior.[21] As we have already seen, rock stars from the 1960s and 1970s still play—and audiences still pay top dollar to hear—their old hits in concert.[22] Elite universities like Harvard and Cornell host archives devoted to hip-hop and offer fellowships for its study; the rapper Nas has endowed one such fellowship.[23] Museums that display the material objects of the popular music past—like the Rock and Roll Hall of Fame in Cleveland, the Museum of Pop Culture in Seattle, and the Country Music Hall of Fame and Museum in Nashville—have become major tourist attractions in the United States and around the world.[24] All three of those institutions were purpose-built structures constructed in the 1990s by major architects to serve important roles in their respective cities' tourism and cultural infrastructures. However, even modest, utilitarian structures like the complex of houses that served as Motown's headquarters on West Grand Boulevard in Detroit and the former theater that housed Stax Records in Memphis have been repurposed as museums, because the music that was recorded there in the 1960s and 1970s is now belatedly viewed as historic and worthy of preservation and veneration.[25] As of this writing, a museum of hip-hop music is being planned to open in the genre's mythical birthplace in the South Bronx.

Depending on one's perspective, this repetition of and homage to popular music's past has been welcomed, warily accepted, or actively resisted—sometimes eliciting all three responses from the same person. The British music critic and historian Simon Reynolds describes this interest in popular music history in his 2011 book *Retromania: Pop Culture's Addiction to Its Own Past*. As suggested by the usage of the word "addiction" in the title and the obvious debt of his new term *retromania* to recognized mental illnesses like kleptomania and pyromania, Reynolds views this preoccupation with the past as a harmful tendency. For Reynolds, retromania afflicts various forms of popular culture (including fashion, theatre, television, and film), but he finds it

> most chronically prevalent in music. That may well be because it somehow feels especially *wrong* there. Pop ought to be all about the present tense, surely? It is

still considered the domain of the young, and young people aren't supposed to be nostalgic . . . the essence of pop is the exhortation to "be here now," meaning both "live like there's no tomorrow" *and* "shed the shackles of yesterday."[26]

Reynolds is voicing widely held notions about popular music's "rightful" associations with youth and the "present tense," that ideology of newness which, as we have seen above, is shared both by those who are supportive and critical of popular music. Yet for all his unease about looking backward to the past to serve needs in the present, Reynolds admits that he himself "pines for the future that's gone AWOL on us, but I also feel the lure of the past."[27] Given the widespread nature of retromania described in his book, it seems that many others feel this lure as well.

Tracy McMullen's *Haunthenticity: Musical Replay and the Fear of the Real* covers similar ground, focusing on live performances of musical reenactment as opposed to the related phenomena of museums, books, documentaries, compilations of recordings, and other commodities. She terms these live performances "Replay" and takes a critical stance toward these musical reenactments influenced by psychoanalytic theory and inspired by various epistemologies—African, African American, and Buddhist—that provide alternatives to what she sees as the dominant liberal or neoliberal worldviews ubiquitous in contemporary North America. For McMullen, the acts of Replay she observes in popular music culture starting in the mid-1990s stem from a deep fear of confronting death and loss; the inevitably of death and loss is a key component of what, borrowing a concept from Lacan, she terms the "Real." For McMullen, live performances of musical reenactment "speak to a time and place when security becomes a paramount concern . . . a world that both felt and was repeatedly described as fragmented, destabilized, and heading toward an uncertain new millennium."[28] Perhaps this sense of uncertainty felt by some in the West was also fed by the cataclysmic events of 9/11 and the 2008 financial crash, what critical theorist Slavoj Žižek, adapting Marx, has respectively called the "tragedy" and the "farce" of our recent history: events that present a dramatic challenge to the idea that subjectivity in the West will be characterized by a stable, bounded, safe, and financially secure sense of identity.[29] In her landmark study *The Future of Nostalgia*, Svetlana Boym notes: "Nostalgia inevitably reappears as a defense mechanism in a time of accelerated rhythms of life and historical upheavals."[30] The "reality" of death and loss are ever more present in our lives, so some listeners and musicians have turned to a fantasy of memories that cannot be forgotten, a musical past that can always be accessed, and nostalgia for a better and more stable time. They find these things, according to McMullen, in the performances of tribute bands like the Musical Box (a Canadian tribute to the British prog rock band Genesis) or re-creations of concerts by artists like the Glenn Miller Orchestra that, through acts of musical verisimilitude, might be able to re-create a fleeting sense of wholeness and stability.

Reynolds and McMullen are the two clearest antecedents in musical scholarship for this current project, and there is much to admire in their research. One key difference with this book is that I trace an interest in the popular music past in a wider temporal context. To be sure, the recent decades of the twentieth and twenty-first centuries have been a time when an interest in the past has been a key part of various popular music scenes, as Reynolds and McMullen document. I will spend a significant amount of this book adding to that documentation. However, I also show how this interest in the past has characterized a variety of other time periods and genres in twentieth-century popular music history.

Where my work differs most strongly is that both scholars ultimately take skeptical or negative views of the acts of retrospection that they analyze. As Reynolds notes, he came of age with two genres of music—punk music in the late 1970s and rave music in the 1980s and 1990s—genres which, as he interpreted them, were about making a swift break with the past. He remains a progressive, someone who believes that popular music should (and must) progress and that recycling, reuse, and nostalgia are antithetical to what should be popular music's fundamental animating spirit: "As a teenager in the postpunk seventies, I immediately ingested a strong dose of modernism: the belief that art has some kind of evolutionary destiny, a teleology that manifests itself though genius artists and masterpieces that are monuments to the future."[31] Acts of musical nostalgia do not fit this modernist vision; perhaps they are more accurately described as postmodern, in which fixed concepts of past and present are unmoored in a kind of free play. In chapter 1 of this book, I question whether this is an accurate description of the ideas and practices of musicians and listeners who have engaged with the popular music past. Nevertheless, practices of musical replay like sampling, karaoke, impersonation, or tribute band performance are commonly viewed as outside popular music culture's normative ideology of newness.

For her part, McMullen is rightfully critical of how easily retrospective culture can be mobilized to celebrate a conservative view of society, one in which privilege and power on the basis of race, class, and gender are buttressed and defended against newness and reality, against challenges to received ideas and values. McMullen's critique is most convincing in her comparison of a reenactment of a 1944 Glenn Miller concert at Yale University in the 1990s with performances given by the contemporary jazz pianist Jason Moran celebrating

Thelonious Monk's famed 1959 concert at Town Hall. Moran's "In My Mind: Monk at Town Hall, 1959" concerts reject the comfort of a direct re-playing or re-creating of Monk's music—though that more conventional path to celebrating Monk had, in fact, been suggested to Moran. Moran shows no attempt to completely know and master the past; his performances instead affirm the way the past is always a messy, fragmentary presence in our lives.[32] McMullen subtly contrasts Moran's tribute to Monk with a more typical "note-for-note" re-creation of an earlier musical event. In McMullen's analysis, the "masterful" re-creation of Miller's World War II–era performance at Yale promoted a vision of American national unity that is decidedly hegemonic, white, and male, leaving little room for other types of identity. While this was unrepresentative of the "real" America even in the 1940s, reenacting this performance in the 1990s— thereby reinstating its political vision and musical values—is even less tenable.

Still, my research on a wide variety of popular music scenes and their engagements with the past guides me to be cautious about ascribing totalizing explanations of the possible motivations and effects of historical consciousness in popular music. Simply put, the uses to which the past can be put are wide and diverse and can inspire a range of actions in the present. The present, the future, the "new," and the "real" may not be uniformly socially positive, and a re-creation or replaying of the past not experienced as negatively as both Reynolds's modernist and McMullen's Lacanian visions would suggest. There is good and bad in every time period, and throughout this book we will see musicians and listeners engaging with the past specifically because there are aspects of it they wish to use as a resource for progressive goals in the present. There is no simple relationship between musical conservatism and political ideology. As a listener, scholar, and musician, I remain agnostic as to whether the interest in the popular music past this book explores is a good thing or a bad thing, but one area where Reynolds, McMullen, and I all agree is that it is certainly a *widespread* thing: a major, if underexamined aspect of genres like jazz, rock, R&B, and hip-hop. It is crucial for us as scholars and observers of popular music, then, to try to better understand the meaning historical consciousness has in people's lives. This book is an attempt to contribute to that understanding.

I began the research that led to this book over a decade ago when I did fieldwork studying tribute bands in the United States and Latin America for my PhD in ethnomusicology. I will save a fuller discussion of this research for chapter 1, in which they take center stage, but what drew me to study tribute bands was how they were involved in many of the most important questions in the study of music and culture; they could be found performing in cities in the United States, Europe, Latin America, Australia, South Africa, and Asia; and yet very few people were taking their impact on popular culture seriously. Even during my first encounters with them, I was immediately struck by how tribute band performances provided important insights into the process of canonization, notions of personal identity and performance, authenticity, the relationship between live performance and recordings, the nature of musical texts and "works," and the spread of popular music both over time and geographic distance.[33] I started graduate school in ethnomusicology as a jazz scholar. Jazz was—and remains—the genre of music closest to my heart and most central to my thinking, and I published my first academic article on the relationship between jazz and hip-hop in the music and social thought of trumpeter Wynton Marsalis.[34] However, I became fascinated by tribute bands early in my time as a graduate student, and given that they had received only limited scholarly attention, they seemed like an obvious choice for my dissertation research.

What came to interest me most in the tribute band scene, in my attendance at concerts and festivals and interviews with musicians and fans, was the relationships with the past that tribute band performances seemed to allow these people to enact. However, after finishing my dissertation and spending more time thinking about tribute bands in the context of other scenes and styles that I was familiar with as a listener and a scholar, I came to the greater realization that these deep relationships with the past were not limited to the tribute band scene but in fact characterized many areas of popular music culture. The purposes of this book are to show how this underappreciated aspect of popular music culture is present in many different scenes and to provide a corrective to dominant ideas in popular music scholarship—absorbed from popular music ideology itself—that youth, novelty, and newness are the only or main defining features of this music, its practitioners, and its listeners.

This book is primarily focused on popular music genres of the United States in the twentieth and twenty-first centuries. I have also done fieldwork as an ethnomusicologist in Mexico City and Buenos Aires, experience I draw upon in my discussion of tribute bands. (Tribute bands to US and UK Anglophone rock bands are common throughout the world, including in these Latin American cultural capitals with complicated relationships to centers of popular music culture in New York, Atlanta, Los Angeles, and London.) But this book is largely an argument about the United States and about how specific kinds of ideas about the past function in that country's popular music. While I hope these ideas can be suggestive and comparative for scholars of other traditions around the world, I believe the specific themes, issues, and nuances are probably most applicable to the particular environment and history of the United States during this time. For that reason, I share the typical ethnomusicologist's qualification about making totalizing or generalizing claims about how popular music will work at other places and times. This is particularly important because popular music from the United States, especially those artists and genres most enjoyed by white middle-class listeners and critics, is often claimed to be universal in appeal and relevance, providing a template for how other kinds of popular music "should" function in society. (I will discuss this more in the book's first chapter, which centers largely on tribute band performances of "classic rock" music from the 1960s and 1970s—the genre of music most often claimed to be "universally appealing" and worthy of historical reflection because it is "objectively great.") However, I do argue that, within the popular music world of the United States itself, historical consciousness is actually fairly widespread—a feature of various popular music genres at different times and places, performed and listened to by people of different race and class backgrounds. This book shows that historical consciousness is a key and underappreciated part of jazz, rock, hip-hop, and contemporary R&B scenes, even though those scenes are sometimes thought of as not having much in common.

My definition of popular music is also broad, encompassing more than just those musical styles referred to as "pop." I take an essentially economic definition of popular music. If it is music that is economically supported primarily by consumers through capitalist exchange, then it is popular music. However, an attention to historical consciousness in popular music opens up a complication in this definition: one key characteristic of historical consciousness is that the historical and aesthetic value of select artists and genres—as attested by government officials, foundation heads, critics, and other elites—exceeds the value given to this music by the "free market." Listeners and musicians make an argument that specific types of popular music should be supported through elite or government patronage, as has typically been the case with art musics like Western classical music and—largely beginning in the 1980s—jazz.[35] Not enough people are listening to the brilliant compositions of Duke Ellington or the creative improvisations of John Coltrane, so courses explaining this valuable music should be taught at educational institutions and performances in these styles should be subsidized by foundation and taxpayer dollars. This move out of the marketplace and into the museum is already happening for rock music, as I detail in chapter 1, and some aspects of hip-hop culture are moving in this direction as well.

Also, as will be most relevant in the book's final two chapters, I typically see less firm borders between the genres of African American music called rhythm and blues or R&B, soul, and funk. To be sure, there are sometimes important musical, social, and economic differences between the musical practices indicated by these terms. But more often, these terms share stylistic traits, performers cross relatively easily between performing songs in these styles, and most importantly, listeners often wholeheartedly embrace a variety of music located across these generic categories, as is perhaps best articulated in Guthrie Ramsey's reappropriation of the term *race music* to analyze the links between "Black cultures from bebop to hip-hop."[36] I try to echo this fluidity in my analysis of how this body of music's influence looms large as a favorite source for samples in hip-hop and for contemporary musicians who do not sample but are still heavily influenced by these sounds from the past.

The first chapter of the book introduces tribute bands: groups of rock musicians who replay the music of other, earlier bands as accurately as possible. I did fieldwork with tribute bands in the United States, Mexico City, and Buenos Aires, attending several hundred performances in venues ranging from dive bars and suburban restaurants to large nightclubs, Broadway-style theatres, and concert halls. By painstakingly and lovingly re-creating music from previous artists, tribute bands are key participants in a discourse that argues that the past in popular music is aesthetically and historically significant. In this chapter, I address the role of the so-called "baby boomer generation": Americans who came of age during the 1960s and 1970s and have remained a consistent audience for rock music from that era even as they have moved through their life cycle from youth to middle age to retirement. The baby boomer generation has been remarkably successful at propagating the popular music of its youth both to successive generations and around the world. While much of the consumption of this music has taken place through mediated commodities like recordings and film, tribute bands have become an increasingly ubiquitous performance format since the 1990s and provide a key example of how this music was experienced in live contexts around the world and by listeners of various ages.

Tribute bands—and many of the other aspects of historical consciousness associated with rock music—came to prominence in the 1990s and have flourished in the decades following. Accordingly, those years have been the focus of much previous scholarship—like that of Reynolds and McMullen—on popular music's relationship with the past. In my examination of other popular music repertoires, I show how the idea that popular music from the past should be honored and preserved—while certainly intensifying in the late 1990s and the first years of the 2000s—in fact characterizes a longer time span of popular music history. The tribute band scene in the United States is largely a white middle-class genre. Even in the Latin American countries I did fieldwork in, where the Black/white binary and the one-drop rule that control much of the discourse around race in the United States do not necessarily apply, taste for the rock music played by tribute bands is heavily influenced by class status—both real and aspirational—which is in turn highly correlated with phenotype.[37] While the rest of the book is concerned with scenes that feature a mix of musicians or are dominated by African American artists, a close analysis of the ways that ideas about present and past, the new and the old worked in a "white" scene like rock music culture is crucial, since many of these ideas have become a tacit norm in much popular music discourse.[38] Close analysis can denaturalize these ideas and point to other possible ways of structuring popular music culture.

The book's second chapter, "Yesterdays: Performing the Past Through the Great American Songbook from Ella Fitzgerald to Bob Dylan," argues that various popular musicians have used the repertoire of the so-called "Great American Songbook" (a set of songs written between the 1920s and 1960) as a way of establishing musical credibility, to enact a relationship with the past, to appeal to older audiences, and to claim artistic depth beyond the popular music mainstream. This chapter examines in detail the performances of artists such as Ella Fitzgerald, Willie Nelson, Linda Ronstadt, and Bob Dylan, all of whom have engaged with the Songbook tradition at key junctures in their careers, ranging over a remarkably long span of time, from Fitzgerald's pioneering albums of this material in the 1950s to the recording of these songs by Dylan and Nelson in the 2010s and 2020s. In the reception of many performances of standards, these songs seem to function as a mark of quality, craft, and seriousness—all of which, according to this view, are present in this music from the past but lacking in more contemporary musical repertoires. Just as in the tribute band scene, and in the continuing reuse of funk and soul in hip-hop and contemporary R&B, the (music of the) past is invoked here by artists, critics, and listeners as a highly valued alternative to the present.

Chapter 3, "Memories and Standards: Miles Davis and 'I Fall in Love Too Easily,' 1963–1970," continues this attention to the performance of "standards" from the past, but shifts slightly to focus on the usage of this repertoire by instrumental jazz musicians. In particular, I examine how and why standards eventually drop out of the repertoire of Miles Davis in the 1960s. Despite the tumultuous changes in his bands, musical style, performance venues, audiences, and recording techniques during this time period, the 1944 standard "I Fall in Love Too Easily," remained a consistent part of his live repertoire through much of this time period. The process of "signifyin(g)" on a jazz standard was (and is) a central part of jazz performance, and this chapter provides a detailed examination of several posthumously released live recordings of Davis and his band performing "I Fall in Love Too Easily." By examining Davis's studio and live recordings, set lists, and interviews, I show that improvising on recognizable popular tunes from the past (such as "I Fall in Love Too Easily" and other standards) becomes less attractive to Davis as he moves away from a traditional jazz audience and toward a younger, countercultural audience. Davis's controversial move away from traditional jazz techniques and toward jazz-rock fusion has been a persistent topic of interest in jazz scholarship and criticism for decades. I argue that this move also must be understood in terms of Davis's stance toward music of the past. This chapter presents an important example of a musician explicitly rejecting the idea that playing music from the past will be the way for him to maintain or recapture aesthetic relevance, not to mention economic stability.

Specifically, Davis's move in the late 1960s was an attempt to establish a younger, Blacker, and more countercultural audience for his music than what he perceived as the whiter, older, middle-class jazz audience that had supported him and his music up to this point in his career.[39] In Davis's calculation, conventional methods of jazz performance and established repertoire from the now "outdated" Great American Songbook were unlikely to appeal to this new audience. Davis provides an early example of a controversial but widespread idea in popular music discourse: that Black audiences and musicians are primarily interested in innovation, while white audiences and musicians are always playing catch-up—or are content to replay, relive, or reexperience prior African American musical styles. Our earlier discussion of the performance of standards by musicians from the pop and rock traditions bears this out. The singer most associated with establishing the Great American Songbook as a performance repertoire, Ella Fitzgerald, was, of course, African American, but many of the musicians who have garnered the most attention for performing this repertoire from the past in recent decades have not been, even when they use styles of singing and playing that are clearly indebted to African American musical techniques.

It is largely white cultural intermediaries with institutional power and networks who have the ability to maintain archives and publish historical accounts of the popular music past, actions that, in conjunction with the re-performances themselves of music from the past, are a crucial part of the historical consciousness in popular music this book analyzes. Indeed, it is something of a truism of popular music discourse that white (especially male) listeners and musicians are interested in conservation, obsessed with the details of the past or obsolete African American musical styles—for example, the Delta blues or Northern soul—while younger, more diverse, and female listeners and musicians are more interested in innovation, following the latest trends, and dancing to the latest hits.[40] It has largely been these older, whiter, middle-class historians, scholars, and critics (all identities this current writer shares) who have had long-lasting influence as the writers of historical narratives, who have determined what exactly of the popular music past has been, and will be, preserved.[41] While there is certainly some truth to this stereotype, those who uncritically subscribe to this idea close themselves off—perhaps unwittingly—to seeing and analyzing the deep relationships with the musical past that African American musicians and listeners enact in various genres. Because of the influence of the ideology of newness and the idea that popular music nostalgia is primarily the province of old white male rock critics or jazz nerds, scholars and critics have been blinded to the sense of repetition and engagement with the past that has often characterized Afrodiasporic culture.[42] Davis, in his abandoning of the jazz standard repertoire and established jazz performance practices, can certainly be interpreted as turning his back on the past, but other Black musicians and listeners have found personally fulfilling ways of engaging with musical history, as I show in the book's final two chapters.

The fourth chapter is titled "Old School: Sampling, Re-Playing, and Re-Hearing the 1970s in Hip-Hop." The creative recycling of preexisting music—through playing breaks from old records, digital sampling, or re-playing music from the past in the studio—has been a fundamental part of hip-hop since its mythological beginnings in 1973. In principle, DJs and producers can sample any available recorded music as the basis for new songs, but in practice, funk and soul recordings from the 1970s have been an overwhelming favorite choice. This chapter argues that music from the 1970s has both political and personal relevance to hip-hop artists. Using evidence from recently published autobiographies by hip-hop musicians, I show how recorded soul and funk music figures heavily in narratives from hip-hop musicians describing their childhoods, their families, and their early musical influences. These domestic experiences represent a key aspect of musical development and enculturation that has not been adequately addressed by scholars of hip-hop. I also analyze the 1970s as a key moment in African American culture, symbolizing a lost "golden age" that, perhaps, the act of sampling music from this period can help recapture. Sampling music from the 1970s, therefore, has become almost a defining characteristic feature of the genre of hip-hop, even for younger artists (and listeners) whose personal connections to the 1970s are more tenuous.

The fifth and final chapter of the book, titled "'I Just Wanna Go Back, Back to the Way It Was': The Past, Activism, and Recent Black Popular Music," brings us up to the contemporary moment. This chapter examines the work of contemporary Black popular music artists such as Prince, Pharrell Williams, D'Angelo, and Janelle Monáe. While not directly sampling music from the past, much of their recent work is clearly indebted to Black popular music from the 1970s in aspects of timbre, groove, and vocal style. This is particularly apparent in songs that address contemporary issues of importance to the Black community, such as police violence and the Black Lives Matter movement. For many artists and activists, movements for civil rights and Black power from the 1960s and 1970s are an important inspiration for their work in the present, and therefore iconic features of music from this time period take on special significance as possibly being able to inspire a similar level of political engagement and activism.

In the conclusion, I consider the future of engagements with the past through popular music. Given the evidence of the case studies examined throughout the book, it is clear that popular music culture is far more interested in events of the "past" than many journalists, critics, and historians had previously considered. This is an interest in the past that is expressed through attendance at popular music museums; the release of commemorative books, films, and box sets; the proliferation of tribute bands both in the United States and abroad; and the continuing influence of Black popular music from the 1970s on contemporary artists. As scholars and listeners, we need to adjust our views of popular music culture to take account of these phenomena; perhaps these acts of retrospection themselves constitute a new norm, a new state of affairs for the production and consumption of popular music.

CHAPTER 1

TWENTY YEARS AGO TODAY

Tribute Bands and Historical Consciousness
in Popular Music

A Tribute Band Performance by Rain

On Sunday afternoon January 15, 2007, Rain, one of the most successful Beatles tribute bands in the United States, was in the middle of their then-annual weeklong run of performances at the Academy of Music on Broad Street in Philadelphia. The Academy of Music is a prestigious concert hall, opened in 1857, where the Philadelphia Orchestra formerly performed and which now hosts the Opera Company of Philadelphia. Rain's residency at the theatre typically happened in January, when the Opera and the other performing arts groups that use the theatre are still on holiday break. As with other tribute band performances I attended during my fieldwork in the United States, the audience for this concert was mostly white, with a wide range of ages. I noticed couples in their fifties and sixties, along with a good number of families with teenage children.

As my fellow concertgoers and I entered and took our seats, two screens flanking the stage were playing 1960s television commercials and excerpts from *The Ed Sullivan Show*. The screens were used as part of Rain's attempt to replicate in live performance what Americans saw on television when the Beatles first performed on that show on February 9, 1964, including the television commercials and footage of other acts that preceded the Beatles that night. Audience chatter was slightly lower in volume than is usual before a concert, as some audience members were intently watching the action on the screen, treating it as an important part of that afternoon's performance. Anticipation in the audience rose as we got closer to the start of the performance, but at the climactic moment when Ed Sullivan on screen announced, "Ladies and gentlemen, the Beatles!" instead of watching the Beatles on the screen, the curtain rose on the members of Rain onstage, four men in matching black suits and skinny black ties, as they performed a note-for-note re-creation of the first song the Beatles played on their first appearance on American television, "All My Loving." While not quite matching the shrieking frenzy of "Beatlemania" that accompanied many appearances by the Beatles during the 1960s, the audience responded with high-pitched cheers and whistles as Joey Curatolo, performing the part of Paul McCartney, sang the song's opening line: "Close your eyes and I'll kiss you, tomorrow I'll miss you." The audience was performing as well, by re-creating the kind of enthusiasm that they themselves (or other teenagers) would have greeted the Beatles with over forty years prior.

The Beatles' first appearance on *The Ed Sullivan Show* is one of the most famous televised performances in popular music history, and many different Beatles tribute bands, like Rain at this performance, open their shows with a replication of the set the Beatles played that night. Reception of the Beatles—in books, documentary films, magazine articles, and fan narratives—has divided their careers into three relatively distinct periods: an early period typified by their performance on *The Ed Sullivan Show*, a middle period marked by their move away from three-minute rock 'n' roll songs to experiments in psychedelia, and a late period consisting of their most critically acclaimed and canonized work, the albums *Sgt. Pepper's Lonely Hearts Club Band*, *The Beatles* (commonly known as *The White Album*), and *Abbey Road*.[1] This periodization is clear in a Rain performance, as the band proceeded chronologically through the music of the Beatles over the course of the afternoon's concert, re-creating songs from each era of the Beatles' career. For each different period, Rain went offstage, changed costumes and hairstyles (Rain and other Beatles tributes make extensive use of wigs), and switched instruments to match the kinds of guitars and drums the Beatles were using at that particular stage in their career, including Gretsch guitars, a Hofner violin bass, and a Ludwig drum set. These instruments, in addition to being visually recognizable to knowledgeable audience members, also have specific sonic characteristics that help tribute bands re-create nuances of timbre as accurately as possible, as my interviews with members of Rain and other tribute bands stressed.

As audience members, we were being taught this history, led through it with the members of Rain acting as skilled lecturers, using their own bodies and changing physical appearances as a visual supplement to the music they played and sang. For the audience, this was likely not the first time they were exposed to this historical narrative. Many in the audience had experienced the events of this history "in person" as fans during the 1960s. Others had read about the Beatles in the hundreds of books and magazine articles that chronicle their career. And likely everyone at the concert had heard countless hours of the music of the Beatles at home on their record, CD, or digital music collections in the ensuing decades since the breakup of the Beatles in 1970. This afternoon's concert joined these other formats in presenting a history of the Beatles with one crucial difference: a Rain tribute band performance presents this historical and musical narrative live onstage.

Rain ended their performance with the final medley from side 2 of the album *Abbey Road*, "Golden Slumbers" / "Carry That Weight" / "The End." In addition to the medley's chronological placement at the end of the last album recorded by the Beatles, it combines several crowd-pleasing elements: the sentimental "Golden Slumbers," the rowdy crowd sing-along on "Carry That Weight," the tom-tom drum solo at the beginning of "The End" (I always see people in the audience air-drumming along to this whenever a Beatles tribute band plays it), and the traded guitar solos and final lyrics of "The End," which have become something of a credo among Beatles fans: "And in the end, the love you take is equal to the love you make."

At the conclusion of the performance, after walking us through the history of the Beatles from their first appearance on television in the United States to their last recordings as a group, the members of Rain broke character and stepped out of the chronological narrative they had been presenting. The screens were used one more time here. Where they had been used earlier in the performance to evoke the ambience of the early 1960s by playing excerpts from *The Ed Sullivan Show*, they were now enlisted for twenty-first-century concerns. After thanking the crowd for the warm reception they had received during their performances in Philadelphia, the members of Rain pointed to one of the screens. On cue, a graphic displaying the band's website, www.raintribute.com, appeared.

Reconfiguring the Past into "History"

The preceding ethnographic vignette—typical of the hundreds of tribute band concerts I attended between 2005 and 2015—concisely exhibits many of the key characteristics of the tribute band scene. Tribute bands are groups of musicians who only play the music of a previous band, usually from the so-called "classic rock" era of the 1960s and 1970s, though tributes to bands like

U2 and Bon Jovi, as well as newer bands like Radiohead, Muse, and Coldplay are now becoming more common. Tribute bands strive to re-create the songs of previous bands "note-for-note" for an audience that is multigenerational but includes many fans who first discovered the music of the "tributed" band as young people, who now attend tribute band concerts in order to reexperience in live performance the music of their youth. Tribute bands sometimes dress up like the tributed band and affect accents to seem as much like the band to which they are paying tribute as possible. Some of the larger-budget tribute bands supplement their stage performances with sophisticated lighting, laser, and video setups, copying video that was used in earlier live performances (for example, the multimedia spectacles that characterized Pink Floyd shows in the 1970s) or by using video that seeks to re-create the feel of an earlier era (old television commercials and black-and-white news footage of historic events from the 1960s are common at Beatles tribute band concerts). In addition, tribute bands often feature elaborate discourses of authenticity and play vintage instruments—like Hofner violin basses, Ludwig drum sets, and Rickenbacker and Gretsch guitars—instruments strongly associated, both visually and sonically, with the bands to whom they are paying tribute.[2] Similar to musicians who specialize in the historically informed performance of Western classical music, tribute band musicians perform with the conviction that it is important that they "authentically" re-create music of the past.

This chapter integrates ethnographic description of several tribute band performances and a critical reading of popular music discourse—including magazine articles, books, and documentaries—in order to explain historical consciousness and examine the role that tribute bands are playing in its construction. In my analysis, I argue that tribute bands are engaged in several important activities: they are key participants in a discourse that argues that the past in popular music is important, they allow audience members to enact relationships with popular music artists through surrogacy, and tribute band performances make use of music from the past for continued economic survival. Perhaps most importantly, tribute bands and their audiences provide an important example of a community for whom an intense awareness of and respect for (a constructed version of) the past is an important part of their lives. In the tribute band scene and in other arenas of popular music culture, we find two contradictory ideas side by side: an ideology of progress and newness confronting a reverential attitude toward the past.

Performances like those of Rain and other tribute bands testify to the importance that some aspects of popular music from the past have now taken on in contemporary culture. As a term, my usage of "historical consciousness in popular music" to describe this attitude unites several disparate developments that have received attention in the study of popular music; these include canon formation, popular music museums, CD reissue projects, and the rise of "classic rock" radio.[3] These developments have been studied in isolation, but I argue that they can be more productively understood as symptoms of the larger tendency to treat popular music with historical legitimacy and respect.

There are at least two aspects to the sense of importance and seriousness that underlies the idea of historical consciousness in the tribute band scene and elsewhere in popular music discourse: aesthetic importance and what I will term *generational importance*. While historical consciousness has become a widespread, prominent feature of popular music culture in recent years, its roots extend back several decades. We can trace one strand of the beginnings of historical consciousness in rock culture to the music criticism that began to be published in outlets like the *Village Voice* and *Rolling Stone* in the mid-1960s.[4] Other, more "respectable" and established publications also began writing about rock music in less hysterical and more laudatory terms around this time. In addition to the voices of younger pop music critics like Richard Goldstein, Robert Christgau, and Ellen Willis—who were largely sympathetic to a wide range of popular music—middle-class critics and intellectuals previously aligned with Western classical music began to find musical worth in some of the popular music developments at this same time. John Lennon, speaking in an interview with *Rolling Stone* founder Jann Wenner in December 1970, describes how this happened for the Beatles:

> There's a guy in England called William Mann who writes in *The Times* who wrote the first intellectual review of The Beatles, which got people talking about us in that intellectual way. He wrote about Aeolian cadences and all sort of musical terms. He's a bullshitter, but he wrote about Paul's album as if it was written by Beethoven, this last one. . . . But it did us a lot of good in that way, cause people—all the middle classes and intellectuals—are going, "Ooh, aren't they clever."[5]

In Lennon's telling, Mann explicitly linked aesthetic merit to the perceived musical sophistication of the Beatles' work.[6] Most contemporary critics and scholars would reject the idea that the ability to describe music using the specific technical language of Western classical music is a sign of musical worth, but Lennon is astutely pointing out that Mann used this vocabulary to confer legitimacy on the previously suspect genre of rock music.

Along with the aesthetic importance given to it by critics and intellectuals (and later claimed by some musicians and fans), there is generational importance: the importance that the members of the baby boomer generation began to place on rock music in the 1960s. Young fans of rock music at this time did not necessarily claim rock to be on an artistic par with the accepted masters of the Western canon; this was not (yet) a battle they were interested in fighting. However, they did often claim that musicians like Lennon, McCartney, Bob Dylan, Paul Simon, and Jim Morrison served an important role as "spokesmen" or "voices" of their generation, despite the fact that this role has been, at times, warily resisted by these figures themselves.[7] Because sheer numbers allowed the baby boomer generation to gain economic and cultural influence in both the United States and in other countries, the words of their "spokesmen" were also taken seriously, in ways that other popular musicians had not been.

From these early beginnings—tentative steps toward viewing rock music as both full of aesthetic worth and as accurately conveying the thoughts and feelings of a coherent generational cohort—historical consciousness in rock music has expanded in the past few decades to become an important feature of the genre. We can date a key milestone in its development to 1995. On September 1 of that year, the Rock and Roll Hall of Fame and Museum opened on the lakefront in Cleveland, Ohio, designed by the star architect I. M. Pei. In November and December, *Anthology*, a multipart documentary series chronicling the career of the Beatles, was broadcast on television in the United States and the UK. These two examples involve several common aspects of historical consciousness: the prestige of museums lovingly presenting the physical artifacts of popular music culture in exalted surroundings, the participation of the mass media through the broadcast of *Anthology* on American television on ABC and ITV in the UK, and the production of commodities for sale in the form of three two-disc CD sets containing outtakes and unreleased performances now thought of as worthy of historical attention—not as scraps or ephemera. 1995 was also the year just before the first members of the baby boomer generation, born in 1946, turned fifty: a time when many of them were marking the end of child-rearing, beginning to reflect on their own past and their future legacy, and with more time and disposable income to devote to the interests of their youth.

Before the intensification of historical consciousness that has characterized the popular music scene since the mid-1990s, popular music in the United States was usually treated as something disposable, something to be momentarily enjoyed but discarded as soon as the next trend appeared or the listener matured into adulthood and, presumably, more adult concerns than following popular culture. In the introduction, we have previously discussed how an ideology of newness is an enduring feature of popular music culture; as a subset of popular music culture, rock is certainly included in this. Describing the way rock 'n' roll was viewed in the 1950s, especially as compared to the more "serious" but less commercially successful genres of jazz and folk music, Keir Keightley writes: "Rock 'n' roll, embodied in ephemeral 45s was dismissed—and not without reason—as a fad and a novelty by those who took music seriously."[8] The short duration of 45s themselves—usually less than three minutes—functions as a metaphor for the status of the music they contained: enjoyable for a few minutes but easily forgotten. This was a genre transmitted in flimsy paper sleeves, lacking the permanence of a more physically substantial LP record—or the heft of a multi-CD box set that would become an important commodity in later rock music culture, once the genre had become heavily influenced by historical consciousness.

Explaining his own indifference to rock during the 1950s, the music executive Clive Davis, who served as president of Columbia Records and later founder of Arista Records, clearly explains the changes in the reception of rock music that occurred in the decades that followed its origins:

> As for rock 'n' roll, I had little interest in it. Today, rock musicians tour and record into their sixties and seventies, and fans in their forties, fifties, and sixties seek out new music, even if only the new releases by artists they grew up with and love. In the Fifties, though, rock 'n' roll was for teenagers. It was inconceivable that an ambitious, married New York lawyer in his late twenties [such as Davis himself] would seriously discuss the latest records by Elvis Presley, Little Richard, or Buddy Holly, let alone adopt their fashions or hairstyles. That would all come later.[9]

The flowering of historical consciousness that dates from around the 1990s represents a fundamental shift in how popular music has been produced and consumed, with important economic and aesthetic consequences across the popular music landscape. That is, historical consciousness—shared to greater or lesser degrees by musicians, producers, executives, critics, and listeners—influences how music will be valued, in both senses of the word. Tribute bands both construct and partake in historical consciousness, in the attitude that treats the events of the popular music past with historical respect and legitimacy. It should be noted that the popular music history discussed in this chapter—as well as its struggle to be taken seriously as "history"—is a very specific narrative whose subjects are almost exclusively white middle-class North Americans and Western Europeans. This music is often claimed to be "universal" by its partisans, and its popularity among many groups of people around the world is undeniable. However, this popularity should be understood both as a function of the power of this "universal" discourse and as a testimony to the reach of multinational record and media companies—and not necessarily due to the innate "genius" of the music itself, as is often claimed. Seen in this way, the continuing popularity of rock music from the 1960s and 1970s both around the globe and with a variety of age groups is the result of a complex interaction between individual taste, marketing, and corporate influence.

Historical consciousness, especially in the sense of taking popular music seriously as an important aesthetic or historical artifact, is not unique to the "classic rock" played by the tribute bands under discussion here. In later chapters in this book, I discuss how other genres of popular music have inspired extensive attention from scholars, critics, musicians, and ordinary listeners, all of whom treat their preferred genres and artists as worthy of sustained analysis and status as properly "historical" phenomena. Classic rock is perhaps unique, however, because in no other genre has a confluence of scholarly, critical, and popular media attention been characterized by such a strong bias in favor of preserving, memorializing, and, indeed, re-performing the past as in classic rock music culture. Although hip-hop may be moving in this direction with the establishment of archives at institutions like Cornell University and the genre's celebration of anniversaries of important albums, as of yet no other genre of popular music has developed the kind of memorializing infrastructure, nor does it undertake this memorializing with the kind of reverent attitude, that I find in classic rock. Classic rock has had a head start on other genres, as some of its fans have taken positions of influence at publishing houses, television and film production companies, and universities. Once in these positions, they have been able to help "naturalize" the importance of the music they happen to be fans of. While I focus in this chapter on rock music as a special case of the development of historical consciousness, more generally my study of tribute bands provides an example of how events from the past can be remade and reconfigured into "history." As I argue above, treating popular music as history is a relatively underexamined feature of popular music, which typically is subservient to an ideology of newness. Scholars of popular music, therefore, would do well to look at how other scholars have examined the relationships between the musical past and the present. For ethnomusicologists, such relationships, although taking different shapes in different contexts, have been a persistent feature in many of the music cultures we have studied, as I discuss below.

Locating Historical Consciousness in Ethnomusicology and Popular Music

Over the history of their discipline, ethnomusicologists have been very interested in attempting to define the field of ethnomusicology and to codify the activities that ethnomusicologists engage in. These attempts have been numerous, diverse, and, at times, contradictory.[10] However, despite these various perspectives, perhaps one of ethnomusicology's most stable disciplinary characteristics has been its focus on musical activities of the present day. If history has been a field defined by reflection on the past, ethnomusicology (as a subfield of anthropology) has been focused on present-day lived experience, with information gathered from fieldwork, interviews, participant-observation, and field recordings. Yet while undertaking this research, ethnomusicologists often encounter cases of their informants interpreting present-day musical activities under the enduring influence of past events.

For example, in her study of salsa music in Cali, Colombia, Lise Waxer found that listeners in the 1990s used salsa recordings from previous decades as a way of recalling an earlier time: "a time of innocence and 'clean fun,' in contrast to the violent ambience established after the rise of the Cali cocaine cartel during the 1980s."[11] Similarly, Kay Shelemay's *Let Jasmine Rain Down: Song and Remembrance among Syrian Jews* examines *pizmonim*, a body of songs brought and preserved by Jewish immigrants from Syria to the Americas, concentrating her research on "individuals to whom the pizmonim are an important aspect of daily life, both in the present and in their memories of past experience."[12] In his study of the legacy of jazz pianist Thelonious Monk, Gabriel Solis "[focuses] on contemporary jazz musicians' experiences of Monk as both listeners and performers, looking at the way their discussions of his performances and their own performances of his music express a way of integrating past and present in their music and in their lives."[13] In all of these cases, a version of the past is constructed by musicians and listeners that is meaningful and useful for their lives in the present, a process which, I argue, shows evidence of a historical consciousness at work. Therefore, these and other ethnographic accounts of people interacting with the past can be useful for us as models for how to understand how various popular music scenes enact relationships with the past.

As I use it to describe trends in the reception of popular music, historical consciousness differs slightly from how the term has been deployed by previous scholars. In Hayden White's *Metahistory: The Historical Imagination in Nineteenth-Century Europe*, historical consciousness refers more generally to "the dominant modes of historical thinking," "the deep structure of the historical imagination," or "the theory and practice of historical reflection."[14] In the work of Peter Seixas, who founded the Centre for the Study of Historical Consciousness at the University of British Columbia and edited the volume *Theorizing Historical Consciousness*, historical consciousness is focused on questions of pedagogy and with the place a historical education has in democracy.[15] He is most concerned with inculcating a historical consciousness in children and students, by which he means an awareness and respect of history as a guide to democratic deliberative decision-making in the present. My own usage of the term is perhaps more modest and is concerned, in this particular case, with the growing ideological position among musicians, critics, journalists, historians, cultural gatekeepers, and listeners that the past in popular music is a proper subject matter for historical thinking and historical study. As with Kirshenblatt-Gimblett's discussion of "heritage," it should be emphasized that historical consciousness is not a natural consequence of the passage of time but results from—and serves to influence—decisions made by specific musicians, listeners, critics, and people involved in the popular music industry.

To use Pierre Nora's term, there are particular "sites" where this historical consciousness can be seen.[16] These sites may or may not be officially recognized by the government or academic historians; nevertheless, they are important places that members of various popular music communities have invested with deep meaning. These include popular music museums such as the Rock and Roll Hall of Fame Museum in Cleveland (opened 1995), the Museum of Pop Culture in Seattle (opened 2000 as the Experience Music Project), and the Country Music Hall of Fame and Museum in Nashville (opened 2001). In addition to these physical "sites of memory," there are metaphorical sites where historical consciousness plays an important role, including the television shows *Behind the Music* and *Classic Albums*, the proliferation of lists printed in publications like *Rolling Stone* enumerating the "500 Greatest Albums of All Time" or "500 Greatest Songs of All Time," and the many box sets, reissue projects, and "special editions" of albums or artists now deemed "classic" in their importance and, hence, worthy of such appreciative treatment.[17]

Many of these developments date from around the year 2000, when there was a particular urge to document and codify a canon of objects from popular music and popular culture. These lists often purported to catalog the "best of the millennium," although in practice they rarely contained items dating from before the year 1950 or 1900.[18] However, this trend of canonization and the treatment of objects from the past in popular music and culture as historically significant has not shown any signs of waning in the years since 2000. Simon Reynolds's *Retromania* was published in 2011, after what he characterizes as a decade (the years 2000–2009) featuring an unprecedented interest in popular culture of the past. He terms this era "the 'Re' decade" and begins his book with a "Retroscape" in which he catalogs a wide array of events from this decade in popular music—openings of museums, record and book releases, reunion tours—that show a retrospective or nostalgic outlook.[19] 2021 saw the release of Peter Jackson's nearly eight-hour documentary *Get Back*, depicting the January 1969 studio sessions of the Beatles in exhaustive detail. The year 2023 featured several celebrations of the fiftieth anniversary of hip-hop's mythical beginnings at the 1973 party thrown by Cindy Campbell and her brother, DJ Kool Herc—including a tribute medley organized by Questlove at the Grammy Awards. The aggregate message from these diverse media is clear: this popular music from the past is worth preserving, collecting, monumentalizing, and knowing about, an attitude that is completely counter to pop's typical ideology of newness but firmly in line with what I describe in this book as historical consciousness in popular music.

Historical Realization, Commoditized Knowledge, and Music Industry Challenges

There are several aspects that have influenced how historical consciousness has developed in the popular music community. First is the realization by listeners that popular music, instead of being an ephemeral entity, in fact has a history. The significance of this change in view has yet to be fully understood by popular music critics, scholars, and fans. The idea of history existing where it had not before is particularly noteworthy in a time when digital technology has allowed the widespread dissemination of what are now seen as historical documents. These documents include the studio and live recorded performances themselves, but also images, films, and first-person accounts of experiences with this music from the past. As should be clear from my description of a Rain tribute band concert, historical consciousness in popular music is not a neutral phenomenon; it is a specific productive force. In the context of rock music culture, historical consciousness produces commodities like commemorative CD box sets and tribute band performances, both of which serve to transmit music of the past in the present.[20] Digital technology also allows this music to be transported, but with one important difference. When the tracks from a box set are transferred to an iPhone or streamed from a digital music service, the carefully constructed historical narrative of the set—often explained in copious detail in the accompanying liner notes—collapses, especially when tracks are listened to using the "shuffle" setting that randomizes the order in which tracks play. Paradoxically, digital objects both resist attempts to construct historical narratives and allow even more access to the raw materials of history itself: the texts (like sound recordings) that are used to build historical narratives, to tell stories.[21]

The realization that popular music is a proper subject for historical reflection occurs simultaneously with the writing of historical narratives themselves by journalists, critical elites, and academics. The writing of music history, however, is never a neutral process and is always a selective one. Indeed, the most prominent historical accounts of popular music, the most respected critics, and much academic scholarship on popular music have focused on a specific set of past events: those occurring in the roughly ten-year period between 1964 and 1974. That this time period overlaps the height of rock music's influence and popularity is no accident. Most critics and historians treat rock music as the most important genre of popular music. This centrality of rock is related to another aspect of popular music. "Rock imperialism"—a tendency to view other forms of popular music as precursors, extensions, or elaborations on a central rock model—is widespread in popular music discourse. For example, James Miller's influential history of rock, *Flowers in the Dustbin: The Rise of Rock and Roll, 1947–1977*, describes "rap, . . . grunge, trance, house, and trip-hop" as "variants of rock."[22] These styles are seen not as self-sufficient genres with their own histories but as supplementary parts of a larger rock tradition. In this vision, the events of the 1960s and 1970s are seen not just as particularly important for rock history, but for popular music history in general. This is because *rock* has come to be understood by some critics and historians as a generic term for all popular music, with rock's fortunes standing in for those of popular music as a whole. According to Miller, rock died (or at least stopped progressing) in 1977 from the twin causes of the release of the punk album *Never Mind the Bollocks* by the Sex Pistols and the death of Elvis Presley. Writing in 1999, Miller described the state of the genre:

> As a mode of social interaction, on the other hand, rock has many of the features of a finished cultural form—a more or less fixed repertoire of sounds and styles and patterns of behavior. . . . Its essential possibilities have been thoroughly explored, its limits more or less clearly established. . . . I believe that the genre's era of explosive growth has been over for nearly a quarter century. Like such other mature pop music forms as the Broadway musical and the main currents of the jazz tradition, from swing to bop, rock now belongs to the past as much as to the future.
>
> My narrative thus ends with the death of Elvis Presley in 1977, because by that time, in my view, the essence of rock and roll—as a musical style, as a cluster of values, as an ingredient in a variety of youthful subcultures around the world—had been firmly established.[23]

If the newly written histories of popular music are not chronicling late-breaking historical developments, what these histories *are* doing is treating events from the 1960s and 1970s as significant and properly historical—not as mere trivia or minutiae. In fact, the vast majority of tribute bands pay tribute to music from precisely this era. To use Pierre Nora's term, tribute band concerts are thus an important "site" where popular music, which was previously associated with novelty, triviality, and ephemerality is acquiring historical weight and depth.

A second aspect of the development of historical consciousness in popular music is the industry's creation and exploitation of the consumer's desire for completion, for a sense of mastery or control, and for a sense of a relationship with a particular favorite artist. A listener can prove their devotion to an artist like Aretha Franklin by owning all of her albums, including all the "special edition," "enhanced," and "with bonus tracks" CD reissues. This is a clear example of commodity fetishism—or, as Muller terms it in a specifically music context, "musical surrogacy"—in which a "real" social relationship with an inaccessible famous artist is replaced with a relationship to a commodity: the recordings of that artist.[24] While Muller's discussion of musical surrogacy described listeners in South Africa separated by geographic distance from the American musicians whose work they admired, her concept can be extended to apply to listeners and artists separated by temporal distance. By consuming commoditized recordings from the past as a surrogate, listeners are able to experience and enact a relationship with past artists and past events. For many who consume these recordings, the act of listening itself is primary, but for other consumers, purchasing and collecting recordings can be equally satisfying. As Baudrillard argues:

> In this respect, the objects in our lives, as distinct from the way we make use of them at any given moment, represent something much more, something more profoundly related to subjectivity: for while the object is a resistant material body, it is also, simultaneously, a mental realm over which I hold sway, a thing whose meaning is governed by myself alone.[25]

For listeners interacting with recordings of music from the past, both types of relationships are possible, and perhaps even likely to be present in the same listener depending on the circumstances.

Third, the record industry participates in the construction of historical consciousness in order to further monetize its back catalog—recordings that recouped their production costs years ago—by marketing reissues, special editions, and box sets. The Recording Industry Association of America regularly releases statements complaining about its loss of revenue in the wake of major changes in music consumption among teenagers and college students, who have traditionally been both the industry's most profitable demographic and its most influential tastemakers. For record companies, making money from a "new" release of old music—particularly a release marketed to members of the baby boomer generation who, as music industry executive Clive Davis points out above, have retained their affinity for popular music—might be a more sound business decision than taking the risk of signing and developing a new artist marketed to teenagers. Indeed, the proliferation of reissues is an important aspect of the contemporary popular music scene, even if consumers have been wary of having to purchase many different versions of an album over the course of a few decades to be able to access all of the authorized recorded material associated with a given project.[26]

Tribute bands are participants in the three components of historical consciousness described above. First, by re-performing verbatim renditions of songs, albums, or "legendary" live performances (such as the Beatles' appearances on *The Ed Sullivan Show* in 1964 or their concert on the roof of the Apple Building in 1969), tribute bands are key participants in a discourse that argues that these objects and events are, in fact, important and properly historical, as my description of a Rain tribute band performance above demonstrated. Second, tribute band performances also enable audience members to enact relationships with popular music icons, through the surrogacy of tribute band performers. If a vinyl record, CD, or digital music file as a commodity can stand in for a relationship to a figure like John Lennon or Bono of the Irish rock band U2, a flesh-and-blood tribute band performer—looking, playing, and singing just like the "tributed" artist—can just as easily perform the same function. The accessibility and lack of ego characterizing tribute band musicians was mentioned several times by audience members I interviewed as one of the things they liked best about tribute band performances. Finally, tribute bands also exploit previous musical material for continued financial gain, just as record companies do with their reissue projects. Jesse Samba Wheeler's research on tribute bands in Brazil discusses how Brazilian musicians subsidize their "original" projects with work as tribute band musicians.[27] I also encountered this economic reality in interviews with tribute band musicians in the United States, as well as in Argentina and Mexico. In popular music scenes throughout the world, the insatiable appetite for (music of) the past makes performance in tribute bands economically appealing to musicians struggling to find an audience for original material.

Aspects of Tribute Band Performances

Tribute band performances take a variety of shapes, owing to the different bands performing, the "tributed" artist, and the constraints of the venue, among many other factors. Some bands strive to look, act, and sound like the original artists onstage: this includes bands like the Doors tribute The Soft Parade, which bills itself as "The World-Famous Authentic Doors Tribute Show" and trades heavily on the resemblance of its lead singer Joe Russo to deceased Doors frontman Jim Morrison. Other bands may attempt as close as possible sonic verisimilitude to the original recordings but pay little attention to similarities in onstage appearance. This would include the Beatles tribute band The Sun Kings, which uses samples to replicate the sounds of the orchestra tuning up at the beginning of *Sgt. Pepper's Lonely Hearts Club Band* and to re-create the dramatic orchestral middle section of the song "A Day in the Life," but does not attempt to mimic the appearance of the Beatles themselves. The decision whether or not to become a "lookalike" (or "clone") band is an important one for tribute bands. Groups that perform in smaller venues and have lower budgets may be dissuaded by the cost of purchasing costumes, wigs, and sets. Such bands may also perceive these visual aspects of the performance as "gimmicks" that distract from the music, which should be left to "speak for itself."[28] But groups like Rain, the Australian Pink Floyd Show, Kashmir (a tribute to Led Zeppelin), and The Musical Box (a Canadian tribute to Genesis) employ both sonic and visual means to create a concert experience that is intended to be more immersive and resemble more closely what a concert by their respective "tributed" bands would have been like.[29] For both types of groups, seriousness and a commitment to a "faithful" reproduction of the music are paramount, but they arrive at this goal in different ways based on their differing conceptions of what elements make up the musical experience.

Exactly which musical parameters of a performance are to be re-created is also an area where tribute bands vary. One of the most financially successful tribute bands, the Dark Star Orchestra, re-creates shows by the Grateful Dead by playing the same songs in the same order as the Grateful Dead originally played at a previous concert, but does not replicate specific improvised solos. In this way, perhaps they are trying to be authentic to the improvisatory nature of the Grateful Dead's live shows, even if their tribute performances fall short of the note-for-note verisimilitude that other tribute bands attempt. Only at the end of their performance does the Dark Star Orchestra announce what concert they were re-creating, but knowledgeable fans can use clues to try to pinpoint what prior show the tribute concert is based on. As Steven Kurutz explains:

> For instance, if only one drummer is onstage the show dates to between 1971 and 1974, when Mickey Hart briefly left the band.... An expert Deadhead can further home in on the date by paying careful attention to the set list and the song arrangements and running times and even instruments onstage—by knowing that, say, the keyboardist Brent Mydland used a Hammond B-3, but earlier Dead keyboard players did not, so if a B-3 is onstage, the show must date to after spring of 1979, when Mydland joined the band.[30]

The Dark Star Orchestra's performances are made possible by historical consciousness. The Grateful Dead and their fans collected a large archive of information about the band's performances—including decades' worth of bootleg recordings and set lists—information that was thought to be historically important enough to systematically collect and which can now be mined by tribute bands to reconstruct and reimagine these performances.[31] Performing in a tribute band is an act based on having a sense of historical consciousness, on an idea that the music of the past is historically important enough to play again. The Dark Star Orchestra takes this attitude one step further than other tribute bands, however. Not content to just pay tribute to the music of the Grateful Dead in a general sense, the Dark Star Orchestra testifies to the historical importance of even individual Grateful Dead performances by recreating them in such a faithful and reverent way.

Perhaps historical consciousness is most evident in performances by Beatles tribute bands like the US-based Rain and BritBeat and bands whose performances I attended during my fieldwork in Argentina in 2008–2009, like The Beats and The Shouts. As I described above, these performances typically feature a three- or four-act structure which moves chronologically from the Beatles' early performances on *The Ed Sullivan Show* in 1964 to the *Sgt. Pepper* period of 1967, with a grand finale of songs from the *White Album/Let It Be/Abbey Road* era. These act changes are marked not only by changes in repertoire but also changes in costume, with matching dark suits for the early Beatles era, brightly colored faux military jackets for *Sgt. Pepper*, and clothing that seeks to mimic the appearance of the Beatles on the *Abbey Road* album cover for the final set. Concerts of this type exist on a different scale than a tribute band performance that takes place in a small bar or rock club. Instead, these concerts are often staged in large theaters or at prestigious concert halls that usually host Western classical music and only rarely feature performances by rock musicians. Tickets to these tribute band concerts are often expensive, with seats ranging from $50 to $100. Yet even at these prices, demand for these bands is high. For example, during the weeklong run of shows at the Academy of Music in Philadelphia in 2007 described above, Rain sold nearly all of its available tickets. Yet in just a few short years, their popularity had dramatically increased such that, by 2011, Rain had performed an extended run at two Broadway theatres in New York, totaling three hundred shows. Like Rain, several Beatles tribute bands (as well as the ABBA tribute Björn Again) feature multiple "casts," so that several versions of the group can play simultaneously, satisfying the demand for these performances in the United States and around the world.

Other tribute band performances in which historical consciousness is foregrounded include the many concerts marking anniversaries: for example, a concert at the 2008 Beatles tribute band festival Abbey Road on the River (AROTR) in Louisville, Kentucky, in which the fortieth anniversary of the release of the Beatles' *The White Album* was marked by a concert performance of the album all the way through, re-created as closely as possible to the original recording by a cast of musicians from various tribute bands, with the addition of a string and brass section. In his spoken introduction to the concert, festival promoter Gary Jacob testified not only to the historical importance of the album itself, but to the historic nature of its reproduction at the festival:

> Thank all of you for making this the biggest night in the history at Abbey Road on the River, that's obvious. And the support we continue to get from all of you is overwhelming. Let's get some of those corporate buildings over there to support this event [gestures to the large office buildings that form a backdrop for the AROTR festival in downtown Louisville]. So we can stay here for another fifty years so all our kids and grandkids can experience what we're all experiencing here [applause]. This should last as long as the Kentucky Derby. This is a great event. And you made it that way.
>
> Ladies and gentlemen, in my opinion, *The White Album* is their magnum opus. I think it is their greatest piece of work. I know that's debatable with some people. But this work, what these people have done to create this piece tonight, with strings and horns and full orchestration, and thirty cast members on and off the stage, and a full reproduction of "Revolution Number 9" [the album's eight-minute *musique concrète* piece, almost never attempted by tribute bands] I promise you it will be one of the greatest rock and roll shows you've ever seen. Ladies and gentlemen, *The White Album*.

Interestingly, Jacob does not introduce the band in his comments; instead he introduces the album. While he certainly gives the performers their due, it is the album itself, and its fortieth anniversary, that are given place of pride. This concert was given prime billing on the festival's main outdoor stage at 9 p.m. on Saturday night, testifying to how important Jacob thought this reproduction was and how many audience members this commemorative performance would draw.

In fact, much of my early fieldwork on tribute bands corresponded with observances of anniversaries for some of the iconic events of the 1960s and 1970s. In 2009, the fortieth anniversary of the release of the album *Abbey Road* was marked by a similar concert at the festival. Several Beatles tribute bands around the world also took the opportunity to re-create the Beatles' final concert on the occasion of its fortieth anniversary, in January 2009. The fortieth anniversary of the release of the rock opera *Tommy* by the Who was also marked by several tribute bands playing the album in its entirety. The historical consciousness that these anniversary concerts are both partaking in and helping to construct now seems to be a persistent feature of popular music culture. Indeed, the 2010s and 2020s also saw forty-fifth and fiftieth anniversary markings of events from the 1960s.

Why do some tribute bands perform in ways heavily influenced by historical consciousness, out of a strong engagement with the past, and with a sense of purpose toward re-performing that history for an audience? There are at least two primary reasons for this. First, every tribute band musician I interviewed spoke of the deep relationship they had to the music they performed, and they described re-creating the history of the music as important and fulfilling work. Second, tribute band musicians are also reacting to audience and market feedback: tribute bands that advertise their concerts as commemorating anniversaries or as a musical journey through the history of a band are able to charge more money and inspire more audience engagement than a band that performs a few rough cover versions.

Victoria, a woman from the United Kingdom I interviewed at the AROTR festival in Louisville who had seen the Beatles themselves perform several times when she was a teenager in London in the early 1960s, told me that she prefers, in her words, the "authentic" tribute bands—that is, those that dress up like the Beatles, play period instruments, and take on appropriate stage personas and mannerisms. However, she did not want Americans to think they had seen the "real thing" if they had only seen a Beatles tribute band performance. These exaggerated performances—in which the "George" in a Beatles tribute band wobbles his leg in time to the music (a move called the "Liverpool leg") and the "Paul" enthusiastically shakes his head back and forth at every opportunity—are based on an overfamiliarity with a limited number of canonized Beatles performances which have been played and replayed over the intervening decades. The historical reality, she maintains, was more complex. Even here, however, she does not call into question the ultimate pursuit of re-creating the past; she only wants this re-creation to be *more* accurate, *more* faithful to the way things actually were.

Tribute bands are willing to take large measures to re-create, re-perform, and allow fans to enact relationships with the popular music past. When I was conducting fieldwork in Argentina in 2008, the Beats, a tribute to the Beatles, played a concert at the Teatro Gran Rex, a large Broadway-style theatre on Avenida Corrientes, the main avenue in the theatre district of Buenos Aires. This performance had been advertised heavily around the city in posters that gave the show's title as "HISTÓRICO" and juxtaposed a full-color image of the four members of The Beats with shaggy hair, dark suits, and skinny ties with

Tribute Bands and Historical Consciousness in Popular Music 39

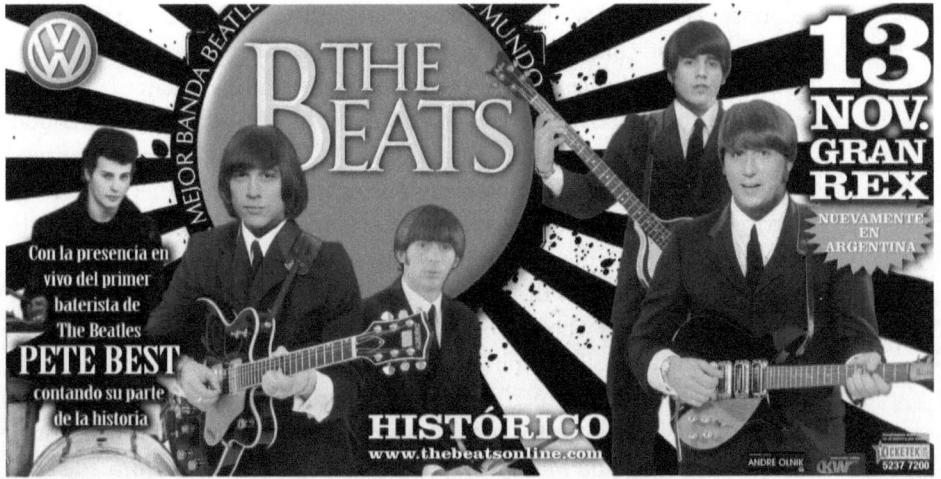

Poster advertising a 2008 concert performance by The Beats in Buenos Aires, Argentina, with an appearance by former Beatles drummer Pete Best.

a grainy black-and-white photo of Pete Best. Text on the posters explained that the concert would feature "la presencia en vivo del primer baterista de The Beatles, contando su parte de la historia" [the live appearance of the first drummer for the Beatles, telling his part of the story].

Best had been the original drummer for the Beatles, but was fired in 1962 and replaced by Ringo Starr shortly before the band became famous. After leaving the music business for several decades, Best had returned, leading a band that performed early 1960s-era rock 'n' roll and cashing in on his association with the most famous rock band in the world, a band viewed by rock music culture as the most historically significant. In fact, I had seen the Pete Best Band perform the previous spring at AROTR. Best, however, did not perform at this concert in Buenos Aires. After the concert, I went to Best's website and found a section describing how Best was available to be booked to appear as a "guest" for public events—one assumes, for a hefty fee—and that was his role at this performance. During the middle of the concert, he appeared onstage with the musicians of The Beats, who asked him a few questions in Spanish about his time with the Beatles. The questions were then relayed to Best by a translator, who also translated his responses in English to the band and the audience. To conclude this onstage interview, the musician who performed the part of John Lennon asked Best to describe Lennon. Best replied, confidently, with one word: "Genius." The translator did not bother to translate this response, but the crowd still burst into immediate applause. "Genius" is a simple cognate of the Spanish word "genio," but phonetic similarity might not be the only reason the response was left untranslated. Perhaps the translator surmised that the crowd at a tribute band concert would be very familiar with the word and concept of "genius," since audience members had paid a substantial amount of money to buy tickets to a concert re-performing the music of musicians now understood, by at least some in rock music culture, as geniuses. This question-and-answer sequence was repeated as the musicians portraying Paul McCartney and George Harrison also asked Best to describe McCartney and Harrison as well. To both questions, Best gave the same reply, "Genius," which was again applauded by the audience. Finally, the drummer in the tribute band asked Best to describe Ringo Starr, the man who had replaced Best in the Beatles after Best had been fired from the band. Best replied simply and confidently, but with a different answer this time: "Drummer," he said with a grin, and the crowd chuckled in response. The band retreated to their instruments and played through Chuck Berry's "Rock and Roll Music," a song the Beatles had often performed in the early 1960s, when Best was a member. Best remained on stage while the Beats played, clapping his hands on beats two and four and smiling. After the Beats finished the song, Best left the stage, having apparently given his seal of approval to the group, blessed the event with his presence, and provided a living connection to an honored past.

The Mythology of the Rock Past

For about fifty years now, consumers of popular culture in the United States—and around the world—have been bombarded with images and sounds from the past: more specifically, from the years of the 1960s and 1970s, years that corresponded to the adolescence and youth of the baby boomer generation, those born between 1946 and 1964. According to these images and the popular historical narratives they accompany, the first performance of the Beatles on *The Ed Sullivan Show* on February 9, 1964, was one of the most important events of the early 1960s, on par with the Woolworth's lunch counter sit-ins, the March on Washington, and the assassination of President Kennedy. Bob Dylan's trio of albums from 1965 and 1966—*Bringing It All Back Home, Highway 61 Revisited,* and *Blonde on Blonde*—marked, as Greil Marcus described them, one of the most intense outbreaks of twentieth-century modernism.[32] In his account of Jann Wenner's *Rolling Stone* magazine (founded 1967), Robert Draper noted that its reporters interviewed Bob Dylan, John Lennon, Mick Jagger, Janis Joplin, Pete Townshend, and Eric Clapton with the sense of purpose a *Time* reporter would bring to an interview with Henry Kissinger, suggesting that these musical figures and their activities were seen as important and generation-defining, creating history that affected young people as much as Kissinger and Nixon's decisions about the Vietnam War.[33] Continuing its run as one of the most influential music publications, *Rolling Stone* still provides serious, in-depth coverage of new pop stars—along with devoting a hefty amount of space to celebrating the music and icons of the 1960s and 1970s, even decades after these figures have left the top of the pop charts, or, in some cases, decades after their deaths.

In this mythology, popular music recordings and events are seen as encapsulating the cultural zeitgeist. The Beatles' *Sgt. Pepper* album ushers in the Summer of Love in 1967—the sexual and spiritual awakening of a generation.[34] The following year, Jimi Hendrix's double album *Electric Ladyland* (especially its cover of Bob Dylan's "All Along the Watchtower") and the Beatles' *The White Album* (another double album, balancing ballads with hard-edged experimental tracks like "Helter Skelter," "Yer Blues," and "Revolution 9") provide the perfect soundtrack for the tumultuous year of 1968—the year of the assassination of Martin Luther King Jr. and student protests at Columbia University and in Paris.[35] The August 1969 Woodstock festival in upstate New York was the apotheosis, a weekend like a return to the Garden of Eden, with peace, love, and music.[36] More than fifty years later, these musical events and recordings have attained the status of an important and profound cultural patrimony—not just through the mere passage of time but because of decisions made by power brokers to venerate these events above others, as Barbara Kirshenblatt-Gimblett describes in her discussion of heritage.

We can see a stark example of the biases of these cultural power brokers by comparing the reception of Woodstock to that of the Harlem Cultural Festival of 1969. With headliners including Stevie Wonder, Gladys Knight and the Pips, Sly and the Family Stone, The Edwin Hawkins Singers, Nina Simone, B.B. King, The Staple Singers, and The 5th Dimension, the Harlem Cultural Festival equals Woodstock as a musical event featuring artists who were both currently popular and highly influential in the decades following. Similar to Woodstock, the Harlem Cultural Festival was filmed by a camera crew and attracted several hundred thousand attendees, many of whom testified to the formative role the festival played in their lives in both musical and social terms. Unlike Woodstock, however, the Harlem Cultural Festival featured primarily Black artists performing for primarily Black audiences. While director Michael Wadleigh was able to convert his Woodstock footage into a widely viewed and critically acclaimed documentary film premiering less than a year after the conclusion of the festival itself, Hal Tulchin's footage of the Harlem Cultural Festival was not able to attract the funding to be widely released, promoted, and viewed. Consequently, while Woodstock became celebrated and canonized, the cultural significance of the Harlem Cultural Festival was largely forgotten and ignored until Ahmir "Questlove" Thompson, drummer for The Roots and well-known curator of the Black musical past, released a documentary film about the festival *Summer of Soul (. . . Or, When The Revolution Could Not Be Televised)* in 2021. The documentary's title is both a reference to Gil Scott-Heron's 1970 song, "The Revolution Will Not Be Televised" and an acknowledgment that it took someone of Questlove's status and influence within the mainstream media to bring this event of Black musical history from fifty years earlier to greater public attention.

However, other events of popular music history—especially those originally appealing to white baby boomers who would come to occupy positions of influence and power in the media industry—have not needed this type of intervention to be viewed as historically significant. Instead, listeners and consumers have heard and seen recycled images and sounds of these albums, hit songs, and live performances for decades. They have been taught to a younger generation—several generations in fact, including my own; I was born in 1983 to baby boomer parents. These events are also familiar to my students, most of whom were born in the year 2000 or later. And images, sounds, and discourse about these events have traveled around the globe via multinational media companies, as well as being talked about endlessly in the United States.[37]

Given the "historic," "generation-defining," "once-in-a-lifetime" character of these events, how terrible it is to have missed them! But many people must have, as these events have acquired much of their renown and status in the cultural canon only retrospectively. Seventy million people in the United States watched *The Ed Sullivan Show* on February 9, 1964, a very high number, but one that represents less than half of the approximately 192 million people living in the United States at the time. The 1969 Woodstock festival in Bethel, New York, looms equally large in the cultural memory, but even by generous estimates, only around five hundred thousand people attended the festival, a tiny sliver of the US population. An equally small number of people played in garage rock bands in the 1960s, moved to Haight-Ashbury in 1967, or listened to the Hendrix albums that critics and historians have, retrospectively, celebrated for their revolutionary qualities. Yet baby boomers have been constantly told that these are the events that define their generation. And those of us born later or in other parts of the world have been told that this is the "real" history, when and where music and culture really mattered. The promise of tribute band concerts is that baby boomers—and others—can experience these events, even if they missed them in the 1960s, with the help of a tribute band dedicated to re-creating this music as closely as possible. For decades, we have been exposed to this history through mediated simulacra. At tribute band concerts, audience members of all ages can "relive" these events for the first time.

Postmodernism and Tribute Bands

In contrast to my argument that performers and audiences in the tribute band scene are motivated by an awareness of and respect for the past as history, the popular music scholar Andy Bennett describes tribute band performance as a particularly postmodern phenomenon in which time and history recirculate in a kind of free play where anything is possible:

> In the course of tribute band performances, dead rock stars are brought back to life, defunct bands are reassembled, and classic live performances of yesteryear are accurately reproduced again and again. Moreover, in revisiting a tributed group or artist's recording and performing history, tribute bands are in the privileged position of being able to creatively play around with that history and will often do so to present an idealized version of events.[38]

Bennett's description of the events that take place during a typical tribute band performance is accurate. Yet, what is important is not just the events that occur onstage, but how these events are presented by musicians and interpreted by tribute band audiences. By breaking down Bennett's discussion, we can more fully understand tribute band performances not primarily, or only, as a postmodern phenomenon but as events presented by musicians and received by audience members deeply concerned with history.

To begin, Bennett is correct that, during the course of a tribute band performance, "dead rock stars are brought back to life." Tribute band concerts seem to feature performances by some of the most iconic musicians of rock music history—including John Lennon, George Harrison, Jim Morrison, and Freddie Mercury. Because of their deep engagement with popular music history and their affinity for the band being "tributed," audience members at tribute band concerts are all too aware that these performers are dead, and no one is fooled that the tribute band musicians portraying these figures represent any kind of reincarnation of the original musicians. Yet, often in tribute band performances, musicians will dress up like these dead performers, affect their accents and stage mannerisms, and, most importantly, attempt to replicate their vocal and instrumental performances as closely as possible. For this, they are rewarded with approval from the audience, in the form of screams of "John!" or "Jimbo!" and an enthusiasm that rarely greets these same musicians when they are performing in bands playing original material. Bernd Gudernatsch, the bassist in the German Beatles tribute band Lucy in the Sky, often exhorts his audience, "Give me a little Beatlemania!" and the crowd responds with shouts and applause.

Furthermore, as Bennett argues, "classic live performances of yesteryear are accurately reproduced again and again." Indeed, as discussed above, specific live performances of bands such as the Beatles and the Grateful Dead are often re-performed at tribute band events. Finally, tribute band concerts do present their audiences with an "idealized version of events," especially a version in which albums like *Abbey Road*, *The Dark Side of the Moon*, or *Led Zeppelin II* were always received the way that they are now received by rock critics, historians, and consumers: as masterpieces and as respected "works" of art deserving of reverential attention and the status of high culture.

The literary scholar David Damrosch's description of the terms *classic* and *masterpiece* can provide useful insights here, especially in reference to the sense of historical consciousness that tribute band culture exhibits with regard to its prized works from the 1960s and 1970s:

> The "classic" is a work of transcendent, even foundational value, often identified particularly with Greek and Roman literature (still taught today in departments of Classics) and often closely associated with imperial values, as Frank Kermode has shown in his book *The Classic*. The "masterpiece," on the other hand, can be an ancient or a modern work . . . The "masterpiece," indeed, came into prominence in the nineteenth century as literary studies began to deemphasize the dominant Greco-Roman classics, elevating the modern masterpiece to a level of near equality with the long-established classics. In this literary analog of a liberal democracy, the (often middle-class) masterworks could engage in a "great conversation" with their aristocratic forebears, a conversation in which their culture and class of origin mattered less than the great ideas they expressed anew.[39]

Allowing for some flexibility in terminology—"classic" and "masterpiece" are not always rigorously distinct in either literary or musical studies—the concepts that Damrosch is describing in the field of literature have clear parallels in the reception of music. In Western music, the classics are those works by composers such as Bach, Mozart, and Beethoven that are often discussed by scholars, critics, and classical music aficionados as being transcendent and foundational, the stuff of which all future music of value will be based.[40] In this view, modern "masterpieces" could very well be those works of popular music—the compositions and recordings of Duke Ellington, John Coltrane's *A Love Supreme*, Marvin Gaye's *What's Going On*, and, most importantly for my argument in this chapter, albums like *Abbey Road, Sgt. Pepper's Lonely Hearts Club Band, Blonde on Blonde,* and *The Dark Side of the Moon*—which, by sheer inventiveness, mastery of formal structure, or presumed authenticity and directness of expression, have been accepted by some critics and cultural gatekeepers as worthy additions to the accepted canon of classical music, existing on its same elevated plane of aesthetic experience. Equating the music played by tribute bands to that performed by symphony orchestras, the tribute band promoter Jeff Parry argues that the new elevated status afforded to (a particular subset of) rock music should be self-evident: "Well, the music is as they say classic. People are still going out to hear Beethoven, Mozart, Haydn, etc., right? And this is the same sort of thing. It's classic music. It's survived the ages. It will survive the ages. And so people want to see it. They can buy the records, download it. But the inevitable experience is seeing something live."[41] For Parry and others who follow his reasoning, this explains the appeal of tribute band performances, which present this rock music live, often in venues, like the concert at the Academy of Music in Philadelphia described at the beginning of this chapter, that are also occupied by ensembles performing the canon of Western classical music.

Bennett's point that tribute bands present an idealized version of history is an important one. For at least several decades, commentators like Allan Bloom, in his 1987 book *The Closing of the American Mind*, have argued that cultural relativism has led an attack on history, and that old truths have now been opened up for debate—especially as these truths were previously transmitted through the "great works" of Western literature, philosophy, and art. This has particular relevance for an ethnomusicological approach to the study of tribute bands and the development of historical consciousness for two reasons. First, cultural relativism has been a central tenet of anthropological and ethnomusicological thought for a century, and a critique of the presumed superiority of Western classical music has been an important part of the ethnomusicological project.[42] Second, the people that Bloom worried about—students who graduated from American universities in the 1960s and in the decades following, for whom "rock music is as unquestioned and unproblematic as the air [they] breathe, and very few have any acquaintance at all with classical music"—make up a large percentage of the audience for tribute band concerts in the United States.[43] These were the middle-class, middle-aged white Americans that I went to concerts with, observed, and interviewed as part of my ethnographic fieldwork on tribute bands in the United States. I drank beer out of glass bottles and wine out of plastic cups with these folks, sometimes sitting quietly in our assigned seats in formal concert halls, sometimes on our feet dancing in the grass on a festival lawn, shouting, and singing along with the band. As participants in the tribute band scene, they do not behave as Bloom might have predicted or as Bennett describes.

If history is under attack, the sense that history is important for day-to-day life is still attractive for a wide range of people, including those engaged in the "retro culture" that Reynolds describes, Civil War "living historians" or "reenactors," amateur genealogists, tribute band fans and musicians, and the other artists and listeners engaged with the popular music past this book analyzes.[44] Instead of Bloom's apocalyptic predictions, "History" may have shifted from being the exclusive property of the ruling class and elite culture to being something that is more appealing and available to the public at large, as Trouillot also suggests in his description of the wide variety of historical narrators discussed in this book's introduction. Jean-François Lyotard called our age a postmodern one and defined postmodernism as "incredulity toward metanarratives."[45] That is, the idea that society is marching along in one recognizable direction, whatever that direction might be: Progress, Conflict, Golden Age Followed by Decadence. Instead, in a postmodern world, we struggle to assign meaning to the events we encounter in our lives and place them into a coherent order. If cultural relativism has influenced academic and political elites to refrain from using metanarratives to classify historical events, partisans of popular culture have stepped into the void left by the retreat of the elites, appropriating these narratives of history and applying them to events in popular culture.

Tribute band performances and other aspects of historical consciousness in popular music I describe in this book are not necessarily the sites of free, postmodernist play that they may appear to be. In fact, many tribute band musicians and audience members take a reverential stance toward history and are not interested in playing with it; instead, they are interested in re-creating that history and re-performing it as authentically as possible. Bennett is clearly right when he points out that tribute band performances can be interpreted as postmodern: after all, bands are attempting to faithfully re-create concerts for audiences who were not originally present. However, I suggest we pay particular attention to the kind of historical knowledge and historical consciousness present in tribute band musicians and audience members. Participants in the tribute band scene know popular music history, and their engagement with the past helps influence their evaluation and enjoyment of music in the present. This is evident when tribute band fans discuss the small details of tribute band performances, argue over nuances in instrumental and vocal techniques, appreciate when bands structure their performances chronologically, and make special effort to attend tribute band concerts devoted to marking anniversaries: all of which I observed during my fieldwork and which are important aspects of the tribute band scene.

Rock music culture may have begun as a postmodern "rupture" against the dominant culture, but as rock music fans have aged and acquired positions for themselves in the economic and cultural mainstream, so has rock music. Many accounts from rock musicians and fans testify to the "shock" they felt on first encountering rock music, whether that encounter was seeing Elvis or the Beatles on television or hearing the Sex Pistols for the first time. These events are portrayed not only as a radical break but as literally "coming out of nowhere," breaking free from both prior conventions and history. Such accounts are encountered less frequently now, and a larger current in the rock world concerns constructing histories and placing those events that "came out of nowhere" into a historical narrative. Tribute bands, by re-playing and re-performing this history, provide a key example of this historical consciousness in the popular music world. For music scholars, the increasing popularity of tribute bands and the spread of historical consciousness in rock music represent a kind of bold-print, spectacular case of contemporary musical activities taking place under the shadow of the past. An attention to tribute bands and historical consciousness in rock very clearly shows a dynamic we can also find at work in other genres and contexts, though sometimes in a less immediately apparent fashion. Additionally, rock music culture exerts an undeniable, if contested, influence on other types of popular music. The *Smithsonian Anthology of Hip-Hop and Rap*, released to great acclaim in 2021, is a case in point: a nine-CD collection of the genre's recorded history, spanning more than forty years, packaged with a three-hundred-page companion book, and retailing for $150. Considering this box set for the *New York Times*, critic Jon Caramanica quotes rapper Chuck D and links the production of this anthology to the memorializing and canonizing impulses of rock: "'I'm envious of what the rock world does,' said Chuck D of Public Enemy, a member of the executive committee, referring to how rock 'n' roll consistently takes stock of, and celebrates, its own history. 'I was interested and jump-started this idea because I got tired of us not being treated like the royalty that the genre is.'"[46]

Still, while rock music culture is clearly influential, ideas about historical consciousness from rock music will also interact with historical thinking that is already a major component of other genres as well. If Chuck D—one of the luminaries who served on the committee that selected tracks for the *Smithsonian Anthology of Hip-Hop and Rap*—points out rock music culture's influence on the historical consciousness shown by this project, we should also remember that the curation of the musical past through crate-digging, DJing, and sampling has always been built into the genre of hip-hop: an engagement with and reverence for the past that developed independently of rock music culture's influence. In this vein, Daphne Brooks also argues that since at least the epoch-defining 1920 recording of "Crazy Blues" by Mamie Smith, Black female musicians "have played crucial roles *as* archives, as the innovators of performances and recordings that stood in *for* and *as* the memory of a people," despite this work often being "trivialized and minimized" by cultural power brokers—largely white men—who write the official histories of popular music (italics in original).[47] As Brooks suggests, musicians and listeners use a wide variety of musical styles to enact relationships with the past.

Before rock's beginnings in the late 1940s and rise to cultural juggernaut status in the 1960s, singers, instrumentalists, producers, and listeners helped construct a repertoire of songs we now know as the Great American Songbook through repeated performance, recording, and listening of this body of material. Exemplifying this book's focus on historical consciousness in popular music, the performance and reception of these songs over the decades have often associated them, either positively or negatively, as inextricably linked to the past. I explore this link between a specific musical repertoire and an imagined version of the past in the two chapters that follow.

CHAPTER 2

YESTERDAYS

Performing the Past Through the Great American Songbook from Ella Fitzgerald to Bob Dylan

Tribute bands came to prominence in the United States and other countries starting in the 1990s, and they have remained an important fixture of live performance scenes. However, tribute bands are certainly not the first instance of popular musicians enacting a relationship with the past through the re-performance of previous musical material, nor the first instance of listeners finding this re-performance to be enjoyable, meaningful, and worthy of their attention. Another feature of the popular music landscape over the last several decades showing a deep relationship to the past has been the recording of albums of songs from the so-called "Great American Songbook."[1] This is the name given to a select body of songs written between about 1920 and 1960 that have been sung by pop singers and improvised on as "standards" by jazz musicians for decades after they were originally written. After a discussion of some of the issues involved in the composition and reception of these songs, this chapter will begin with an analysis of Ella Fitzgerald, the musician probably most responsible for establishing the Songbook tradition as a coherent, venerable recording and performance repertoire—and not just a stack of musty old songs from decades prior. Over the past seventy years of musical history, there have been hundreds of singers and instrumentalists for whom this repertoire is their "home turf," the main body of songs that they sing or perform. The next chapter will focus on a period in the career of trumpeter Miles Davis, who was strongly associated with performing tunes from the Songbook for much of his career, but slowly deleted these songs from his setlists during a time when his music and desired audience changed dramatically in the late 1960s and early 1970s.

The majority of this chapter, however, will be focused on artists who came to prominence in other genres of music—including genres of music that are typically thought of as very different from the Songbook tradition—but who have reached back to the past and recorded albums of material from the Great American Songbook at crucial junctures in their careers. A list of well-known artists who have recorded such albums would include some of the most commercially successful artists in genres such as rock, folk, country, pop, R&B, and hip-hop: Bob Dylan, Gloria Estefan, Bryan Ferry, Art Garfunkel, Queen Latifah, Cyndi Lauper, Annie Lennox, Paul McCartney, Willie Nelson, Linda Ronstadt, Seal, Carly Simon, Rod Stewart, and James Taylor, among others. For many of these artists, this was not an aberration or one-off left turn, as we will see. Linda Ronstadt made three albums of this material with arranger Nelson Riddle in the 1980s, Rod Stewart recorded five Songbook albums between 2002 and 2010, and Bob Dylan released five discs (two full-length albums and one three-CD set titled *Triplicate*) of standards in the 2010s. Willie Nelson has also returned many times to the Songbook over the course of his own long career, ranging from his 1978 *Stardust* album to the 2021 *That's Life*, Nelson's second album of songs sung by Frank Sinatra and named after one of Sinatra's signature tunes. (*My Way* was the first, in 2018.) Recording a standards album has become almost an expected path for aging pop and rock musicians, such that it is viewed by some critics as notable or commendable when musicians *do not* follow it. Discussing Madonna's 2019 album *Madame X* that featured Latin pop influences, collaborations from contemporary hip-hop artists, and was released when Madonna was sixty years old, Ben Beaumont-Thomas of the British newspaper *The Guardian* writes: "To her credit, she has not done what many in her position would then do: lick their wounds and sell a jazz standards album to Radio 2 listeners."[2]

The reception of Songbook albums by aging pop and rock musicians has been mixed. Some of these records have been hailed as artistic and commercial triumphs, featuring great artists showing how their talents can be applied to a body of material outside of their typical comfort zone. For some sympathetic critics, these recordings also demonstrate the sturdiness or "timelessness" of the material itself—which is both flexible enough to accommodate the wide-ranging, idiosyncratic approaches of pop stars and as relevant now as it was decades previously. Other releases, perhaps Rod Stewart's albums most notoriously, have received less positive attention from critics. Alexis Petridis summarizes the critical reaction to many of these projects: "Most great American songbook albums feel grafted on to the artist's career: too obviously glommed together as a money-making exercise or a means of tiding them over when inspiration fails to strike."[3] Even more damning is Jesse Cataldo: "Few things symbolize creative death as succinctly as the standards album, now a frequent terminal point for aging artists who seek to forestall the end of their productive output by capitalizing on the golden-hued nostalgia of bygone hits."[4]

These are typical critiques, and they very clearly contain what we have discussed as the widespread ideology of newness in popular music discourse. We can see this ideology expressed in the highly charged language used by these critics: "inspiration fails to strike," "creative death," "terminal point," and "aging artists." These are all negative things to be avoided at all costs. There is also the idea of the profit motive—"a money-making exercise," "capitalizing on the golden-hued nostalgia"—in contrast to the idea of doing new things out of creative compulsion, a compulsion that is not tainted by the capitalist profit-seeking impulse that raids the past for any scrap of profitable raw material it might still contain.[5] For many influential critics and writers (and doubtless for some ordinary listeners), this is the worst fate that can befall a musician: performing old music for money, rather than out of creative necessity, at the end of one's career.

But let us not be unduly influenced by anticommercial sentiments and ideology. Just like any recording released by a popular music artist, these Songbook albums are intended to make money for their creators as commodities, and their success (or lack thereof) will be a major focus of analysis in this chapter. Contrary to Petridis's claim, by no means have these albums been universally successful or a surefire money-making proposition for their creators. In addition to serving as commodities in the marketplace, these albums perform cultural work for the artists who produce them and for the listeners who purchase and listen to them. The recording of standards by musicians originally associated with other repertoires (especially songs which they themselves wrote) troubles our conventional notions of firm generic boundaries and hierarchies in popular music.[6] These albums also serve as an important site of historical consciousness in popular music, by salvaging songs from the past and lovingly re-presenting them to listeners. With a focus on these themes, recordings of the Great American Songbook take on an importance in cultural understandings of popular music not commensurate with the limited level of engagement they have previously received from scholars and critics.

The Songbook Tradition

There is now a well-developed industry of books, articles, and songbooks themselves (books with lyrics and piano accompaniment meant for amateur home performance) that aim to describe and honor the Great American Songbook and the tradition of standards. In the fields of music criticism and appreciation, Alec Wilder, Will Friedwald, and Philip Furia have been key figures in these tasks. Published in 1972, Wilder's *American Popular Song: The Great Innovators, 1900–1950* is a foundational source of information about these songs, but also an important primary source document itself: an early example of the attempt to define and codify this tradition as a venerable body of work from the past.[7] Wilder provides over five hundred pages of analysis and explanation of songs, but leaves a specific discussion of his methods and premises to be written by James T. Maher, the book's editor, in a seventeen-page introduction. Maher explains that the book is organized around the work of individual songwriters in what we would now recognize as a familiar kind of "Great Man" history of American music. That this book was published in the early 1970s, just after this tradition had largely been superseded in popularity and importance by developments in rock, soul, and R&B is not incidental. Wilder's exploration of these songs roughly ends in the 1950s, because, according to Maher, "The rock era was about to begin."[8] Maher provides a further example of the ideology of newness in popular music with his claim that the "professional tradition in song writing was nearing its end" at this time period due to the "pop audience, a predominantly young consumer group that is notorious for its short attention span, and its insatiable hunger for the *new* [emphasis in original]."[9] Will Friedwald has followed in Wilder's footsteps with several well-researched books defining and honoring this tradition, shifting slightly from Wilder's composer-centric view to focus on the songs, the singers who performed them, and the recorded albums on which these performances are eventually contained and canonized. We can clearly see this division of focus in three of the books Friedwald has published: *Stardust Melodies: The Biography of Twelve of America's Most Popular Songs, A Biographical Guide to the Great Jazz and Pop Singers*, and *The Great Jazz and Pop Vocal Albums*.[10] Friedwald has also turned his attention to two of the singers most associated with popularizing the Great American Songbook, writing a biography of Frank Sinatra and collaborating with Tony Bennett on the singer's autobiography.[11] Throughout his work, Friedwald is writing as a historian, but also as a critic who is a celebratory champion of the musical quality of this material. Furia supplements Wilder's near-exclusive focus on the music of this tradition by devoting his 1990 book to *The Poets of Tin Pan Alley: A History of America's Great Lyricists*.[12]

The commercial publishing and sheet music world, typified by companies such as Hal Leonard, also often uses these terms "Great American Songbook" and "standards" in book titles and anthologies. Such books go in and out of print as their contents are packaged and repackaged to stimulate consumer demand, but a 2007 anthology from Hal Leonard is a representative example of the type of language used to describe this body of material: *The Great American Songbook—The Composers: Music and Lyrics for Over 100 Standards from the Golden Age of American Song.* For such publishers, more so than academics and critics, naming and defining this tradition is central to their main task of marketing products to be purchased by consumers. However, even the "noncommercial" world of academic music theory scholarship has also participated in defining and describing the distinctive features of this body of music, most notably with the work of Yale music theorist Allen Forte (1926–2014), a scholar better known for his dense studies of early twentieth-century atonal classical music.[13] Forte turned his attention to the Songbook tradition late in his career and produced two books analyzing it: *The American Popular Ballad of the Golden Era, 1924–1950* and *Listening to Classic American Popular Song*.[14]

Wilder, Friedwald, Furia, Forte, and others seem to think that there is a "there" there: that distinctive features exist that mark out the Great American Songbook as a stable, bounded tradition, a "discrete musical entity," to use the definition from Maher's introduction to Wilder's *American Popular Song*. Whether this is true or not matters less than the fact that the Great American Songbook has become a social reality, something that, even if it did not exist based on the essential or internal characteristics of the songs themselves, has been socially constructed through artifacts like these books analyzing and describing it—and the dozens of recordings that specifically pay homage to it by name. Readers interested in the history, development, and features of this body of material would do well to consult some of the sources cited here that explore the characteristics of songs and this tradition in more exhaustive detail than I can do in this chapter. However, some aspects of these songs and their history will be crucial for us to understand when we analyze how the recording of albums of this material fits into historical consciousness in popular music.

Ben Yagoda lists three main sources for the body of songs that come to be known as "standards": "Broadway shows, Hollywood movies, and one-off Tin Pan Alley compositions."[15] In all cases, these songs would originally be distributed to audiences in a variety of ways. Listeners might first hear them in a kind of "one time only" unique performance environment, such as hearing a song at a Broadway show or movie theatre. These two modes of listening have an important difference, of course, in that a song presented on film and heard in a movie theater does not have the performer in person, sharing what Walter Benjamin famously referred to as the performer's "aura" with the audience.[16] But movies and theatrical performances are similar in that they are essentially nonrepeatable events for the listener or viewer. Audience members buy their tickets and sit down, and they hear the song once in the course of a performance—barring a reprise or, more rarely, an encore. If they want to hear the song again, they have to buy another ticket. Importantly, these are events that take place in the public sphere outside the intimate confines of the home; audience members do not have to "imagine" themselves as part of the greater community of listeners, they can see and hear for themselves the other people present at this performance or screening and observe and be influenced by the reactions of other people.[17]

There are three other primary ways for audiences to originally encounter these songs. None of these means are exclusive; they all worked together in concert to create a large body of songs that listeners interacted with in various formats over the span of several decades, a kind of multiple exposure that almost certainly contributed to this music's longevity and emotional power. The first one is perhaps the most surprising to twenty-first-century readers: sheet music. Reflecting the massive boom in piano production and ownership in the first decades of the twentieth century, sheet music was the primary commodity of the music industry for much of its early history. Sheet music was an important way for audiences to interact with the body of songs that would eventually be canonized as the Great American Songbook, either through browsing titles in a music store or seeking out specific songs to perform at home after initially hearing them in a different venue. Radio has its early beginnings in 1920 and spread quickly throughout the United States in a few years, such that hundreds of radio stations were licensed, and home radios became common. For our purposes, one of the most important radio programs got its start in 1935: *Your Hit Parade*, an hourlong show that presented the top songs of the week. In its beginnings, the *Your Hit Parade* tabulation was based on the statistics for best-selling sheet music, not recordings. For the listeners of *Your Hit Parade*, the vision of popular music culture they were presented with was one in which songs were more important than any one particular performance of them. On the program, songs were performed by a rotating, largely anonymous stable of singers—not necessarily the artists who had recorded them or performed them in films or Broadway shows.

In their early years, radio programs heavily emphasized live musical performances over the playing of recordings. Eventually, however, this convention—enforced by various government restrictions—was lifted and recorded music became ubiquitous on the airwaves.[18] Recordings eventually overtook sheet music as the best-selling and most lucrative commodity in the music industry—and as a key site for listeners to encounter the body of songs eventually known as the Great American Songbook. In his discussion of how recordings allow listeners different ways of interacting with music (as compared with live performance), Mark Katz analyzes seven "causes," properties of recordings that then have "effects" on the ways that listeners experience music: tangibility, repeatability, manipulability, portability, receptivity, (in)visibility, and temporality.[19] Repeatability is particularly important for the development of historical consciousness this book analyzes. This property of recording describes the fact that recordings can be replayed a seemingly infinite number of times, even decades after their original release. With the widespread popularity of recordings and playback equipment in the early twentieth century, for the first-time listeners were able to listen to their favorite songs almost at will. This bred a familiarity with the body of songs composed during this era that is called upon and reinforced by the later retrospective recordings of songs from this time period.

The time between the 1920s and the early 1960s—the years that gave birth to the Great American Songbook—was clearly a period of dramatic change in the United States: the ongoing Great Migration of African Americans from the rural South to the urban North and West; the Depression in the 1930s; the entry of the United States into World War II; the readjustment to postwar life and the beginnings of the baby boom; and activism for civil rights. Many of the technologies of production and dissemination used in the entertainment industries also underwent dramatic shifts during this time: shifts in record length and playback speed (78s, 45s, and later 33 RPM LPs), the switch from acoustic to electrical recordings, the adoption of microphones, and the transition from silent to sound films. Musicologist Charles Hamm argues that, surprisingly, the style of popular songs did not change very much during this period, despite the vast changes in the societal fabric generally and the music industry specifically. Taking the career of Irving Berlin as a primary example, Hamm notes: "Songs written by Irving Berlin in 1915 are essentially the same as those written thirty years later; continuity of musical style is one of the most striking features of the Tin Pan Alley era."[20] Surveying the popular music scene at the beginning of the 1950s, Hamm summarizes: "The song style that had served Tin Pan Alley so well had changed very little, except in details, for almost half a century."[21]

What was this style? Hamm offers a concise description of the rough musical form of songs from the Great American Songbook: "With almost no exceptions, they are in verse-chorus form, the verse sketching a dramatic situation or an emotional vignette, . . . and the chorus following as a 'set piece,' a more lyric section, elaborating on the situation set out by the verse."[22] Choruses themselves take on a limited number of forms, the vast majority of them lasting thirty-two measures, with eight-measure sections arranged in typical patterns like AABA or ABAC. In performance, these choruses were often themselves repeated several times, especially when performed by jazz musicians. A fair bit of musical repetition at various levels of structure is already baked into the form and performance of these songs, then, even before we take into account the repeatability of the songs once recorded. Rhythmically and harmonically, there was space for innovation. Composers such as George Gershwin, Jerome Kern, and Richard Rodgers moved away from songs harmonized by simple major and minor triads, and rhythms adapted from ragtime and the nascent genre of jazz made these songs rhythmically distinct from earlier styles of American popular song. In performance, these elements could be amplified, with instrumentalists largely free to further enrich notated chords with additional notes or substitutions. Melodies could also be interpreted rhythmically as individual performers saw fit, and the unique sense of time or "swing" that performers like Louis Armstrong, Billie Holiday, Frank Sinatra, and Miles Davis brought to their performances of standards is one of the main features that contemporary and later listeners find most valuable in these musicians. Hamm notes that the lyrics of these songs tended toward a narrow range of topics, "dealing almost exclusively with personal emotions, almost never with events outside of the person.... One searches almost in vain for songs touching in any way on the great social and political issues of those years."[23] This primary focus on romantic love rather than social issues fit the prerogatives of the growing media industry and its sense that popular culture was best suited for entertainment and escapism, not edification or activism.

Ella Fitzgerald, Norman Granz, and the Codification of the Songbook Tradition

The raw material for the Great American Songbook tradition dominates the American popular music scene for decades in the middle of the twentieth century. But more than just being a vast quantity of songs within a particular style, musicians and listeners begin to think of this music as a tangible and venerable tradition. Ella Fitzgerald was perhaps the musician most associated with the Great American Songbook, and especially with the idea that the Songbook was a coherent entity of songs from the past, worthy of being presented respectfully in comprehensive recordings. Her association with the Songbook comes primarily from her set of albums devoted to the work of individual composers (or composing teams) that were conceived of as unified projects and recorded when Fitzgerald was already both a veteran of the industry for twenty years and a commercially successful artist. The impact of these albums is the result of an interaction between the music contained on them and important aspects of listening and consumption practices, demographic trends, and new technology in the 1950s and 1960s.

The question of who created jazz is a notoriously unsettled one for jazz fans, critics, and musicians, but Fitzgerald is never seriously advanced as one of the genre's originators. Even such early figures as Louis Armstrong, Bessie Smith, and Duke Ellington are typically not thought to have invented the genre, though they are certainly among the genre's earliest critical and popular successes. Those musicians were all born around the turn of the twentieth century and were old enough to profit from the emergence of jazz and other related styles as major commercial forces in popular culture in the 1920s and 1930s. Fitzgerald was born roughly a generation later, in 1917. Her adolescence and musical development, therefore, took place at a time when jazz had been established as a style and, importantly, key recordings had been made and distributed on records and radio. One of Fitzgerald's biographers, Stuart Nicholson, argues that these new means of musical distribution were critical for both her own musical development and that of her audience:

> As a child Ella was among the first generation of youngsters to grow up with both the radio and the phonograph. For the first time music for the masses was freely available, revolutionizing popular song and popular singing, changing and transforming people's lives forever. Like the emergent cinema in relation to theater, records and radio brought music within everybody's reach.... It ushered in the age of the vernacular performer, but it did something more: It gave the audience a license to dream, to imagine that they, too, could become one of those performers, become famous, become a star.[24]

Fitzgerald's career began with her big break on November 21, 1934, when she won the famous Amateur Night competition at the Apollo Theater on 125th Street in Harlem. Winning this contest eventually brought her to the attention of Chick Webb, who was already a well-known bandleader around Harlem and had a regular gig at the Savoy Ballroom but had yet to make as much of an impact nationally as contemporary rivals like Duke Ellington. According to Nicholson, "Charlie Buchanan, the black manager of the Savoy Ballroom ... began urging Webb to add a female vocalist to his lineup. Buchanan could see the commercial potential a girl singer might make in creating a bridge between bandstand and audience."[25] Charles Linton, who was already singing with Chick Webb, explained the musical division of labor: "I did the classics and the ballad tunes, and they wanted me to find someone that I liked to do the swing tunes."[26] It was Linton who eventually put Fitzgerald and Webb in contact with each other, and in Linton's telling, commercial appeal and musical style were key determinants in the decision to hire Fitzgerald. Linton differentiated his singing of "the classics and the ballad tunes" from Fitzgerald's assignment of "the swing tunes": apparently those songs that had audience appeal but less timeless musical worth and seriousness. Christi Jay Wells has convincingly demonstrated how gendered notions of popularity, commercialism, and hierarchy are attached by critics to Fitzgerald's performances early in her career. For Wells, such critics link "popularity with femininity, deploying romanticized notions of anticommercialism and authenticity."[27] Though gendered roles are not my main focus in this chapter, we can also see that reactions to Fitzgerald concerning the "timelessness," or the "classic" qualities of her later performance and recorded repertoire—when, not incidentally, she devoted albums to individual "Great Man" male composers in a familiar canonizing move—also clearly contain gender politics.

In the 1930s, so-called "girl singers" had particular roles in swing bands, and we can hear this in "Love and Kisses," the first recording Fitzgerald made with Webb's band in June 1935. Nicholson's assessment of the song is that it clearly fit the commercial purposes that motivated Fitzgerald's hiring: "There could be no doubting Webb's intentions. 'Love and Kisses' was a commercial dance band arrangement with no pretensions to jazz. Webb, on recordings at least, was intent on appealing to the broadest audience possible."[28] Nicholson notes that, on the seventy-four full-band recordings that Webb would make over the rest of his career before his untimely death four years later on June 16, 1939, Fitzgerald would be featured on more than fifty of them. For Nicholson, this is clear evidence that Webb was moving toward a more commercial, pop-oriented direction and that Fitzgerald was key to these plans.

This shift in direction started to be noticed by those who had been longtime devotees of the Chick Webb Orchestra, including the critic and record producer John Hammond. In 1937, he took square aim at the songs recorded and performed by Fitzgerald and Webb, writing in *DownBeat* of his disappointment that commercial gimmicks and "badly written 'white' arrangements" have replaced the level of musicianship that Webb had earlier been known for—though Hammond also writes that Fitzgerald was "so great a personality that crowds usually overlook such deficiencies."[29] Hammond himself was white and a scion of the wealthy Vanderbilt family, but he disapproved of what he interpreted as Webb's turning away from the audience of Harlem dancers that he had cultivated at the Savoy: "In commercializing his band for the broadest possible appeal, Webb was focusing on white America, the constituency that could provide the biggest paychecks."[30] Again, Wells is crucial here for our understanding of this dynamic in the reception of jazz and other popular music genres: ideas about Blackness, masculinity, and anticommercialism are often linked together and set against whiteness, femininity, and mass commercial popularity. Hammond's critiques are an early example of a widespread phenomenon in the reception of music from African Americans by white audiences: the notion that these audiences will only accept something less than the real thing, which they will then support with their large buying power, while other more authentic artists will languish in obscurity and comparative poverty. The undeniable commercial success of white musicians like Paul Whiteman and Pat Boone certainly gives evidence for claims like Hammond's, and such musicians are usually depicted in historical narratives as villains—or at least as charlatans—for their commercial success at playing a watered-down version of Black musical innovation for white audiences. White Americans, of course, are not monolithic, and there will be different white audiences that Fitzgerald will appeal to at different times; Hammond himself might have represented white jazz fans who had different tastes from those of the average listener at this time. For our purposes, what is key is that different repertoires are viewed by influential critics as having vastly different potentials to be high art and, eventually, historically important. For these critics, one way of charting Fitzgerald's career would be from these early beginnings of "commercial," disposable music and toward the historically significant and worthy-of-canonization Great American Songbook later in her career.

After Webb's death in 1939, Fitzgerald herself had enough star power to continue leading the band, first under Chick Webb's name but eventually as Ella Fitzgerald and Her Famous Orchestra. But for many critics and historians, the trend toward commercialization and trying to appeal beyond an imagined core jazz audience continued. Nicholson is unenthusiastic about her repertoire at this time, singling out "My Wubba Dolly" (1939) as particularly egregious:

> The problem was that no thought had been given to creating a context for Ella's singing by employing sympathetic arrangers and expanding her role within the band with suitable, specially arranged material. She continued to operate as she had done with Webb, as a band singer, albeit with the band in her name, grinding out the pop songs with no apparent discrimination between good and bad.[31]

For Nicholson, this situation largely held for the next few years. Describing Fitzgerald's repertoire in 1946, he writes: "Her stage performances were a mixture of ballads, novelty numbers, current pop songs, and scat features. But there was no sense of any underlying aesthetic direction. Rather, her performances celebrated her talent by pushing in several directions at once with a childlike exuberance."[32] I am less interested in deciding whether Nicholson's judgement is correct or true; more important is that it represents an influential critical assessment of Fitzgerald's work. Nicholson also clearly sets up the (apparent) change that would happen in Fitzgerald's career once she got, in his words, "sympathetic arrangers," "specially arranged material," and "aesthetic direction." In most tellings of Fitzgerald's career, that happened when she eventually came under the management of Norman Granz and made her series of Songbook albums for Granz's Verve Records. In his narrative of Fitzgerald's life, Nicholson contrasts her early career and the later Songbook albums with Granz that would be influential in establishing her reputation and canonizing her—and which also served to help establish the canon of the Great American Songbook itself.

Norman Granz entered the Fitzgerald story in 1949, by which time she had been singing professionally for fifteen years. Granz was also experienced in the music business; he had organized his first Jazz at the Philharmonic (JATP) Concert at Philharmonic Auditorium in Los Angeles in 1944, part of his lifelong goal of getting jazz musicians bigger paychecks, better treatment, and presented in circumstances that suited what he believed was their status as great artists and musicians.[33] He established JATP as a brand name, one that followed him and his all-star caravan of musicians around even when they performed at different prestigious venues around the United States and the world—that is, at venues not necessarily with the word "Philharmonic" in their name. Fitzgerald performed in her first JATP concert on February 11, 1949, at Carnegie Hall in New York and eventually started touring with the JATP entourage. Fitzgerald was a big box-office draw, but some reviewers still had the same critique of her repertoire that we have already seen from Hammond and Nicholson: admiration for her vocal technique and performance, but a dismissal of her song choices. After a performance in Chicago, a critic for *DownBeat* wrote: "Ella Fitzgerald sang what was generally regarded as a crummy selection of songs with delicacy and personal appeal ... Just how 'Old Mother Hubbard,' 'Mr. Paganini,' and 'A Little Bird Told Me' got into her repertoire we don't know."[34]

In addition to her association with Norman Granz and JATP, technological developments and music-industry changes would also affect Fitzgerald's career in the late 1940s and early 1950s. The long-playing (LP) record format had been recently developed, and record companies and musicians were beginning to take advantage of the creative and marketing possibilities offered by this format.[35] The ways that jazz was being presented live were also changing. The declining fortunes of big bands meant that ballrooms and dancehalls—such as those Fitzgerald had performed at with the Chick Webb Orchestra at the beginning of her career—were closing around the United States. Jazz could still be heard at clubs, of course, but Granz and the JATP enterprise also led the way in proving that jazz could also be economically successful (and aesthetically appealing) in larger halls and more formal concert settings. Festivals would also become major sites for jazz performance and live recordings in the 1950s and 1960s, with many of the genre's figures making some of their performances that are most beloved by critics and fans in festival settings. In 1954, Fitzgerald and her trio performed at the George Wein–organized Newport Jazz Festival, the first major jazz festival in the United States. The

Members of the Jazz at the Philharmonic group on tour in Europe in the 1950s. From left: (standing) Norman Granz, Gene Krupa, Ella Fitzgerald, Ray Brown, J. C. Heard, Barney Kessel, Oscar Peterson, Lester Young; (kneeling) Flip Phillips, Charlie Shavers, Willie Smith. Photo by Pictorial Press.

LP format, concert hall presentation, and performances at large festivals all went together as steps away from small clubs and ballrooms and toward a middlebrow, middle-class audience for jazz.

In September 1950, Fitzgerald recorded her first LP, the ten-inch *Ella Sings Gershwin*. A few aspects of this recording are notable: first, it only features piano accompaniment from Ellis Larkins, as opposed to either a piano-bass-drums rhythm section or a larger orchestra, as would be typical of her later Songbook albums. Second, this is only a ten-inch LP with less running time than the soon-to-be-standard twelve-inch LP. While on a smaller scale than her later Songbook albums in terms of instrumentation and length, *Ella Sings Gershwin* can be seen as kind of a test case, figuring out whether a collection of the work of a single composer can be shaped into a coherent aesthetic statement and a saleable commercial product. Nicholson certainly seems to approve of this project, describing *Ella Sings Gershwin* as a recording in which "Ella's talent is seriously and conscientiously employed on material with which she was in total sympathy."[36] Given that George Gershwin had died thirteen years before this album collecting some of his songs in a unified package was released, this was also clearly a retrospective project characterized by historical consciousness, a sense that music from the past was worthy of commemoration.

Taking stock of Fitzgerald's career in the late 1940s and early 1950s, Nicholson writes that Milt Gabler, her producer at Decca Records, "laid the foundation for her later triumphs in the fifties and sixties by building a huge popular audience for her, far beyond that customarily associated with a jazz singer," even if that meant that she recorded a large quantity of material that Nicholson and some contemporary critics viewed as overtly commercial and not worthy of her artistic talents.[37] At the end of 1953, Fitzgerald signed with Norman Granz as her manager, and eventually she also shifted over to recording for his newly established Verve Records. *Ella Fitzgerald Sings the Cole Porter Songbook* is the first proper album she recorded for Granz on Verve Records in 1955. By then, the concept of recording a Songbook album had already been tentatively established. Fitzgerald herself had already recorded *Ella Sings Gershwin* in 1950 for Decca. And in 1953, Granz had started to record the jazz pianist Oscar Peterson on a series of albums that would ultimately feature the work of composers like Cole Porter, Irving Berlin, George Gershwin, and Jerome Kern, among others.

However, *The Cole Porter Songbook* exists on a much larger scale than these previous recordings. Fitzgerald is accompanied here by a large orchestra arranged and conducted by Buddy Bregman—not just the solo piano accompaniment of *Ella Sings Gershwin*. With this large orchestra, Fitzgerald, Bregman, and Granz ended up recording enough music to fit not just one twelve-inch LP, but two—thirty-two songs in total. One reason why these songs now filled up more running time was because Fitzgerald was singing *more* of each song. According to Granz's biographer, Tad Hershorn: "Granz also pushed Fitzgerald to sing all the verses to the songs to feature the full scope of the lyricist's art and make the albums that much more distinctive and authoritative."[38] As we have already seen in Hamm's description of these songs, many songs in the Great American Songbook tradition have introductory verses that give exposition of the song's situation—particularly important in a musical theatre context, from which many of these songs originated—while the choruses are catchier, more tuneful, and express the song's main sentiment. It is common practice for singers and jazz musicians performing these songs outside of their original musical theatre context to delete their opening verses and skip right to the repeating chorus. For Hershorn, Fitzgerald's choice to include this typically excised material and to sequence Porter's songs one after another on an LP provided evidence of Porter's artistic and historical merit: "The collection revealed the depth and craftmanship of Porter's art by demonstrating in retrospect how time and again Porter had adapted his music and lyrics to fit the narrative of stage and film productions, some of which had sunk without a trace apart from his music."[39] The end result of this creative labor by Fitzgerald, Bregman, and Granz was a product that, at least in heft, certainly gave the impression that Porter's music was historically important and worth taking seriously: a double-LP set comprised of thirty-two fully orchestrated songs. As Hershorn argues, this album helped rehabilitate Porter as a composer of sturdy songs that deserved to be reheard, even if the productions for which they were originally written were perhaps not up to this standard of High Art and had rightfully languished in obscurity. Such a rehabilitation would also set up Porter as a figure worthy of being paid tribute to in further Songbook albums and other aspects of historical consciousness—not as just a composer of disposable popular songs from decades past.

Granz was a skilled promoter, and he purchased advertisements for the album in a variety of mainstream publications: *Esquire*, the *New Yorker*, and *High Fidelity*, along with many newspapers. Fitzgerald was hardly an obscure name; indeed, she had sold records in quantities that contemporary jazz singers and instrumentalists can only dream about. But even by the standards of Fitzgerald's career up to this point, *The Cole Porter Songbook* album was wildly popular, finishing 1956 as the #18 best-selling LP of the entire year. Following the commercial success of *The Cole Porter Songbook*, Fitzgerald would go on to record seven more Songbook albums between 1956 and 1964, each one devoted to the work of a single composer or composing team. In August 1956, Fitzgerald and Bregman were back in the studio recording *Ella Fitzgerald Sings the Rodgers and Hart Songbook*, another two-LP set. Again, this did well commercially, reaching #11 on the *Billboard* albums chart. In the summer and fall of 1957, Fitzgerald recorded four LPs, spread over two volumes of *Ella Fitzgerald Sings the Duke Ellington Songbook*, with the participation of the composer and bandleader himself. In March 1958, she recorded *Ella Fitzgerald Sings the Irving Berlin Songbook*. This album was nominated for Album of the Year at the first presentation of the Grammy Awards that took place in 1959. Though she lost this award to Henry Mancini's soundtrack to *Peter Gunn*, Fitzgerald did win Best Vocal Performance, Female for *The Irving Berlin Songbook*; also in 1959, *The Duke Ellington Songbook* would earn Fitzgerald the Grammy for Best Jazz Performance, Individual.[40]

Since the Songbook series was proving to be such a popular and critical success, Fitzgerald and Granz continued with several more albums in this vein. In 1959, she recorded five LPs worth of material for *Ella Fitzgerald Sings the George and Ira Gershwin Songbook*. This album featured the musical direction of Nelson Riddle, probably the arranger most well-known for his work on the Songbook tradition. Riddle had a longstanding collaboration with Frank Sinatra on Capitol Records, and this Gershwin project would be the first of several albums he would record with Fitzgerald, including two more Songbook albums: *Ella Fitzgerald Sings the Jerome Kern Songbook* in 1963 and *Ella Fitzgerald Sings the Johnny Mercer Songbook* in 1964.

Between these projects with Riddle, Fitzgerald also recorded *Ella Fitzgerald Sings the Harold Arlen Songbook* in 1961, with arrangements by Billy May. All told, between 1956 and 1964, Fitzgerald recorded eight projects with "Songbook" in their titles devoted to individual composers or composing teams for Verve Records.[41] Other high-profile projects by Fitzgerald during this time period were similarly "backward-looking," including duet albums with Louis Armstrong and other standalone projects that still focused on a narrow range of the Great American Songbook repertoire from between 1925 and 1950. These albums were only slightly distinct from the Songbook albums discussed above in that they featured the work of several composers within that time frame and style, rather than the "single-author" focus of her Songbook series. To the relief of those critics who had earlier condemned her choice of material and arrangements, Fitzgerald was no longer recording many newly written songs, hopeful to catch the public's ear and score a hit with a fresh melody.

Fitzgerald's Songbook albums were part of a general LP boom in the late 1950s and early 1960s. Authors such as Robert Fink and Janet Borgerson and Jonathan Schroeder have described this moment as one in which listening to LPs on a home hi-fi system became a key defining characteristic of middle-class, largely white society in the United States.[42] While a wide range of musical genres were issued on LP and eagerly incorporated into this audience's lifestyle, Nicholson has strong ideas about how middle-aged listeners specifically consumed and appreciated Fitzgerald's recordings:

> They had great appeal for a whole generation brought up in the era of big bands who were now feeling disenfranchised from popular music by successive waves of bop and rock 'n' roll. In their youth they lindy-hopped in the aisles of the Paramount and the ballrooms across middle America. Now they had sons and daughters of their own who were jiving to Elvis Presley or to Milt Gabler's latest signing, Bill Haley. The music was a million miles from the sounds of their youth. Still with an interest in popular music, they found it easy to identify with Ella's cool breeze or the engaging humor and charm of her duets with Louis. Unlike the music of the new generation, it was noncombative, nonthreatening, and the ideal accompaniment for a chat around the coffee table or a dinner party with friends. The songs of the Broadway composers from the late 1920s, the 1930s, and the early 1940s were the pop music of their salad days, the music with which they identified. Now they could hear those numbers again, tastefully updated on LP by

a singer who let the songs speak for themselves rather than imposing on them the subjective baggage of her own life experiences.[43]

Nicholson makes a hard left turn at the end of that description, perhaps alluding to the idea that Fitzgerald's recordings were supposedly less concerned with deep emotions and drama than recordings made by her peers like Billie Holiday and Nina Simone. If Nicholson is correct in his interpretation of Fitzgerald's audience, there may also be political and racial undertones to these listening preferences. Holiday and Simone both recorded Abel Meeropol's antilynching song "Strange Fruit." Simone additionally recorded a variety of songs with direct political messages, was closely associated with civil rights struggles in the 1960s, and her musical activism has been a key part of her legacy for later musicians and listeners. However, even on recordings and live performances by Holiday and Simone of ostensibly nonpolitical songs more focused on individual romantic relationships, many listeners have interpreted their vocal style as being suffused with pain borne out of race- and gender-based oppression.[44]

Fitzgerald's performances, however, have largely not been interpreted in this way, even on repertoire sung in common by all three singers, such as the Gershwin ballad "I Loves You, Porgy," a song with lyrics that clearly allude to sexual violence. This song was Simone's breakout hit from her 1959 debut album, and the widely viewed 2015 Netflix documentary *What Happened, Miss Simone?* shows her performing it on Hugh Hefner's *Playboy's Penthouse* television show, the only woman of color on the set designed to portray a fantasy of white male power and subservient female sexuality. Holiday had also performed the song in a dramatic context in the 1940s and 1950s; in his autobiography, Miles Davis explains: "Whenever I'd go see her, I always asked Billie to sing 'I Loves You Porgy,' because when she sang, 'don't let him touch me with his hot hands,' you could almost feel that shit she was feeling. It was beautiful and sad the way she sang that."[45] Later, when discussing his own recording of this song, Davis seems to allude to the amount of emotion that Holiday was able to infuse into her performance: "The hardest tune I ever had to play in my life was 'I Loves You Porgy,' because I had to make the trumpet sound and phrase just like a human voice."[46] Fitzgerald herself recorded "I Loves You, Porgy" as part of her duet recording with Louis Armstrong on the score of *Porgy and Bess* in 1957 for Norman Granz and Verve Records.[47] To my knowledge, no contemporary critic or later historian has singled out Fitzgerald's performance of "I Loves You, Porgy" as being particularly emotionally affecting, though certainly this album—like all of her albums in the late 1950s and early 1960s for Verve—was well received by audiences and critics. The relative popularity of Fitzgerald over Holiday and Simone—at least for this mass audience that Nicholson is describing—can then be viewed as a turning away from the difficult questions of violence and inequality that their performances sometimes raise. In this interpretation, Fitzgerald's recordings would more easily fit a social context in which listeners were not expected to listen carefully and emotionally invest in these songs, but to appreciate them as pleasant background accompaniment for friendly conversations and dinner parties. This, however, is *not* how the Great American Songbook is always interpreted by musicians or listeners: the meaning that the Songbook has would change over the decades and with shifting contexts in popular music, based on what it was being compared to. Later in this chapter, we will specifically see performers like Linda Ronstadt turning to the Songbook repertoire *because* they view it as able to express deeper emotional truths than other musical styles.

In the most influential narratives of Ella Fitzgerald's career, she was an immensely talented singer who was recording inferior, disposable songs during her tenure in the Chick Webb Orchestra and as a solo artist on Decca in the 1940s and early 1950s. In our discussion of various time periods of popular music history, we will see that what exactly counts as "frivolous" music is a moving target; its actual musical and aesthetic qualities matter less than how this music is treated in the marketplace and in the critical establishment. Granz was able to leverage her undeniable popularity, new technology, and new listening contexts to set her up doing Songbook albums that presented the works of individual composers as "Great Men," in the style of Western classical music. Granz's strategy of rehabilitation is not so different from the tribute band model analyzed in the previous chapter. Their obvious differences aside, composers like the Gershwins, Cole Porter, and Irving Berlin were musicians working in a heavily commodified industry eager for massive popularity, the same way that the Beatles, Pink Floyd, and Led Zeppelin were. In both cases, historical consciousness in popular music works such that the passage of time, plus elevation over their peers, reveals them to be great artists worthy of having their work taken seriously and reverently presented. The main difference between these two cases of historical consciousness in popular music is that Fitzgerald herself is not erased in the process of paying tribute to these composers, as tribute band musicians sometimes are. She is held up as a top interpreter of these timeless works, such that her albums themselves later would take on the aura and status of prized documents. It is no surprise, therefore, that Fitzgerald's recordings of the Great American Songbook albums have become heavily canonized, reissued in lavish box sets and compilations, as commodities within the ideology of historical consciousness.

Fitzgerald recorded the last of her single-composer albums marketed with "Songbook" in the title in 1964, although she still performed and recorded various songs from this tradition for the rest of her career. 1964 is a pivotal year in popular music history: the year of the first appearance by the Beatles on *The Ed Sullivan Show*, the "British Invasion," and the subsequent massive rise in popularity of rock 'n' roll among adolescents, teenagers, and young adults. Fitzgerald's career continued, but in this new popular music landscape, she did not receive nearly the amount of commercial and critical attention that she did in the 1950s. Still, the songs from the Great American Songbook did not disappear from sheet music, even if performances of them began to disappear from the *Billboard* charts. The fact that these songs had been extensively recorded by hundreds of musicians, including Fitzgerald, meant that nostalgic listeners could easily listen to this music on their personal record collections, and the Songbook did not vanish from the minds and memories of listeners and musicians. The Songbook remained ripe to be re-performed and listened to again, and the cultural issues at stake in its rediscovery—especially by artists and their audiences more associated with other styles of popular music—will be the focus of the remainder of this chapter.

"Sometimes I wonder why I spend the lonely night dreaming of a song"

The formulaic quality and stylistic consistency of the songs that would come to be known as the Great American Songbook begs the question: great according to whom? Linda Martin and Kerry Segrave have an answer, explaining: "The music strove for a broad, mass appeal only among white adult society. It was WASP culture the music spoke to, and it did so in the most benign way. It sang of no taboos, nor did it question any values."[48] If Hamm is correct that the relatively static musical style of the Great American Songbook does not reflect vast societal and technological changes, and if Martin and Segrave are correct that this musical style was viewed as banal, bland, and limited in its appeal to narrow demographics, this may help explain why the Songbook comes to be seen as increasingly obsolete as the tumultuous political and social changes of the 1960s continued. Recordings and performances of standards did, in fact, lose their overall popularity over this period, especially compared to the enormous rise in popularity and commercial success of R&B, rock 'n' roll, and Motown. But soon after the material from and performing styles of the Great American Songbook lost their dominant role in the marketplace, they would acquire a nostalgic potency and signification for musicians and listeners, such that these "classics" from the past were ripe for periodic rediscovery, re-performance, and repeated listening. Carmen McRae's 1972 album *The Great American Songbook*, a double LP recorded live in Los Angeles, was the first time that this term would be used in the promotional materials of this repertoire. But McRae was already fifty-two years old when this album was released and a longtime veteran of the jazz world. This album was not a dramatic departure in repertoire, only a conscious choice to name it and market it in a specific way.

Willie Nelson, however, occupies an important place as a musician from outside the pop/jazz tradition who has nevertheless turned multiple times to recording songs from the Great American Songbook and whose 1978 album *Stardust* is perhaps the most critically and commercially successful example of this type of genre crossing and historical consciousness: a re-performing of prior musical material based on the conviction that this material is historically important, and therefore can be made relevant to contemporary audiences. By the time he recorded *Stardust* in the late 1970s, Nelson's career had already taken many twists and turns. Starting in the mid-1950s, he worked variously as a radio DJ, singer and guitarist, and songwriter. He had a run of success in the country industry in the early 1960s, most notably with his composition, "Crazy," an enormous hit for singer Patsy Cline in 1962 and a song that is still part of Nelson's live repertoire sixty years later. As a performer, Nelson never fit in well with the country music establishment in Nashville, and by the early 1970s had relocated to Austin, Texas.[49] Two notable albums came from this period: *Phases and Stages* (1974) and *The Red-Headed Stranger* (1975), music which, in the words of Atlantic Records producer Jerry Wexler, had the effect of "coalescing of his audience, where the rednecks and hippies came together" in the subgenre he would be known as one of the founders of: "outlaw country."[50]

The 1970s was also a time of legal and managerial uncertainty for Nelson, which would culminate a decade later with the IRS seizing some of his assets to pay back taxes.[51] Throughout his career, Nelson frequently switched record companies: his own idiosyncratic musical tastes, eccentric singing, and failure to conform to prior models would often sour his relationships with record company executives searching for a more predictable and easily marketable musician. Still, he was clearly a talented singer and songwriter, so there was always a new record company eager to sign him if a relationship with another company headed south. Starting in the 1950s, Nelson moved through several record companies, including Liberty, RCA Victor, and Atlantic Records' short-lived country division, before finding a relatively stable home on Columbia Records between 1975 and 1993.

It is under this mixed set of circumstances that Nelson decided to record the material for the album that would eventually become perhaps the most well-known album of standards by a musician from outside the Songbook/jazz tradition: *Stardust*. The album was produced by Booker T. Jones, whom Nelson originally met when they both lived in the same condo building in Malibu, California, in the late 1970s. Jones was a keyboardist, songwriter, and producer best known for his work with Booker T. and the MG's in the 1960s: a group with two white and two Black members that seemed to epitomize the spirit of interracial cooperation that was part of the Memphis-based Stax Records mythology.[52] Nelson tasked Jones with arranging and producing the record for him, relying primarily on Nelson's touring band as the backing musicians. On this album, Nelson and Jones recorded ten songs from decades past, including "Stardust" (1929), "Georgia on My Mind" (1930), "Blue Skies" (1926), "All of Me" (1931), "On the Sunny Side of the Street" (1930), and "Someone to Watch Over Me" (1926). Arrangements of songs from the Great American Songbook do not always go for understatement, so Nelson was satisfied that Jones was willing to avoid the syrupy strings that had overwhelmed some of Nelson's recorded performances when he was working in Nashville earlier in his career. Approvingly, Nelson notes: "Booker kept it basic. No soaring string sections, not a single backup singer."[53] While the strings certainly are not "soaring" or prominent in the mix, they do make occasional appearances, particularly under Mickey Raphael's harmonica solo on "Georgia on My Mind." A horn section also adds warmth to that song's coda vamp. But how these instruments are used differentiates these arrangements from other arrangements that use similar instrumentation. Jones's horns play mid-register "pads" as opposed to high-register, intricate obbligato melodies more typical of arrangements for Frank Sinatra, Tony Bennett, and Dean Martin.

Columbia Records, however, was skeptical of this body of material, which represented an apparently dramatic turn away from his outlaw country songs—a genre that Nelson had helped establish just a few years before, and for which he was still in the process of constructing the audience. If the influential music executive Jerry Wexler called this audience a coalescing of rednecks and hippies, it was not clear to Columbia Records executives that these same people were interested in hearing and buying Nelson perform songs like "Moonlight in Vermont" or "Georgia on My Mind." Insofar as songs like these were associated with the educated, middle-class popular music of older generations, this was in fact the opposite of the type of music Nelson's audience might seem likely to buy; this establishment identity was antithetical to both rednecks and hippies. In the next chapter of this book, we will see that jazz trumpeter Miles Davis had a closely related dilemma a decade earlier, when he also had to decide what kind of performance repertoire would most appeal to a countercultural audience that he was seeking to cultivate. The audiences for Nelson's outlaw country and Davis's fusion experiments are certainly different sectors of the counterculture, but they are both alternatives to the older, middle-class, white audience that is imagined to be the most likely audience for songs from the standards or Songbook tradition. In his 2015 autobiography, Nelson reconstructs a debate that he had about the album with a skeptical unnamed record executive, one of "the boys at Columbia":

> [Nelson:] People loved these songs. They were so good they lasted. And now there's three or four new generations of fans who haven't heard them. I don't think it's a stretch to say that those fans are bound to love this music....
>
> [Columbia Executive:] These new generations you're talking about look at you like an outlaw guru.... They relate to you because you're a nonconformist. Believe me, they don't want to hear you doing songs they associate with their fathers or grandfathers.[54]

Whether this conversation actually took place or whether it instead represents Nelson's after-the-fact justification for this unlikely career move, several aspects are notable for our concerns. Nelson makes a claim for the musical quality of the Great American Songbook, pointing out that the songs contained in it have endured for a long time because of what he views as their intrinsic aesthetic worth, possibly differentiating them from other songs composed during prior decades and songs composed during the then-present day, the 1970s. Plenty of songs written in the 1920s, 1930s, and 1940s have not lasted, and perhaps all or the vast majority of songs written in the 1970s are not likely to endure for decades, either. Nelson argues for the inherent quality of the body of songs that he is singing on *Stardust* as members of the Great American Songbook, elevating them above these two other repertoires of material. Another aspect of this brief conversation addresses an important topic we have already discussed: the ideology of newness and the strong youth bias in the production and reception of popular music. Closely related to this emphasis on newness and youth is a narrative of music consumption being a battleground between generations and a way for listeners to differentiate themselves from the mores and traditions of the past. For baby boomer hippies especially, breaking away from their parents' generation, from the so-called "Greatest Generation" of World War II, was—at least according to popular music ideology—a main goal accomplished by consuming popular music. The fathers and grandfathers associated with the Great American Songbook and mentioned by the Columbia executive represent patriarchal male authority; it is probably not incidental that mothers and grandmothers are not discussed in this reported conversation.

Elsewhere in his writing, Nelson deconstructs the idea that his home genre of country music is so far removed from the Great American Songbook tradition. Nelson was born in 1933 in rural Abbott, Texas, and he notes that the "country" music that he and other people growing up in the 1940s listened to was itself a product of Tin Pan Alley and Hollywood, some of the same origins that Yagoda mentions as sources for the Great American Songbook. "They didn't start calling it country western music until the singing cowboy movies of the thirties and forties. This was not real country or cowboy or western music, for the most part, that Gene Autry or Roy Rogers and Dale Evans or the Sons of the Pioneers sang around their movie campfires. These were movie tunes by pop songwriters who tried to sound country."[55] There are parallels, Nelson argues, between the production and dissemination of the country music of his youth and other popular song traditions at that time. *Stardust* features ten songs from the Great American Songbook. "Unchained Melody," written by Alex North and Hy Zaret in 1955, is the only relatively later song in this collection; the other nine are songs Nelson would have heard during his childhood, as they were written in the 1920s, 1930s, or 1940s.

Stardust sold over five million copies, won Nelson a Grammy award for his performance of "Georgia on My Mind," and is perhaps the best-loved release in his extensive catalog of over one hundred studio and live albums. *Stardust* itself has been canonized; in 2008, a special thirtieth anniversary edition of the album was released. This edition of *Stardust* is typical of the kind of historical consciousness discussed in the previous chapter, in which important anniversaries of recordings or important events are marked, in this case with what we might call a celebratory commodity. In fact, one could argue that Nelson's *Stardust* participates in historical consciousness in two ways. The original 1978 recordings testified to the historical importance of songs from previous decades by re-performing them. But enough time has passed such that by 2008, even those 1978 recordings are viewed as historic and worthy of commemorating with an "anniversary edition."

It has been over four decades since *Stardust*, and Nelson has remained an enigmatic figure in the popular music world. He records prolifically and tours frequently, making him a seemingly ubiquitous presence in small arenas, minor league baseball stadiums, and summer festivals across the United States. Given the overwhelming commercial and critical success of *Stardust*, it is no surprise that he has returned several times to recording Songbook albums. Indeed, though Nelson is a gifted songwriter, he is also one of relatively few star musicians equally comfortable playing and recording songs written by other composers, as compared with musicians like Bob Dylan or James Taylor; these

Songbook albums are, therefore, less of a dramatic departure for him. In addition to *Stardust*, Nelson has recorded at least nine additional albums devoted to the Great American Songbook repertoire: *Somewhere Over the Rainbow* (1981), *Without a Song* (1983), *What a Wonderful World* (1988), *Healing Hands of Time* (1994), *Nacogdoches* (2004), *American Classic* (2009), *Summertime: Willie Nelson Sings Gershwin* (2016), *My Way* (2018), and *That's Life* (2021). Most of these albums seem to be an attempt to recapture the formula that was so commercially successful on *Stardust*: uncluttered arrangements featuring Nelson's touring band and his distinctive reedy voice.

Occasionally, however, Nelson has stepped out of this comfort zone to release a standards album that sounds quite different from his typical fare and is perhaps meant to appeal to a slightly different audience than the (now-aging) rednecks and hippies who attend his concerts and shout "Willie!" at him as his band cranks through the beginning of his typical set-opener "Whiskey River." *My Way*, released in 2018, is a good example of this attempt to stretch Nelson's stylistic wings. Titled after Frank Sinatra's signature anthem of perseverance and only featuring songs associated with Sinatra, the album opens with a version of "Fly Me to the Moon." The Count Basie Orchestra, with an arrangement by Quincy Jones, accompanied Sinatra on his 1964 recording of this song. Nelson's version on *My Way* is much closer to this typical brassy, midcentury style than the "basic" arrangements that Booker T. Jones provided for Songbook tunes on *Stardust*. The rest of the songs on the album are arranged in the same manner and represent a great change from Nelson's usual aesthetic on recordings or in live performances. A few tracks later, the Gershwin standard "A Foggy Day" is typical of Nelson's approach on this album: a quick tempo with swinging drums, a prominent piano solo, and a horn *soli* section. Heard in 2018, such arrangements call to mind the Canadian crooner Michael Bublé, the artist known—and sometimes criticized—for being an unoriginal imitator of Sinatra's sound and style. Bublé's conventional good looks and rich baritone voice help him appeal to middle-class yuppies perhaps more than Nelson's grizzled, eighty-something visage and long braids.

Stardust provided an example for other musicians from the country, rock, and pop fields that recording material from the Great American Songbook was a viable aesthetic and commercial strategy. Other musicians would certainly follow in those footsteps, and critics and listeners were open to following them down this path. However, the choice of arrangements and approaches to these songs would heavily influence how these projects would be received. The Songbook tradition seems to have at least two faces: it can be a repository of timeless, deep emotional truths, or it can be another pop culture artifact glibly and cynically designed to manipulate our emotions.

The Passions of Adolescence and the Great American Songbook

Born in Tucson, Arizona, in 1946—the first year of the post–World War II baby boom, Linda Ronstadt began her musical career in the mid-1960s as the singer of a folk-rock trio called the Stone Poneys. They had moderate success, most notably with the single "Different Drum," which peaked at #13 on the *Billboard* Hot 100 in 1967. Ronstadt moved to Los Angeles and became associated with the constellation of musicians living in the Laurel Canyon neighborhood north of Hollywood, a colony of artists including Crosby, Stills, and Nash; Joni Mitchell; and James Taylor.[56] As a solo artist in the 1970s, her music straddled the pop, rock, folk, and country genres. Ronstadt's major commercial breakthrough came in 1974 with the release of her album *Heart Like a Wheel*, which hit #1 on the *Billboard* 200 chart of best-selling albums and was nominated for the Album of the Year Grammy Award. Subsequent albums in the 1970s would be similarly successful, and by the end of the decade she had cemented for herself a rare position in the popular music world. She was a singer who could appeal to audiences across the divided listenerships of the pop, rock, and country genres, and in the male-dominated rock world, she was a "girl singer" (a term that Ronstadt herself often would use to self-identify, perhaps in tribute to and solidarity with the "girl singers" of the big band era) who could fill the large auditoriums and arenas that were beginning to be staples of the popular music touring infrastructure. But according to her autobiography *Simple Dreams*, she was not content to just repeat this pattern of recording and touring for increasingly larger audiences and increasingly larger monetary rewards.

By the early 1980s, Ronstadt was in her midthirties, coming off a decade of working as a solo artist and several years of overwhelming success. While she may not have been young by the standards of the youth-oriented popular music world, she was at the height of her popularity and not at a loss for ideas, inspiration, or talent. Turning her back on this megastardom, Ronstadt began working on several projects in the early 1980s that were personally fulfilling but less likely to garner massive popular success. She performed in an extended run of a Broadway production (and later film version) of *The Pirates of Penzance*, an operetta by Gilbert and Sullivan that originally premiered in 1879. While she was living in New York and performing in *The Pirates of Penzance*, Ronstadt began to think of recording an album of standards. As we have discussed above in the negative reactions to some standards albums by critics, such albums are sometimes viewed as a way of invigorating a moribund career, consolidating a shrinking fan base around a body of songs and performance techniques that have an established, "timeless" appeal, or as something that is age-appropriate both for the performers and their audiences. As popular musicians get older, there is more of a sense that certain types of music—comprising certain performance styles and expressing certain sentiments—are more appropriate for them, as we have already seen with Strausbaugh's claim that the blues is an appropriate genre for an aging Mick Jagger and Keith Richards to play, but not rock 'n' roll.

These usual explanations do not seem to be the case for Ronstadt during this stage of her career, so what explains her eventual recording of three Songbook albums during the 1980s? First, there is family and personal influence; the standards tradition is one that she was exposed to as a child growing up in the 1950s. Describing her interest in exploring popular music history, she writes: "The pop singers that came before me were the interpreters of the American standard song. I started thinking about the records that my father had brought home to play on the big high-fidelity monaural record player he bought in 1957: Ella Fitzgerald and Louis Armstrong duets, Peggy Lee, Chris Connor, June Christy, and Billie Holiday."[57] Ronstadt's account of the history of American popular music—"the pop singers that came before me"—is selective, not complete. After all, there were plenty of popular singers who came before her and sang a wide variety of repertoire, such as Elvis Presley, Hank Williams, and Bessie Smith, to name only a few. Instead, Ronstadt is choosing her ancestors, particularly because she is being influenced by family connections and personal history; this is music she remembers from her childhood, and that she warmly associates with a particular time period and technology: the LP boom and the rise of home listening that we have already discussed in reference to Ella Fitzgerald on Verve Records. Throughout the case studies presented in this book, we will see the influence of family members and older generations on a musician's musical development and taste, and Ronstadt here provides another example of this key and underexamined aspect of popular music culture. Ronstadt positively associates the repertoire of the Great American Songbook with her father. Recall that the Columbia Records executive skeptical of Nelson's *Stardust* album also had the same association of this music with older generations, which led him to be dubious that such an album would appeal to the younger audiences for Nelson's outlaw country. Ronstadt would face similar resistance from music industry professionals for her own standards projects in the 1980s.

The late 1950s was a fruitful time for the standards tradition and for an adolescent Ronstadt to be overhearing her father's records on his new turntable. While rock 'n' roll was certainly gathering steam by this point, several landmark recordings in this older Songbook style were also released around this time, including some by artists that Ronstadt specifically remembers her father owning. The first two of three duets albums by Ella Fitzgerald and Louis Armstrong had been released on Verve in 1956 and 1957. (The third, a version of *Porgy and Bess*, would follow in 1959.) Peggy Lee's *Black Coffee* was reissued as an LP in 1956. Billie Holiday's late-career landmark *Lady in Satin* was recorded and released in 1958, just a year after Ronstadt's father bought his turntable, and may very well have been one of the releases by Holiday that Ronstadt remembers him having in his collection.

Despite her successful career in other genres, the Songbook musical style and repertoire remained familiar to Ronstadt over the decades that followed. According to the author Peter J. Levinson, Mick Jagger "gave [Ronstadt] a Norman Granz–produced jam session album of standards featuring saxophonists Charlie Parker and Ben Webster, which she played constantly" in the late 1970s.[58] This was likely the 1952 Verve album *Jam Session*, which features a seventeen-minute ballad medley of the assembled musicians taking turns performing a chorus of a series of Songbook standards. This was one of several such albums that Granz produced in the 1950s, expanding the format of his live JATP concerts to LP records: gather top musicians together and let them play with minimal oversight or direction. Ben Webster, known for his tenure with Duke Ellington in the 1940s and widely recognized as one of the best tenor saxophone balladeers in jazz history, plays "What's New" during this medley, which trumpeter Charlie Shavers immediately follows with a chorus of the Gershwin standard "Someone to Watch Over Me." Ronstadt would eventually record both of these songs for her *What's New* album of standards. Other influences on Ronstadt's decision to record standards include her friendships with several men. Ronstadt met the famed R&B producer Jerry Wexler, best known for his work on Atlantic Records, when she was living in New York in the early 1980s and performing in *The Pirates of Penzance* on Broadway. At this time, she was dating the journalist Pete Hamill.[59] Both Wexler and Hamill had wide-ranging musical tastes, particularly in midcentury jazz and Black popular music, and Ronstadt writes about spending time absorbing music with both men.

In addition to these social ties, Ronstadt also had musical and aesthetic reasons for making a dramatic shift in her repertoire. Her popularity in the 1970s had risen to great heights, but that meant that she was booked in larger and larger venues, a situation with challenging acoustics that bothered her as a performer. She explains: "The sound in those enormous places was kind of like being in a flushing toilet with the lid down.... The audience was getting a sound mix that was so distorted by the acoustics of the building that any delicate passages or musical subtleties were lost."[60] Recording standards might shrink the audience for her live performances, but given the technical and acoustic difficulties that had frustrated her as an artist, this downsizing was not necessarily lamentable. Ronstadt also explains that she was looking for songs that were more expressive emotionally. Describing the repertoire that she recorded on her three standards albums, she writes: "The sophisticated sweep of melody and complex layers of meaning in the lyrics meant that I could tell a richer and more nuanced story—and the story wasn't stranded in the passions of adolescence."[61] This is a common theme in the performance and reception of these songs: a mythology that portrays popular music of whatever particular style ("novelty" pop recordings in the 1930s and 1940s, rock 'n' roll in the 1950s, contemporary pop in the 1960s and later) as crassly commercial, youth-oriented, and hopelessly "stranded in the passions of adolescence," while music from the past (the standards tradition, in this case) can express a "richer and more nuanced story"—one associated with mature, adult concerns.

When Ronstadt began to work on recording this body of material, Wexler, an industry veteran, put together a band of jazz musicians to serve as her accompaniment. Unfortunately, the arrangements were not satisfactory for Ronstadt, and Wexler was content to delegate these decisions about arrangements and mixing to other people, without consulting her. In this conflict over artistic direction, she began to view Wexler as a holdover from a previous era, not in a positive way but as a throwback to a time when singers were largely at the mercy of producers and executives for how songs would be recorded and presented. While she was critical of some aspects of the rock genre—such as its use of reverb-heavy arenas as performance venues and what she views as its limited emotional palette—she still wanted to keep the artistic empowerment and independence she credited rock music with bringing to the industry. Instead of a situation in which musicians were dictated to by A&R men like the infamous Mitch Miller at Columbia: "Artists like Bob Dylan and the Beatles changed all that. They wrote or selected their own material and musical direction, becoming enormously successful in the process. David Geffen's label, Asylum [to which Ronstadt was signed], was founded on the premise that the artist's vision would be respected and supported."[62] Ronstadt remained interested in this repertoire, but she decided to scrap these recordings with Wexler and pursue a more equitable musical partnership.

For her next attempt at making recordings from the Songbook, she decided to collaborate with Nelson Riddle, who had done arrangements for Frank Sinatra in the 1950s and 1960s—and for Ella Fitzgerald on Verve Records, as discussed above. By the early 1980s when Ronstadt contacted him, however, he was not nearly as busy as he had been in earlier decades. Ronstadt summarizes why Riddle was available and willing to work on this project: "Nelson's phone hadn't been ringing that much in the past several years. The rock-and-roll revolution had swept away most of his employment."[63] This was largely due to the decline in popularity of songs arranged in Riddle's style—classical orchestra

Album cover of Linda Ronstadt's final collaboration with Nelson Riddle, *For Sentimental Reasons*. Riddle died in 1985, before this album's release in 1986.

with additional horns and the rhythm section of a jazz band—in favor of guitar-based accompaniment for rock music and singer-songwriters, that is, exactly the musical tradition that Ronstadt made her name with in the 1970s. Again, Ronstadt was interestingly caught between two worlds and the drastic changes the popular music industry had witnessed over the previous decades. This is a recurring theme in the recording of these standards albums: to greater or lesser degrees, many of the musicians who record standards albums later in their careers—such as Ronstadt, Nelson, Bob Dylan, Paul McCartney, Rod Stewart, James Taylor, and Art Garfunkel—were part of the musical movement that dethroned this tradition from its place of prominence a few decades before.

Ronstadt found a more collaborative partner in Riddle, and the end result was not only *What's New* in 1983 but two more albums, *Lush Life* in 1984 and *For Sentimental Reasons* in 1986, all featuring Riddle's arrangements of tunes from the Great American Songbook. In many ways, reception of these albums was very positive. *What's New* sold over three million copies in the United States and peaked at #3 on the *Billboard* albums chart, behind only Michael Jackson's *Thriller* and Lionel Richie's *Can't Slow Down*, two of the biggest hits of the 1980s. The sequels fared less well commercially, but still sold over a million copies each, with *Lush Life* also earning Ronstadt a Grammy nomination for Best Female Pop Vocal Performance. But these projects faced resistance as well, as Ronstadt explains in two revealing excerpts in her autobiography. Even before the recording sessions for *What's New* began, the music industry executive Joe Smith attempted to dissuade Ronstadt from moving forward with the project, arguing that her fans would be alienated from this work and her career would suffer major damage. This argument echoes the concerns of one of the "boys at Columbia" in regard to Nelson's *Stardust* album; in both cases, figures in the music industry worried that recording material from the Great American Songbook would not appeal to the audiences these artists had worked hard to consolidate. Ronstadt herself was conscious of the resistance this music might face from critics and listeners. She explained her motivations for recording this material in her autobiography: "Rock-and-roll diehards in the music press wondered why I had abandoned Buddy Holly for the Gershwins. The answer is that there was so much more room for me to stretch and sing."[64] This is an interesting answer, even if it is not self-evidently true. If Ronstadt was strictly speaking about showing off the power and skill of her singing—"stretching" her vocal muscles, so to speak—the pop-rock genre that Ronstadt had been a part of before recording the standards albums offered plenty of space for her to do that. Joni Mitchell, Robert Plant, Stevie Wonder, Aretha Franklin, and Janis Joplin had all demonstrated that wide-ranging, virtuosic vocal technique could fit in pop-rock music. But Ronstadt here may also have been referring to a wider emotional range that these songs—and not her earlier repertoire—apparently allowed her to reach. This interpretation of her words is in line with her earlier quoted claim that these songs were not trapped in adolescence the way that pop-rock was. This, again, is a common attitude in the reception of music from the Great American Songbook: that these older songs are, in fact, "timeless" and speak of more enduring and mature emotions than the fleeting passions of youth. Therefore, they deserve to be repeated and re-performed.

Still, the likely disconnect between Ronstadt's retro-styled recordings of these songs and the audience that had followed her until this point in her career was something that critics noticed. In a three-star review in *Rolling Stone* magazine, Christopher Connelly summarized the disjuncture between Ronstadt's audience and her "new" recordings:

Ah, but what's the point of this record, anyway? If this were your favorite type of music, you probably wouldn't be reading this magazine. An album of standards may not have been a bad idea, but recording them with the Nelson Riddle Orchestra was. Sure, the arrangements are nice, but they'd suit Eydie Gormé just as nicely. Not to place these songs into some kind of contemporary context—as Rickie Lee Jones did on *Girl at Her Volcano*—is to turn them into museum pieces, and to make Ronstadt's own contribution into a feat, a stunt, fascinating but lifeless.[65]

Here Connelly draws a distinction between recording standards in a relatively straightforward way—as they had been recorded in, say, the 1950s and 1960s, with the Nelson Riddle Orchestra standing in for a midcentury aesthetic conservatism—and recording the songs in "some kind of contemporary context." With dramatic string and wind crescendos supporting her voice on sustained syllables or when she reaches for a high note, Ronstadt is definitely in the former camp. The mention of Eydie Gormé (1928–2013) seems to be meant as an insult: she stands in as a generic singer in this tradition, someone who was a relic from a bygone era.[66] Given the widespread character of the ideology of newness in popular music culture, it is no surprise that *Rolling Stone* magazine, in the early 1980s at least, was at pains to distance itself from this nostalgic vision of the popular music industry world. However, the commercial success of Ronstadt's collaborations with Riddle shows that at least some listeners were open to other ways of engaging with popular music and appreciated the "museum pieces"—self-consciously retrospective music—that Ronstadt and Riddle put on display in these albums.

Bob Dylan: Bringing It All Back Home

To end our discussion of Songbook albums, I want to take a closer look at the recent catalogue of Bob Dylan. Dylan is, of course, one of the most influential and famous musicians and popular culture figures of the past sixty years. His life and career have been documented in hundreds, perhaps thousands of books. In the work of influential critics like Greil Marcus, Dylan's music has been a key site for the argument that works of popular music have deep aesthetic and historical significance.[67] His shifting styles over the years and decades of his career have been closely analyzed by critics, and scarcely any serious review or consideration of a particular new Dylan album or live performance will fail to situate it within the context of landmark albums in his career like *Blonde on Blonde, The Basement Tapes, Blood on the Tracks, Time Out of Mind*, or "*Love and Theft,*" secure in the knowledge that readers will know these albums from decades past intimately and understand the comparisons to Dylan's current work. The immense corpus of scholarship and criticism interpreting Dylan's music, the continuing entries in "The Bootleg Series" from Columbia Records documenting outtakes or live performances from his decades-long career (up to Volume 17, as of this writing), and his enduring place in contemporary culture all point to intense historical consciousness in the reception of Bob Dylan. He is a popular musician who first came to prominence in the 1960s and whose past musical endeavors are still the focus of deep interest and appreciation. His turn to recording material from the Great American Songbook in the 2010s shows Dylan himself interested in engaging with, honoring, and replaying the musical past.

While a full accounting of Dylan's sixty-year career in the public eye is unnecessary for my argument, briefly discussing a few important highlights will serve to better illuminate how his series of standards albums fits in his work, and how his fans and followers might interpret these albums. His 1997 album *Time Out of Mind* began a late-career upswing for Dylan, after several decades of albums and performances that were not generally well received by critics and fans. *Time Out of Mind* won the Grammy Award for Best Contemporary Folk Album and beat Radiohead's *OK Computer* for Album of the Year. The album also contributed a new song to the Dylan songbook canon—and arguably a late entry to the Great American Songbook itself. Its ninth track, "Make You Feel My Love," has been widely performed by over 450 artists, including Billy Joel, Garth Brooks, and Adele.[68] Since the late 1990s, Dylan has garnered an array of awards and plaudits from critical institutions. "Things Have Changed," his contribution to the soundtrack of the film *Wonder Boys*, won an Oscar for Best Original Song in 2001; later that year his album "*Love and Theft*," released on the same day as the 9/11 terror attacks, topped the *Village Voice* Pazz and Jop Poll of critics. His 2004 autobiography *Chronicles Volume One* was a finalist for the National Book Critics Circle Award. In 2008, the Pulitzer Committee awarded him a special citation. Finally, in 2016 Dylan won the Nobel Prize in literature—not for *Chronicles Volume One*, but for his songwriting: the first time that any musician had been so recognized. While there have been some controversies over Dylan incorporating the words of novelists and poets into his songs without giving them credit, these various awards have been given to Dylan for his own original, creative work—not for his interpretations of others' songs. His own rough, limited-range singing voice is, legendarily, an acquired taste. However, generations of critics and fans have valued Dylan for the unique performances of his own songs, secure in the belief that he really feels the emotions contained in these songs because he wrote them, and that his "authentic" vocal performances themselves enhance the beauty of the thoughts and ideas expressed in his lyrics.

Therefore, it is surprising that, starting in 2015, Dylan chose to release five discs—the albums *Shadows in the Night*, *Fallen Angels*, and the three-disc *Triplicate*—of Songbook material written by other people. While Dylan's popularity in the 2010s was not near the heights it reached in the mid-1960s, the level of esteem his work received was still quite high. He was not aging out of prior youth-oriented material; his original songs, especially since *Time Out of Mind*, are typically about mortality, fate, relationships, and existentialism—not dancing and partying. It seems likely that Dylan could have continued to release an album of original songs every few years (like *Time Out of Mind* in 1997, "*Love and Theft*" in 2001, *Modern Times* in 2006, *Together Through Life* in 2009, *Tempest* in 2012) and continued to play these new songs, as well as mixing in others from earlier in his career, to medium-size, appreciative crowds around the world on his so-called "Never-Ending Tour" for as long as he wanted to.

On the other hand, perhaps we should not have been surprised with this turn in Dylan's career. His recent catalogue includes 2009's *Christmas in the Heart*, an album featuring Dylan's voice in particularly rough shape making his way through traditional carols including "Hark! The Herald Angels Sing" and "O Little Town of Bethlehem," along with pop tunes like "Winter Wonderland" (1934) and "I'll Be Home for Christmas" (1943). Many of the performances on this album are sweetened with background vocals from an Andrews Sisters–style choir. Dylan also recorded two albums of solo folk and blues covers in the early 1990s, *Good as I Been to You* and *World Gone Wrong*, both of which were met with modest acclaim. These albums suggest that Dylan was interested in singing other people's songs and in what he could add as a vocalist and performer to another body of work that was not his own. In contrast to his Christmas album, the two folk albums were shorn of instrumental and vocal frills, featuring only Dylan with an acoustic guitar and a harmonica. This, of course, is how Dylan got his start on the folk scene in Greenwich Village in the early 1960s, a scene in which it was customary to perform older songs written by other people. Still, a song like Woody Guthrie's "Pastures of Plenty" occupies a very different place in American culture from one like "Autumn Leaves," the fourth track on *Shadows in the Night*; they appeal to different audiences, express different emotions, and are situated in very different political economies.[69]

Dylan's performances on his standards albums stay in a narrow lane. All of the songs on these five discs were recorded by Frank Sinatra, and the albums were received in the press specifically as Dylan's homage or tribute to Sinatra. That is not terribly surprising for an album of standards; Sinatra recorded prolifically, so any album that presents this body of material is bound to have some overlap with Sinatra's repertoire. What is more surprising is that Dylan closely copies the arrangements that Sinatra used for his recordings of these songs, matching tempos and form, and transcribing instrumental parts for the members of his touring band, transferring winds, brass, and strings to a conventional rock instrumentation. For example, Donnie Herron on pedal steel guitar sometimes stands in for sections of violins, violas, cellos, and basses. Similar to those string instruments, pedal steel guitar can sustain notes for long periods of time and play dramatic crescendos and decrescendos easily, and these were typical devices of arrangers like Nelson Riddle when orchestrating instrumental accompaniments to Sinatra's vocals. Bassist Tony Garnier often plays an upright bass with a bow to mimic the timbral qualities of some of Sinatra's arrangements. Dylan further limits the range of these recordings by overwhelmingly choosing songs with slow tempos and melancholic lyrics.

By performing some of Sinatra's repertoire and adapting Sinatra's arrangements for his own rock-influenced backing band, Dylan presents a history of American popular music in a relatively faithful, reverent way. Still, the story these recordings tell about Sinatra and about the Great American Songbook itself is necessarily a partial one. Stephen M. Deusner, writing for *Pitchfork*, notes that *Shadows in the Night* presents a vision of the past "as though this style of American pop songwriting was good only for providing ruminative ambience rather than sophisticated humor, feisty insight, or infectious rhythm"—and this description could also be applied to Dylan's subsequent albums of standards.[70] These recordings are not leavened by the up-tempo, finger-snapping, "Chairman of the Board"–type numbers that Sinatra himself would have inserted into his albums and live performances; tunes like "Luck Be a Lady Tonight," "The Best Is Yet to Come," or "I've Got the World on a String" are absent from Dylan's homage to Sinatra. Dylan is constructing a selective version of Sinatra and the Great American Songbook, one that focuses squarely on romantic love (usually lost or unrequited), loneliness, aging, and mortality. Kyle Anderson summarizes the overall aesthetic: "This isn't the *Ocean's 11* Sinatra drinking dry martinis with Dino at the Copa."[71]

Dylan takes a strategy different from Willie Nelson's 2018 Sinatra tribute, which *does* seem to be invoking Sinatra in his role as ambassador of the good life, especially through its brassy arrangements. Sinatra himself is not the one-dimensional stereotype some of his contemporary fans have made him out to be: the Rat Pack Sinatra. Indeed, many other listeners and critics have found Sinatra's more introspective, sentimental, and lovelorn performances to be equally of value. This is the version of Sinatra that Dylan conjures here, but is one that existed in his own lifetime, one that Sinatra himself helped create, that writers like Pete Hamill mythologized, and which was recognized and consumed by fans.⁷² The way that Sinatra presented himself and has been received by his audiences is complex, and Dylan here is choosing the particular aspects of Sinatra's music and cultural mythology with which he wants to engage. However, Dylan also articulates a vision of the musical past, and specifically the Great American Songbook, that we have already seen before: this music from the past deserves our attention even now because it expresses deeper, truer emotions than other styles. Artists like Dylan use this particular constructed version of the past for their own purposes in the present. That does not make their performances any less real or authentic. In fact, the opposite seems to be the case: the selective and constructed vision of the popular music past that Dylan presents in his standards albums is usually viewed by sympathetic listeners and critics as *more* authentic.

Any new release by Dylan gets extensively covered in the press, and the reviews of Dylan's standards albums have tended to focus on a few important issues, including the idea that these old songs of romance gone wrong are appropriate for a man in his seventies to sing and that Dylan's vocal performances add to the timeless quality of these songs. Writing for *MOJO* magazine, a publication with a clear orientation in favor of white classic rock masculinity, Michael Simmons writes: "When he wavers or doesn't quite hit or hold the designated note, it's in keeping with Bob's lifetime fealty to artistic realism . . . Dylan's handful of mistakes are part of his art—a human element in a corporate world that places a premium on assembly-line sameness."⁷³ This is an explicit critique against pop music that is believed to be technically perfect, but artistically vapid and therefore aesthetically lacking. Douglas Heselgrave concurs: "The results haven't always been pretty, but I'd venture that Bob Dylan at his most vocally eccentric and grating is far more interesting than any of the pitch-perfect dross that passes off as singing these days."⁷⁴ These reviewers are expressing ideas that are widely shared among a certain set of listeners about what is most interesting and valuable in the performance of popular music. These ideas are perhaps even shared by readers of this book; certainly, at times, they are shared by its author. However, these ideas are also an aesthetic ideology that does work in the world, not a neutral or a universal truth that should be taken for granted.⁷⁵

In addition to highlighting the "authentic" qualities of Dylan's voice that are appropriate for this repertoire, Heselgrave also notes that Dylan's age gives him special access to this material: "These songs are so lived-in and well-worn; they weren't written for a young man to sing."⁷⁶ This is not literally true. Many of the entries in the Great American Songbook were written by young men, and they were certainly sung by plenty of young men (and young women) during their first years of popularity in the 1920s, 1930s, and 1940s. Other critics, however, agree that Dylan's age makes his performances of these songs more effective. Jim Farber writes: "Dylan is singing of a long-ago love recalled, not one lived in now. He delivers the songs at an age—73—when longing has a very different pull on the soul."[77] Corbin Reiff argues: "The weight of his experience is present in every line, every vocal tic, and every exhale . . . lending a discernible authenticity to the weight of emotion in Dylan's sometimes-frail, sometimes-raspy delivery."[78] Alexis Petridis draws together these two aspects, age and vocal quality: "A lot has been written about the state of Dylan's voice in recent years, but if any songs suit a ruined voice, they're those assembled here. Most of their authors were half Dylan's age when they wrote them, but they sounded much older: everything is suffused with world-weariness and regret."[79] Finally, Matt Melis finds that the aspects of Dylan's approach helps us as listeners appreciate the "historic" or "timeless" qualities of these songs: "instead of sanding down the rust or touching up the paint on these antiquities, he strips them clean of yesteryear's lush orchestration and flashy adornments to find their cores—what makes them work for all eras."[80]

Why do Dylan's albums of standards get such generally positive reviews? It could be that critics were used to Dylan zigzagging through styles and identities over the previous decades, so they were primed for this shift—especially if they have attended any of Dylan's live concerts, in which he seems to delight in performing unrecognizable versions of songs from his own vast back catalogue. It could also be that these performances of songs from the Great American Songbook sounded similar to Dylan's recent albums, especially since "*Love and Theft*" and *Modern Times* liberally employed swung eighth notes and electric guitar timbres much more associated with jazz and the blues than with rock. It could be that critics are willing to give Dylan wide latitude late in his career, because he has built up a large amount of goodwill and he appeals to the largely white, middle-aged, male critical establishment. Relatedly, critics and listeners themselves may have aged or mellowed right along with Dylan; perhaps Dylan has his audience perfectly figured out and knows that these nostalgic songs associated with love and a rosy view of the past would now appeal to the fans who have been following his career for decades.

There is also a Dylan doppelgänger whose vastly different approach to recording Great American Songbook material may influence the reception of Dylan's recordings. Lurking in the background of some of the reception of Bob Dylan is Rod Stewart, another aging white male rock star from the 1960s who also recorded several albums of material from the Great American Songbook in the 2000s. It is easy to see how Stewart can be viewed as the kind of anti-Dylan on these projects. Over the course of five albums, all released on longtime industry mogul Clive Davis's J Records, Stewart is backed by subdued strings and drums played lightly with brushes. Dylan's recordings of standards were supposedly recorded in one take with no overdubs. Whether this is literally true or not, they certainly contain slight rough spots and some imprecise playing from his backing musicians. Stewart's recordings were certainly *not* recorded in one take, and the credits for each album are long, with many musicians credited with arranging, keyboard and synthesizer programming, and conducting—along with more conventional instruments like piano, guitar, and bass. The final results are much more polished; listeners would be hard-pressed to find any obvious "mistakes" on these recordings.

Stewart's performances were critically panned, but they sold well. As is usually the case with a series of albums like this, their sales figures eventually dropped off, but the first volume *It Had To Be You: The Great American Songbook*, released in 2002, sold over three million copies in the United States. By the time the fifth and final volume of this series *Fly Me To the Moon: The Great American Songbook* was released in 2010, sales numbers were down across the entire music industry, as consumers shifted dramatically away from CD sales and toward downloading and streaming. Still, even this album peaked at #4 on the *Billboard* Top Albums chart, and the other albums in this series had a similar level of commercial success. What this means for Dylan is that when he started releasing albums of this material in 2015, Stewart's albums had been in the air for a decade as the best-selling and most ubiquitous version of these songs sung by an artist in Dylan's age and gender demographic. These performances were literally in the air—they were frequently played at grocery stores, coffee shops, pharmacies, and department stores. Stewart and Dylan were obvious foils for each other, and the different critical reactions they received can tell us much about the specific type of historical consciousness that critics find valuable in this repertoire.

Steve Smith explicitly contrasts these two artists, finding Dylan's relatively unpolished versions of these songs "far from an indulgent wallow in saccharine nostalgia—and disproving absurd accusations of a quick-buck dip into a fountain of easygoing oldies a la Rod Stewart."[81] Janne Oinonen writes: "By power-hosing these standards clean of the string-soaked syrup they've been drowning in for years, the songs are allowed to breathe, to reveal the raw hurt that's been buried under bombastic arrangements and technically excellent yet lifeless, smug delivery of the contemporary titans of traipsing down the middle of the road."[82] For critics like these, recordings of standards from the past, at least if done in certain ways, have the potential of providing hard-won, timeless truths. For those who value a sense of historical consciousness in popular music, a too-glib, "technically excellent" performance of these songs is as unsatisfying as the rest of the "frivolous" world of new contemporary pop music.

The first two chapters of this book have primarily focused on white performers of material by white composers for (largely) white audiences. There are some exceptions, to be sure. Ella Fitzgerald and other Black singers such as Louis Armstrong, Billie Holiday, and Sarah Vaughan were important figures in first performing and codifying the Songbook tradition. Jimi Hendrix is certainly an essential figure in historical consciousness in rock music; the three studio albums he released before his untimely death in 1970 have been reissued in many commemorative editions, along with multiple CD sets chronicling live performances and studio outtakes. His performance at the 1969 Woodstock festival—especially of "The Star-Spangled Banner"—helped cement that festival as one of the key moments, aesthetically and politically, in rock music's constructed canon. One of the most important physical sites for historical consciousness in rock—the Museum of Pop Culture in Hendrix's hometown of Seattle—effectively doubles as a shrine to the guitarist.[83]

At the beginning of this chapter, I listed many prominent musicians from a range of pop genres who have turned to recording albums from the Great American Songbook at some point in their careers. Relative to Black musicians' importance to popular music culture, few of them have made the choice to record standards, as compared to their white counterparts. Consider a sampling of Black artists who came to prominence since the 1970s and have enjoyed long, commercially successful careers. Neither Whitney Houston nor Michael Jackson recorded a standards album before they died. Of prominent living Black popular musicians—Erykah Badu, Anita Baker, Beyoncé, Mary J. Blige, Brandy, Toni Braxton, Mariah Carey, Al Green, Janet Jackson, Alicia Keys, Brian McKnight, Lionel Richie, Rihanna, Sade, Usher, Vanessa Williams, and Stevie Wonder—none of them has yet devoted an album to Songbook material. One reason explaining the paucity of Songbook albums by Black musicians may be that there is a specific nostalgia embedded in these songs that is not appealing to Black performers (and/or Black audiences), that the impulse to pay homage to the standards traditions is a nostalgia for a "whitebread," segregated America. The Great American Songbook occupies an ambiguous position in American popular culture. The songs are sometimes criticized as expressing only the thoughts and feelings of middle-class WASP culture, though they were written largely by Jewish songwriters. For listeners in the twenty-first century, performances of standards are often associated with the genre of jazz, a genre with clear African American roots and whose most heralded exponents are Black. Yet in the middle decades of the twentieth century, jazz and the popular music worlds of Broadway, film, and Tin Pan Alley were distinct. Duke Ellington is one of very few Black composers whose work has been adopted into the Great American Songbook. Scholars such as Yagoda and Zak have examined the racism, elitism, and regional bias in this time period that kept the most prestigious and lucrative parts of the songwriting industry largely closed to nonwhite composers.

White critics and listeners often associate the Songbook with a rosy "simpler time" of peace and prosperity of the postwar United States, a time which often corresponded to the youth and adolescence of aging listeners. This time, however, was not such a rosy time for African Americans and may bring to mind the exact opposite kind of memory, as Badia Ahad-Legardy argues: "for many Black Americans, 1950s America triggers black-and-white images of state-sanctioned violence and repressions—kitchenette buildings, *Amos 'n' Andy*, and the innumerable indignities of Jim Crow."[84] Similarly, if these songs are associated with a kind of glamourous supper-club nightlife that systematically excluded Black audience members—such as Las Vegas casinos in the 1950s—perhaps it becomes more obvious why Black performers would be less interested in fondly remembering this period by paying homage to this repertoire. However, a relative lack of interest in further mythologizing the Great American Songbook does not suggest that Black musicians and listeners are never nostalgic or do not participate in historical consciousness in popular music; Ahad-Legardy's work extensively documents writers, visual artists, and musicians who construct and express "romantic recollections of the past in the service of complicating the traumatic as a singular black historical through line."[85] One crucial lesson from Ahad-Legardy and from considering Black and white engagements with the past together is that we should not expect that everyone is going to be nostalgic about the same things that white culture, white artists, white listeners, and the white critical establishment are nostalgic about. Instead, Black creators and audiences may be looking for a more positive, affirmative version of the past to draw inspiration from, to be nostalgic for, and to re-create. We can expect relationships with the past to be varied and not totalizing; certain aspects of it are relevant for particular aesthetic, economic, and social goals, but these relationships with the past may alter when these goals shift: from community to community, person to person, and even within the varied stages of an individual's life. In the next chapter of the book, I will closely examine the musical choices of one prominent Black musician whose relationship to the repertoire of the Great American Songbook changed dramatically over the course of his career. In the final two chapters, I will examine how contemporary musicians and listeners in hip-hop and R&B draw on a specific, but different version of the musical past than we have analyzed thus far.

CHAPTER 3

MEMORIES AND STANDARDS
Miles Davis and "I Fall in Love Too Easily,"
1963–1970

Locating Miles Davis at a Precarious Time

The contemporary world of jazz is often backward-looking and deeply concerned with its own rich history. In his 2018 study of jazz in the twenty-first century, critic Nate Chinen notes that the genre is "enshrined in the popular imagination as a historical practice, a set of codes to be reenacted endlessly," with many listeners, critics, and jazz neophytes sharing "a common perception that the music reached its peak in a distant golden age."[1] Perhaps this sense of nostalgia is inevitable, given that so many of the acknowledged jazz greats—Charlie Parker, Fats Navarro, Clifford Brown, John Coltrane, and Billie Holiday, to name only a few—died at young ages, leaving both their fans at the time and later listeners to fondly remember the creative heights they achieved during their lifetimes and wonder at the body of work they might have produced later in their careers. Many contemporary fans of jazz—myself included—may also feel a sense of nostalgia for a time when jazz was a more prominent part of the musical and cultural landscape: when cities supported numerous jazz clubs, when jazz was more frequently encountered on radio and television, when developments in the music were more frequently discussed and debated in the public sphere, and seemingly every month brought a new landmark recording or a now-legendary live performance.[2] A variety of figures in the jazz world—listeners, critics, historians, musicians, publicists, and record company executives—exhibit the historical consciousness I analyze in this book: a conviction that the music from the past is worthy of study, reflection, and replaying, whether that means recording a tribute album to an earlier musician, playing a bebop tune from the 1940s at a jam session, or settling in with a multidisc box set compilation on the home stereo. However, not all jazz musicians at all times look back to the genre's past so warmly or so frequently, or with such a sense that the music literally deserves to be re-played.

On the subject of his relationship to the past, jazz trumpeter Miles Davis's most revealing insight comes from a conversation with the writer Eric Nisenson in the late 1970s. At the time, Davis was in the middle of a six-year, self-imposed exile from performing and recording. In a cocaine-addled state, Davis got into a debate with Nisenson about what day of the week it was. When Nisenson finally pulled out a copy of the newspaper to prove that Davis was mistaken, Davis seemed unfazed, explaining: "Do you see all those awards on my wall, Eric? The reason I won them is because I can't remember anything worth a damn."[3] That is to say, Davis was unsentimental about the past—his own or anyone else's, musical or otherwise. Significantly, this lack of remembrance was framed by Davis as the reason that he has been successful (as evidenced by the plaques and awards he had won), because he had not been content to revisit or re-create past musical accomplishments he cannot even remember anyway. Instead, he had no choice but to move forward, to progress, in line with the ideology of newness shared by some—but by no means all—jazz musicians and critics at that time.[4]

According to this version of Davis's career—a narrative that Davis himself played a role in constructing—his reluctance to repeat his earlier musical triumphs is what pushed Davis to create such widely divergent, critically acclaimed (and award-winning) works such as *Birth of the Cool* (1949), *Walkin'* (1953), *Porgy and Bess* (1959), *Kind of Blue* (1959), *Sketches of Spain* (1960), *Miles Smiles* (1967), *In a Silent Way* (1969), and *Bitches Brew* (1970). Davis's influence and long-lasting popularity stands in stark contrast to a contemporary like Dizzy Gillespie. For all the plaudits Gillespie's work in the late 1940s has received, his music is viewed to have been codified by the early 1950s, and his later career (until his death in 1993) has largely been ignored by jazz critics, historians, and record buyers.[5] Listeners may be divided on their opinions of Davis's albums *On the Corner* (1972), *You're Under Arrest* (1985), and *Tutu* (1986), but they clearly represented a musician taking very different approaches to music-making over the course of his career. Love him or hate him, Davis's ever-changing music—and Davis himself—have been impossible for critics, fellow musicians, and even casual listeners to ignore.

Another well-known quotation from Davis regarding his relationship to the past is his claim that, "I have to change. It's like a curse."[6] These changes themselves seem to be indicative of his relationship to the past: he is weary of playing the same ways that people have heard him play before, reluctant to perform old music that audiences might remember. Yet in any musician's career, there is a balance of change and stasis, and even if we accept the narrative of Davis as a stylistic chameleon and innovator, some aspects of his performances were slower to change than others. Several musicians stayed in his band for extended stints (including saxophonist Wayne Shorter, who joined in 1964 and made his final live performances with the band in the spring of 1970), and he had professional relationships with collaborators like producer Teo Macero and arranger Gil Evans for long periods of time.

In this chapter, I focus on a period of Davis's career—the 1960s and early 1970s—in which the questions of sameness and difference, past and present, innovation and tradition are particularly acute. He began the early 1960s as perhaps the most famous musician in jazz, a genre that was still a major commercial and cultural force in the United States and abroad. British jazz writer Richard Cook describes Davis's position in 1961, on the heels of the *Someday My Prince Will Come* album:

> Davis's stock as a celebrity and a media personality as well as a jazz musician had continued to grow, as had his personal fortune: he was probably making more money from jazz record sales than any of his contemporaries with the possible exception of Dave Brubeck, whose star had perhaps waned a little since the late 1950s. As far as Columbia [Records] were concerned, he was a guaranteed source of income. Album sales of rock 'n' roll records had yet to make a significant impact—it was still seen as very much a teenage, singles-based music—and Davis could lay title to a business stature on par with that of many leading American entertainers.[7]

However, by the early 1970s, several developments had occurred that threatened both the prestige of jazz and Davis's status as the genre's most important figure. Jazz's economic and cultural position was challenged both by music coded as "white" (the rock music performed by artists like the Beatles, the Doors, and even Jimi Hendrix) and "black" (Motown, soul, and funk of artists like Sly and the Family Stone and James Brown).[8] The teenaged singles buyers of the early 1960s mentioned by Cook above had matured into the baby boomer generation, which made its presence felt through massive attendance at rock music festivals and spent a good portion of its income on purchasing recorded music, particularly rock LP records. In a not unrelated development, white critics and intellectuals began treating rock music as a credible artistic medium, instead of as a novel, disposable commodity. For some Western classical music composers and musicians, rock began to replace jazz as a kind of favorite hobby: the music that they spoke about in interviews or public appearances and seemed to hold in a similar high esteem as the accepted classical canon. For example, beginning in the late 1930s, the composer Ned Rorem was obsessed with the music of Billie Holiday, and during the late 1950s, Leonard Bernstein intently followed the developments of musicians like Ornette Coleman.[9] By the end of the 1960s, however, these same men were paying more attention to rock music played by and targeted to the white counterculture.[10] As Keir Keightley notes, jazz was no longer the only popular music genre which could be taken "seriously."[11] For a classical musician or a middle-class intellectual to claim some populist credibility, rock may have been even a more effective choice than jazz. In many ways, this was the beginning of treating rock music as a genre with artistic significance and historical legitimacy, as I described in relationship to tribute bands in chapter 1. However, before rock music could gain the *historical* legitimacy it acquired in the 1990s and beyond—as an honored part of the past worth remembering and replaying—it had to first acquire *aesthetic* legitimacy, which was already starting to happen by the end of the 1960s, as Rorem and Bernstein exemplify.

To a certain extent, Davis was able to navigate—and even profit from—this shifting musical and cultural landscape of the late 1960s with his shifting music. For an album released by a "jazz" musician, *Bitches Brew* (recorded in August 1969 and released in April 1970) enjoyed unprecedented commercial success. However, subsequent recordings, including 1972's *On the Corner*, failed to duplicate those sales figures. Davis's status as the biggest star in jazz had also been challenged by the rise of other musicians, including his former pianist Herbie Hancock, who had more success marketing his music to the large young Black audience that Davis coveted.[12] Aesthetically, Davis's music had changed in two important ways, compared to his music of ten years prior: with his incorporation of electric instruments into his touring and recording bands (including electric guitar, Fender Rhodes pianos, and various pedals used to manipulate his own trumpet sound) and his eschewing of many of the formal conventions of jazz performance (such as head-solos-head form, discrete songs, fixed chorus structures, and functional harmony) in favor of long, groove-oriented performances organized around bass ostinatos, short melodic fragments, or free improvisations.

These musical changes introduced Davis to potential new audiences for both record sales and live shows, but they also created a major fault line in the reception of his music. At the time, and in the decades since these important developments, Davis's musical changes in the late 1960s have alienated many listeners, critics, and fellow musicians who otherwise placed his earlier work in the jazz pantheon. Perhaps the most polemical of these critics was Stanley

Crouch in a 1990 essay that described *In A Silent Way* (recorded in February 1969 and released in July 1969) as "no more than droning wallpaper music." Davis's next studio album, *Bitches Brew*, with its "multiple keyboards, electronic guitars, static beats, and clutter," confirmed, for Crouch, that Davis was "firmly on the path of the sellout."[13] In Crouch's assessment, this is the path Davis would continue to follow for the rest of his career.

While perhaps uniquely sharp-tongued, Crouch is not alone in his assessment of Davis's music. Even some of Davis's musical peers and friends, while quick to underscore their personal respect and admiration for him, also admitted to a certain bafflement at his new musical style from the late 1960s and onward. A 1972 profile of Davis by the jazz critic Leonard Feather collects a few of these reactions to Davis's new sound, with Dizzy Gillespie affirming, "I know he has something in mind, whatever it is. I know he knows what he's doing, so he must be doing something that I can't get to yet." By contrast, Gillespie's own relationship to the past was clear. He spent much of 1971 and 1972 touring with a band under the name of Giants of Jazz, including Thelonious Monk, Sonny Stitt, and Art Blakey—all veterans of 1940s and 1950s bebop—playing old warhorse tunes like "Straight, No Chaser," "'Round Midnight," and "Blue 'n' Boogie."

Clark Terry similarly withholds judgment of Davis's music, claiming, "I don't know whether or not I'm musically mature enough to understand it," before noting that one of the reasons Davis's fusion jazz might be attracting a comparatively large audience is because it lacks, "the real balls of jazz, the chord progressions, the structures, and so forth." Note the masculinist language Terry uses to describe "the chord progressions, the structures, and so forth" of "real" jazz. For Terry, Davis's new music is viewed as musically simple, appealing to a wide audience, and perhaps therefore, feminine. While not as derogatory as Crouch would be twenty years later, Terry also advances the idea that Davis's new musical direction might be a calculated move to reap the financial rewards of attracting a larger audience:

> Maybe he's doing it sincerely, but I do know that it's a much more lucrative direction for him. I happen to know that there was a period when in spite of all his many possessions—investments, home, car—there was a period when he needed to bolster these; he really needed to get into a higher financial bracket. And there was an opportunity for him to get into this kind of thing, so he took the opportunity to jump out and do it.[14]

Despite these critiques, Davis's early fusion years are not without critical and scholarly supporters. These supporters include, perhaps most notably, Greg Tate (1957–2021) and Gary Tomlinson, a Black public intellectual known for his provocative writing on contemporary popular culture and a white musicologist best known for his scholarship on Renaissance music, respectively. In *Bitches Brew*, Tate hears "James Brown's antiphonal riffing against a metaphoric bass drone with Sly's minimalist polyrhythmic melodies and Jimi's concept of painting pictures with ordered successions of electronic sounds."[15] While Tomlinson's prose is decidedly less colorful, he notes a surprisingly similar "rich dialogue of musical voices that went into the making of Davis's new styles" which "opened lines of communication between traditional jazz, with its blues background and improvisational impetus, on the one hand, and rhythm and blues, funk, and white acid rock on the other."[16] Tomlinson and Tate, along with more recent work by scholars such as Eric Porter, Jeremy A. Smith, Victor Svorinich, and George Grella have contributed to a reevaluation (and, perhaps, a vindication) of Davis's early fusion period.[17] In these various narratives, the story of Davis's career, either as tragedy or triumph, has largely been told through his studio recordings, especially concerning the late 1960s and the (apparently) radical shift of albums like *In a Silent Way* and *Bitches Brew* as compared with his earlier acoustic work. This is problematic because, as Chris Robinson notes in a review of recently released Davis live recordings from 1967 through 1970, "most of what has been [previously] available for listeners who were unable to hear his groups live barely resemble the [studio] albums made during this time."[18] Close listening to some of this newly released live material, along with Davis's studio albums and other live recordings, can further illuminate how Davis's music was changing—and what was staying the same—at this controversial time. Looking only at Davis's studio recordings gives an image of a musician playing primarily new compositions by his younger bandmates and undertaking experiments based on new studio and postproduction technology. His live recordings, however, tell a different story about Davis's relationship to his earlier repertoire and to the jazz past.

This chapter examines Miles Davis's studio and live repertoire during the time period from 1963 until 1970, particularly his performances of the ballad "I Fall in Love Too Easily," a tune from the Great American Songbook that was a remarkably persistent presence in his sets, despite the myriad of other changes that took place during this time period. Indeed, listening to multiple versions of "I Fall in Love Too Easily" reveals clear differences in musical parameters such as form, tempo, rhythm, timbre, and orchestration. But the fact that many performances of "I Fall in Love Too Easily" over a long span of time even exist—in settings as diverse as a recording studio in Los Angeles, a jazz club in Chicago, major concert hall stages in Europe, and the Fillmore East and Fillmore West rock clubs—provides a compelling case study for scholars and listeners alike. In a sense, Davis undertook a kind of experiment, holding "I Fall in Love Too

Easily" constant as part of his repertoire but varying the contexts in which it was performed over a period of seven years. Examining Davis's performances of "I Fall in Love Too Easily" enables us to focus on what, according to both jazz critics and jazz historians, is a crucial turning point, not only for Davis's career but for the genre as a whole. Through detailed examination of various performances of "I Fall in Love Too Easily," we can also concentrate closely on how exactly Davis's relationship to the musical past was changing during this period, even as one song remained a part of his repertoire. In my analysis, I show that "I Fall in Love Too Easily," more so than any other standard, served as a durable vehicle for Davis's musical goals throughout the mid-1960s. By 1970, however, these goals seem to have shifted as Davis moved, step by step, away from the time-tested model of jazz performance based on improvisation on a familiar, preexisting tune or structure: such as a standard from the Great American Songbook. Hence, "I Fall in Love Too Easily," and all other jazz standards were dropped from the band's book as Davis pursued other means of performing that did not depend on—and help perpetuate—a relationship between his audience and music from the past.

"I Fall in Love Too Easily" Joins Davis's Repertoire

"I Fall in Love Too Easily" was written by Jule Styne and Sammy Cahn and first performed by Frank Sinatra in the 1945 MGM musical *Anchors Aweigh*. As Yagoda explains, such movie musicals were a typical source for the songs that would be re-performed by a variety of singers and instrumentalists and would take their place in the constructed tradition of the Great American Songbook. Over the next ten years, the song was recorded by several jazz musicians, including the singer Johnny Hartman in 1955 and by Davis rival Chet Baker, who sang and played trumpet on a recording of the song for his 1956 album *Chet Baker Sings*.[19] Davis first recorded "I Fall in Love Too Easily" for his 1963 album *Seven Steps to Heaven*. This album found Davis at an unsettled time in his career, between his groups featuring John Coltrane and Cannonball Adderley of the late 1950s and early 1960s (with which he recorded the celebrated 1959 album *Kind of Blue*) and the successes of his "second great quintet" of the mid-1960s, with Wayne Shorter, Herbie Hancock, Tony Williams, and Ron Carter. Health problems were also bothering Davis, making it difficult for him to keep a regular schedule of recordings and live performances. Davis was also a victim of his own success in that members of his bands—such as Coltrane, Adderley, Bill Evans, Wynton Kelly, Jimmy Cobb, and Paul Chambers—often used the exposure they gained from playing with Davis as a springboard to leave the band and form their own successful groups. As a consequence of this instability of personnel, Davis experimented with various musicians to fill out his bands for gigs, tours, and recordings in the early 1960s.

"I Fall in Love Too Easily" was recorded in Los Angeles in 1963 as part of the initial recordings for *Seven Steps to Heaven*. Davis used a quartet instrumentation, with his own Harmon-muted trumpet accompanied by the expatriate English pianist Victor Feldman, Ron Carter on bass, and Los Angeles–based Frank Butler on drums. This performance begins with a rubato piano and bass introduction before a sixteen-measure statement of the song's melody by Davis at the tempo of around 50 beats per minute. Davis then plays two solo choruses, Feldman takes a chorus and a half solo, and finally Davis returns to play the melody for the second half of this chorus to end the piece. Perhaps the most notable feature of this version is that Butler goes in and out of a double-time feel seemingly at random and not necessarily coinciding with important structural signposts (e.g., falling out of double time two measures before the end of Davis's solo, only to return to double time during the second measure of the piano solo that follows). Carter never follows Butler's lead to walk in medium 4/4 time—unlike the later studio and live recordings of the Carter-Williams-Hancock rhythm section, in which changes in feel and texture, while sometimes abrupt, are usually followed by other members of the rhythm section. In a contemporary review of the album for *DownBeat*, Don DeMichael noticed: "Butler occasionally seems at a loss as to what to play behind Davis, sometimes double-timing for a few bars and then dropping back; he sounds more comfortable backing Feldman."[20]

Earlier in his career, Davis had often recorded songs from the Great American Songbook, perhaps most notably on the albums that completed his contract with Prestige Records. These albums—*Workin'*, *Cookin'*, *Relaxin'*, and *Steamin'*—replicated Davis's nightclub sets at the time, and were recorded quickly in two sessions in May and October 1956 so that Davis could fulfill his obligations to Prestige and move on to a more lucrative contract with Columbia Records, beginning with his album *'Round About Midnight*.[21] In contrast to these albums for Prestige, the albums Davis would go on to record for Columbia did not feature Songbook tunes. Most of the tunes recorded by Davis during this time period (from the mid-1950s until the mid-1960s) were either his own original compositions, compositions by members of his band, or compositions by other contemporary jazz musicians who could be considered his peers (for example, Thelonious Monk's "'Round Midnight" or Jimmy Heath's "Freedom Jazz Dance").[22] *Seven Steps to Heaven* marks something of a departure, then, as three of its tracks, "Baby Won't You Please Come Home," "Basin Street Blues," and "I Fall in Love Too Easily" were well-known standards. And "I Fall in Love

Too Easily" would remain a part of Davis's live sets during the mid-1960s, with the "second great quintet" and during the early years of his fusion period until 1970, when he jettisoned all other jazz standards or songs from the Great American Songbook.

Standards and Signifyin(g)

What kind of cultural work is accomplished when a jazz musician plays a standard, replays a tune from the near or distant past that his or her audience is likely to have heard before? Given that the performance of standards was (and is) such an important part of jazz, but that it vanished almost entirely from Davis's playing after 1970, right at the time his music attracted new fans and alienated some of his old followers, it is worth pausing and considering what is communicated when a jazz musician like Davis plays a standard—and what the absence of this practice in his playing would have meant for his audiences.

Playing a jazz standard allows for the possibility of a moment of recognition from the audience, and this is true if we consider the experiences of both attending a live performance and listening to recordings. Davis was notorious for not announcing the titles of the songs that he was about to play during live performances, but audience members could still recognize opening melodic gestures and respond with applause when they recognized the piece from prior audition. This recognition can be heard in numerous live recordings by Davis, even in live recordings made in Europe and Japan, showing that the global distribution of Columbia Records was able to make his studio recordings available and familiar to a wide international audience.[23]

In other genres of music, such as rock or pop, audiences at live performances largely expect to hear songs that they know, either from that artist's recorded catalog or covers of other well-known songs. In his study of the relationship between music and recording technology, Mark Katz has detailed how this expectation could be one result of what he terms a "feedback loop" operating with recorded music. Because recordings are repeatable in ways that live performances are not, listeners can become habituated to hearing the same songs (and even minute details of the same performances) over and over. They then expect to hear these same performances replicated in live settings. Even in music that is so ideologically connected to the idea of improvisation as jazz, this same kind of feedback loop is possible through what Katz terms the "repeatability" of recorded music, through which, "unique spontaneous acts, then, may come to be regarded as fixed."[24]

More generally, audiences in a variety of Western musical genres over the past century have become used to the idea of hearing songs, compositions, or melodies in live performance that they have some prior experience with. This has become such an engrained part of musical experience that musicians, listeners, and scholars only rarely remark on what a fundamental change this is from prior practice. The classical music critic Alex Ross has noted that, for much of its history, Western classical music was characterized by an insatiable desire for new music and that the works by the previous generation's acknowledged masters were, within a few decades time, often seen as hopelessly old-fashioned and left to gather dust.[25] Such revivals or a more general audible presence of music from the past in the soundscape are now a common occurrence for listeners, aided by the advent and spread of recording technology from the early twentieth century onward. The music critic Simon Reynolds argues that audio recordings are "what ultimately created the conditions of possibility for retro," by which he means a general predilection for cultural artifacts from the past, a predilection that is "based . . . on obsessive repeat-play of particular artifacts and focused listening that zooms in on minute stylistic details."[26] Extending Reynolds's analysis, this "zoom-in and rewind" allows listeners to become obsessed with (and therefore demand to hear in live performances) familiar music.

This is not a neutral development. Critics such as Ross and Reynolds seem to be at least slightly critical of this tendency to repeat and replay music from the past, taking a critical stance that can be categorized as progressivist or modernist, in favor of new music and development; Reynolds himself fully admits to this ideological position.[27] However, there can also be great power in the reuse of prior musical materials, and there may be particular reasons why musicians replay and repeat (and why listeners find this appealing) that may not line up with critical prerogatives.

The theory of Signifyin(g), as proposed by Henry Louis Gates Jr., has been used as a compelling explanation for the creative reuse of prior materials in a variety of African American artistic traditions, including literature, the visual arts, and music.[28] In Gates's theory, texts signify on other texts, playing with an audience's expectations, alternately highlighting and withholding aspects of the signified-on text that are already familiar to the listener, reader, or viewer. For a jazz musician, this could be as simple as delaying notes of a melody or words of a song by a few beats to create a sense of anticipation that is eventually fulfilled. In the bebop era, jazz musicians signified on standards such as "How High the Moon" by adopting their chord progressions and writing new melodies to place on top of these chord progressions; such was the case with Charlie Parker's composition "Ornithology." However, this relationship to a previous text from the past can be limiting. A song may have associations that an artist does not want to have and is unable to subvert even through his or her "signifying" on it. In the case of music, intellectual property and the payment of royalties are also major issues. For recordings, artists (or their record companies) will have to pay royalties to the owners of the song's copyright, even if the melody is embellished, improvised on, or otherwise "signified" on. Conversely, the royalty income earned from recordings of one's own composition can be an important source of income for musicians. Since a chord progression cannot be copyrighted, bebop musicians were able to claim copyright by writing a new "head" or melody over an existing familiar chord progression. Moving forward twenty years to the 1960s, such concerns remained important for African American jazz musicians, at a time when Black ownership and Black capitalism were promoted as important strategies in the fight for civil rights and respect. In the record industry in particular, many African American musicians such as Davis complained about economic slights from the white-owned companies (like Columbia) for which they were earning money. Therefore, the decision to record and perform tunes written by oneself or to use Tin Pan Alley tunes composed largely by white songwriters has to be viewed as a political one.

Throughout his career, Davis has been widely hailed as an interpreter of songs, particularly of ballads. He is not typically held up as a major jazz composer, and few of his compositions (with the exceptions of "So What," "All Blues," and "Milestones") have been frequently performed by other jazz musicians—in contrast to peers like Charles Mingus, Thelonious Monk, or Charlie Parker. It is primarily through his versions of songs written by other people, particularly Great American Songbook standards such as "My Funny Valentine," that Davis's formidable reputation as a trumpeter and bandleader rests. Up to a certain point in his career, until about the mid-1960s, this made sense for Davis. To perform such standards, particularly in live settings, was typical practice for jazz musicians. Indeed, Davis's performances of jazz standards were highly regarded by contemporary listeners, lauded by jazz critics, and have been analyzed in great detail by jazz scholars in the intervening decades. In 1983, Howard Brofsky published a music-theoretical analysis of solos by Davis from 1956, 1958, and 1964 recordings of the ballad "My Funny Valentine" in *Black Music Research Journal*. While the subject of his analysis was a novel one for a music theorist in the early 1980s, Brofsky's analysis otherwise uses the typical tools and methods of music theory to aesthetically validate Davis's performances, concluding that "there is, among these three versions, a kind of progression from improvisation to composition, from unique moments in the earlier pieces to the global conception of the 1964 performance."[29]

While examining in detail one of these same performances (the 1964 version of "My Funny Valentine" recorded live at Philharmonic Hall in New York), Robert Walser takes a very different approach in his 1995 article "Out of Notes: Signification, Interpretation, and the Problem of Miles Davis." Walser discusses both the specific ways that Davis performs the notes (necessitating a detailed transcription and a prose description of aspects of the performance difficult to capture in Western notation) and how these performances functioned in a greater cultural context. Crucially, Walser's analysis suggests that the ways in which Davis approached particular notes—bending them, using false fingering, rushing or playing behind the beat—are in fact meaningful and dialogical, communicating with the audience and their sense of expectation built on their prior musical knowledge. In so doing, Walser adapts Gates's theory of "Signifyin(g)" as an analytical tool. Comparing Davis's performance of "My Funny Valentine" to that of the jazz singer Tony Bennett, Walser asks:

> Now can we say that Davis is signifyin' on—commenting on, in dialogue with, deconstructing—Bennett's version? The question is made more complex by the idea that as a performer, Davis is signifyin' on all of the versions of the song he has heard, but for his audience, Davis is signifyin' on all the versions each listener has heard. What is played is played up against Davis's intertextual experience and what is heard is heard up against the listeners' experiences. Moreover, Davis is no doubt engaging the many Bennett-like performances of "My Funny Valentine" he must have heard, but he is also signifyin' on many jazz versions, including his own past performances. This chain of signifyin' spins out indefinitely, though most fundamentally Davis is in dialogue with the basic features of the song itself, as jazz musicians would understand them and as listeners would recognize them. The whole point of a jazz musician like Davis playing a Tin Pan Alley pop song can be understood as his opportunity to signify on the melodic possibilities, formal conventions (such as the AABA form of the 32-measure chorus), harmonic potentials, and previously performed versions of the song.[30]

With only a few substitutions (Chet Baker or Johnny Hartman for Bennett, the sixteen-measure form of "I Fall in Love Too Easily" for the thirty-six-measure AABA' form of "My Funny Valentine"), Walser's description of Davis's signifying here could easily apply to his performances of "I Fall in Love Too Easily," including the studio recording from 1963 and the live versions he played of the piece in the years that followed.

As has been well described both in *Miles: The Autobiography* and in a wide variety of literature by scholars and critics, Davis's music began to change in the mid-1960s.[31] On the studio recordings made with his quintet of Shorter, Hancock,

Williams, and Carter, many of the markers of codified jazz style (twelve- or thirty-two-bar forms, functional harmony, head–solos–head arrangements) are not present or are radically altered. But what has not been well described is the fact that Davis and his quintet still performed jazz standards, including "I Fall in Love Too Easily," in these new performance styles during live gigs at clubs and concert halls. The Davis quintet in the mid-1960s and earlier bebop musicians were both signifyin(g) on jazz standards, in the sense of using an audience's prior familiarity with a text (the expected melodies and chord progressions of a particular Tin Pan Alley song) as a basis for creating a richly layered new performance.

During his lifetime, a handful of live recordings of Davis were available. Since his death in 1991, Columbia Records has been engaged in a process of monetizing recordings made of him during his lifetime, since he remains a highly bankable commodity as a musician. A steady stream of reissued CDs, new archival recordings, and box sets have been issued.[32] These releases themselves should be viewed as part of a growing historical consciousness in the music industry, as more and more music is viewed as historically significant and (therefore) economically valuable. For scholars, this means that a profusion of live recordings have become available, and we can now hear more clearly how Davis and his quintet were playing (and, indeed, signifying on) standard tunes during the 1960s, how their performances of these tunes varied over the course of several years, and what points of continuity existed in their live repertoire that are obscured by only listening to their studio albums. We can also see that, as much as Davis's music was changing during the late 1960s, some unexpected connections to the past remained.

The "Second Great Quintet" at the Plugged Nickel

Davis assembled the "second great quintet" in the fall of 1964, with Wayne Shorter becoming a permanent replacement for George Coleman on tenor saxophone, Ron Carter remaining with the group on bass, and Herbie Hancock and Tony Williams joining on piano and drums, respectively. The group, now in its final form, quickly made both live recordings (*Miles in Berlin*, recorded at the Berliner Philharmonie, on November 4) and studio recordings for the album *E.S.P.* in January 1965. However, Davis was again experiencing health issues that prevented the group from touring or recording for much of 1965. The members made use of this free time to work with other musicians and pursue their own projects, which included several Blue Note albums made by members of the group during this time: Hancock's *Maiden Voyage*, Williams's

Spring, and Shorter's *The Soothsayer*, *Etcetera* and *The All Seeing Eye*. Perhaps more importantly, they had the opportunity to play with musicians associated with more experimental styles of jazz: Ron Carter worked with the saxophonist Charles Lloyd, Wayne Shorter played with Roy Haynes at Slugs (a Lower East Side club favored by members of the avant garde such as Albert Ayler and Sun Ra), and the trio of Williams, Shorter, and Carter did a gig together in Boston playing free improvisations.[33]

While the members of the quintet picked up other playing experiences, Davis slowly convalesced, and in December 1965, he took his now-solidified quintet into the Plugged Nickel club in Chicago. Columbia made recordings of the group and, in 1995, released a box set of thirty-nine tracks, documenting two complete nights (seven sets total) of playing.[34] In his autobiography, Davis describes the band's repertoire at the time, drawing a distinction between the music that the quintet played live and what they had been recording in the studio for Columbia:

> My playbook, the songs we would play every night, started to wear down the band. People were coming to hear those tunes that they heard on my albums; that's what was packing them in the door: "Milestones," "'Round Midnight," "My Funny Valentine," "Kind of Blue" [sic]. But the band wanted to play the tunes we were recording which we never did live, and I know that was a sore point with them.... Instead of developing the new music live which we were playing on records, we found ways to make the old music sound as new as the new music we were recording.[35]

Davis seems to admit that commercial concerns—and, broadly speaking, a consideration of his audience—motivated his repertoire choices. This fits in well with Crouch's idea, quoted above, of Davis being a "sellout" for performing rock-influenced music from the late 1960s onward, but it does not fit most descriptions of Davis in the early and mid-1960s. For example, the journalist Lionel Olay began a 1964 profile of Davis by describing him as someone who "is distinctly anti-performance" and "barely masks his contempt and hostility for the fans."[36] Writing in 1964, this was already the conventional wisdom about Davis, but it was conventional wisdom that, at times, Davis was at pains to dispute. In a 1968 interview with the drummer Arthur Taylor for the latter's *Notes and Tones* book, Davis seems to take direct aim at critics and journalists like Olay:

> Most guys want to know about ... well, they say I'm rude, and that I turn my back on the audience, and that I don't like white people. And that I don't like the audience. But the thing is, I never think about an audience. I just think about the

band. And if the band is all right, I know the audience is pleased. I don't have to hold the audience's hand.[37]

Davis in 1965 seemed to be at a crossroads. He was caught between his bandmates' desire to perform the new material on his studio albums, his audience's desire to hear familiar songs that they knew from his prior albums, his reticence as a performer to "hold the audience's hand," and his knowledge that these people were the ones who were buying his albums and "packing" his clubs and concerts. His approach these two nights that we have recordings of, December 22 and December 23 at the Plugged Nickel, was to play mostly pieces he had first recorded in the late 1950s and early 1960s, not the newer compositions by Shorter, Hancock, Carter, and Williams. Even of these older pieces, his set lists were heavily weighted toward Songbook standards. His typical sign-off "The Theme" closes all seven sets (with lengths varying from a cursory thirty seconds to over ten minutes). Otherwise, Songbook tunes make up nineteen of the remaining thirty-two performances, including four versions of "I Fall in Love Too Easily."

On a large scale, these four versions share a basic shape. Davis always plays the opening chorus, solos for a few choruses, and then Shorter and Hancock play solos, before Davis returns to reprise the melody to end the piece before going quickly into the next song—which, in these recordings, was either "No Blues" or his set-closer, "The Theme." This is the usual head-solos-head form that had become a cliché by 1965 and against which certain jazz musicians, including free jazz musicians and even Davis himself, would rebel. Beyond the general structure of the performance, there are distinct similarities in execution between these four versions. For the opening melodic chorus, Davis always clearly plays the first eight notes (which correspond to the title lyrics, one note per syllable). For a group that was often working without breaks between songs—and certainly without spoken introductions from its leader—this helped signal, both to his fellow band members and to the audience, that the band will now be playing "I Fall in Love Too Easily." During his opening melodic statements, Davis is always accompanied by Hancock on piano. Carter on bass usually begins playing around the fifth measure, while Williams on drums will either play very sparsely with brushes on the snare drum or lay out entirely. Without Carter anchoring the ensemble, Davis and Hancock typically play rubato, without a discernible 4/4 metrical structure or steady pulse. When Carter is playing, the quarter-note tempo is slow, around 60 beats per minute or less.

On all versions of "I Fall in Love Too Easily" from the Plugged Nickel, Davis continues his solo for a few choruses after the opening melodic head chorus. During these solos, Williams provides the most contrast, usually playing in double time, making choices to go back and forth between brushes on the snare and sticks on cymbals. Carter often plays a walking bass line to go along with the feel set by Williams. Within this framework, however, Williams was notorious for being a particularly interactive drummer, switching his patterns and accents often. Shorter always solos on tenor saxophone after Davis, and during these solos the rhythm section texture is similarly varied. During the first set on December 22, Williams goes into a quick waltz time on the ride cymbal (with each measure of 3/4 equivalent to one quarter note of the initial slow tempo) at the end of Davis's solo and keeps this going for the beginning of Shorter's solo, with Carter playing double time against it, for a composite 3 against 2 feel in the rhythm section.

For the members of Miles Davis's quintet, these were no ordinary performances. In his autobiography, Hancock recounts that the group of Davis, Carter, Williams, Shorter, and himself had been playing together for a year by the time of these late-1965 gigs. They had figured out how to respond to each other on the bandstand almost too well, and the Plugged Nickel provided an opportunity for them to stretch their creativity:

> We needed to put the challenge back in, to figure out ways to take more risks. I had noticed that our playing had gotten a little too comfortable, but on the flight to Chicago it was Tony who started the conversation.
> "I've got an idea," he said. "Let's play some anti-music." He wanted us to promise that during our sets at the Plugged Nickel, whatever anybody in the band expected us to play, we would play the opposite. Some people have suggested that Tony was trying to sabotage the band by doing this, but really he was only trying to sabotage our comfort level, to break us open again. It was just another step in trying to push our boundaries as musicians and as a band....
> We knew we were using the audience as guinea pigs for our experiment, but this was a way to break the habits we had formed—by destroying the structure, then picking up the pieces and building something new.[38]

Hancock's role in this music is usually to add ambiguity by drastically reharmonizing the tune's lead sheet chords, rather than the harmonic grounding a pianist would be expected to provide in a more traditional jazz combo. As free as the Plugged Nickel performances of "I Fall in Love Too Easily" are harmonically and melodically, there is still a discernible chorus structure: in this case the sixteen-bar structure of the tune. In fact, Davis even telegraphs this chorus structure by often playing relatively clear paraphrases of the tune's opening eight-note melody which coincide with the beginning of choruses; this is true even for his "solo" choruses, when he would otherwise be expected to mostly stay away from the tune's composed melody in favor of improvising on the tune's underlying harmonic structure. During the Plugged Nickel gigs, however, this familiar harmonic structure itself was often all but unrecognizable.

The "Second Great Quintet" in Europe

Whether or not one characterizes the band's playing of ever-more-abstract versions of old jazz standards as "anti-music" (as Williams proposed), they finished their residency at the Plugged Nickel on January 2, 1966. Health problems continued to bother Davis throughout the first few months of 1966, but the quintet played a West Coast tour in the late spring and the Newport Jazz Festival in July.[39] Davis returned to the studio in October 1966 to record *Miles Smiles*. Along with tunes written by quintet members ("Circle" by Davis, "Dolores," "Footprints," and "Orbits" by Shorter), two other compositions were recorded and released: "Gingerbread Boy" by Jimmy Heath and "Freedom Jazz Dance" by Eddie Harris. As with all other studio albums made by the group, no jazz standards were recorded. In May 1967, the quintet recorded the music that would be released as the *Sorcerer* LP. A month later, the quintet was back in the studio recording the *Nefertiti* album. Davis had fallen into a pattern of recording new compositions by his band members in the studio (and releasing these on his albums), but filling out his live set lists with a mix of originals and standards.

In the fall of 1967, Davis and his quintet toured Europe with a package of other jazz artists, including Thelonious Monk, Sarah Vaughan, and Archie Shepp. On several of the concerts, the Davis quintet was paired with Shepp and his band, a pairing which Davis biographer Jack Chambers attributes to the "recognition ... of Davis's recent alliance with freer jazz, a recognition not nearly as widespread as it should have been, perhaps because most jazz fans and many reviewers were still smitten with Davis's earlier records and had not caught up to him in the interval."[40] In 2011, Columbia Records released a four-disc set, *The Bootleg Series Volume 1: Live in Europe 1967*, compiling live recordings made by the quintet on this tour in October and November 1967 in Antwerp, Copenhagen, Paris, Karlsruhe, and Stockholm. Discussing the quintet's playing in his autobiography, Davis writes: "I loved that band, man, because if we played a song for a whole year and you heard it at the beginning of the year, you wouldn't recognize it at the end of the year."[41] This is at least a slight exaggeration. Nevertheless, now that many of Davis's live recordings are widely available, we can hear for ourselves how these songs were changing from night to night and year to year. "I Fall in Love Too Easily" is a particularly good

Miles Davis, Ron Carter, and Wayne Shorter performing in London, UK, in 1967. Photo by Brian Foskett.

case study because it was a consistent presence in Davis's sets and recordings of it are available from a comparatively long range of time.

For at least these five sets from the spring of 1967 released on disc, the band's repertoire fell into a predictable pattern, even if what they did with these pieces from night to night was fluid. "Agitation," a Davis original released on *E.S.P.* that had been performed twice on the Plugged Nickel recordings, had been promoted to being the group's usual set-opener. "Agitation" was always followed by "Footprints," a Shorter composition released both on the composer's 1967 *Adam's Apple* album and on *Miles Smiles*. Other quintet originals performed on the European recordings include "Riot" and "Masqualero"; together with "Agitation" and "Footprints," recent compositions by the band total fifteen of the thirty-four tunes on these recordings. "Gingerbread Boy," a Jimmy Heath tune recorded on *Miles Smiles*, is also played twice. This is a marked departure from the Plugged Nickel gigs in which "Agitation" was the only tune from the group's recent studio recordings that was performed.

However, some material would still have been familiar to fans who, in Chambers's words, "were still smitten with Davis's earlier records and had not caught up to him in the interval." The Thelonious Monk composition "'Round Midnight," which Davis had recorded with his "first quintet" for Columbia Records in 1956, is played three times over the span of five gigs. "No Blues" appears three times, and an even older blues composition, "Walkin'," is performed once. The standards "On Green Dolphin Street" and "I Fall in Love Too Easily" are each performed twice. Finally, "The Theme" still serves as a set-closer for most of the sets, ranging dramatically in length (as it had during the Plugged Nickel gigs) from thirty seconds to more than eight minutes. Davis therefore had a rather limited repertoire of pieces for these concerts, even if they did span a wide chronological range of his career, from pieces that he had only released within the past year to songs he first recorded more than ten years earlier ("'Round Midnight" and "Walkin'"). Comparing the song selection from this European tour to the set lists from the Plugged Nickel two years earlier, we can see how the group was changing. Most of the standards performed in 1965 at the Plugged Nickel had permanently vanished from Davis's repertoire. Songs like "If I Were a Bell," "All of You," and "I Thought About You" received their last performances by Davis at the Plugged Nickel, while others like "Autumn Leaves" and "My Funny Valentine" would be gone by the summer of 1966.[42] When these standards were no longer performed by Davis, a particular type of communication with his audience based on a shared knowledge of and history with the Great American Songbook was gone.

"I Fall in Love Too Easily," however, was one of the survivors, and the quintet played it on November 6, 1967, at the Salle Pleyel in Paris. For this performance, Davis is accompanied only by Hancock on piano for the first two choruses, lasting nearly two minutes. (This duet orchestration can be seen as a precursor to later versions of the piece, discussed below.) The first eight measures are a fairly clear presentation of the tune's written melody. During the second eight measures of the sixteen-bar chorus structure, fewer of Davis's melodic choices match up with the composition's written melody, but experienced listeners would still be able to pick out occasional references to the tune. A second chorus starts at 1:06, still rubato with only Hancock and Davis playing. Carter and Williams join on bass and drums at 1:52 to begin another chorus, playing in double time at about 144 beats per minute. Davis's solo hangs over into the next chorus, starting at 2:43, but Shorter enters in the sixth bar of the sixteen-measure chorus at 3:00. By the time the next chorus begins at 3:36, Carter and Williams have doubled the tempo again, and shortly thereafter, Hancock stops comping. For the next minute and a half, accompanied only by Carter and Williams playing at a very fast tempo, Shorter's solo is in a context that sounds very close to free jazz, as Chambers's description above suggests. Williams and Carter stage a dramatic deceleration and diminuendo at the end of Shorter's solo, eventually leaving Hancock to play an unaccompanied rubato solo. At 7:55, Hancock's playing suggests the comfortable double-time tempo from the beginning of the piece, which acts as a cue for Williams and Carter to rejoin the performance.

Davis reenters at 9:42 and finds himself in three different rhythm section textures in quick succession. The rhythm section maintains its double-time tempo for the first 8 measures of this chorus, with Williams greeting Davis's arrival with several loud bass drum hits and cymbal crashes. Hancock and Williams seem to jointly decide to switch the feel to 12/8 for the next four measures of the chorus, beginning at 10:00. But by 10:10, Williams has dropped out and Hancock and Carter are playing out-of-time accompaniment for Davis to end the piece. In less than thirty seconds, then, the rhythm section has shown three of its seemingly infinite ways of interpreting the structure of a song like "I Fall in Love Too Easily." Davis repeats a cadential figure four times, each time ending on the third degree of the scale but neglecting to resolve down to the tonic. Instead, he moves immediately on to the next composition, "Riot."

Davis and the quintet performed "I Fall in Love Too Easily" the following night in Karslruhe, Germany, on November 7, 1967. In Karlsruhe, the performance begins with Davis by himself for the first 8 measures, before Hancock joins him to finish the second half of the first chorus. This time, however, Davis and Hancock play three choruses by themselves before Davis plays a short phrase that cues Carter and Williams to come in at double time. Williams seems eager to play even faster, however, so he redoubles the time, which Carter eventually follows. Once Carter is walking in 4/4 at this very quick tempo, Williams takes this as a license to play loud flourishes on the snare and cymbals which threaten to disrupt the meter, though he keeps a steady tempo on his hi-hat. For Shorter's tenor solo, Williams's playing again provides sharp contrasts, dropping out entirely at 18:30, playing out-of-time snare drum rolls at 18:55, and locking into a steady groove on his ride cymbal at 20:00.[43] Hancock plays a comparatively brief solo starting at 22:08. Davis returns to finish the piece, this time ending on the tonic at 25:14. The sense of repose is short-lived, however; almost as soon as the trumpet leaves Davis's lips, Williams begins the drum solo that introduces "Gingerbread Boy."

Comparing the live recordings of "I Fall in Love Too Easily" from this tour in Paris and Karslruhe with those from the Plugged Nickel, we can hear important differences. Davis's playing sounds much stronger and more confident in the 1967 European recordings. There are just as many, if not more, shifts in tempo, texture, and feel as the "anti-music" of the Plugged Nickel performances, but they are accomplished much more smoothly than the 1965 recordings. The context is also quite different. At the Plugged Nickel, "I Fall in Love Too Easily" was just one standard among many played; listeners at the Chicago performances would have heard other Songbook tunes like "If I Were a Bell," "Stella by Starlight," "All of You," "I Thought About You," "When I Fall in Love," and "Autumn Leaves" during the same set as "I Fall in Love Too Easily." By 1967, as I noted above, set lists were dominated by quintet originals. "I Fall in Love Too Easily" would therefore take on added significance for the audience as one of only a few familiar scraps of melody in a night of newer, and probably less recognizable, music.

New Experiments

Both contemporary reviews of the quintet's concerts in Europe in 1967 and reviews of the 2011 release of these recordings agree that the band's performances were at a remarkably high level.[44] Once Davis returned to the United States, however, he was not content to rest on his laurels. (Perhaps we can recall his claim, quoted above: "I have to change. It's like a curse.") Instead, he seemed eager to change and expand his ensemble's timbral palette. In December 1967, he began bringing in a series of guitarists for recordings in the studio, including Joe Beck, Bucky Pizzarelli, and George Benson. Davis also purchased a Fender Rhodes piano for Hancock to play. Hancock eventually took to the electric piano—and has had a deep interest in various kinds of technology in his ensuing career—but Carter was less enthusiastic about the electric bass that Davis had him play on several tracks recorded at this time. Hancock and Carter left the band, and by the September 1968 sessions that yielded "Felon Brun" and "Mademoiselle Mabry" for the *Filles de Kilimanjaro* album, Chick Corea on electric piano and Dave Holland on bass had become permanent members.

In February 1969, this group, augmented in the studio by Joe Zawinul on organ, Hancock returning on electric piano, and John McLaughlin on electric guitar, would record what Crouch termed the "droning wallpaper music" of *In a Silent Way*. After these sessions, Williams left the group and was replaced by Jack DeJohnette on drums. This group, with Shorter remaining on tenor and soprano saxophones, is sometimes known as Davis's "lost quintet" because few recordings of the band exist. Davis writes in his autobiography, "Man I wish this band had been recorded live because it was really a bad motherfucker.... Columbia missed out on the whole fucking thing."[45] In fact, after bootleg recordings of the group had circulated among collectors for years, in 2013 Columbia officially released a few of these performances as *The Bootleg Series Volume 2: Live in Europe 1969*. Davis was certainly correct in that the live performances of this group are a revelation. They provide a fascinating link between the music of the mid-1960s quintet and Davis's controversial fusion albums from 1969 and later.

This band's live repertoire was decidedly mixed, with selections from the quintet's mid-1960s albums, newly recorded (or yet-to-be-recorded) tunes from *Bitches Brew* and *In a Silent Way*, and even venerable, familiar songs like "'Round Midnight," "No Blues," and "Milestones." On recordings from performances at jazz festivals in Juan-les-Pins, France, and Berlin, the group also performs "I Fall in Love Too Easily," the only remaining Tin Pan Alley standard in the band's book. Listening to full sets from this group, the sound of the "lost quintet" is a striking shift from both Davis's quintet with Hancock, Williams, and Carter and from the studio sessions that produced *In a Silent Way*. DeJohnette plays the opening of "Directions" (the group's new set opener) with sustained loud snare rolls punctuated by cymbal crashes, seemingly even less interested in serving as a steady timekeeper than Williams had been. Crouch criticized *Bitches Brew* for having "static beats," and it is certainly true that the steady, chugging grooves on much of that album are far more regular and easy to follow than DeJohnette's playing in live performances during 1969. In context with these live recordings, the steadiness found in *Bitches Brew* could be heard as necessary for keeping the large ensemble of multiple drummers, keyboard players, and bassists together in a way that was less of a concern for the quintet instrumentation. Additionally, those who think of Davis as a trumpet player who lacks technical proficiency or power will also be surprised by these recordings, as he seems to effortlessly hit and sustain high notes and play quick runs.

The two performances of "I Fall in Love Too Easily" captured on *Live in Europe 1969* are equally revealing, and quite different from the 1965 and 1967 live quintet recordings. Their instrumentation consists only of Corea on electric piano and Davis on trumpet. Their running times are also significantly shorter, clocking in around three minutes in length rather than the ten-minute excursions with long solos by Davis, Shorter, and Hancock the group performed in 1965 and 1967. The July 26, 1969, performance at the Juan-les-Pins festival consists only of two choruses and an extended tag. Corea and Davis play rubato, with Davis playing a fairly straightforward version of the melody for the opening chorus. Perhaps most interestingly, he repeats a cadential figure that goes up to the third scale degree several times, as was also present in the live recording from Paris in 1967. Unlike most of his other live performances, however, Davis actually resolves and ends on the tonic and waits a few seconds before proceeding to the next number. The effect is a performance of "I Fall in Love Too Easily" far more wrapped up and neat than had been his usual practice.

Four months later in Berlin on November 7, "I Fall in Love Too Easily" found its way into his set again. Still a rubato duet between Davis on open horn and

Corea on electric piano, the tune's opening melody is only recognizable for the first four measures. After that, neither Davis nor Corea make much audible effort to follow the tune's melodic structure or sixteen-measure chorus form. Most significantly, "I Fall in Love Too Easily" now serves as an introduction to the Shorter composition "Sanctuary," a place it would have in the repertoire before being dropped from the book entirely (and with it, the last of the Great American Songbook standards from Davis's repertoire).[46]

In the 1965 and 1967 live recordings, a performance of a ballad like "I Fall in Love Too Easily" could be used for several purposes. It could serve as a reminder of different times and musical styles. For at least some portion of Davis's audience, a live performance of "I Fall in Love Too Easily" would have recalled the song's genesis in the 1940s, earlier recordings of the tune by other artists, and Davis's own recording of the song in 1963. Perhaps the central paradox of jazz improvisation is that by playing something "old" and familiar to an audience, musicians can also show off their creativity, their ability to perform a familiar text in a multitude of inventive new ways. Certainly this was the case for "I Fall in Love Too Easily" in the mid-1960s for the Miles Davis Quintet. In 1965 and 1967, "I Fall in Love Too Easily" is mobilized to showcase the quintet's wide range: its ability to shift between vastly different tempos, dynamic levels, pitch ranges, and time signatures.

By 1969, however, "I Fall in Love Too Easily" is used for a more limited function in live performances: to act as a period of relative calm in terms of its tempo (rubato), its orchestration (electric piano and trumpet), and its volume (without the snare drum and cymbal punctuations heard on other tunes in Davis's sets).[47] In 1965 and 1967, Davis and his quintet were taking harmonic and melodic structures from the honored past tradition of the Great American Songbook, structures that would have been familiar to at least part of their audience and manipulating them—signifying on them—in various ways.[48] By 1969, the pieces Davis and his new quintet were playing would likely have been less familiar to their audiences: tunes like "Directions," "Spanish Key," "Miles Runs the Voodoo Down," "It's About That Time," "Sanctuary," and "Bitches Brew" had not yet been commercially released by the time of these performances in France. Even tunes that Davis's earlier bands had recorded and released (such as "Milestones," "'Round Midnight," "No Blues," and "Footprints") were probably less well known than the Songbook standards Davis played in 1965. As described by Gates, Signifyin(g) is a broad artistic practice, and one could still describe Davis here as Signifyin(g): putting the performance conventions of jazz, rock, and free jazz into dialogue with each other. However, this dialogue was based less and less on shared knowledge between Davis and his audience of a preexisting text, perhaps less and less based on a relationship between the past and the present, and more on the relationship between the present and the future: the new musical and social world that was to come and which Davis himself heralded.

Final Performances

By the time of the Berlin performance in November 1969, *In a Silent Way* had been released, giving both Davis's fans in the jazz community and other interested listeners a chance to hear his new musical direction, in which electric instruments were foregrounded and postproduction editing was used to assemble a final product from various takes in the studio.[49] In the world outside jazz, the Woodstock festival had taken place, finishing up on Monday morning August 18, the same morning that Davis would take a group of musicians into the studio for the first of the sessions that would eventually yield *Bitches Brew*. His 1968 marriage to Betty Mabry and his friendship with Jimi Hendrix assured that Davis was well aware of events in the youth counterculture.

Whether one credits this development to pressure from Columbia label executives, Davis's desire for a wider audience, or his own wandering muse, Davis began to perform in new venues associated with the rock counterculture, most notably Bill Graham's Fillmore East in New York and Fillmore West in San Francisco. In March 1970, the Davis group, now augmented by Airto Moreira on percussion, opened for Neil Young and Crazy Horse and the Steve Miller Band for two nights at the Fillmore East. A month later in San Francisco, Davis and the sextet, now with Steve Grossman on saxophone, opened for the Grateful Dead and Stone the Crows at the Fillmore West in San Francisco for four nights. The April 10 show was released by Columbia as *Black Beauty: Miles Davis at Fillmore West*. Davis's performance of "I Fall in Love Too Easily" from this gig fits the pattern established during the Berlin recording; it serves as a brief rubato electric piano-and-trumpet introduction to "Sanctuary."

In June 1970, Davis and his group, now with Keith Jarrett joining Chick Corea on keyboard, were back in New York at the Fillmore East, opening for the folk-rock singer Laura Nyro. At the June 19 performance at the Fillmore East, the group played "I Fall in Love Too Easily" as an out-of-time interlude for keyboards and trumpet, with Moreira adding occasional comments on percussion. The performance only lasts for one chorus before quickly transitioning to "Sanctuary." DeJohnette taps at his cymbals and Moreira's moaning contributions on cuica are more conspicuous during the following evening's performance of "I Fall in Love Too Easily" on June 20. Davis, however, abandons the tune before completing a full chorus, moving on to "Sanctuary." Later in 1970, Davis played at the Isle of Wight festival in the UK on August 29. With performances by artists like Jimi Hendrix, the Who, the Doors, and Sly and the Family Stone, the Isle of Wight festival is perhaps second only to Woodstock itself in the counterculture mythology. For the estimated crowd of six hundred thousand, Davis's set consisted entirely of recent material from *Bitches Brew* and *In a Silent Way*, along with Joseph Zawinul's "Directions." All jazz standards, including "I Fall in Love Too Easily," had now been dropped from Davis's repertoire.

Leaving the Jazz Past Behind

The gigs that Davis and his band played in high-profile rock venues had important consequences. As Davis notes in his autobiography, playing on the same bill as the Grateful Dead at the Fillmore West in California

> was an eye-opening concert for me, because there were about five thousand people there that night, mostly young, white hippies, and they hadn't hardly heard of me if they had heard of me at all.... The place was packed with these real spacy, high white people, and when we first started playing, people were walking around and talking. But after a while they all got quiet and really got into the music.... After that concert, every time I would play out there in San Francisco, a lot of young white people showed up at the gigs.[50]

Some of these "venturesome white rockers willing to try something new" (as Tomlinson describes them) made up a good portion of the record sales for *Bitches Brew*.[51] Indeed, playing concerts in these venues lined up with what Jeremy A. Smith argues was "Columbia's broader interest in exposing the entirety of its roster to the newly recognized, and predominantly white, youth market."[52]

While Davis was no doubt happy with the increased record sales from this new audience, he also began to be increasingly interested in appealing to a young Black audience. Smith has extensively discussed the marketing of Davis's music in his article, "'Sell it Black': Race and Marketing in Miles Davis's Early Fusion Jazz." Both Davis and Columbia Records were interested in expanding his audience beyond the traditional jazz audience to a youth market, but Smith warns us against the tendency to "conflate a musician's interests and goals with those of a record company."[53] Instead, Davis, as he mentioned in various interviews during the 1970s and in his autobiography, specifically wanted a young Black audience for his new music.

The tendency in the reception of early fusion, from Clark Terry to Stanley Crouch, is to assert that Davis's music changed for the worse because he wanted a new, bigger audience. A viewpoint that is more sympathetic to Davis's music or to an ideology of autonomous art would suggest that concerns about audiences (white or Black, large or small) were incidental to Davis's shift in musical direction. Determining causality can be a tempting path. Did Davis change his music (to electric instruments and away from standards) to appeal to a new audience? Was his new audience a result of the change in Davis's music? However, I want to suggest that understanding causality in this case is less important than understanding consequences. Simply put, continuing to perform standards from the past would likely not have been an effective communicative strategy for Davis with the audience he was playing to in 1970. Similarly, the comparatively massive audience (for a "jazz" musician, at least) he attracted for his performances and recordings would likely not have been interested in his music had he continued with his older repertoire.

Where does this leave Davis's performances of "I Fall in Love Too Easily" between 1963 and 1970? Given the frequency with which he performed it, Davis clearly believed that "I Fall in Love Too Easily" was uniquely adaptable to the quicksand-like textures of the second quintet in 1965 and 1967. Though his studio albums almost exclusively featured quintet originals, Bob Blumenthal, in his liner notes to the 1995 release of the *Plugged Nickel* box set, suggests several possible reasons Davis continued to play standards in live performances in late 1965: "[1] a continued fondness for the likes of 'Autumn Leaves' and 'If I Were a Bell,' [2] a conviction that they could be molded to more abstract ends, and [3] a realization that the audience expected at least this much familiarity in a Davis performance."

Of these three reasons, the first two could just as easily apply to the quintet's European tour of 1967, Davis's "lost quintet" protofusion heard in Europe in July and November 1969, or his live performances at the Fillmore West and Fillmore East in 1970. As for Blumenthal's third reason, "familiarity" is exactly what is necessary for the particular kind of signifyin(g) that Walser has located in Davis's performances and which Davis seems to suggest in his autobiography was one of the main reasons that people sought out his live performances—at least in the mid-1960s. However, this familiarity and the process of signifyin(g) that it affords becomes less and less of a factor for Davis's live performances as his audiences—or least the audiences he desired—changed. Whether his audiences in 1969 and later were white rock fans or young Black followers of soul and funk, neither of those two potential audiences would likely have had a prior familiarity with Tin Pan Alley songs such as "Autumn Leaves," "If I Were a Bell," or, indeed, "I Fall in Love Too Easily."[54] Perhaps this is why his performances of "I Fall in Love Too Easily" at rock venues were so cursory and why Davis did not interpret the song's chord changes and melody in the various tempos and rhythmic feels that had characterized his performances of the song a few years earlier, when he was playing to a "jazz" audience. The form and melody of "I Fall in Love Too Easily" may still have been attractive to Davis, but it was apparently no longer necessary or desirable to extensively signify on the song's structure.

Conversely, the February 1964 recording of "My Funny Valentine" analyzed by Walser and Brofsky comes from a concert performance by the Davis quintet at a benefit concert for the NAACP at Philharmonic Hall. The audience for such a concert would likely have been middle- and upper-class elites, a far cry from the Black youth audience that Davis was courting by the end of the 1960s or the white rock audience that Columbia was pushing him toward. The middle- and upper-class, older audience that likely attended the Philharmonic Hall concert would probably have been familiar with tunes like "My Funny Valentine" and "I Fall in Love Too Easily." Insofar as this audience was a jazz audience, they would have also been intimately familiar with the idea that jazz musicians signify on standards in their performances, even if they would not have used the language adopted by Gates (and later Walser) to describe this practice.

"I Fall in Love Too Easily" was the last jazz standard in Davis's book, and by dropping it from his repertoire in the summer of 1970, Davis left behind this particular kind of communication with his audience. In Tomlinson's and Tate's appreciations of Davis's electric music quoted above, neither writer is dismissive of audiences. However, the communication, dialogue, signifying, and mixing they are most concerned with celebrating is between musical styles and techniques—rock, funk, jazz, Black musicians and white musicians, "Black music" and "white music"—not between musicians and their audiences or between a musical memory of the past and a contemporary performance in the present. Perhaps this is one of the reasons that Davis's music from this time period has been so controversial: it represents a shift in the materials and methods of jazz performance away from signifyin(g) based on the audience recognizing a relationship between a previously known tune and an improvised performance and toward a conversation of musical styles and genre conventions. As the 1960s continued, Davis became less and less interested in replaying music from the past in live performances—in this case, a tune from the Great American Songbook—despite the fact that his performances of "I Fall in Love Too Easily" bore little resemblance to the original Sinatra recording of the song from 1945 or Davis's own studio recording from 1963. In the 1970s and beyond, however, other African American musicians would be more interested in incorporating aspects of the popular music past into their own new creations, as I illustrate in the following two chapters.

CHAPTER 4

OLD SCHOOL

Sampling, Re-Playing, and
Re-Hearing the 1970s in Hip-Hop

Youth and Newness in Hip-Hop

Ever since the genre's mythological beginnings on August 11, 1973—when DJ Kool Herc spun records for partygoers in the recreation room of his housing project building at 1520 Sedgwick Avenue in the South Bronx—hip-hop music has been a genre which, almost by definition, has reused the catchiest, most interesting parts of other preexisting songs for its own funky ends.[1] Unlike other popular music genres, the building blocks for the creation of hip-hop in the mid-1970s were not abstract notes and chords but portions of songs: verses, choruses, or, especially, percussion "breaks" from already existing records played live and manipulated in various ways by DJs at neighborhood parties and, later, in clubs.[2]

When considering the ideas of musical innovation and re-creation, it has become something of a truism to say that musicians have only a limited amount of chords, notes, rhythms, and timbres at their disposal, so of course they are going to borrow, re-create, and be influenced by music of the past—in the same way that hip-hop DJs and producers use music from the past during their sets or on new recorded tracks. Other genres of popular music in the twentieth century, however, have made newness and a break from the past an explicit part of their ideology and appeal. As I discuss in chapter 1, accounts of rock music, for example, often testify to the shock of first encountering the music, such as hearing the Beatles or Elvis Presley on *The Ed Sullivan Show*. Presley himself, when asked by Marion Keisker, an assistant at Sun Records in Memphis, who his influences were, famously replied, "I don't sound like nobody."[3] This denial of musical antecedents and influences was, to be sure, disingenuous. Presley's debt to the blues singer and guitarist Arthur "Big Boy" Crudup (born 1905) is clear in that Presley (born 1935) covered Crudup's song, "That's Alright Mama" as his first released single in 1954. Overt musical "borrowings" (sometimes characterized as "theft") from Crudup and other African American musicians have been a consistent source of controversy in critical assessments of Presley for decades.[4] Yet despite these contradictions even in its most celebrated founding figure, rock music culture, as most forms of popular music in the United States, advances an ideology of newness and youth as an important part of its aesthetic and commercial appeal.

Hip-hop's association with youth in the early 1970s is clear; Herc (born Clive Campbell in Jamaica in 1955) was only eighteen years old at the time of this first party, and the party itself was a fundraiser for his younger sister, Cindy, to participate in that quintessential ritual of twentieth-century American teenage consumerism: buying clothes for the upcoming school year.[5] However, hip-hop's claim to newness lies on shakier ground, since its earliest musicians played not conventional instruments that produced notes and chords but turntables that could only play preexisting, recorded, and commodified sound. At that first party in August 1973, and at other early hip-hop events, DJs like Herc played records like the Incredible Bongo Band's "Apache" and "Bongo Rock," "The Mexican" by the band Babe Ruth, and the Jimmy Castor Bunch's "It's Just Begun" for an appreciative audience of listeners and dancers.[6] In 1973, there was no such thing as a "hip-hop record." The recording commonly viewed as the first hip-hop record, "Rapper's Delight" by the Sugar Hill Gang (1979), was still six years away.[7] Starting with the commercial success of "Rapper's Delight," hip-hop would begin the slow but steady process of becoming the global, influential musical genre and culture we know it as today: a culture whose primary calling cards are commodities and products for sale or streaming. During its beginnings in the early 1970s, however, *hip-hop* was a verb, not a noun; to be a hip-hop musician meant to be a DJ who played a particular set of records in particular locations, for a particular audience of dancers, listeners, and partygoers. In the first few years of hip-hop during the mid-1970s, these records were primarily soul and funk records from the recent past—that is, the 1960s and 1970s. The settings were parks and community centers in the Bronx and a few receptive clubs in Manhattan. The listeners were mostly Black and Latino teenagers for whom DJs assumed the status of neighborhood heroes.

Most of these aspects of hip-hop culture have dramatically changed since the 1970s. Hip-hop's audience in the United States is no longer majority Black and Latino.[8] Hip-hop has expanded beyond its birthplace in the Bronx and New

York City; listeners today are found across the United States, and influential artists have hailed from nearly every corner of the country. Outside the United States, vibrant hip-hop scenes exist in countries around the world.[9] DJs are also no longer the undisputed stars of hip-hop culture, having been superseded by rappers—a development related to the fact that hip-hop music is no longer exclusively or primarily experienced through live events but through sound recordings and music videos. However, one important sonic aspect of hip-hop from its beginnings did not change: sounds from soul, funk, and R&B records from the 1960s and 1970s have remained a key building block in hip-hop, as the most important source for samples in the production of hip-hop tracks over the forty years since hip-hop's emergence in the South Bronx. This chapter aims to understand how and why.

This chapter has two main objectives. I will first show that samples from 1960s and 1970s soul, funk, and R&B are particularly prominent in hip-hop songs.[10] This should be a relatively uncontroversial claim, as scholars such as the musicologist Joanna Demers have already explored this topic at some length. Demers summarizes the influence of this music on hip-hop in her 2002 dissertation: "Hip-hop relies to a great extent on a patriarchy of black soul and funk musicians who legitimize and authenticate the tracks on which they are re-used."[11] In addition, a more general musical aesthetic of the 1970s has been a key feature of recent popular music in the United States, including not only hip-hop but related genres such as R&B and the aptly named genre of neo-soul. Some of the most popular and critically acclaimed music of the 2010s, including releases by Pharrell, Daft Punk, Janelle Monáe, D'Angelo, and Kendrick Lamar—while not directly sampling recordings from the 1970s—are clearly indebted to the decade for specific timbres, grooves, and vocal styles, as I will discuss in the next chapter. Second, I examine some of the possible reasons *why* these recordings from the 1960s and 1970s have had such a rich second life in hip-hop over the last fifty years. I will consider signifyin(g), the influential theory of creative reuse and appropriation in various African American artistic traditions advanced by Henry Louis Gates Jr. and productively deployed by several music scholars to explain traditions including jazz and hip-hop.[12] As discussed in the previous chapter on Miles Davis, signifyin(g) depends on listeners having familiarity with a previous text (such as a funk or soul song) so that they can recognize when aspects of this text are being reproduced, subverted, or otherwise "played" with. I will consider family influence, the underacknowledged fact that many contemporary hip-hop musicians began their crate-digging in their mother's or father's record collections.[13] I will also examine the place of the 1970s in the African American imagination as a possible motivating factor for the continued reuse of recordings from this time period in hip-hop.

Sampling, replaying, and reusing music from the 1970s in hip-hop therefore provides another important example of historical consciousness in popular music at work—perhaps the most important because it concerns the genre which is arguably the most globally influential musical movement of the past fifty years. Hip-hop forces us to complicate our understandings of how race influences the relationships that musicians and genres have with the past. White musical practices (and musicians) are often painted as retrospective and interested in living in the past. Hip-hop, however, shows primarily African American DJs, producers, and rappers engaging in meaningful ways with a prior African American musical tradition. Putting hip-hop in comparative perspective with other popular music traditions can also be compelling. Looking broadly at genres like jazz, rock, R&B, and hip-hop, we can see intriguing similarities in the way these genres, initially viewed as threatening and rebellious—often with clear racist overtones—gradually became domesticated and integrated, however warily, into critical and scholarly canons. As this book shows, a greater sense that the history of these genres is important enough to be "re-played" in some way—through instrumental and vocal re-performance, sampling, sonic allusion, and canonization—can be a key component of this general rise in respectability.

"The *Killa* Beats from Back in the Day"

Scholars such as Jeff Chang and Joseph Schloss have described the excitement DJs were able to produce among dancers and listeners at parties in the 1970s by playing and manipulating relatively recent soul and funk records.[14] In his book *Foundation*, Schloss details how even the dancers he did fieldwork with in the early 2000s—thirty years after the first hip-hop parties, and twenty years after b-boying's first rise to national prominence in the 1980s—still enjoyed dancing to those songs played by DJs like Kool Herc in the early 1970s. Schloss clearly illuminates the historical consciousness at work in hip-hop culture and argues that this sonic consistency should challenge dominant views of the genre:

> For those who see hip-hop as a wild, anarchic expression of youthful abandon, brutal materialism, criminality, or even political change, this may seem odd. Could today's rebellious b-boys really be so mindful of history—so culturally conservative—that they insist on dancing to the *exact records* that brought the form to life 35 years ago, long before most of them were born? [emphasis in original][15]

One song with particular staying power is the 1973 recording of "Apache" by the Incredible Bongo Band, a recording sometimes referred to as the "national anthem of hip-hop."[16] Schloss quotes one b-girl as saying that dancing to songs like "Apache" or "It's Just Begun" was especially meaningful to her because they were the same songs that earlier b-boys and b-girls had danced to, and therefore placed her contemporary work in a longer tradition and history of dancing: "It's important, in the aspect that it [b-boying] does have history behind it. And to think that you're getting down to the same beats that the pioneers of the dance got down to before. Like the *killa* beats from back in the day . . . it's important to remember not to forget songs like that. It's history."[17]

However, hip-hop culture is not only a museum for the preservation of 1970s funk, nor were funk records the only kind of records that DJs were using in the beginnings of the genre. Consider another early hip-hop DJ icon, Afrika Bambaataa. His fellow DJ, Grandmixer D.ST, credits Bambaataa with creating the "genre-less" conception of hip-hop: an omnivorous style that takes delight in recontextualizing compelling bits of musical material from seemingly any genre ever pressed on wax: rock music, speeches, blue-eyed soul, and novelty records, to name only a few of the genres that Bambaataa would spin at parties and gigs. In Mark Katz's excellent history of hip-hop DJing, Grandmixer D.ST explains Bambaataa's musical style: "Bambaataa was a musical record connoisseur, he was a genius, he understood variety, he understood the genre-less concept of music—that's real hip-hop. And that's what he taught all of us."[18] Herc, Grandmaster Flash, and Bambaataa are sometimes known as the "holy trinity" of early hip-hop DJs, and each is revered for a specific contribution to the art form. Herc is the originator. Grandmaster Flash is known for his technical innovations in spinning and manipulating records. But both Flash and Herc themselves recognize Bambaataa's eclectic musical taste as his most unique contribution to the budding hip-hop culture of the 1970s.[19] Bambaataa continued his eclecticism even when he made the transition from live performances to making recordings of his own. For example, Bambaataa's best known song, "Planet Rock" (1982), copies its distinctive high-register chromatic riff from "Trans-Europe Express" by the German electro-dance band Kraftwerk. The beat of "Planet Rock" was also a reprogrammed copy (using a Roland TR-808 drum machine) of the beat of another Kraftwerk song, "Numbers." While "Planet Rock" was a commodified recording, Robert Fink explains that it "was an attempt to capture in the studio the unpredictable range of Bambaataa's live DJ-ing. Bambaataa enjoyed throwing stuff like Kiss, the Monkees, calypso tunes, bongo breaks, movie soundtracks, even the Pink Panther theme into a funky set."[20] This is exactly Bambaataa's "genre-less" conception of hip-hop music as described by Grandmixer D.ST, in which a track from a German electro band might find an unlikely home. Indeed, the recording of "Planet Rock" was not the only time that Bambaataa reused music from Kraftwerk. According to Fink, "one of his early-1980s Zulu Nation tricks was layering the fiery rhythms of speeches delivered by Malcolm X over the unbroken thirteen minutes of 'Trans Europe Express' plus 'Metal on Metal' as they followed one another on the B-Side of [the 1977 Kraftwerk LP] *Trans Europe Express*."[21]

Following Bambaataa's lead, hip-hop DJs and producers certainly have repurposed music from a wide variety of genres in the five decades since DJ Kool Herc's party in the Bronx, and some DJs seem to enjoy turning unlikely source material into the basis for a hip-hop track, song, or performance. In the 1970s, a time of interethnic tensions between Puerto Ricans and African Americans in New York City, Latino DJs such as Charlie Chase took delight in getting primarily Black audiences to respond to the grooves of salsa records. Discussing the salsa song, "Tu Coqueta," Chase notes: "I throw that sucker in, just the beat alone, and they'd go off. They never knew it was a Spanish record. And if I told them that they'd get off the floor."[22] In retrospect, this seems not all that radical. Similar to funk, soul, and hip-hop, salsa was, after all, another urban, Afrodiasporic dance genre in which percussion breaks played an important musical role. More surprising might be the 1998 Jay-Z hit single "Hard Knock Life (Ghetto Anthem)," for which producer The 45 King (born Mark James) sampled a children's-sung chorus from the musical *Annie*. These examples, and dozens of others like them, show that the idea that anything already recorded can be sampled or reused in creating hip-hop music is an important part of the genre's identity, as Jay-Z himself confirms when explaining the usage of the *Annie* sample:

> Any artist should be able to touch any type of music, as long as it's done in a way that feels natural. If you're not doing it solely for the intention of selling records. There are plenty of records that came to me with big hooks, and I was like 'I can't do that.' I'd know the record could be big but it didn't fit me. The *Annie* sample fit me. It was from another world, but it had an underlying theme that connected. Being an underdog, always getting kicked in the face, shunned by society—it all relates to me and a huge group of people I was speaking to.[23]

Jay-Z's discussion of the sample from *Annie* in "Hard Knock Life (Ghetto Anthem)" shows how an omnivorous aesthetic is an important part of hip-hop ideology. In practice, however, listeners, DJs, and producers cannot seem to resist coming back for their favorite meal. A large amount of the songs that producers continue to rely on, that b-boys and b-girls continue to dance to, and that hip-hop listeners continue to find appealing as backing tracks for contemporary releases actually comes from a relatively narrow range of music: that of soul, funk, and R&B recordings from the 1960s and 1970s.[24] Perhaps the continued reuse of these songs is because these records tend to, in Jay-Z's words, "feel natural," "connect," and "relate" to hip-hop artists and producers more than other records. (Later in the chapter, I will discuss why that might be the case.) The focus on this narrow range of music to sample and replay is all the more remarkable given how much hip-hop culture has changed and expanded since its beginnings, from a local practice in the South Bronx to a global multi-billion-dollar industry. These were new recordings when they were first spun at parties, but over the years of their continued reuse, they became old records—"the *killa* beats from back in the day"—that can still get the party started, get dancers out on the floor, and give inspiration to an MC. This continued veneration of music from the past through its incorporation into new tracks shows historical consciousness to be a key aspect of hip-hop culture.

Replaying and Musical Conservativism in Early Hip-Hop

In this chapter, I consider together various forms of musical re-creation used in hip-hop, including DJs replaying old records, musicians re-creating instrumental parts in the studio, or producers using a digital sampler to grab drum breaks or a bass line from an earlier track. There are clear differences in these musical practices, as I will discuss below. Sampling gets the most attention in both scholarly and journalistic discourse, likely because it has been the greatest source of legal controversy over copyright infringement.[25] However, I consider these uses together in this chapter to show that, using various techniques, hip-hop music has been consistently characterized by the reuse of prior musical material. Hip-hop culture itself sometimes blurs the lines between these practices: some producers, most notably Dr. Dre, are known for using a hybrid approach in which instrumental parts from old recordings are re-performed in studio by conventional musicians, and then altered and manipulated at will by producers, as if they were samples themselves. In some cases, listeners themselves might not be able to distinguish between sampling and replaying on a finished track, especially when other audio processing or filtering is also present. A larger argument of this chapter is that hip-hop belongs to a broad general category of reusing music from the past in order to create new music.

Throughout most of the 1970s, the reusing of music in hip-hop was based on playing vinyl records on turntables at parties. Within this analog world, DJs would often play fragments of songs, using a mixer and two turntables to cue up the next musical selection and switch to playing music from the second turntable smoothly, hopefully without leaving any musical space or silence. Following Lydia Goehr, scholars have defined the "musical work" as an abstract musical object—not any one particular recording, score, or performance.[26] In the early years of hip-hop before 1979, there does not seem to have been a sense of creating some sort of new musical composition or "work" out of these fragments of records. Instead, hip-hop DJs at parties functioned like radio DJs: their job was to provide the soundtrack for the dancing at the party out of songs the audience either knew and liked or did not know but would find appealing once they heard them—such as the salsa records sometimes "snuck in" by the DJ Charlie Chase. The job of the DJ—and at least initially, the MC—was to supplement this recorded music with exhortations over the microphone, stock party chants, or commentary. Bootleg cassettes of live performances by DJs and MCs did circulate in the underground economy of New York City in the 1970s, providing a fascinating precursor to the more "official" hip hop recordings released on vinyl starting in 1979. However, these cassettes seem to have functioned for their listeners as a snapshot in time of an essentially fleeting experience—not as self-sufficient works in themselves.

In most accounts of the genre's history, the first hip-hop record was "Rapper's Delight," but almost everything about the circumstances of its production was very different both from later commoditized forms of hip-hop and from the party scene of the 1970s. Recorded in August 1979, its producer, Sylvia Robinson, was a newcomer to hip-hop culture, having only been introduced to the phenomenon of rapping by a trip to the Harlem World disco in Manhattan in June of that year, where she happened to see a performance by Lovebug Starski.[27] None of the rappers featured on the recording—Big Bank Hank, Master Gee, or Wonder Mike—had been established members of New York hip-hop crews. The recording itself was done not in the Bronx, Harlem, or even a midtown Manhattan studio, but across the Hudson River in suburban Englewood, New Jersey. Using "neutral" descriptive language, we could state that Big Bank Hank re-created or borrowed rhymes from his acquaintance Grandmaster Caz of the Cold Crush Brothers to record on "Rapper's Delight." Within the ethical world of hip-hop, however, it is more common to say that Hank—an amateur without extensive experience as an MC—stole or "bit" rhymes from Caz. For hip-hop "heads," two aspects of Hank's theft are particularly egregious. At the beginning of his first verse, Hank raps, "Well I'm the C-A-S-A-N, the O-V-A, and the rest is F-L-Y." Hank apparently did not realize this was Caz's way of introducing himself by an alternate nickname, Casanova Fly. In a later verse, Hank purports to relay some advice his father gave to him: "But whatever ya do in your lifetime / you never let an MC steal your rhyme," a declaration that seems ironic, to say the least.

The musical basis for "Rapper's Delight" was the contemporary disco/funk song "Good Times" by the band Chic. There are several ways this backing track could have been constructed. Sylvia Robinson could have used a DJ to play the break for this song, perhaps using two turntables and "doubles" (two copies) of the record and a simple two-channel mixer equipped with a fader to cut the feed back and forth from one turntable to another. This would have been most similar to the techniques of live hip-hop performance. Robinson and her engineers could also have used magnetic tape to cut and splice together a backing track for "Rapper's Delight" from a recording of "Good Times." By the late 1970s, this was not a new or radical technique, and had been used prominently in record releases by artists such as the Beatles and Miles Davis. Splicing would have required equipment not available to DJs rocking park jams or playing gigs in the rough-and-tumble world of Manhattan and Bronx clubs, but certainly would have been possible in the controlled confines of a recording studio. Instead, Robinson chose a more traditional way to create the backing track: she used musicians from the funk band Positive Vibration to replay instrumental parts from Chic's recording in the studio, which Hank, Master Gee, and Wonder Mike then rapped over. This production choice was no doubt influenced by Robinson's long career in the music industry as a singer, songwriter, and producer using traditional studio recordings techniques before her involvement with hip-hop. In the mid-1950s, she had several hits as part of the duo Mickey & Sylvia, including "Love Is Strange." In the 1960s, she and her husband Joe Robinson started a soul music label, All Platinum Records. As a solo artist, Robinson had an unlikely hit with the innuendo-laced 1973 track "Pillow Talk."

Robinson was an experienced music industry professional, and the recording of "Rapper's Delight" shared much in common with earlier forms of pop music (including R&B or soul) in which a hit song would be re-recorded by many different singers and instrumentalists on different record labels in the hopes of cashing in on a trendy melody and appealing to the different audiences associated with particular genres. While both disco and hip-hop relied on DJs spinning records for dancing, there was a generational divide between the genres' audiences in the late 1970s. Disco generally appealed to an older, more affluent crowd that could afford to wear flashy clothes and buy drinks at fancy nightclubs in New York. Hip-hop in the 1970s, on the other hand, was almost exclusively music for Black and Latino youth, more frequently performed in parks, outdoor parties, or neighborhood clubs. If Chic's "Good Times" appealed to the adult disco/funk crowd, by combining its re-created bass and drum part with rapped vocals, the same song might appeal to the youth audience for hip-hop. David Toop suggests that early hip-hop, in terms of its musical development and means of production, also drew on an older form of African American popular music: doo-wop. According to Toop, while disco was associated with high-tech studio production and the "high-living trappings" of Manhattan nightclubs:

> Rapping, by comparison, bore a striking resemblance to the street-corner harmony era. Just as the 115th Street Tin Can Band had honed their routines in their playground at Wadleigh Junior High (later becoming The Harptones) back in 1951 so, 25 years later, it would have been possible to peer through the wire-mesh fence of a similar schoolyard and hear schoolfriends and neighbours struggling to arrange ensemble raps and solo verses in preparation for a block party.[28]

"Rapper's Delight," then, is a surprisingly conservative record, and on hip-hop's first recorded release, the genre already begins its long history of reusing funk and soul. Even if here the chronological gap between "Good Times" and "Rapper's Delight" is only a few months, hip-hop would retain its privileged relationship with soul and funk from the 1970s for decades to come.

Sampling the 1970s: Eric B and Rakim to Kanye West

A catalogue of all usages of soul and funk samples in hip-hop recordings would be enormous and beyond the scope of this chapter. I therefore just want to discuss examples of a few of the most prominent usages of music from the 1970s by hip-hop artists and producers. Other than the fact that they all reused music from the 1970s, perhaps the most important thing that the hip-hop artists under discussion here have in common is that they were popular and influential among both listeners and critics. Otherwise, the musicians discussed below belong to different subgenres of hip-hop, have different images, address divergent topics in their lyrics, and even sometimes have strong rivalries with each other. Their employment of music from the 1970s, however, is a common attribute they share, testifying to the wide-ranging impact of this music on the genre of hip-hop.

After the initial success of "Rapper's Delight" at the end of 1979, the decade of the 1980s marks the symbolic beginning of hip-hop's breaking into the mainstream. Importantly, it did this primarily as a recorded commodity. In chapter 2, I introduced Mark Katz's scholarship on seven key differences between recordings and live performances—he terms these differences "causes"—that have wide-ranging effects on musical life.[29] One of these causes—*repeatability*—is crucial for our discussion of the construction of the Great American Songbook through the multiple exposure to this music that records enable. More generally, repeatability is a key contributor to the historical consciousness present in *all* of the popular music scenes and genres analyzed in this book. For the increasing popularity of hip-hop in the 1980s, another cause is also particularly salient: the *portability* of recorded music as compared to live performance. By recording hip-hop music in the 1980s, the music is now able to travel far more widely than before recordings. With the advent of hip-hop recordings, audiences around the United States (and eventually around the world) unable or unwilling to go to a park jam or a club to hear DJs and MCs perform were able to hear and participate in nascent hip-hop culture.

But what did the new, broader, and more geographically diffuse audience for hip-hop hear? Drum machines, like the famous Roland TR-808 or Oberheim DMX, allowed hip-hop musicians to construct drum parts in the studio, even without conventional training on percussion instruments. This was a departure, both in terms of sound and technique, from hip-hop in the 1970s. On important recordings made in the early 1980s like "I Need a Beat" by LL Cool J (1984) and "Sucker M.C.'s" by Run-DMC (1983), recycled breaks spun from turntables were not the source of these tracks' rhythmic foundations. The drum timbres from early drum machines also did not sound like the drums from 1970s soul and funk records played at early hip-hop parties—or, for that matter, like the drums recorded in the studio by a live musician for "Rapper's Delight."

Beginning in the mid-1980s, the invention and adoption of digital samplers changed the techniques and sonic characteristics of hip-hop again. Digital sampling technology allowed hip-hop musicians to record excerpts (drum parts, guitars, horn lines, vocals, etc.) from their own vinyl record collections into the sampler's digital memory. They could then trigger and manipulate these sounds at will. This was a change in technique, to be sure, from the DJs' practice of laying hands on vinyl, but it also allowed for a return to hip-hop of specific timbres and sounds from the 1960s and 1970s. While production practices in the 1980s are diverse, the music of artists like James Brown and other funk and soul musicians was a consistent presence in the hip-hop soundscape.

We can hear this presence in the 1987 track "I Know You Got Soul" by Eric B and Rakim. The drums for this song are sampled by an E-Mu SP-12 sampler from the Funkadelic recording "You'll Like It Too" (1980), while a drum and guitar riff from Bobby Byrd's "I Know You Got Soul" (1971) are also added. The resulting sound of tracks like this, as Loren Kajikawa argues, "helped usher in a new stylistic era where the distinctive timbres and 'live' rhythmic feel of 1960s and 1970s soul and funk recordings permeated rap music."[30] In 1988, the rap group Stetsasonic sampled, among others, Sly and the Family Stone and replayed a bass line from a 1975 recording by jazz/funk organist Lonnie Liston

Smith for their song "Talkin' All That Jazz." In the lyrics, they also specifically refer to Eric B and Rakim's usage of the Bobby Byrd recording, as well as the more general power of rap to "bring back old R&B" into the soundscape:

> Tell the truth, James Brown[31] was old
> 'Til Eric and Ra came out with "I Got Soul."
> Rap brings back old R&B
> And if we would not, people could have forgot.

In the early 1990s, the Los Angeles–based producer Dr. Dre sampled (and replayed) the work of George Clinton and his groups Parliament and Funkadelic to produce the subgenre of rap known as G-funk. Loren Kajikawa brilliantly traces the differences between Dre's productions for his 1992 solo album *The Chronic* and his earlier productions for the group N.W.A. He describes the sound of N.W.A's track "Straight Outta Compton" as "full of rhythmic stabs and staccato attacks" in which the "sonic space seems filled to maximum capacity."[32] Some of the samples that Dre used for his N.W.A productions have already been discussed above, including the oft-sampled "Amen, Brother" break by the Winstons and "You'll Like It Too" by Funkadelic. For *The Chronic*'s hit singles "Nuthin' But a 'G' Thang" and "Let Me Ride," Dre still samples (or has studio musicians replay) music from the 1970s—as in his productions for N.W.A— but to radically different sonic ends. Perhaps most obviously, longer samples are used on *The Chronic*, rather than the chopped-up breakbeats of his earlier work. For example, the chorus from the 1975 Parliament tune "Mothership Connection (Starchild)"—"Swing down sweet chariot, stop and let me ride"—is repeated four times in the chorus of Dre's "Let Me Ride." George Clinton is often associated with the Afrofuturist movement, in which political and spiritual transcendence is imagined for Black people through technology, possibly to reach into space or other planets. "Mothership Connection (Starchild)" is clearly referencing the spiritual "Swing Low Sweet Chariot" to suggest a parallel between the deliverance from nineteenth-century slavery and an escape through the "mothership" away from the oppressive reality of twentieth-century America. By sampling "Mothership Connection (Starchild)" for "Let Me Ride," Dre brings this metaphor back down to Earth, replacing Clinton's mothership with his own "six-four": a 1964 Chevrolet Impala, which promises a slightly different kind of liberation and mobility.

On the East Coast during the 1990s, the producer Chucky Thompson sampled the Isley Brothers tune "Between the Sheets," taking its harmonically rich keyboard chords featuring 7ths and 9ths as the basis for the 1994 song "Big Poppa" by the Notorious B.I.G. For all of the rhetorical (and actual) violence between East and West Coast hip-hop in the 1990s, musicians from both camps drew on a similar body of material for new tracks. "Big Poppa" and Dre's "Let Me Ride" share much in common, sonically. Both tracks eschew the frenetic sound of late 1980s gangsta hip-hop in favor of slower tempos, longer melodic lines, and less quick-cutting between samples. Both tracks are also built around the soundscape of the R&B/funk canon.

In the early 2000s, Kanye West first came to prominence as a producer in his work for the rapper Jay-Z, including several tracks on Jay-Z's 2001 album *The Blueprint*. These tracks deserve some discussion because *The Blueprint* was a critical and commercial success for Jay-Z, it catapulted West to fame as a producer and prepared the way for his breakthrough as a solo artist, and the album is especially known for the fact that it features samples from 1970s soul on nearly every one of its tracks. West's production of the track "Izzo (H.O.V.A.)" samples the Motown song "I Want You Back" by the Jackson 5, released in 1969 and a #1 hit on the *Billboard* chart in January 1970. Motown Records, the most successful Black-owned label of the 1960s and 1970s, holds special weight in hip-hop culture, as an example of the power of independent Black entrepreneurship and the potency of Black popular music to help achieve material success. In the business endeavors of various figures associated with hip-hop culture (such as record labels, label imprints, clothing lines, ownership stake in other companies), we can see hip-hop artists trying to re-create the success of Motown founder Berry Gordy, whom they often invoke by name in lyrics or in interviews as a model. The Motown sound—"the sound of young America," according to the company's marketing campaigns in the 1960s and 1970s—was fertile ground for West and Jay-Z, as West also sampled former Temptation David Ruffin's 1973 track "Common Man" on *The Blueprint*'s "Never Change." As a commentary on his stubbornness, the stability of his artistic vision, or the continued relevance of soul music from the 1970s for contemporary hip-hop production, Jay-Z's rapped chorus is particularly telling on that song: "I never change / I'm too stuck in my ways."

Once West began his own solo career as a rapper, the artists he sampled on his own first two albums, *The College Dropout* and *Late Registration*, include canonical R&B figures such as Chaka Khan, Aretha Franklin, Gil Scott-Heron, Curtis Mayfield, and Ray Charles. By sampling these artists, West can suggest a similarity or lineage between himself and these exalted figures. Of course, sampling is not the only way this can be accomplished: liner notes, interviews, or physical presentation can also say much about the artists to whom you feel kinship. (This is a topic we will return to in the next chapter.) West also invokes musicians he wants listeners to consider his artistic peers and ancestors by namechecking them in his lyrics. West's "Slow Jamz" from his debut album

The College Dropout is particularly noteworthy in this regard. The song begins with a spoken introduction by Jamie Foxx, describing a situation in which a woman at a club is lamenting the focus on fast songs and requests something slower. West seemingly acquiesces to this demand with the music that follows this introduction. "Slow Jamz" is therefore self-aware of the genre conventions of Black popular music to include a slower, "more romantic" song "for the ladies" either on an album, at a live performance, or within a DJ's set at a club. The song's chorus, sung by Jamie Foxx, dramatizes this desire by naming the specific type of artists this woman is requesting:

> She said she want some Marvin Gaye, some Luther Vandross
> A little Anita would definitely set this party off right
> She said she want some Ready for the World, some New Edition
> Some Minnie Ripperton will definitely set this party off right.

The song itself is built on a sample from Luther Vandross's 1981 cover of "A House Is Not a Home," originally recorded by Dionne Warwick in 1964. In the song's verses, many other artists are invoked by name by West or by the rapper Twista, who contributes a guest verse. These include Gladys Knight, Smokey Robinson, Freddie Jackson, Ashford & Simpson, Al Green, the Isley Brothers, Evelyn "Champagne" King, the Whispers, Isaac Hayes, the Spinners, Earth, Wind & Fire, Keith Sweat, Maze, Jodeci, and Teddy Pendergrass. Vandross and Warwick themselves are of course also invoked; "Slow Jamz" samples Vandross's recording, and Vandross's recording, a cover, would have also brought to mind Warwick's 1964 version of the song. Released in 2003, the song is a veritable roll call of the soul music pantheon of previous decades. The majority of the artists mentioned by West and Twista had the peak of their careers during the 1970s, and for those from the 1980s or later, I would argue that they partake of a sound world that is highly identifiable with Black popular music of the 1970s, in its emphasis on emotive vocals, high-fidelity clean production, and analog instruments—as opposed to digital keyboards or synthesized drums that characterized, for example, the "Minneapolis sound" of Prince and his collaborators in the 1980s.

West takes several different approaches to his historical source material. One of the most common manipulations West makes to the music he samples is to shift their tempos into the typical medium tempo range for hip-hop of around 80–110 beats per minute (bpm). For DJs operating conventional turntables—either in the 1970s or today—tempos of source material could be changed using adjustments on the turntable to increase or decrease the speed of a record by 10 percent. Taking a record meant to be played at 45 RPM and playing it at 33 RPM (or vice versa) would have an even more dramatic effect, but these wide tempo manipulations would also change the pitch of voices and instruments, sometimes in ways that were viewed as undesirable distortions.[33] In the digital era, however, pitch and tempo can be adjusted independently. Because of this increasing manipulability that digital technology allows, hip-hop producers can make a wider variety of source material fit the typical genre parameters of hip-hop.[34] "Touch the Sky" by West from his 2005 *Late Registration* album shows this approach. For this track, West samples a four-measure horn loop from Curtis Mayfield's 1970 song "Move on Up." Mayfield's track is at the brisk tempo of 138 bpm, but West slows the sample down over 20 percent to 110 bpm—a much more common tempo for hip-hop during this era—without dramatically altering the pitch and timbre of the sample.

"Slow Jamz" and "Touch the Sky" are from West's first two albums, *The College Dropout* and *Late Registration*, respectively. West continued to incorporate soul and R&B from decades past into his productions for the next few years. Perhaps the clearest example of this is a track that samples "Try a Little Tenderness" as recorded by Otis Redding and released on Stax Records in 1966. West's track—a duet with Jay-Z from their 2011 *Watch the Throne* collaborative album—is simply called "Otis" as if nothing else needed to be said by way of explanation or introduction: he is assuming that his listeners know exactly who the "Otis" in question is and have a set of associations with him and his music. As for West's associations with Redding, his attitude toward the recording seems to verge on reverence. West does slightly slow down (and lower the pitch) of Redding's recording, from 103 bpm to 95 bpm, about an 8 percent drop. Otherwise, the first thirty seconds of "Otis" is an unornamented sample of "Try a Little Tenderness," as if West did not want to alter the well-known, canonical recording. The warm timbres of organ, electric guitar, horns, piano, and Redding's vocals have clear associations with classic soul music, and West seems to be placing himself and Jay-Z in Redding's exalted company.

Together with his work on Jay-Z's albums in the first years of the 2000s, this can be seen as an early phase of West's career, in which he was coming to prominence and was known for repurposing soul music for hip-hop tracks. Since that time, there have been radical changes in West's life and career, including his professed political beliefs, religious fervor, public image, mental health, and celebrity status. His sonic palette has also changed, and his later albums are largely built around newly composed elements, not samples. It is unclear what the relationship is between West's personal changes and the changes in his musical style, but West is well aware that certain fans would have preferred he retain the same musical techniques and personality that originally brought him to fame in the hip-hop world. On his 2016 song, "I Love Kanye," he performs lyrics from the perspective of one of these disappointed fans:

> I miss the old Kanye, straight from the go Kanye
> Chop up the soul Kanye, set on his goals Kanye
> I hate the new Kanye, the bad mood Kanye
> The always rude Kanye, spaz in the news Kanye

Since 2018, West has been increasingly vocal about his Christian religious beliefs in interviews, social media posts, and in his music and live performances. In the summer of 2018, he was involved in the release of five separate albums, including *ye* under his own name, the duet album *Kids See Ghosts* with Kid Cudi, and West-produced albums by Pusha T, Teyana Taylor, and Nas. Together with his own gospel-influenced album *Jesus Is King* released in October 2019, this would seem to be a formidable body of work. Yet all of these albums have short running times (less than thirty minutes), feature a limited number of tracks, and seem cursory, as if they were unfinished sketches for songs that just happened to be formally released to streaming platforms when an imposed deadline approached. Still, some of this work also samples Black music from the 1970s, incorporating recognizable timbres like acoustic pianos and choirs—and the recognizable cultural associations of these sounds with the political and social climate of the time period that originally produced them. The main difference is that the new sources for West's 1970s samples are from the genre of gospel music, rather than the secular music he largely depended on during the first decade of his career. Even this, however, is only a slight shift; while secular music dominated West's early work, his first major hit as a solo artist, "Jesus Walks," was built on a sample from the song "Walk With Me" by the ARC Gospel Choir. "No Mistakes" from *ye* samples a piano riff from the 1971 song "Children Get Together" by the Edwin Hawkins Singers. The massive crossover success of another song by the Edwin Hawkins Singers, "Oh Happy Day," shows that the sonic characteristics of this type of gospel music—including repeating ii-V and I-IV chord progressions—were largely shared with ostensibly secular genres like soul. Another prominent example of West's reusage of gospel music is "God Is" from *Jesus is King*, which samples a 1979 gospel song of the same name by Reverend James Cleveland and the Southern California Community Choir. On this track, West even performs the production trick that helped nickname the style of hip-hop he was known for early in his career: "chipmunk soul," in which emotive vocals from Black popular music were slightly sped up to give them an obvious "altered" quality and then incorporated into hip-hop beats. Cleveland's original recording is at the slow tempo of 41 bpm in the key of B-flat major. West's "God Is" is pitched-up three half-steps to the key of D-flat, with an increase in tempo to 53 bpm; it sounds as though the pitch and tempo were increased in tandem, as in the days of analog hip-hop. This increase in speed serves to further emphasize soloist Dora Pickett's already expressive vibrato and other vocal flourishes as she sings the lyrics "God is my light in darkness oh, God is, He is my all in all" to open West's new production. Much has changed about Kanye West's status in hip-hop culture over the course of his career, but for listeners, at least some of his later music still incorporates vocals and instrumental timbres from the recognizable and venerated sound world of 1970s Black popular music.

How do I as a scholar—or ordinary listeners—get information about these sampling practices? One of the most interesting developments in hip-hop culture since the late 2000s has been the rise in prominence of websites such as Genius and WhoSampled. Genius is primarily devoted to explicating the language used in hip-hop song: transcribing lyrics and providing hyperlinked explanations of slang. However, it also lists who produced a particular song and notes any musical samples used or lyrical allusions to other songs. WhoSampled is devoted to, in its own words, "exploring the DNA of music," a powerful metaphor that could mean many things. Perhaps it brings to mind traditional harmonic or melodic analysis of music, understanding the building blocks—things like chords and scales—that have the possibility to generate music. For WhoSampled, however, these building blocks exist on a slightly larger scale: there is no discussion of chords, scales, melodies, or rhythm patterns on WhoSampled. Instead, users can look up the Notorious B.I.G. song "Big Poppa" on WhoSampled and see that it samples the Isley Brothers' 1983 track "Between the Sheets." WhoSampled tells us exactly where this sample shows up in "Big Poppa" and where it came from in "Between the Sheets" in the form of time codes keyed to YouTube clips. Users wanting to further "explore the DNA of music" could click on hyperlinks showing other songs by the Isley Brothers that have been sampled, other songs that have sampled "Between the Sheets," or other songs that were sampled in Notorious B.I.G. songs. Before websites like WhoSampled, some of this information had been minimally available in the copyright clearance notices printed in liner notes, and hip-hop heads and aspiring beatmakers prized and traded this knowledge among themselves. WhoSampled, however, allows for users to more fully immerse themselves in the vast web of allusion and quotation of sounds from the past that characterizes much of hip-hop music.

Signifyin(g)

Henry Louis Gates's theory of signifyin(g) may help explain the tendency to sample and replay songs from the Black popular music canon over and over in hip-hop. As has been well described in a variety of secondary literature since Gates's influential theory was first published in 1988, signifyin(g) refers to the creative reuse and re-signification of texts that is one of the most salient characteristics of Black artistic production, including literature, the visual arts, and, most importantly for our purposes here, music.[35] In Gates's theory, texts signify on other texts, often taking a stance of irony or parody toward them. Texts that reproduce dominant norms or values are subverted in the practice of signifyin(g), often to produce an ironic or critical commentary on these norms. Signifyin(g) is in many ways an explicitly musical theory, and while Gates is focused primarily on African American and Afrodiasporic literature, he also writes eloquently and convincingly about music:

> Because the form is self-evident to the musician, both he and his well-trained audience are playing and listening with expectation. Signifyin(g) disappoints these expectations; caesuras, or breaks, achieve the same function. This form of disappointment creates a dialogue between what the listener expects and what the artist plays.[36]

Signifying can help explain the prevalence of sampling in hip-hop. To recall our description of pioneering DJ Afrika Bambaataa from the beginning of this chapter, signifying may also explain the "genre-less" concept of hip-hop that Grandmixer D.ST attributes to Bambaataa. This is because an attitude that treats previous texts or recordings as ripe for reinterpretation, re-signification, or ironic commentary may very well take its source material from genres or styles that, otherwise, might seem unlikely. Depending on the scale that we want to look at, signifyin(g) can illuminate various kinds of hip-hop musical practices. Signifyin(g) can describe a more active DJ or producer, rapidly cutting and mixing between records before the listener can feel too comfortable with any particular groove. Signifyin(g) could also describe Chucky Thompson's production of "Big Poppa," in which the keyboard and drum parts are sampled from the Isley Brothers but not the vocal melody or text. For listeners familiar with "Between the Sheets," those elements are present or implied, just as Gates describes that the "form" is implied for a "well trained audience." However, signifyin(g) alone does not necessarily explain why specific recordings or styles have remained so popular as a source material for samples. In the theory of signifyin(g) as explained by Gates and expanded on by later commentators, signifyin(g) is convincingly proposed as a common feature of African American creative production. However, the theory does not explain why, in the context of hip-hop, producers, DJs, and MCs continue to sample a relatively narrow range of music for a large amount of their new creations.

Good Times?

Why the specific continued emphasis in hip-hop on soul and funk from the 1970s? The 1970s is an ambiguous time in African American culture. Chronologically, the 1970s is situated after the assassinations of Malcolm X and Martin Luther King Jr. in 1965 and 1968, respectively. However, the 1970s is also after some of the tentative gains of the civil rights movement, as codified in various pieces of legislation such as the Civil Rights Act of 1964 and the Voting Rights Act of 1965. For at least a portion of Black Americans, the 1970s was a time of relative stability, advancement, and unity, before the ever-widening inequality gap of the 1980s. The hip-hop scholar Tricia Rose describes this time as "the twilight of America's short-lived federal commitment to Black civil rights and during the predawn of the Reagan-Bush era."[37]

A look at the work of the influential Black sociologist William Julius Wilson can be instructive here in tracing some of the successes and challenges shaping African American life in the 1970s and beyond. These successes and challenges, I argue, are crucial for how the decade is remembered and why music from this time period might have special significance for hip-hop DJs, producers, and listeners. Wilson's second book, *The Declining Significance of Race: Blacks and Changing American Institutions* (1978), shows how the gains made by members of the Black middle class during the preceding years were not spread to lower-income African Americans.[38] His argument was that the mere existence of racial difference and racism themselves were not solely responsible for holding back African Americans but that other factors were contributing to a dramatic split between upper-income and lower-income Black people. Wilson's later books summarize his arguments even in their titles: *The Truly Disadvantaged: The Inner City, The Underclass, and Public Policy* (1987) and *When Work Disappears: The New World of the Urban Poor* (1996), both of which describe how factors such as the shift from a manufacturing to a service economy and the flight of jobs from inner cities to inaccessible suburbs combined to disadvantage African Americans living in urban ghettos.[39] The 1970s, however, was a time just before these changes were happening, or when they had only just started to occur.

In the early 1980s, several important changes occurred that had both real and noticeable impact on the African American communities that would nurture the hip-hop musicians who were growing up during this time. Once these musicians began their careers in the late 1980s and the 1990s, they would craft some of hip-hop's most-recognized aesthetic achievements and cement hip-hop as a major commercial force in American culture. In January 1981, Ronald Reagan was inaugurated as president of the United States. During his campaign, Reagan had used ostensibly race-neutral "dog-whistle" language about "welfare queens" and "young bucks" buying T-bone steaks with welfare checks as a way of consolidating the white vote against government antipoverty programs perceived as benefiting Black people at the expense of white workers and taxpayers.[40] Drug use was certainly not new in American culture—heroin took a massive toll in the 1970s—but the influx of cheap crack cocaine beginning in 1985 devastated Black communities. This devastation was caused both by the negative effects of the drug itself and the punitive enforcement efforts of mass incarceration directed against drug addicts as part of the "War on Drugs." Deindustrialization in the 1980s also hit African Americans especially hard, since manufacturing jobs were an important way for them to get a foothold into the stability of the middle class without the educational benefits and access to government-sponsored mortgages that white workers more often had. For sociologist Mitchell Duneier, the timing is suspicious; he notes that mass incarceration from the War on Drugs occurs in concert with large-scale global economic changes "only after deindustrialization rendered poor urban Blacks increasingly superfluous."[41] These destructive developments of the 1980s, I argue, are one of the main reasons that the 1970s looms so large in African American culture and in hip-hop; in comparison to the 1980s and 1990s, the 1970s can be seen and mythologized, accurately or inaccurately, as a lost "golden era." Music, then, takes on special significance as something that can sonically recall this time period and, perhaps, heal the social bonds that have been fractured. To loop an organ riff or a drum pattern is to repeat, over and over, artifacts from this earlier exalted time and to call on their powers once again.

For hip-hop producers, sampling accomplishes several artistic tasks. To be sure, an effective sample—a great horn riff, catchy guitar pattern, sonorous organ chord, or a funky rhythm—can be enjoyed purely for aesthetic purposes. To some ears, the music of the 1970s has much to offer sonically, placed at an important point in the maturation of the recording industry and studio technology. While developments in 1980s digital technology arguably shifted the soundscape, the 1970s was very much a "high-fidelity" era, as skilled producers, mixers, and engineers made use of the capabilities of multitrack recording and relatively large budgets to clearly capture acoustic signals and mix them into attractive recordings. On the listener/consumer end, the 1970s was an era of relatively high-quality sound reproduction, whether that was enjoyed through sophisticated home stereo systems or the powerful speakers of discos. By the 1970s, some of the most iconic settings for listening to recorded music of the 1950s and 1960s were largely superseded: tinny transistor radios, AM signals on car radios, and mono recording mixes. Simply put, music from the 1970s "sounds good" and has a reputation for sounding good. The 1970s also has an important role in African American culture, not only as a time of relative stability and prosperity, but also as a time when many hip-hop musicians came of age and, in family settings, formed the musical tastes that would guide their later artistic practices.

Family Business

Contrary to both stereotypes of African American youth and ideas about isolated, solitary genius, hip-hop artists' musical development does not take place in a vacuum. Instead, hip-hop artists' formative musical experiences take place in an environment shaped intimately by their immediate and extended families. Parents, siblings, aunts, and uncles feature prominently in hip-hop artists' accounts of their early experiences with music. Families are a particularly fraught topic when discussing African American culture. Chattel slavery was often explicitly used to break up family structures or any other kind of bond that might interfere with the primary task of creating wealth for the enslaver.[42] In the early twentieth century, the Great Migration of African Americans out of the rural South and into the urban North and West provided new opportunities, but also fresh challenges for family and community life.[43] In the middle decades of the twentieth century, academic and government researchers worked to understand Black family life, particularly Black family life in the urban areas that gave rise to hip-hop culture—and to hip-hop musicians themselves. In addition to the scholarship of William Julius Wilson, described above, these various researchers include Daniel Patrick Moynihan's oft-debated 1965 report *The Negro Family: The Case for National Action*, psychologist Kenneth Clark's *Dark Ghetto*, the work of the anthropologist Oscar Lewis examining what he termed the "culture of poverty," and the interventions of activist Geoffrey Canada.[44] Perhaps more influential in the public sphere than these academics and educators have been the unabashedly negative portrayals of Black family life by conservative researchers like Charles Murray, championed by politicians such as Ronald Reagan.[45] For Reagan, it was exactly the government's permissive aid programs that led to the "welfare queens," single mothers, and general lack of personal responsibility that he viewed as characterizing Black families in the 1960s, 1970s, and 1980s. Murray, Reagan, and various later conservative commentators have largely ignored white supremacist government policies and pointed to the breakdown in Black families as itself a cause for poverty, crime, and violence in Black communities. In the context of this widespread stigmatization of Black families, then, hip-hop can be an important visible and audible counterexample to dominant narratives, showing the positive influence of Black families to help create a significant musical and cultural movement. For the creation and the perpetuation of hip-hop—and especially for the deep relationships with music of the past that hip-hop both expresses and depends on—Black families matter.

Many figures involved in hip-hop culture have talked about their early experiences with music involving family connections. These include Ahmir "Questlove" Thompson, drummer for the Philadelphia-based hip-hop band the Roots. In his 2013 memoir, *Mo' Meta Blues: The World According to Questlove*, Thompson describes his parents as "this funky, hip, post-civil rights, postrevolutionary bohemian black couple. They listened to all the cool music and wore all the cool clothes and had all the cool attitudes."[46] In the early chapters of the book, Questlove describes being born into this family in 1971 and listening to this "cool music" that his parents and others in his family played around the house. The first narrative chapter of *Mo' Meta Blues* contains a section in which he discusses, year by year, albums that were influential to him growing up. His musical tastes, and those of his family members, were eclectic, but his musical memories are heavily weighted toward 1970s soul and funk.

His first entry is *Music of My Mind*, the album by Stevie Wonder. Questlove writes: "I know this record was played right around the time of my birth, and for years after that. I encountered it very early, at a point when I was still judging records not by how they sounded but by how they looked."[47] His second entry, for 1972, is the Sly and the Family Stone album *There's a Riot Goin' On*. For this album, though, he qualifies and explains his relationship to it. "Though it came out in 1971, I remember hearing this record in 1972."[48] Though I do not want to discount the possibility that Questlove actually remembers those records being played from when he was only a few months old, it seems more likely that they were in heavy rotation around his family's turntable for years to come, and he is retrospectively pointing to their influence before he actually could have been conscious of and remembered them. It is clear from reading the rest of his autobiography that family, including his professional musician parents, were heavy influences on him growing up. His mother's tastes were particularly influential: "As it turns out, many of those records [jazz-funk records from the 1970s that his mother purchased] would be used as break beats in the future, so in a way it was an early education for my career in hip-hop."[49] While this early musical exposure helped Questlove develop into the skilled musician he would become, he recognized that his family was particularly obsessed and interested in music: "I loved the way that music was the center of our house, though I think I knew even at the time that it wasn't normal."[50]

Perhaps the lengthiest and most poetic description of a hip-hop artist discussing his childhood experiences with music from the 1970s influenced by his family comes from the rapper Jay-Z. In his autobiography, *Decoded*, which he coauthored with hip-hop journalist dream hampton, Jay-Z writes: "When I was a kid, my parents had, like, a million records stacked to the ceiling in metal milk crates." He then goes on to list some of these records and artists.

> I remember "Walking in Rhythm," by the Blackbyrds, "Love's Theme," by the Love Unlimited Orchestra, "Dancing Machine," by the Jackson 5, "Tell Me Something Good," by Rufus, "The Hustle," by Van McCoy and the Soul City Symphony, "Slippery When Wet," by the Commodores, "Pick up the Pieces," by the Average White Band, "It Only Takes a Minute," by Tavares, "(TSOP) The Sound of Philadelphia," by MFSB (Mother Father Sister Brother), the *Superfly* soundtrack by Curtis Mayfield, James Brown, Billy Paul, Honeycomb, Candi Staton, Rose Royce, the Staple Singers, the Sylvers, the O'Jays, Blue Magic, Main Ingredient, the Emotions, Chic, Heatwave, A Taste of Honey, Slave, Evelyn "Champagne" King, Con Funk Shun.[51]

Decoded is not a typical celebrity autobiography. The book combines standard autobiographical narratives, footnoted explanations of his lyrics, and photographs and other images. A sense of how words would look printed on the page is clearly not incidental to the creative vision of *Decoded*, and it is therefore important to note that about a third of a page is spent just naming all these songs and artists Jay-Z remembers from his youth. Considering this list, he summarizes: "If it was hot in the seventies, my parents had it." Of course, just having access to a library of records does not guarantee a career in hip-hop. Therefore it's important that Jay-Z talks about the meaning those records had for his family, the significance of how they worked in his family life, and what he would do with them as an adult:

> My parents would blast those classics when we did our Saturday cleanup and when they came home from work. We'd be dancing in the living room, making our own *Soul Train* line . . . My mother would play "Enjoy Yourself," by the Jacksons, and I would dance and sing and spin around. I'd make my sisters my backup singers. I remember those early days as the time that shaped my musical vocabulary. I remember the music making me feel good, bringing my family together, and more importantly, being a common passion my parents shared.
> That music from my childhood still lives in my music. From my very first album, a lot of the tracks I rapped over were built on a foundation of classic seventies soul. On *Reasonable Doubt* [Jay-Z's debut album, released in 1996], we sampled the Ohio Players, the Stylistics, Isaac Hayes, and the Four Tops. . . . The songs carried in them the tension and energy of the era. The seventies were a strange time, especially in black America. The music was beautiful in part because it was keeping a kind of torch lit in a dark time.

Jay-Z finishes this discussion by highlighting the connections between these two eras: the 1970s of his childhood and the 1990s and 2000s, when he evoked the sounds and associated memories of that earlier time period in his artistry, to critical and commercial acclaim:

> I feel like we—rappers, DJs, producers—were able to smuggle some of the magic of that dying civilization out in our music and use it to build a new world. We were kids without fathers, so we found our fathers on wax and on the streets and in history, and in a way, that was a gift: We got to pick and choose the ancestors who would inspire the world we were going to make for ourselves. That was part of the ethos of that time and place, and it got built in to the culture we created. Rap took the remnants of a dying society and created something anew. Our fathers were gone, usually because they just bounced, but we took their old records and used them to build something fresh.[52]

In another passage, Jay-Z clearly describes the sonic impact this "classic seventies soul" had when incorporated into hip-hop tracks. Summarizing what he refers to as "the Roc-a-Fella" sound (named after his record label imprint), Jay-Z says that it consists of "manipulated soul samples and original drum tracks, punctuated by horn stabs or big organ chords. It was dramatic music: It had emotion and nostalgia and a street edge, but . . . combined those elements into something original."

These excerpts from Jay-Z's *Decoded* are one of the lengthiest examples of a very prominent hip-hop musician describing his musical upbringing. It also important to notice here that Jay-Z is, at least, what we might call a second-generation hip-hop artist. He was born in 1969, whereas DJ Kool Herc was born in 1955, Afrika Bambaataa in 1957, Grandmaster Flash in 1958. For these earlier figures, the soul and funk recordings they played at parties in the 1970s was, for them, recent popular music. The same is true for "Good Times," which had only been released for a few months before it was re-played in the studio to serve as the instrumental basis for the Sugar Hill Gang's "Rapper's Delight." For a chronologically later artist like Jay-Z, this is music that he remembers from his childhood that remained an important part of his life, but he still has enough distance from it to refer to it as "classic seventies soul." He is not the owner of this music; "If it was hot in the seventies, my parents had it," he writes—not *I had it* or even *we had it*. Hip-hop would not exist without Black families, and it is especially in the continued audible presence of music from the 1970s in hip-hop that we can see the influence of Black families on the shape of hip-hop culture.

An important part of the mythology of many popular music styles in the United States—hip-hop and rock music chief among them—is that listeners to these styles are engaging in youthful rebellion against their parents. The dominance of this mythology, however, has deafened us to the many instances in which popular music is passed down from generation to generation, something I observed during my fieldwork with tribute bands in which parents and children often made up a large portion of the audience for concerts. We have also seen this in our discussion of Linda Ronstadt, who was first introduced to the repertoire of the Great American Songbook she would record in the 1980s when she was a child in the late 1950s, listening to LPs of this material with her father. Such a sharing of popular music between generations does not fit the narrative of a teenage boy blasting Led Zeppelin from his bedroom stereo system while an angry parent yells at him to turn it down, but that narrative springs from a specific raced, classed, gendered, and generational experience of popular music and should not be applied universally and uncritically to all experiences of popular music. As with many aspects of popular music discourse, the widespread character of this rebellion ideology may be a product of the white baby boomer generation, specifically its conflict with its parents in which rock and other genres of popular music formed a particularly audible flashpoint of conflicts over a wide variety of social mores, including attitudes on race, gender, and sexual behavior. This is the influential mythology that popular music consumers from a variety of race, gender, and age backgrounds have been exposed to in the half century since the end of the 1960s.

A testimony like Jay-Z's from *Decoded* suggests, at the very least, that popular music recordings are not, as their detractors have sometimes claimed, disposable ephemeral commodities. They can take on a second life when reused or sampled. But their first life can extend for years or even decades after their release, remaining an audible presence in the soundscape. This is an important shift from pre-1960s understandings of popular music, which generally treated pop music as exclusively associated with youth and as something that was outgrown as quickly as its listeners moved through developmental stages to adulthood. These extended first lives and second lives through sampling and reuse are part of what I am calling "historical consciousness in popular music." In hip-hop, we can see this with the opening of archives at elite institutions like Harvard and Cornell and the publication of books like *The Anthology of Rap*, an over eight-hundred-page tome that offers a chronologically arranged canon of rap lyrics from 1978 to 2010.[53] The history of hip-hop is now being viewed as something that is worth remembering and knowing about; this is what is behind the construction of archives, canons, and museums devoted to hip-hop. Hip-hop is gaining respect from some of the traditional "mainstream" gatekeepers of culture, similar to the way that rock music gained respect in the 1990s. What makes hip-hop unique is that such a retrospective outlook has been part of the culture since its beginnings: it is not being imposed upon hip-hop from the outside. As this chapter shows, a large part of hip-hop culture has always been devoted to remembering and re-presenting music of the past through playing old records at parties, rerecording music in the studio, and sampling soul and funk from the 1970s in contemporary releases.

Conclusion: Youth and Newness in Hip-Hop Reconsidered

Perhaps one of the most interesting things about this musical conservatism is its influence among contemporary global youth cultures, of which American hip-hop is perhaps the lingua franca. For just one example of this surprising influence of older soul music filtered through contemporary hip-hop, consider the Twitter account of user @j_tsar. On the afternoon of Monday April 15, 2013, two bombs were detonated close to the finish line of the Boston Marathon, killing three people and injuring 280. A few hours after the bombings occurred @j_tsar tweeted, "Ain't no love in the heart of the city, stay safe people," in an apparent attempt to show solidarity with the victims of the bombing. At the time, the user @j_tsar, whose real name is Johar Tsarnaev, had not yet been identified as a suspect in the bombing, and perhaps his tweet was an attempt to throw authorities off his trail or to feign a lack of involvement in the attack. On the morning of Friday April 19, 2013, when Johar and brother Tamerlan Tsarnaev led police on a car chase through the Boston suburbs and Johar was still a fugitive, various media outlets began investigating the identities of the alleged bombers. The Tsarnaevs were ethnic Chechens who had received asylum in the United States. Johar, a nineteen-year-old college student at the nearby campus of UMass Dartmouth, was reported by his friends and acquaintances to be a typical young man, with many reports noting his affinity for hip-hop. This affinity was taken as evidence of his identity as an assimilated, unremarkable American college student, such that his acquaintances were shocked to hear him being accused of such a heinous crime.

It is worth pausing over this remarkable development. Hip-hop, which has often been mobilized as an all-purpose scapegoat for youth of color, was now being used as a suggestion for why Tsarnaev was *not* likely to be guilty of a crime. No doubt the racial politics of the United States, in which a light-complexioned Tsarnaev could be viewed as "white" (that is, until his Islamic faith was known, at which point he is more easily racialized as "Muslim" or, inaccurately, "Arab") has much to do with hip-hop being seen as a positive sign of his American assimilation. For Black youth, on the other hand, affinity for hip-hop is still largely viewed as evidence of pathology. As proof of Tsarnaev's love for hip-hop, some media outlets reported the first half of his tweet from Monday evening—"Ain't no love in the heart of the city"—as a quotation from the rapper Jay-Z. However, any hip-hop producer or aficionado will note that this attribution is not quite accurate, although a Jay-Z song is likely to be the source of where Tsarnaev first heard those words. In fact, the refrain for the 2001 Jay-Z song "Heart of the City" ("Ain't no love / in the heart of the city / ain't no love / in the heart of town") was sampled by producer Kanye West from a 1974 recording by the singer and guitarist, Bobby "Blue" Bland, originally written by the songwriters Michael Price and Dan Walsh. When heard in the context of Jay-Z's verses, this sampled chorus takes on a meaning significantly different from that of Bland's recording. In Jay-Z's song, the love he expects is from his fans and from the larger hip-hop community. His topic is, as he writes in *Decoded*, the classic theme of hip-hop:

> When we take the most familiar subject in the history of rap—why I'm dope— and frame it within the sixteen-bar structure of a rap verse, synced to the specific rhythm and feel of the track, more than anything it's a test of creativity and wit. It's like a metaphor for itself; if you can say how dope you are in a completely original, clever, powerful way, the rhyme itself becomes proof of the boast's truth.[54]

"Heart of the City" is about all the great things Jay-Z has done, exhorting listeners not to be jealous, not to be haters, but to respect his greatness. Summarizing the years of hits he has already provided for listeners, he raps: "Jigga held you down six summers; damn, where's the love?" Bland's version is a more typical sentiment of R&B, in which the singer laments, presumably, the end of a romantic relationship. What Tsarnaev tweeted was only secondarily a lyric from a hip-hop song; it was first a quotation from an R&B song from the 1970s. Read in the measured tones of a newscaster or NPR host, those words no doubt seemed abstractable. Heard in the context of Jay-Z's song, with its electric guitar chords, swirling strings, and the distinctive gritty timbre of Bland's voice, those lines, I would argue, unmistakably call upon an historical, aesthetic, and ideological past: the 1970s.

Popular music genres—and particularly hip-hop—are often painted as being radically new, cutting-edge tools with which contemporary global youth construct new identities and make a swift break with the past. This is no doubt part of the allure of popular music for listeners and, for some critics, part of its danger. The examples in this chapter show that this understanding of the cultural work performed by an engagement with popular music is incomplete. In his tweet, Tsarnaev uses the language of the 1970s himself, perhaps without even consciously realizing it. Record geeks like Questlove certainly do recognize allusions to or outright samples of earlier Black popular music in culture—because they have been socialized into knowledge of this music from a young age. For those without this socialization, a variety of new tools are available for interested listeners to connect the dots back from today's radio and YouTube smashes to their source materials. Sampling in hip-hop can be heard as a direct allusion to and insertion of the past into new music; however, other genres of Black popular music find alternative ways to enact a relationship with history, as I explore in the next chapter.

CHAPTER 5

"I JUST WANNA GO BACK, BABY, BACK TO THE WAY IT WAS"

The Past, Activism, and
Recent Black Popular Music

"We All Know It's Derivative"

In March 2013, the white R&B singer Robin Thicke and the African American producer, artist, and songwriter Pharrell Williams released the song "Blurred Lines," a track with many sonic characteristics of 1970s R&B and disco. Instrumentally, "Blurred Lines" featured the buzzy timbre of the Fender Rhodes electric piano playing in the key of G major and a percussion track with a bass drum playing steady quarter notes ("four-on-the-floor"), an active cowbell part, and occasional hits on a hi-hat cymbal (on the "and" of beat 4, every other measure) at the danceable tempo of 120 beats per minute. Vocally, the song contained Thicke's mid-range and high-register falsetto vocals, various background shouts and whoops from Pharrell, and a guest verse from the rapper T.I.

On its initial release, the song performed in line with the moderate-but-not-overwhelming success that Thicke had enjoyed to that point in his career. However, after Thicke and Pharrell performed "Blurred Lines" on the NBC music competition television show *The Voice* on May 14 and on *The Ellen DeGeneres Show* on May 16, the song quickly gained popularity, eventually becoming the best-selling song of 2013 in both the United States and the UK.[1] The song was critically acclaimed as well, ending up as #5 on the *Village Voice*'s annual Pazz and Jop Poll of critics.[2] Despite these markers of critical and commercial success, the song also faced considerable negative attention for its lyrics and music video. The music video for "Blurred Lines" exists in two versions, and in both versions, Thicke, Pharrell, and T.I. are fully clothed in fashionable suits watching three female models (Emily Ratajkowski, Jessi M'Bengue, and Elle Evans) pose and dance around for their enjoyment.[3] In the official version, the models are wearing few clothes. In the unrated version, the models are topless and wearing flesh-colored thongs. The song's title—perhaps referencing vision blurred as a result of heavy drinking or an unclear boundary between consent and coercion—and its repeated lyric "I know you want it . . . but you're a good girl"—suggested to many listeners that the sexual encounter described in the song amounted to rape. In a June 17, 2013, article in *The Daily Beast*, Tricia Romano summarized what she took as the content of the track: "The song is about how a girl really wants crazy wild sex but doesn't say it—positing that age-old problem where men think no means yes into a catchy, hummable song."[4]

In response to this critique, over twenty student unions at British universities banned the song from being played at public events.[5] Pharrell Williams, the song's producer and cowriter, ultimately admitted that the feminist criticism of "Blurred Lines" made him better understand the sexist nature of contemporary culture and how popular music helps contribute to and normalize predatory attitudes toward women. In a 2019 interview with the men's fashion magazine *GQ*, Williams described what he had learned from the controversy over this song: "I realized that we live in a chauvinist culture in our country. Hadn't realized that. Didn't realize that some of my songs catered to that."[6] Significantly, Williams's apparent feminist awakening happened after the publicity given to the 2017 #MeToo movement and concerns over the sexual exploitation of women in the entertainment industry by powerful men. The "Blurred Lines" music video depicting Thicke, Williams, and T.I. eyeing the topless or scantily clad young female models is close to the type of predatory behavior engaged in by figures like Harvey Weinstein.[7]

Another controversy also followed "Blurred Lines," one especially germane to the topic of this book. As analyzed in Katherine M. Leo's *Forensic Musicology and the Blurred Lines of Federal Copyright History*, legal proceedings over songwriting credit and copyright infringement began in August 2013, when "Blurred Lines" was in the middle of its twelve-week run at the top of the *Billboard* Hot 100.[8] These initial legal proceedings stretched on for nearly two years, but in March 2015 a jury found Thicke and Williams liable for $7.4 million in damages to the estate of Marvin Gaye on the basis of the apparent musical similarities between "Blurred Lines" and Marvin Gaye's 1977 song "Got to Give It Up," another R&B/disco hybrid with falsetto vocals and a Fender Rhodes electric piano. Thicke and Williams openly acknowledged their influence from Gaye (1939–1984), and the song's instrumentation clearly references the sound world of 1970s Black popular music. However, Thicke, Williams, and many other musicians have defended the idea that this influence and sonic reference to the musical past does not constitute illegal copyright infringement under US law. During the appeals process after the initial verdict, over two hundred musicians joined an amicus brief in support of Thicke and Williams. Significantly, the amicus brief was signed both by younger musicians (such as Jennifer Hudson, Katharine McPhee, and Aloe Blacc) and older musicians (including members of Earth, Wind & Fire and John Oates). That is, the brief was supported by musicians who are in the beginning or middle stages of their careers *and* musicians who have created a large body of popular songs, but whose days writing potential new hits are probably behind them. Members of Earth, Wind & Fire and John Oates are exactly the type of musicians who might be motivated to zealously protect their old intellectual property from serving as uncompensated inspiration for future new songs. In addition, they are artists who wrote songs in the same broad genre category—R&B from the 1970s and early 1980s—that Thicke and Williams were accused of infringing on in their "Got To Give It Up"–influenced track. Instead, these older musicians joined an amicus brief that argued:

> The verdict in this case threatens to punish songwriters for creating new music that is inspired by prior works. All music shares inspiration from prior musical works, especially within a particular musical genre. By eliminating any meaningful standard for drawing the line between permissible inspiration and unlawful copying, the judgment is certain to stifle creativity and impede the creative process.[9]

Though he did not join the amicus brief, Questlove, the drummer and bandleader of the Roots, agreed that Thicke and Williams should not be liable for copyright infringement. As someone who is both intimately involved in various aspects of music production and has a deep knowledge of music history, Questlove explained how he interpreted Williams's creative process in the composition and production of "Blurred Lines" and other tracks:

> There's a thin line, but for the sake of hip-hop culture: Look, technically it's not plagiarized. It's not the same chord progression. It's a feeling. Because there's a cowbell in it and a Fender Rhodes as the main instrumentation—that still doesn't make it plagiarized. We all know it's derivative. That's how Pharrell works. Everything that Pharrell produces is derivative of another song—but it's an homage.[10]

Questlove here combines a specific technical interpretation—that having similar instrumentation does not constitute musical plagiarism and copyright infringement—with a general theory of how Williams works as a producer and songwriter. According to Questlove, Williams's typical method is to make songs that are "derivative" "homages" to other songs. This could also largely describe Questlove's own creative process. The Roots mostly do not use samples of music from the past, as is typical for some other hip-hop artists (and discussed in the previous chapter). One of the reasons Questlove gives for this is that the cost of sampling is too high for them to afford as artists without the massive sales numbers of musicians like Jay-Z, Kanye West, or Lil Wayne.[11] Still, because specific timbres and styles of playing are so important for certain subgenres of hip-hop, Questlove and his bandmates in the Roots incorporate these sounds in their recordings through their playing of conventional musical instruments, not through samples. In a time when the holders of copyrights can heavily police hip-hop and R&B musicians for uncleared samples, Questlove argues "for the sake of hip-hop culture" that musical "feeling"—if not specific notes or "chord progressions"—must be allowed to be freely borrowed from the past by contemporary artists. There is also a slight Freudian slip here in Questlove's invoking of "hip-hop culture" in his discussion of "Blurred Lines." Despite featuring a guest verse from the rapper T.I., "Blurred Lines" is otherwise an R&B/pop song, not a hip-hop song. Perhaps Questlove is suggesting that there is a continuum of musical genres between hip-hop, R&B, and pop that all feature sonic references to the past as a key element. Finally, he also hints that the audible homage to beloved past work in "Blurred Lines" was recognized by listeners, and possibly part of its wide appeal: "We all know it's derivative."

The fact that a huge pop hit and a substantial amount of songwriting royalties were involved in the court case gave this topic more interest than an abstract philosophical debate on the line between musical influence and copyright infringement, and the case was extensively covered and commented on in the media. Despite the amicus brief and the arguments of musicians like Questlove, the judgment in favor of the Gaye estate was upheld, though the amount of damages was lowered to $5.3 million. Closely imitating a musical style from decades before was an effective strategy for Thicke and Williams to create a new hit song, but the legal system determined that "Blurred Lines" in 2013 sounded so similar to "Got to Give It Up" from 1977 that Thicke and Williams were forced to compensate the Gaye estate.

"Blurred Lines" serves as a good example of three characteristics of pop music in the 2000s. First, it exemplifies, through both its lyrics and its wildly popular music videos, popular music's general heteropatriarchal tendency toward women: a world in which women exist primarily as objects for sexual domination by men.[12] In this, it was certainly an extreme case, but not an outlier. Second, "Blurred Lines" participates in the ongoing "love and theft" of Black popular musical style by non-Black musicians.¹³ Thicke is a white artist who was able to become highly successful performing music clearly influenced by (and, depending on one's opinion, possibly infringed from) a prominent African American musician, Marvin Gaye. Thicke seems to be another in a long line of white artists who were able to be more commercially successful playing Black music than the Black artists who created these styles.¹⁴ Debates over questions of influence, appropriation, and infringement occur frequently in popular music discourse, especially as musicians, listeners, and critics are increasingly aware of the white supremacist origins and contemporary racist biases of the marketing of popular music. However, these debates only rarely move into the judicial realm where large sums of money and legal precedent are at stake. The legal battle over the proceeds of "Blurred Lines" also forced listeners and critics, supporters of Thicke and Williams and supporters of the Gaye estate, to consciously grapple with a third aspect of the contemporary pop music world: the large extent to which recent popular music engages with music of the past, especially finding "inspiration"—to quote the amicus brief—in music from the 1970s. This is the aspect of popular music culture I will focus on in this chapter, examining sonic evocations of the 1970s as another important example of historical consciousness in popular music.

In this chapter, I analyze recent Black popular music artists that invoke music from the 1970s in their recordings, videos, and live performances without directly sampling this music. In attempting to sonically re-create music from this time period, Thicke and Williams are not unique, and my focus in this chapter will be on the work of some of the most popular and critically acclaimed artists of the past twenty years, including Prince (1958–2016), Janelle Monáe (b. 1985), D'Angelo (b. 1974), Beyoncé (b. 1981), Bruno Mars (b. 1985), and Kendrick Lamar (b. 1987). In invoking the past, these musicians are at least as obvious or upfront about their musical and cultural influences as the hip-hop musicians we examined in the previous chapter who directly sample or re-play music from this same time period. In their study of the legality of sampling in hip-hop, McLeod and DiCola note that some hip-hop songs "combined many ... musical fragments at once, often rendering the original sources unrecognizable."¹⁵ Sampled or replayed sources are sometimes obscured by hip-hop musicians to stay one step ahead of the copyright lawyers, to avoid giving away trade secrets to rival musicians, or simply to keep the focus on themselves and not their sources. This hiding of sources probably has its roots in the DJ culture of the 1970s that gave birth to the recorded and commercialized hip-hop of the 1980s and beyond. One technique of DJs at this time was to remove the labels from the records they would spin at parties, so that rival DJs would not be able to easily discover where a particularly compelling sound came from and then use that in their own live DJ sets.[16] In contrast, the musicians I analyze in this chapter who do not directly sample music are typically more open about the sources of their musical influences, especially in interviews, liner notes, or other areas of popular music discourse in which they describe their creative process. (It is certainly possible that, in the wake of the settlement Thicke and Williams were forced to pay, they may be more reticent to discuss musical influence in the future.) Telegraphing such influence can be a way of claiming roots in an honored past tradition. These influences can sometimes also be more audible and visible for their audiences to become aware of; tracking down obscure samples in hip-hop tracks may or may not be an activity that casual listeners engage in, but aspects of timbre or stage presentation, for example, might be more obviously perceptible to audiences.

As discussed in the previous chapter, changes in the performance and recording techniques of Black popular music in the 1970s and 1980s had drastic consequences for how the past could be engaged in sonic practice. These changes were physical and technological as well as ideological. Ever since recording and playback equipment were developed, it was theoretically possible to use prerecorded sound in the performance and recording of "new" music in either live or recorded settings. The first composer in the Western classical tradition to integrate playback technology into live performance was Ottorino Respighi, whose 1924 piece *Pines of Rome* called for the playing of a nightingale's song in the score during the third movement. Respighi even specified the particular recording by catalog number that should be played during the performance of this piece, which otherwise featured conventional orchestral instruments.[17] However, a consideration of *Pines of Rome* shows that it is not sheer technological possibility that determines changes in music. While incorporating recorded music into live performance and new recordings was possible for composers in the Western classical tradition early in the twentieth century, it did not become a dominant or widespread part of this tradition. Instead, the Western classical tradition has been relatively conservative over the past century, only slowly admitting new performance techniques and new instruments—such as recording and playback equipment—into its accepted practices.[18]

However, other genres of music have been more willing to incorporate new musical practices and techniques. After digital sampling became possible and prominent in hip-hop in the 1980s, sampling became perhaps the primary way a relationship with the past is understood in popular music—due to the fact that hip-hop became arguably the most influential genre in the popular music world. Sampling also occupies a prominent position in the critical discourse and reception of popular music because it is so directly tied into hot-button issues like intellectual property, appropriation, and genre and race "crossover."

However, sampling—integrating old recordings into new recordings and performances—is not the only way to engage with the past: there are other ways for performers to invoke the past in musical performance and recording, and other ways for listeners to hear these invocations. I have discussed some, but by no means all, of those ways in this book. When jazz musicians and pop singers approach the Great American Songbook, they are considering repertoire that was typically written decades earlier, and their decision to perform or not to perform these songs is influenced by its historical status and its associations with earlier eras. Tribute bands face a similar choice, but with the added idea of trying not just to re-perform new versions of the past but to copy the nuances of prior performances as accurately and authentically as possible in their live shows. In some sense, hip-hop musicians carry on this increasing verisimilitude, since they can actually take the recorded sounds themselves and integrate them into a new performance or recording; but of course, in addition to verbatim quotation, hip-hop musicians also often alter these sounds and add new vocal and instrumental elements on top of them. In addition, even the mere act of replaying these sounds in new historical, geographic, and generic environments changes how audiences will interpret the meaning of these sounds.[19] Perhaps R&B and hip-hop musicians who do not directly sample prior recordings are not as able to directly incorporate the past into their contemporary work as those who make use of sampling technology, but as I show in this chapter, they have found other ways to invoke and find meaning in the past in their songs and live performances. This has been a key aspect of some of the most critically and commercially successful popular music of the past twenty years, even among those musicians who are otherwise viewed as groundbreaking, revolutionary, or radical, in line with popular music's usual ideology of newness. Attention to the evocations of the past in the work of these artists shows that they are even more complicated than scholars and critics have typically thought.

"Kick the old-school joints, for the true funk soldiers"

Born in Minneapolis, Minnesota, in 1958, and passing away in that same city in 2016, Prince Rogers Nelson is doubtless one of the most popular, influential, and groundbreaking musicians of the past fifty years. There is now a well-developed and growing scholarly literature aiming to understand his diverse contributions to the cultural arena.[20] Among the many topics of discussion, writers have often focused on his flouting of gender/sexual norms and his outspoken attitude to the music industry, since these were some of the most controversial and spectacular aspects of his life.[21] In this section, I focus on a relatively short and underexamined moment of his career: the period from roughly the year 2000 until his death when he was actively engaging with the popular music past in his albums and live performances.

A full consideration of Prince's impact and legacy is beyond the scope of this chapter and this book, but a brief summary of Prince's career will be helpful for understanding the subtle shift in his performances in the years after 2000, especially what I argue is his audible relationship to 1970s funk during this time period. Prince released his first album, *For You*, in 1978 and became a superstar in the mid-1980s. His success can be measured most easily by the 1984 album and film *Purple Rain*, in which he portrayed a fictionalized version of himself ("The Kid") trying to make it as a musician in Minneapolis. With *Purple Rain* the film, the album, and title track, he achieved the rare feat of having the #1 album, #1 song, and highest-grossing movie in the same week. Throughout the early part of his career, Prince was known for his sexually provocative performances and lyrics. For example, his song "Darling Nikki" (which also appeared on the album and film *Purple Rain*) was one of the inspirations for the 1985 Congressional hearings on censorship spearheaded by Tipper Gore, wife of then-Senator Al Gore, and her Parents Music Resource Center.[22] A few years later, he performed the song "Gett Off" in bright yellow assless chaps on television at the 1991 MTV Video Music Awards Show. Perhaps the danger of Prince, to his conservative critics, was that he was able to couple these sexually explicit songs and "shocking" performances with undeniably catchy pop hits like "Kiss" and "Raspberry Beret" that appealed to a wide audience of teenagers and young adults.

After these successes of the 1980s, the mid-1990s saw Prince in something of a slump. Hip-hop rose in commercial popularity, and Prince had a famously strained relationship with the genre and the hypermasculine bravado of its sexual politics.[23] He also started a protracted business dispute with his record company Warner Bros. about royalties and creative control. While the exact details of this dispute may have remained obscure to fans and casual observers, some of Prince's public actions would certainly not have gone unnoticed. In 1993, he changed his name to an unpronounceable symbol that combined the biological signs for male and female. Around this time, he began appearing in public with the word "slave" written on his cheek, as a protest against what he claimed were the exploitative business practices of Warner Bros. He also started covering the 1969 Staple Singers song "When Will We Be Paid?" during his concerts, an overt protest against the long history of economic exploitation of African Americans and a call for just compensation.[24] As these last two examples show, Prince at this time began to draw connections between his own perceived plight as a musician being taken advantage of by a white-controlled media industry and patterns of systemic discrimination experienced by African Americans for centuries, reaching back to slavery.[25] Such political and economic concerns would remain an undercurrent throughout the rest of his career, including his decision, in 2015, to place his music on the Jay-Z-owned Tidal streaming service and the negotiations for the publication of his autobiography, *The Beautiful Ones* (published posthumously in 2019).[26] "When Will We Be Paid?" remained a part of his live repertoire, including serving as the opening song for his final concert on April 14, 2016, in Atlanta, just a week before his death.

By the late 1990s, Prince had established a core audience of devotees who still flocked to his live performances, but he did not enjoy a radio hit during these years. His personal life also saw great changes. Perhaps most importantly, he began practicing as a Jehovah's Witness in 2001, thanks to the mentorship of Larry Graham, the former bassist for Sly and the Family Stone, who himself had been a Witness since 1975. To adhere to the Witnesses' teachings, Prince no longer cursed or used specific language to describe sexuality—though, to be sure, sexual matters and sexuality, though described in less graphic ways, still featured heavily in his live performances and recordings.[27] In this way, it is as if he were going back to the 1960s and 1970s high-water mark for funk music, when the performances were still dripping with sexuality, but at times expressed through innuendo, with a veneer of plausible deniability. This is certainly different from Prince's work in the 1980s, in which explicit language was used and specific sexual acts were described in his songs—much to the consternation of Tipper Gore and the rest of the Parents Music Resource Center.

It is always difficult to determine causality, and assigning motivations to an artist as mysterious and mercurial as Prince is particularly challenging, but two sets of facts are true concerning Prince's career in the 1990s and beyond. The first is that Prince stopped having radio hits around the late 1990s, and he largely stopped writing and releasing three-minute pop songs; none of his singles released after 1995 charted higher than #60 on the *Billboard* singles chart. The second is that he started collaborating more and more with an older generation of musicians, including Larry Graham and saxophonist Maceo Parker—who had performed with James Brown in the 1960s, George Clinton in the 1970s, and was rightly viewed as a kind of funk godfather. The resulting differences in Prince's sound were subtle, but present. Drum machines were featured less prominently in Prince's songs and live performances—live drums sets were used instead. Horn sections, including saxophone and trombone solos, were present in his live performances and recordings. Keyboard synthesizer timbres were largely traded for acoustic pianos or vintage electric keyboards like Fender Rhodes or Wurlitzer pianos. All of these timbres have very different temporal referents; they no longer reference the 1980s, when Prince first gained his massive popularity and used then state-of-the-art Linn drum machines and Yamaha DX7 synthesizers.[28]

How can we understand this shift in sound over the course of Prince's career? Griffin Woodworth's dissertation extensively discusses Prince's usage of various timbral possibilities in ways that have significance to Prince and are meant to signify specific things to his audience. According to Woodworth's analysis, Prince's usage of synthesizers and keyboards early in his career in the late 1970s and early 1980s was meant to distance his music from funk bands that prominently featured horns like Earth, Wind & Fire and Tower of Power. There are also racial components to this: as a Black artist, Prince was pushed by Warner Bros. to first appeal to a Black audience, before being given the promotional resources to crossover to a "mainstream" (read: white) audience. This type of barrier and recording company control was something that Prince resisted throughout his career, and his use of specific timbres can be viewed through this economic and racial lens.[29] Given the concerns of this chapter and this book, we can also view it through a historical lens. When Prince released his first two albums, *For You* in 1978 and the self-titled *Prince* in 1979, funk music was still recent popular music. Similar to the ways that early hip-hop DJs spun James Brown, the Jimmy Castor Bunch, and Sly and the Family Stone records, funk was still youth culture, for both Prince and his listeners in the late 1970s and early 1980s. It had not yet acquired the nostalgic meanings it would take on in the 1990s and beyond. Prince's move to distance himself timbrally from this music can be seen as a young artist trying to establish himself as making a unique contribution to the popular music scene, in line with the dominant ideology of newness that often characterizes popular music culture.

Woodworth also examines Prince's eventual adoption of horns into his bands in a 2013 article, "Prince, Miles, and Maceo: Horns, Masculinity, and the Anxiety of Influence."[30] As scholars such as Portia Maultsby have extensively discussed, funk music in the 1970s is highly associated with working-class African American identity and heterosexual male desire.[31] In Woodworth's analysis, the adoption of horns into his bands can be tied to Prince adopting heteropatriarchal norms, in that his relationship to funk instrumentation should be viewed as a relationship with the sexual politics that this genre largely represents for its performers and listeners. Woodworth's argument is compelling, but I want to extend his discussion to include some of the musical choices that Prince would make in the 2010s, when he both continued his usage of horns in recordings and live performances and gave a series of significant live performances in which themes in addition to gender politics and heteropatriarchy were foregrounded. Specifically, what was prominent in this time period was Prince's explicit historical consciousness, his drawing up a narrative of a chunk of Black musical history and skillfully placing himself at the center of it through live performances and recordings.

Prince was a prolific artist, as tales about his vault of unreleased material at his Paisley Park compound can attest. Even if we limit our discussion to songs and albums that he released during his lifetime, there is a very large amount of material to come to terms with. The amount of material Prince recorded and released was, in fact, a major point of contention between him and executives at Warner Bros., who wanted him to conform to a more easily marketable schedule of album releases and tours. Therefore, what follows is necessarily a simplification, but hopefully useful for teasing out the important historiographical turn in Prince's music and reception in the last fifteen years of his career. An analysis of Prince also sets us up for a consideration of the historiographical turn in other artists around this time as well, especially since Monáe, D'Angelo, Mars, and Beyoncé all specifically attest to Prince's influence on their own musical direction, and a sonic reference to Prince's music itself is frequently part of their own historical consciousness.

Prince's album *The Rainbow Children* was released in November 2001. The album is a concept album heavily influenced by Prince's newfound religious beliefs as a Jehovah's Witness, but also drawing parallels between the fate of African Americans in the United States through the transatlantic slave trade and the biblical Israelites—a comparison also prominent in a wide variety of Black Protestant theology. Much of this narrative is provided by voiceovers at the beginning and ending of songs delivered by Prince in a voice that has been digitally altered to sound very low-pitched. Prince did little to promote this album, and coupled with its rather esoteric narrative, this probably helped ensure that it did not sell well, beyond the core audience of fans that Prince had already cultivated by this time, more than twenty years after the beginning of his career.

Still, for our focus on historical consciousness in popular music, this album is highly significant for its sonic textures. The sound of many of its tracks is clearly indebted to funk from the 1960s and 1970s, especially the music of James Brown and Sly and the Family Stone. "The Work, Pt. 1," the album's fourth track, is especially notable in this regard. Even its title is rich in significance. The "Pt. 1" is a reference to the common practice of splitting a long funk performance over two sides of a 45-rpm single, because each side could only hold about three and a half minutes of music, not long enough for the extended workouts that artists like James Brown liked to release.[32] In Prince's case, this was clearly "just" an homage to Brown and not a necessary descriptive part of the title, since there is no "The Work, Pt. 2" and the song instead comes to a firm close at the 3:45 mark, not fading out over a groove only to fade back in on "Pt. 2" as Brown's "Pt. 1" tracks often did.[33] In the song's lyrics, Prince declares that he is "willing to do the work"—in this case, the work of deconstructing the false narratives about Black people that circulate in the media (what is referred to as "the digital garden" on the previous song on the album). Additionally, "the work" could also be a reference to one of Brown's many nicknames: "the hardest-working man in show business." The song's assertiveness and pro-Black politics are also similar to many songs by Brown: "Get Up Offa That Thing" (1976), "Get Up, Get Into It, Get Involved" (1970), and even "Say It Loud (I'm Black and I'm Proud)" (1968).

Sonically, the track also clearly shows Brown's influence. It is a medium-tempo funk groove (111 beats per minute), nearly the same as Brown's iconic "Cold Sweat" (113 bpm) from 1967: a track that has been suggested by the writers Nelson George and Rickey Vincent to be the birth of funk as a recorded genre.[34] Prince shouts, screams, and grunts "Oww," "Huh," and "Ooh-uh" similar to Brown's vocal style. The verses feature hits from the four-member horn section of the Hornheadz; later in the song there is a short trombone solo, similar to those provided by Fred Wesley on classic recordings by Brown.[35] And Larry Graham himself, former bassist with Sly and the Family Stone, plays bass guitar on the track. Nearly all of the other guitar, keyboard, and bass parts on the album are played by Prince, and Prince's facility at playing a wide variety of instruments is a key part of his mythology as a musical polymath. The bass guitar is one of the most important defining instruments of funk, and having Graham provide the bass line further cements the track's connection to funk's past. The composite instrumentation for this track released in 2001 clearly echoes 1960s and 1970s funk: electric bass and guitar, organ, drum set, horn section, Prince's lead vocal, and back-up singers who respond to him in call-and-response style.

"The Work, Pt. 1" is not the only track on *The Rainbow Children* to explicitly call back to the sounds of an earlier funk era. "Family Name" and "The Everlasting Now" also do this, especially with their use of bass lines and horn section parts, again provided by the Hornheadz. Vocal references to earlier performance practices and formal structures are also present in these songs. For example, on "Family Name" Prince calls out when to go to the bridge of the song, as Brown had often done in live performances and on recordings, either out of necessity—because the performance was being improvised—or to give a feel of spontaneity and improvisation to a planned performance. For Prince on "Family Name," this marking of formal structure is almost certainly functioning more as an evocation of Brown and a signal to listeners about Prince's homage to the musical past than a necessary direction to his other musicians:

this is not an improvised jam but a meticulously planned recording in which Prince overdubs himself performing multiple instrumental parts.

An even more telling moment happens around the six-minute mark of "The Everlasting Now." After an instrumental interlude, the texture thins out to just John Blackwell on drum set and a spoken-word voice (Prince's voice, digitally altered) is heard saying: "You know this is funky, I just wish he'd play like he used to, old scraggly head son of a . . ." This voice is then dramatically stopped before it could finish the end of that epithet with the sound of a slap being delivered across the cheek.[36] (Recall that after Prince became a Jehovah's Witness, there was no longer any profanity on his records.) Immediately after this interruption, the song's chorus comes in with lyrics that combine funk's typical attitude of partying and having a good time, with the album's particular religious message:

> Don't let nobody bring you down
> Accurate knowledge of Christ and the Father will bring the everlasting now.

This is a remarkable moment because it shows that Prince was aware that however much listeners might appreciate his obvious musicianship, virtuosic instrumental solos, and funk grooves, there was a portion of his audience that longed for him to return to his earlier, 1980s-era style of dependable pop hits—and not the long, multisection, funk-meets-prog-rock-and-musical-theater conceptual tracks of *The Rainbow Children*.

Following the release of *The Rainbow Children* album, Prince embarked on a tour of North America, Europe, and Japan in 2002 with essentially the same funk instrumentation as characterized the album; for live performance, that meant other musicians had to join him on stage, instead of Prince himself overdubbing multiple keyboard and guitar parts. Prince made it a point to play these old-sounding new songs on tour, along with other instrumental funk grooves. This tour was documented on a three-disc box set *One Nite Alone . . . Live!*, which was originally available in limited release and likely only purchased by die-hard fans.[37] "Xenophobia"—a newly composed instrumental funk tune that allows various members of the band to take extended solos—is the third song on this compilation, matching its typical place on the tour's setlist. That is, it was played early in the show, setting up what audience members should expect from the rest of the performance. During the spoken introduction to this song from the *One Nite Alone* box set, Prince says: "Welcome to the power of surrender. First things first: you must surrender your expectation. For those of you expecting to get your 'Purple Rain' on, you in the wrong house. See, we're not interested in what you know, but what you are willing to learn." As with many of Prince's enigmatic pronouncements, this is a complicated utterance to parse. Similar to tribute bands that lead audience members through the history of rock 'n' roll by re-creating iconic albums or live performances onstage, Prince seems to be calling out to audience members "willing to learn" funk history (and maybe even some *Rainbow Children*/Jehovah's Witnesses theology) from him. Prince is less interested in playing his own big hits from the 1980s ("what you know," songs like "Purple Rain"); instead he is interested in playing his new material from *The Rainbow Children*. However, while this material was newly released, it is also clearly "old" in terms of its sound. In instrumental timbre, vocal style, and arrangements, this music references 1970s funk more than Prince's 1980s pop music.

One of the ways we can see this reference to the funk past is in the musicians he hired to play with him at this time, including saxophonist Maceo Parker, who joined Prince's band for this tour and would play on and off with him during live performances and recordings over the next decade. With Parker in his band, Prince could claim a real living connection to the origins of the funk genre, and a distinguished pedigree of funk associates; in addition to Brown, Parker had also played with Parliament-Funkadelic and, since the 1990s, had successfully toured leading his own bands playing, in his words, "2% jazz, 98% funky stuff."[38] Prince would affectionately refer to Parker as "The Teacher" onstage, telegraphing his importance to the work that Prince was undertaking. In his live performances over the last fifteen years of his life, Prince seemed to take particular delight in presenting and teaching music history to his audiences, and if audiences did not know a particular song, lyrical reference, or dance step, he would playfully taunt them with, "If you don't know, you better ask somebody." Not only were his own songs distinctly funk-influenced on this tour, but Prince and his band would also cover iconic funk songs during these shows: "Pass the Peas" by the JBs (1972), "Love Rollercoaster" by the Ohio Players (1975), and Sly and the Family Stone's "Sing a Simple Song" (1968) all made frequent appearances on this tour's setlists.[39]

Musicology, Prince's next studio album after *The Rainbow Children*, was a dramatic departure in terms of the work done to publicize the album.[40] Prince made a music video for its title track. He also did a rare television appearance on *The Tonight Show with Jay Leno* in February 2004, showing off his well-rehearsed band (including Maceo Parker, whom he introduced by name to take a solo, just as James Brown would), stylish clothes, and slick dance moves before sashaying to the couch to chat with Leno and fellow guest Mel Gibson. Gibson and Prince have some surprising commonalities: they are similar in age, came to prominence in the 1980s as sex symbols, and are both deeply religious, with Gibson appearing on the program to promote his then newly released film *The*

Passion of the Christ and Prince's prior album being the heavily spiritual and mythological *The Rainbow Children*. Their brief interaction is telling:

> LENO: Now, Mel, why can't you dress like that? See how cool—
> GIBSON: I don't know. It doesn't work on me.
> PRINCE: Mel Gibson! What's shaking, baby? What you doing after the show?
> GIBSON: What am I doing after the show? Dancing, I guess.[41]

Though visibly awkward and clearly unsure of how to interact with Prince, Gibson has figured out a key characteristic of the *Musicology* album and Prince's career at this time in 2004: this is an album about dancing and funk. None of the songs feature any of the conceptual elements that characterize *The Rainbow Children*, and there is no mythological story, narration, or reference to religious doctrine. Sonically, however, the album closely follows the template laid out by *The Rainbow Children*, and perhaps pushes it even further. Once again, funk from the 1960s and 1970s is a key reference. "Musicology" as a field is usually defined as the study of music history. In the title track's lyrics, Prince goes further, calling musicology "just another one of God's gifts." While Prince does not seem to be referring to the academic field of musicology, this album certainly does show him continuing his interest in music history, in knowing and paying homage to one's musical elders.

Serving as both the opening song on the album and the song Prince chose to perform on *The Tonight Show*, "Musicology" begins with a typical funk bass line, a repeating four-beat pattern of eight notes in which beat 1 ("The One") is accented, while syncopations dominate the rest of the measure. In the lyrics, Prince asks: "Don't you miss the feeling music gave you back in the day?" before name-checking the songs "September" (1978) and "Let's Groove" (1981) by Earth, Wind & Fire, "Hot Pants" (1971) by James Brown, and Sly and the Family Stone's "I Want to Take You Higher" (1969) as the kind of songs Prince wants to hear at his parties. The song and the album as a whole works to place Prince in the lineage of funk history and as the genre's most reliable modern-day purveyor. Maceo Parker again joined Prince on several songs on the album, and he also played with Prince on the "Musicology Live 2004ever" tour that followed the album's release.

This tour was even more successful than the 2002 *One Nite Alone* tour, with Prince playing to larger venues, a total of eighty-eight shows over the spring and summer of 2004. This was the second highest-grossing tour of 2004 at over $90 million, and the one that sold the most tickets, with 1.5 million tickets sold. The *Musicology* album and tour seemed to be Prince taking one more shot at mainstream popularity, after several years, if not decades, of indulging his wandering muse: instrumental jazz albums, concept albums, and limited releases only available to members of his fan club. However, he did not chase popularity by re-creating the sound of his 1980s hits or attempting to imitate the sound of contemporary pop music radio. Instead, *Musicology* was his attempt to win fans on his own terms, by going back to his own musical ancestors and heroes, such as James Brown and Sly and the Family Stone. It was explicitly an appeal to a "lost" "classic" style, what he called in the lyrics for the song "Musicology" "old-school joints for the true funk soldiers."[42]

Prince contains multitudes, to be sure, and any attempt to neatly fit his career into a box is going to run into serious problems. Consider, for example, a project he released in March 2009, at a time when, I have argued, he was very interested in sonically referencing the 1970s in his music. He released three albums together as a set, one of which was *MPLSoUND*, a reference to the so-called "Minneapolis sound" of the early 1980s that Prince created through his own work and the sound of his protégés and associated artists like Morris Day and the Time. This album features timbres from 1980s electronic keyboards, drum machines, and synth strings, when Prince had largely abandoned these timbral elements in his other albums and live performances. The album's fifth track is a ballad called "Here," that employs most of these features. However, even at the end of this song, he includes a seemingly ad-libbed "Donny Hathaway's 'A Song for You' ain't the same without you here," referencing a 1971 recording by the soul singer Donny Hathaway. Hathaway's dramatic, stirring vocals over piano and string orchestra backing made this song one of his best-loved performances. It is clear for Prince that 1970s soul/funk remains a touchstone and, perhaps, his own personal romantic soundtrack.

For one final look at the later career of Prince, I want to turn our attention to the series of shows that he presented under the "Welcome 2" brand.[43] Continuing for almost two years (from December 2010 to September 2012), the tour was primarily made up of multiple shows in the same location or metro area as a kind of residency. The tour began with six shows in the New York metro area, four at Madison Square Garden and two across the Hudson River in East Rutherford, New Jersey, at the Izod Center. (I attended the December 29, 2010, show at Madison Square Garden, with Mint Condition and Janelle Monáe as opening acts.) In April and May 2011, he played a total of fifteen shows at the Forum in Inglewood, California, former home of the Los Angeles Lakers. The tour finished in September 2012 with three consecutive shows at the United Center in Chicago. Prince used these concerts as perhaps the most specific instance of invoking the musical past, arguing for his place at the center of this musical story, and pointing to younger artists that he influenced as implicit proof of his greatness and legacy.

He did this both through his own band's instrumentation and through his curation of opening acts and duet partners during these performances. The older generation of Prince's influences were well represented. Larry Graham's band Graham Central Station was often the opening act. Maceo Parker, a Prince collaborator in addition to leading his own band, took over opening duties on some nights, and the Minneapolis-based R&B band Mint Condition opened some shows. Younger artists showing Prince's influence on their own music were also often featured as openers, including Cee-Lo Green and Janelle Monáe (to whom our attention will turn later in this chapter). The retro-soul of Sharon Jones and the Dap Kings and the classical- and pop-influenced jazz of Esperanza Spalding opened for Prince on December 15, 2010, at the Izod Center in East Rutherford; two months later Spalding would come to wide notoriety by beating Justin Bieber for the Best New Artist Grammy Award. The idea of Prince's sphere of influence stretched even beyond music for this tour. For the New York area shows, the ballet dancer Misty Copeland also performed during Prince's set: she danced while Prince played his ballad "The Beautiful Ones." While openers are sometimes selected haphazardly or for the commercial desires of a record company, at this point in his career Prince had much more agency to decide who would be opening for him and who would be part of the sense of community and historical narrative he was creating onstage. By choosing these particular opening acts, Prince seems to have been curating a narrative of Black musical history, with his influences, his offshoots, and himself at the center. The artists who he chose to surround himself with seemed to largely agree with this Prince-centric view. After opening for another Prince concert on December 29, 2013, Janelle Monáe tweeted:

> 12/29/10=1st time we opened for our musical hero PRINCE at Madison Square Garden. Now again on same date, 3 yrs later. #blessed #thankful[44]

There are many different ways to tell the history of African American music: centering certain artists and styles, deemphasizing others, and drawing connections across ostensible boundaries. This is a familiar dilemma faced by every historian, textbook author, documentarian, or college professor when deciding how to do their work.[45] What does Prince put into this narrative, and what does he leave out? The 1970s funk and R&B style (themselves both highly influenced by jazz, among other genres) is at the core of this narrative: in Prince's musical style throughout the last fifteen years of his career, in the work of the older generation of artists who opened for him on the "Welcome 2 America" tour, and in the sound of the younger artists who are heavily influenced both by Prince's own work *and* that of his recognized predecessors.[46] Women—Jones,

Spalding, Monáe, and Copeland, along with some of the celebrated female artists Prince has collaborated with over the years including Mavis Staples and Chaka Khan—are also given a surprisingly prominent place in Prince's musical universe and historical narrative, relative to the ways in which they have been written out of many journalistic and scholarly accounts of Black popular music.

Perhaps the most obvious missing element in this narrative is hip-hop, and its exclusion does not seem accidental; its mainstream public debut in 1979 with the release of the Sugar Hill Gang's "Rapper's Delight" and its rise to popularity in the mid-1980s behind artists like Run-DMC almost exactly parallels Prince's own career trajectory. In the 2004 song "Musicology," Prince does give shout-outs to Jam Master Jay of Run-DMC and Chuck D of Public Enemy in his pantheon of past musical heroes, along with the already-mentioned lyrical references to the work of James Brown, Earth, Wind & Fire, and Sly and the Family Stone. Chuck D had previously collaborated with Prince on the track "Undisputed" from the 1999 *Rave Un2 the Joy Fantastic* album.

However, these limited engagements with hip-hop culture fit a predictable pattern. Jam Master Jay had been recently murdered in 2002, and Prince's mention of him in the lyrics to "Musicology" can perhaps be seen as a tribute to a fallen fellow musician. Chuck D was far from being a commercial mainstream star by the time Prince collaborated with him in the late 1990s and acknowledged him by name in 2004. Even at the height of their commercial popularity in the late 1980s, Public Enemy constantly sampled the music of James Brown and were interested in renewing the Black political activism that flourished in the 1960s and 1970s. Chuck D was therefore a natural fit for Prince's explicitly history-based vision at this time in the 2000s that looked back to prior decades as a source of musical and political inspiration. A younger and more commercially successful hip-hop artist—someone whose songs were primarily about partying and consuming substances—would not have fit into Prince's narrative at this time, especially as he was performing a kind of "respectable" Black musical and social history.

The vision of Black musical and cultural history that Prince advanced in the years around 2010 did not exist in a vacuum. The first Black president of the United States had been elected, and then reelected—someone only three years younger than Prince who seemed to largely share his musical taste of 1970s soul and funk music. This is the president who gave an unaccompanied impromptu performance of the opening lines of Al Green's 1971 song "Let's Stay Together" at a campaign fundraising event at the Apollo Theater in Harlem in 2012, even in the original F major key of Green's recording. Similarly, Stevie Wonder made frequent appearances at Obama campaign rallies and other events, and Prince himself was even invited to the White House to perform. To be sure, Obama also made some tentative forays into hip-hop culture, and hip-hop artists and fans were largely supportive of Obama himself.[47] However, much of Obama's public life, including his aesthetic choices, were marked by a politics of respectability, as writers such as Ta-Nehisi Coates have argued.[48] Songs about love and romance were acceptable if they came from stars like Wonder and Green who had been largely canonized and accepted by the mainstream—and who were, themselves, approaching senior citizen age. Younger artists like Monáe, Common, and Kendrick Lamar were admittable to this vision so long as they adopted the codes and respectable cultural politics of their elders. Obama publicly chose Lamar's "How Much a Dollar Cost?" as his favorite song of 2015, announcing his choice in *People* magazine—not exactly a publication venue known for its discussion of figures like Lamar, arguably the artist with the most credibility among various subgroups of the hip-hop community. Yet the song from Lamar's *To Pimp a Butterfly* album was an explicitly Christian message, adapted from Matthew 25:32–46, about the responsibility to help those less fortunate than ourselves. Ronald Isley of the canonical and longstanding R&B band the Isley Brothers sings the song's outro, and the easily recognizable guitar chords of the Isley Brothers' 1973 recording of "That Lady" provide the basis for another track on the album, Lamar's anthem of self-empowerment, "i." Prince, Lamar, and Obama were all key figures in promoting a specific narrative of Black history drawing on the politics and cultural aesthetics of the 1960s and 1970s, but channeling them to an optimistic viewpoint in the 2010s.

African American families suffered heavy losses in the financial collapse of 2008–2009 and its uneven recovery in the years following. But whereas previous economic insecurity or perceived government indifference or incompetence had inspired strong political and artistic criticism from Black Americans, at this time, the figurehead of the US government was the first Black president: a man who inspired fierce loyalty from the majority of African Americans, widespread approval from independents that led to his lopsided victories in two elections, and paranoia that shaded into racism and xenophobia from conservatives. However, this optimistic vision of the present—one heavily inspired by the past, specifically the 1970s—would shift around the year 2013, and another movement, decidedly less optimistic but no less political, would come to strongly influence conversations about Black political and expressive culture.

"Does anybody hear us pray, for Michael Brown and Freddie Gray?"

On February 26, 2012, Trayvon Martin, an unarmed seventeen-year-old African American high school student was shot and killed by George Zimmerman while walking back from a convenience store in Sanford, Florida. This killing took place just over a year after Prince began the "Welcome 2" tour in December 2010. On July 13, 2013, Zimmerman was acquitted of second-degree murder charges. In response to this verdict, Alicia Garza, Patrisse Cullors, and Opal Tometi began organizing around the hashtag #blacklivesmatter, eventually forming a loose coalition of activist groups with the same name.[49] A year after the Zimmerman verdict, another unarmed African American teenager, Michael Brown, was shot and killed, this time by a white police officer, Darren Wilson, in Ferguson, Missouri, a majority-Black suburb of St. Louis. In response to this death, large protests were organized by a variety of activists, including those identified with the Black Lives Matter movement.

What does all of this have to do with Prince, and the invocation of the past? At the time, the protests around these killings—and many others, including those of Eric Gardner, Sandra Bland, and Freddie Gray—represented the most prominent movement for racial justice in the United States since the civil rights movement of the 1960s and 1970s forty years before, the exact time period Prince is musically invoking with his live performances that also looms large as a source for samples for contemporary hip-hop. The 2020 protests galvanized by the murder of George Floyd by the police officer Derek Chauvin in Minneapolis drew energy from the original Black Lives Matter protests of 2013 and 2014, though these 2020 protests were even larger in scope. The strength of this movement is that it did not stay cloistered among a small group of concerned activists but expanded to grab the attention of a relatively large number of people. Some of the people who were influenced by the Black Lives Matter movement were musicians and listeners; this should not be surprising, since music has often occupied a prominent place in African American protest movements. Musicians in the years 2012 and after wrote and performed music that was explicitly connected to the concerns of the Black Lives Matter movement, and even more songs that were generally "socially conscious" could be interpreted and reused by activist audiences for political purposes.

Prince's clearest contribution to this political movement was the release of his song "Baltimore" in 2015. The song featured a classic Prince electric guitar melody and a plaintive question in the opening verse: "Does anybody hear us pray / for Michael Brown and Freddie Gray?" Later in the song, a chant clearly modeled after group protests slogans is repeated several times: "If there ain't no justice then there ain't no peace." This song was primarily spread as a music video on YouTube, where an official video authorized by Prince and directed by Ralston Smith combines the song's lyrics with still images of protest and Prince's own "Rally 4 Peace" benefit concert that he performed in Baltimore in May 2015, after the death of Freddie Gray due to injuries suffered in police custody and widespread protests in the city. During that concert, Prince again performed the Staple Singers' "When Will We Be Paid?," this time as a duet with the R&B singer Miguel, a younger musician whose fusion of funk, rock, and overt sexuality is clearly modeled after Prince himself. In his comments at the concert, Prince expressed a message of racial justice through economic empowerment: "We need new ideas, new life. Most of all, we need new piece. And the kind of piece I'm talking about is spelled 'P-I-E-C-E.' Next time I come to Baltimore, I want to stay in a hotel owned by one of you. I want to play in a building owned and operated by one of you."[50] Such messages of systematic inequality, owning and controlling institutions, and generational wealth have become key parts of recent activist discourse, but they also have a long history in the Black freedom struggle, perhaps most spectacularly in the 1960s and 1970s that Prince actively invokes with his musical choices in the last fifteen years of his career. Prince, however, would not be the only artist in the 2010s and beyond to draw inspiration from the sounds and politics of this earlier era.

Janelle Monáe, the "Funkiest Horn Section in Metropolis," and Memories That Cannot Be Deleted

Janelle Monáe came to prominence in the early 2010s with two critically acclaimed albums, *The ArchAndroid* and *The Electric Lady*. While neither album became a hit on the scale of work by other Black female R&B artists like Rihanna or Beyoncé—her highest chart performance on the *Billboard* albums chart is only #17—Monáe's work received critical acclaim and generally positive reaction from listeners willing to engage with her multialbum mythological story of a robot in a dystopian future who falls in love with a human. If listeners were unwilling to take that deep dive into Monáe's work, they may still have encountered her 2010 breakout hit, "Tightrope." Sonically, much of Monáe's music in the beginning and middle stages of her career was highly indebted to midcentury funk. "Tightrope" in particular is an obvious homage to James Brown, similar to the ways that much of Prince's work from the 2000s until his death in 2016—such as "The Work, Pt. 1"—referenced Brown's musical legacy. In his exploration of Janelle Monáe and what he terms "Afro-sonic feminist funk," Matthew Valnes describes several aspects of "Tightrope."[51] It opens with high-pitched, trebly electric guitar, drum set, and Monáe wailing. Its verses feature a repeating two-measure bass riff that outlines one chord, and its instrumentation includes well-rehearsed horn riffs from saxophones and trumpets: "the funkiest horn section in Metropolis," as she introduces them. Speech-song declamation, in the style of Brown, alternates

Janelle Monáe performing at the 2011 Wireless Festival in London, UK. Photo by James Linsell-Clark.

with more conventionally virtuosic and melismatic figures on "Tightrope." In the popular music video for this song, Monáe is wearing her "uniform" of "black-and-whites," a black tuxedo with white shirt and two-tone black and white shoes. In interviews, Monáe has described how this is both an homage to James Brown's stage presentation style in the 1960s and to her mother, who worked as a janitor and also wore a "uniform" to work every day; instead of a never-ending parade of couture outfits expected of other female artists, Monáe simply wears her tuxedo uniform to her job as a musician. While her physical performance does not quite match the energetic frenzy of Brown in the 1960s, the camera does at times zoom in on her feet executing intricate dance steps.[52]

"Tightrope" was the biggest hit of Monáe's early career and a clear example of generic features of funk forming an important part of her sound. However, numerous other songs from Monáe's first two albums also showed a strong influence from 1970s Black popular music, including "Dance or Die," "Q.U.E.E.N.," and "Ghetto Woman," among many others. If Monáe's invocations of music from the past were an important part of her career from the beginning, her involvement with politics and politically inspired music came about more gradually. After the death of Sandra Bland in police custody in Texas on July 13, 2015, Monáe released a stand-alone track, "Hell You Talmbout," a clear protest chant. Over a 12/8 percussion groove, Monáe and other members of her group shout out the names of Black people killed in racially motivated violence. Of the songs inspired by police violence in the 2000s, "Hell You Talmbout" is probably closest to the freedom song tradition of the civil rights movement. No melodic or harmonic instruments are prominently used in the performance. It shares this in common with the mass freedom song tradition, in which songs would be sung in meetings, or in warm-up to the meeting, but not usually in contexts where piano, guitar, or other instrumental accompaniment was present. In the style of freedom songs like "We Shall Overcome" or "We Shall Not Be Moved," the song is lyrically repetitive, easily allowing for mass participation from the audience, and not depending on the expert performance technique from a highly skilled musician. It alternates a chorus expressing outrage and disbelief over injustice with verses that are similarly repetitive: following a simple pattern that drops in a different person's name at the beginning of the lines.

> Sandra Bland, say her name
> Sandra Bland, say her name
> Sandra Bland, say her name, say her name, won't you say her name?

Throughout her career, Monáe has combined sonic and visual references to 1960s and 1970s Black popular music genres like funk with other elements that suggest a futuristic or fantasy world. The allegorical relationship between this world and contemporary American society has influenced journalists, critics, and listeners to view Monáe's work through the critical lens of Afrofuturism: an artistic and philosophical movement that imagines a scientific or otherworldly existence for Black people as a critique of the present's failures. In her recent book *The Meaning of Soul: Black Music and Resilience Since the 1960s*, Emily J. Lordi proposes a modification or addition to this widespread interpretation of Monáe. Instead of emphasizing Afrofuturism, Lordi includes Monáe in her grouping of Black musicians who express what she terms an "Afropresentist" usage of soul music and its related cultural and political associations:

> Afropresentists use the past (in the works I discuss, "the past" means citations of soul music) as a resource for rethinking this world. . . . Afrofuturism is too often the go-to paradigm for talking about new world orders, as if radical change were necessarily an otherworldly project. . . . The works I highlight, in contrast—by Beyoncé, Erykah Badu, and Monáe herself—seek to provoke change in the present.[53]

Lordi analyzes Monáe's 2013 album *The Electric Lady* in this light, describing it as "less about androids and fantastic other worlds than it is about the unrealized futures that shape the present."[54] Lordi admits this is a "cheeky, if not downright perverse" interpretation of Monáe, who is usually viewed as an

Afrofuturist *par excellence*. I am hesitant to fully endorse Lordi's interpretation of *The Electric Lady*, if for no other reason than the fact that the album's liner notes and three different "interludes" continue the story of Cindi Mayweather, an android from the future who falls in love with a human. This does not mean that the relationship of the soul past to the contemporary present does *not* characterize *The Electric Lady*, only that Afrofuturism should also remain a key lens through which to interpret Monáe and her listeners' engagements with her work. Monáe remains such a fascinating figure because her work invokes at least three different realms: the futuristic dystopia of Cindi Mayweather, the soul/funk musical and political past of the 1960s and 1970s—and our present-day society, which is illuminated and critiqued by its comparison with these two other times and places.

Perhaps Monáe's next album, 2018's *Dirty Computer*, most strongly reflects a concern with the contemporary political world, especially that world epitomized by the 2016 election of Donald Trump as president of the United States. For years, Monáe parried questions about her sexuality in interviews, usually replying to such inquiries with, "I only date androids." However, in the aftermath of the 2016 presidential election, Monáe felt called upon to be more personally and politically outspoken. In an interview with *Rolling Stone* to promote the release of *Dirty Computer* in April 2018, she came out as a "pansexual free-ass motherfucker," and the album had clear political overtones.[55] Prince had guested on vocal and guitar on "Giving 'Em What They Love," the second track on *The Electric Lady*. *Dirty Computer*, released two years after his death, continues to show his influence. Its lead single "Make Me Feel" has a similar bass, drums, and electric guitar groove to that of Prince's "Kiss." The title *Dirty Computer* is probably also a reference to Prince's 1980 album *Dirty Mind*. The surviving artist most associated with soul and funk from previous decades, Stevie Wonder, makes a brief cameo appearance on *Dirty Computer* in the form of a phone message he apparently left for Monáe. For this forty-six-second interlude, Wonder's spoken words are backed by a clavinet, an instrument that Wonder often used in the 1970s on songs such as "Heaven Is 10 Zillion Light Years Away."

Monáe's relationship to the past is clearest on the *Dirty Computer* project when examining its companion forty-five-minute "emotion picture." In the film's narrative, Monáe is confined in some sort of prison or mental institution, captured for being different, for not fitting into the machine of society, for being a "dirty computer," in need of being cleaned. In the film's opening narration, Monáe's voice can be heard setting the scene: "They started calling us computers. People began vanishing. And the cleaning began. You were dirty if you looked different. You were dirty if you refused to live the way they dictated. You were dirty if you showed any form of opposition at all. And if you were dirty, it was only a matter of time." While Monáe is lying on an examination table, two technicians in an adjoining room carry out the cleaning process of going through her memories and manually deleting them. Monáe, or Jane 57821, as she is called here, has a brain-controlling cap fitted on her skull, and a gas floods the room, which she inhales. From there, the technicians scroll through her memories, displayed on a screen in the control room. As these technicians delete memories, however, the memories themselves are displayed on the technician's screen, and that is how we as viewers are able to enter into Monáe's inner mental world: the memories that need to be "deleted" because they are "dirty" are in fact the music videos for the songs on the *Dirty Computer* album.

The first memory that is accessed by the technicians—in order to be deleted—is of Monáe and a companion out for a joyride, grooving along on the car stereo to the dancehall-flavored song "I Got the Juice," the ninth track on the album. (Incidentally, this song features a guest appearance by Pharrell Williams, another contemporary musician whose interest in the Black musical past we have already analyzed in this chapter.) Within seconds a siren interrupts the groove, and Monáe curses to herself as she is pulled over by a flying drone. After checking their identity cards and scanning their retinas, the drone lets Monáe and her companion go. Once the drone has left and the coast is clear, the music for "I Got the Juice" returns, Monáe gets out of the car and opens the trunk, and three more friends emerge. Generally speaking, the videos that make up Monáe's memory, such as the video for "I Got the Juice," depict Monáe and her multigender, multiracial group of friends having fun, dancing, and partying. What needs to be deleted by the technicians is any memory about having fun, expressing oneself, hanging out with friends, partying, dancing, joyriding, having unconventional clothing or hairstyles. It is these memories of events that Monáe experienced, apparently, that are so "dirty" and threatening to the ruling regime that they need to be deleted.

The next video that we access through Jane 57821's memory is for the song "Crazy Classic Life," in which Monáe sings the lyrics: "I am not America's nightmare / I am the American dream." However, despite these optimistic lyrics, danger lurks overhead, in the form of police helicopters shining lights on the outdoor party the video depicts. Eventually, the party is busted, which is surely a reference to the contemporary overpolicing of communities of color, and possibly to immigration raids that intensified in the early years of the Trump presidency. Monáe herself is initially apprehended, but one of her companions is able to physically overpower an officer, allowing her to temporarily escape. In between cleaning sessions, Monáe recovers in a private room where she is attended to by a nurse-type figure, played by Tessa Thompson. Thompson introduces herself as Mary Apple 53, though Monáe calls her Zen.

Zen had been a key figure in Monáe's memories that had flashed across the technician's screen, and Monáe is highly distraught that Zen doesn't remember her or their previous relationship.

In the final scenes before the credits roll, there are hints that Mary Apple 53/Zen may be beginning to remember her relationship with Monáe, but she is apparently powerless to stop the continuation of the cleaning Monáe will be subjected to. In the last scene, we see Monáe again, after she has apparently undergone a successful final cleaning. But instead of being Jane 57821, she introduces herself to a new patient as Mary Apple 54—apparently the next nurse in sequence, with the job of guiding another patient through the cleaning process. The film's credits begin to roll on this rather bleak outcome. When Monáe is at this institution being cleaned, her memories are erased; the message "Memory Deleted" flashes on the technician's screen after individual memories are apparently taken from her brain. But this description is not true. At the end of the film, Monáe and the nurse who had been overseeing her cleaning—Mary Apple 53/Zen—make a break for it and escape the hospital, along with the new patient, the new "dirty computer" they had been supposed to help clean. The memories that Monáe had—of being free, being able to express herself sonically, being able to express her sexuality, being able to flout standards of visual conformity—have *not*, in fact, been successfully deleted.

This triumphant switch is soundtracked by the album's final song, "Americans," a celebratory anthem that Monáe also closed her live performances with during the summer of 2018 on her "Dirty Computer" tour. Prince's influence is again clear on this song, which sonically recalls "Let's Go Crazy" from the *Purple Rain* album and film. Both are nearly the exact same tempo of about 98 beats per minute, which can be felt in double time at 196. They also have similar orchestration: "Let's Go Crazy" opens with sustained organ chords and Prince's famous sermon beginning: "Dearly beloved, we are gathered here today to get through this thing called life." Monáe's "Americans" opens with stacked vocal harmonies, promising listeners that they'll "find a way to Heaven." In terms of narrative arc, however, "Let's Go Crazy" and "Americans" are placed differently in their respective musical-dramatic projects. "Let's Go Crazy" opens the album (and film) *Purple Rain*, introducing us to its cast of characters getting ready and making their way to Minneapolis's First Avenue club, the central setting for the film. "Americans" comes at the end of the *Dirty Computer* album, during the final credits of the "emotion picture," after the film's characters have escaped the prison/institution for a life of freedom. When Monáe sings, at the end of the song's chorus, "I'm not crazy, baby, I'm American," perhaps she is singing for all of the freaks, all those wanting to live a "crazy classic life," those "dirty computers" that the rest of the work introduces us to.

For Monáe as an artist, then, the past has multiple resonances. The slightly distant past of the 1960s and 1970s can be a musical and political resource and source of inspiration. Her collaborations with and homages to Prince and Stevie Wonder situate her in an honored narrative of Black musical genius stretching back several decades and continuing into the twenty-first century. In the film and album *Dirty Computer*, a greater emphasis is placed on the personal memories that Monáe, Jane 57821, and the rest of us "dirty computers" possess. Perhaps Monáe is suggesting that these personal memories are not faulty and cannot be deleted, denied, or ignored so easily. Instead, as she demonstrates with her prison break at the end of the film, these memories of the past can be used as a resource to imagine and enact a more liberated future, even in a time of darkness.[56]

Back to the Way It Was

Born Michael Eugene Archer in 1974 in Richmond, Virginia, the musical artist known as D'Angelo came onto the music scene in the mid-1990s, when he was marketed as a "neo-soul" musician. The music executive Kedar Massenburg is credited with popularizing the term and applying it to two artists that he managed—D'Angelo and Erykah Badu—though the term would eventually also be applied to other musicians like Angie Stone, Jaguar Wright, Jill Scott, and even John Legend. To some, the "neo" in the genre's name marked a rupture between the originators of the genre of soul music and musical practice in the 1990s. Critics of this term instead viewed music by D'Angelo, Badu, and other related artists as proceeding directly in an unbroken lineage from an earlier soul music past and acknowledged greats like Sam Cooke, Smokey Robinson, and Aretha Franklin. In an article examining the genre, Phillip Lamarr Cunningham takes direct aim at its name, summarizing the concerns of many of the artists who felt the term was an inaccurate description of Black musical history: "What makes the term so problematic is the popular belief that it is a new form of R&B/soul rather than a continuance of it. However, as I contend here, neo-soul is just soul music that both reflects and advances the tradition."[57] For our purposes in this book, I am less interested in arbitrating this debate than I am in noting that a widespread consensus existed that D'Angelo's music in the 1990s was closely related to the Black popular music past.

The past, however, is a diverse resource for artists and listeners to engage with. What aspects of the past were so-called "neo-soul" artists like D'Angelo and their listeners hearing during the genre's height of popularity in the late 1990s? In 1995, D'Angelo released his debut album *Brown Sugar*, and the title track and its accompanying music video provide one clear example of how the past in soul music is invoked by artists. The video opens with a conversation between D'Angelo and an older African American man in an elevator who immediately begins to tell D'Angelo about "Back in the days, when I was a teenager, brother." The man continues: "Awww, shoot, brother, you should have been around in those days, those were the good old days." D'Angelo is shy and relatively unresponsive, but he finishes their conversation with, "Alright, pop." However, the two men get off the elevator at the same floor, and are in fact heading to the same place, the club where D'Angelo will be giving the performance that makes up the main action of the video: the implication being that the same type of "back in the days" feeling the older man spoke about will also be provided here. The performance venue is a small club with red curtains. The club's tables have individual lamps, and the musicians are backlit onstage by overhead lights and shot such that their faces are sometimes only a faint outline in shadows. D'Angelo is accompanied onstage by an electric bass player and drummer, while he performs on a Wurlitzer electric piano, the brand name of which is prominently displayed at the 3:20 mark of the video. The band settles into a slow, sparse, 83-beats-per-minute soul groove while D'Angelo on vocals extols the virtues of "brown sugar," likely meant to refer both to sexual attraction and to a strain of marijuana. The crowd listening to his performance certainly seems to be under the influence of both of these mind-altering substances: camera shots switch back and forth between the band onstage, audience members nodding their heads appreciatively to the music, and couples dancing together or hooking up in the club's bathroom, all while a persistent cloud of smoke adds visual atmosphere. "Brown Sugar" presents one vision of the Black popular music past that D'Angelo was interested in re-creating: the good life, romantic love and sexuality, head-nodding grooves, obvious chops on conventional instruments, and highly skilled melismatic vocals.

Voodoo, the follow-up to *Brown Sugar*, was released in 2000 and was even more commercially and critically successful than its predecessor. Following the album's release in January, D'Angelo and a supporting cast of musicians including Questlove, trumpeter Roy Hargrove, and bassist Pino Palladino embarked on an ambitious tour in the spring, summer, and early fall of 2000. One stretch saw them perform twenty-seven shows in twenty-six cities in the span of only thirty-nine days. Despite this brutal schedule, the show received rave reviews, drawing comparisons to performances by Marvin Gaye, Sly and the Family Stone, and Parliament-Funkadelic. Unfortunately, a variety of personal and health problems led to D'Angelo taking a roughly decade-long hiatus from performing and recording for the rest of the 2000s and the early years of the 2010s. However, during the first decade of the 2000s, other artists

The Past, Activism, and Recent Black Popular Music 173

Album cover for D'Angelo and The Vanguard's *Black Messiah*, 2014.

were still carrying the torch of recordings and live performances that paid obvious homage to R&B history of the 1960s and 1970s, including, as we have already seen, Prince and Janelle Monáe, along with fellow "neo-soul" artists like Erykah Badu.

D'Angelo made an unexpected return to prominence in the music industry with the December 2014 release of *Black Messiah*. Little advance promotional or publicity work was done prior to the album's release, and the enthusiastic fans and critics that D'Angelo had cultivated earlier in his career were met with a slightly inscrutable product. Shot in black-and-white, the cover photo of *Black Messiah* shows no faces or bodies, only hands raised in the air, possibly in a gesture of surrender, praise, or supplication—though closer inspection reveals two of the hands are clenched into fists in a gesture of defiance often associated with calls for Black power.[58] D'Angelo's title is provocative, perhaps paralleling the Isaac Hayes album *Black Moses* from 1971. On that classic album from the soul music canon, the cover unfolds into a large photograph in the shape of a cross, with Hayes dressed in a hooded robe and sandals with his arms open, seemingly beckoning viewers and listeners to him.[59] For some listeners, D'Angelo's title might have also called to mind a cult favorite but relatively obscure Cannonball Adderley live album *The Black Messiah*, also released in 1971. Combining these two words, "Black" and "Messiah" together forces the listener to confront some questions: in response to what has the Black Messiah returned? Who is the Black Messiah here to redeem? And is D'Angelo himself claiming to be the Black Messiah? If curious listeners wanted to know the answers to these questions, they had to buy the CD in which D'Angelo explains what he means by this title on the first page of the liner notes:

> Some will jump to the conclusion that I'm calling myself a Black Messiah. For me, the title is about all of us. It's about the world. It's about an idea we can all aspire to. We should all aspire to be a Black Messiah.
>
> It's about people rising up in Ferguson and in Egypt and in Occupy Wall Street and in every place where a community has had enough and decides to make change happen. It's not about praising one charismatic leader but celebrating thousands of them. Not every song on this album is politically charged (though many are), but calling this album *Black Messiah* creates a landscape where these songs can live to the fullest. *Black Messiah* is not one man. It's a feeling that, collectively, we are all that leader.

Listeners with a background in the history of government intervention in the civil rights movement of the 1960s and 1970s—at least some percentage of the target audience for this album—would also have recognized "Black Messiah" as a term from J. Edgar Hoover and the FBI's COINTELPRO (counterintelligence program) designed to stifle radical movements. In a March 1968 internal directive, one of the long-range goals of COINTELPRO was stated as to "prevent the rise of a messiah who could unify, and electrify, the militant black nationalist movement."[60] The Black Panther leader Fred Hampton might have been one of these figures, and, true to the goals of COINTELPRO, he was shot and killed by Chicago police under highly questionable circumstances on December 4, 1969.[61] While Hampton's death is not as well known in the general public as those of Martin Luther King Jr., Malcolm X, or Medgar Evers, his legacy is often referred to in recent Black popular music, with the rapper Jay-Z claiming a kinship to Hampton on his 2011 collaboration with Kanye West, "Murder to Excellence," based on the fact that Jay-Z was born on the same day as Hampton's assassination. It is not insignificant, then, that D'Angelo chooses to include a speech from Fred Hampton on "1000 Deaths," the second track on *Black Messiah*. The lyrics to the song's chorus could be seen as a fitting eulogy for Hampton: "A coward dies a thousand times / but a soldier only dies just once." Listeners who did not initially make these connections would still have recourse to sites like Genius, Twitter, and Wikipedia, which can serve as an explanation for these references, as well as an interpretive community for listeners to argue and debate the meaning of these texts. While I do not wish to reproduce a naïve techno-utopianism, it is clear that these sites do provide new forums for commentary, explication, and interpretation that were not possible under previous media regimes.[62]

The timing of the release of *Black Messiah* is also critical for understanding its reception, its message, and the way it depends on listeners making connections between present-day situations and the past. While D'Angelo had not released a studio album since 2000's *Voodoo*, *Black Messiah* had been in the works for several years, and at least one of the reasons motivating its release in December 2014 was the non-indictment of Ferguson police officer Darrell Wilson that same month, in connection with the death of Michael Brown. *Black Messiah* was apparently rushed into release in response to this non-indictment, without any of the usual long-term promotion that typically accompanies a new release. Perhaps this rush is evidence that D'Angelo was ready to claim a position for himself as a leader in the long tradition of Black activism. It is no accident that in one of the few interviews the notoriously media-shy D'Angelo did to promote *Black Messiah*, he is in the company of Bobby Seale, a former Black Panthers leader, and it is Seale's ability to inspire protests for political and social change that most interests D'Angelo during this conversation. For a June 2015 article, Seale, D'Angelo, and a *New York Times* reporter drove around Oakland, California, as Seale pointed out important sites in the history of the Black Panthers. In the joint interview that *Times* journalist Dan Hyman conducted with D'Angelo and Seale, D'Angelo laments the paucity of artists who seem to be addressing important social issues in 2015: "Kendrick Lamar, he's an example of someone who is young and actually trying to say something. Who else? You got Young Jeezy and Young Thug. You know what I'm saying? It's stupid. It's ridiculous."[63] D'Angelo explains further:

> Now more than ever is the need to sing about [social change] and to write songs about [social change]. And no one's doing it. There's only a chosen couple of people. I think it just takes one little snowflake to start a snowball to go down the hill. My contribution and say, Kendrick Lamar's and some chosen others start the snowball. That's all I can hope for. I don't know if I'm comfortable being quote-unquote a leader. But I do realize and understand that my role as a musician, and

in the medium that I am, that people are listening to me. Kids are listening to me. We have power to influence minds and influence lives.

However, only a few of the songs on *Black Messiah* actually seem to address questions of racism, police brutality, or equality directly in their lyrics. One of the few that does is "The Charade," a three-minute track with a prominent melody in the bass guitar and electric sitar, and D'Angelo singing in falsetto. In a line from the chorus, D'Angelo sings: "All we wanted was a chance to talk / 'stead we only got outlined in chalk." When I saw D'Angelo perform "The Charade" during his concert at the Royal Oak Theatre outside of Detroit on June 27, 2015, he introduced this song by dedicating it to Michael Brown and other victims of police brutality. Yet when it came time to sing the chorus's lyrics, which certainly could have acted as a rallying cry for the enthusiastic, racially diverse audience at this concert, he only half-sang the lyrics into the microphone, turning away and letting his back-up singers sing the lines for him. I do not want to overgeneralize from this one ethnographic observation, but it points to a general problem in the reception of *Black Messiah*: many of the lyrics on the album are incredibly difficult to make out, due either to D'Angelo's lack of enunciation—his mumbling, as he calls it in interviews—or his layering and layering of overdubbed harmony voices that obscures the text. This seems to be a deliberate aesthetic choice by D'Angelo and not an example of "bad" or "incompetent" performing or recording. D'Angelo clearly thought deeply about the production of this album, even including a kind of manifesto in the liner notes explaining: "No digital 'plug-ins' of any kind were used in this recording. All of the recording, processing, effects and mixing was done in the analog domain using tape and mostly vintage equipment. For best results, listen at maximum volume." However, text intelligibility is an issue that ordinary listeners and professional critics have lamented, and it perhaps points to D'Angelo's general reluctance to take a leading role as a musical or activist figure, despite his claim in the 2015 interview with Bobby Seale. While D'Angelo toured the United States and Europe in support of *Black Messiah* in 2015, playing theatres and festivals, he has otherwise kept a relatively low profile in the years since, only occasionally showing up on other artists' recordings and releasing one song under his own name, a contribution to the Daniel Lanois–produced soundtrack to the video game *Red Dead Redemption 2*. If activism around the Black Lives Matter movement in 2014 inspired the release of *Black Messiah*, the large-scale protests in 2020 did not motivate a similar musical response from D'Angelo.

However, as with his earlier hiatus, it is not as though D'Angelo's absence leaves the popular music scene lacking for artists who strongly engage with the past of funk, soul, and R&B from the 1960s and 1970s as an important legacy for musicians in the twenty-first century. The uses of the past by these artists varies widely: at least some of the works of Prince, Janelle Monáe, and D'Angelo used musical invocations of the past as a direct or indirect commentary on contemporary political struggles. For other artists, however, references to the musical past are still ubiquitous, but seem to be more about the pleasures of pastiche and showing off musical chops. Perhaps the clearest example of this would be the 2014 song "Uptown Funk" by Mark Ronson and Bruno Mars, which quickly became one of the most popular songs of the 2010s. While the song interpolates a vocal hook from a 2012 track by the rapper Trinidad James, journalists and critics have pointed out the instrumental and timbral references to a panopoly of funk artists from the late 1970s and early 1980s, including the Gap Band, Cameo, Morris Day and the Time, and Zapp. Mars has continued to reference music from this time period in his other recordings to phenomenal pop success: such as his multiple Grammy-winning album *24K Magic* and his 2021 collaboration with Anderson .Paak, *An Evening with Silk Sonic*, an album that also features narration from funk legend Bootsy Collins. These invocations, however, do not seem to be politically motivated; Mars has largely steered clear of politics and has not been a prominent advocate for social causes. His lyrics focus on the ostensibly nonpolitical topics of dancing, partying, and sexual pleasure. If harnessing music of the past to inspire energy for contemporary political and social movements does not characterize Mars's work, he certainly does provide an example of a musician who has been able to sonically re-create music of the past to catapult himself to widespread popularity.[64]

Another pop megastar, however, has occasionally made invocations of the Black (musical) past of the 1960s and 1970s as a political statement. Beyoncé's every utterance, interview, song, album, and live performance are dissected by her large group of enthusiastic fans and a growing collection of engaged scholars.[65] Her musical palette is wide and diverse, but perhaps her most celebrated invocation of the Black past in her performance was not even audible. In February 2016, Beyoncé performed at the Super Bowl halftime show for a large, worldwide audience. Though the British rock band Coldplay was ostensibly the headliner (and Bruno Mars and Mark Ronson performed "Uptown Funk" just before her appearance), Beyoncé's performance, accompanied by a drum line and thirty Black female back-up dancers, received far more attention than these other artists. She sang an excerpt from her song "Formation," whose controversial video had just been released on YouTube the same weekend as the Super Bowl. The lyrics of "Formation" testify to Black Southern female empowerment, and several images from the video allude to contemporary protests against police violence. In this context, the outfits her back-up dancers wore during the Super Bowl—monochromatic black leather outfits and high-heel combat boots, with natural hair peeking out from the sides of the tight-fitting berets they wore on their heads—were widely perceived as referencing the sartorial style and radical politics of the Black Panther Party from the 1960s and 1970s. Lordi explains the parallels between this past moment and our contemporary world to hypothesize about why artists might be drawn to referencing the past in their work: "Insofar as soul artists working in the 1960s and 1970s were navigating a sociopolitical landscape that resembles our own—in its spectacular anti-black violence as well as its radical mobilization—the soul revival reflects an effort to reclaim soul artists as models of expressing black resistance, joy, and togetherness through the medium of popular song."[66] In addition to responding directly to a specific political moment, invocations of the Black musical past by artists like Prince, Beyoncé, Monáe, D'Angelo, and Mars also fit the widespread historical consciousness that describes a variety of recent and historical engagements with the popular music past, across boundaries of race, gender, generation, and genre.

CONCLUSION

The Future of Old Music

Musical engagements with history are not themselves consigned to the past; despite the prevalence of the ideology of newness in much popular music discourse, such engagements are likely to remain a vibrant and substantial part of popular music culture. The past, however, is not singular and uniform; scholars will especially want to pay attention to *which* past or pasts are evoked by musicians and reckoned with by listeners and critics, which pasts are intelligible and help to guide thought and action in the present.

Consider a hip-hop album that gained widespread critical acclaim: *Eve*, released in 2019, by the North Carolina–based rapper Rapsody. One of the features of the album that listeners are likely to notice first is that every one of its tracks—other than an interlude featuring the spoken word artist Reyna Biddy—is named after an important woman from Black political, musical, or pop cultural history. Over the course of the album, Rapsody and her collaborators are highly interested in situating her music in relation to the past and to a narrative of Black musical and social history. They do this in a multitude of ways: celebrated guest artists, production choices, samples, and, perhaps above all, copious and intricate lyrical references. In recognition of her lyrical skill as an MC, Rapsody was named "Lyricist of the Year" at the 2020 BET Hip Hop Awards. What sets *Eve* apart from other engagements with history that we have examined thus far in this book is that there are at least two distinct eras of the past that are referenced in *Eve*.

To be sure, there are clear references to the "golden age" of 1960s and 1970s music and Black social activism, as we have already seen and discussed in a wide variety of hip-hop and R&B. The album opens with a sample of Nina Simone's 1965 cover of the antilynching song "Strange Fruit," a song originally composed by Abel Meeropol and famously performed by Billie Holiday beginning in 1939.[1] Rapsody's track is simply titled "Nina," and Rapsody has spoken eloquently about her personal discovery of and admiration for the music and activism of Simone.[2] Several further references on *Eve* make clear that Rapsody is interested in linking her life and work to the crucial period of Black activism in the 1960s and 1970s. A lyric on "Nina" imagines an aging member of the Black Panthers asking, "Who gonna come after us?" with the implication that it is Rapsody and members of her generation who will carry on the struggle. Another song later on the album is titled "Myrlie" after Myrlie Evers, widow of the assassinated civil rights leader Medgar Evers. In this song, Rapsody expresses clear links between the deaths of Black men like Evers, Malcolm X, Martin Luther King Jr. and more recent deaths of Eric Garner and Trayvon Martin. In keeping with the album's female-centered focus, the song's lyrics primarily describe the families who mourn for these lost Black men, with Rapsody imagining that she herself might someday be in the position of Myrlie Evers, Betty Shabazz, or Coretta Scott King:

> We saw people cry, think about all our people's wives
> Raise the kids in a world they know ain't safe to live
> Like Myrlie, emergency
> The mirror me said I could be her, too, the day I say "I do."

The album's final track is titled "Afeni" after Afeni Shakur, Black Panther and activist in the late 1960s and early 1970s—but perhaps best known in hip-hop culture for being the mother of rapper Tupac Shakur. A live performance of Tupac performing his song "Keep Ya Head Up" is sampled on "Afeni," further signaling this connection for listeners. Tupac Shakur is a significant figure in hip-hop culture—and perhaps for Rapsody herself—not only because he came to aesthetic and commercial prominence in the 1990s, but also because he could trace a direct family connection back to this venerated earlier time of Black activism.[3]

Indeed, we could view Tupac as a fulcrum around which the album turns; in addition to the earlier activist eras that are part of the legacy that he inherited and expressed in his music, the 1990s time period of Tupac's popularity and success as an artist is also strongly evoked in *Eve*. Rapsody was born in 1983. She came to adolescence in the 1990s and, on this album released in 2019, she references, plays with, signifies on, and pays tribute to the popular culture that she grew up with from that time period. Therefore, a more recent canon of heroes and venerated figures is also constructed in this album. One song takes its name from the character played by Queen Latifah in the 1996 film *Set It Off* ("Cleo"); another ("Hatshepsut") features a guest appearance from Latifah herself, someone whose musical activism around Black and female empowerment were highly prominent in popular culture in the late 1980s and 1990s.[4] The song "Whoopi," named for the comedian and actress Whoopi Goldberg, includes a clever pun on the title of her biggest popular culture success, the 1992 film *Sister Act*. "Whoopi" also samples the bass line and beer bottle riff from Herbie Hancock's 1973 recording of "Watermelon Man," the second track on Hancock's canonical jazz-funk album, *Head Hunters*.[5]

The album's first single, "Ibithaj," is a direct call back to the 1995 track "Liquid Swords" by GZA, member of the Wu-Tang Clan hip-hop collective. On this song, Rapsody features the R&B artist D'Angelo—in a rare guest appearance—singing a vocal hook from "Liquid Swords" and GZA also performs a guest verse. In addition to having two highly celebrated artists of the 1990s hip-hop/R&B continuum contribute to this song, Rapsody's producer 9th Wonder builds the track for "Ibithaj" around the same sample that RZA used in the construction of "Liquid Swords" from 1995: Willie Mitchell's 1967 recording of "Groovin'." In the chorus for "Ibithaj," Rapsody adapts a line from another mid-1990s hip-hop classic, "Things Done Changed" by the Notorious B.I.G. (born Christopher Wallace in 1972). Biggie's line "Back in the days when n***as had waves / Cazal shades and corn braids" becomes "Back in the days when n***as wore fades / silk-tied caps just tryna catch a wave" for Rapsody. What is notable is not just that Rapsody honors the Notorious B.I.G. by mimicking his line, but that both rappers use this "back in the days" lyrical construction to describe a warmly remembered scene from the past. Cazal eyeglasses were an iconic staple of Darryl McDaniels from hip-hop superstars Run-DMC, whose height of popularity overlapped with Wallace's youth in the 1980s. As the title of his song makes clear, a radical shift had happened from this nostalgic childhood scene to the early 1990s adulthood that Biggie describes in the rest of the song's lyrics: a time of desperate violence spurred on by the crack epidemic.[6] In "Things Done Changed," differences in circumstances and lifestyles even have the potential to rupture family bonds: "Back in the days our parents used to take care of us / Look at 'em now, they even fucking scared of us," a potential development that seems especially significant since, as we have seen, families are a key site where artists and listeners are enculturated into the Black musical past they often draw upon in their later creative work and engagement with the genre of hip-hop. But Biggie's 1990s adulthood is the time of Rapsody's youth, and she recalls the music and culture of that time period fondly, through her explicit homage to the Notorious B.I.G., the Wu-Tang Clan, and guest appearance by

D'Angelo on this particular track—as well as her engagement with 1990s pop culture on other songs mentioned above. Rapsody's *Eve* follows the path we explored in chapters 4 and 5: an evocation of the 1960s and 1970s musical and political past by rappers and R&B artists through means such as sampling, timbre, and lyrical references, but she adds to this a deep awareness of a more recent past in the hip-hop and pop cultural world of the 1990s.

The canon constructed here by Rapsody and her collaborators is largely, if not exclusively, an African American one, but listeners from a wide variety of backgrounds and engaging with a wide variety of genres continue to find deep meaning in the musical past. For many younger musicians and listeners interacting with popular music in the twenty-first century, the past is not a foreign country, especially given how easily the digitization of music and streaming services offer access to the raw materials of history—like sound recordings—at least for the growing number of people with access to computers, smartphones, and broadband internet.

The 2010 film *The Social Network* is another example of a pop culture text that illustrates and depends on the relationship of Millennials to popular music history. In the film's final scene, Jesse Eisenberg, who plays Facebook founder Mark Zuckerberg in a fictionalized depiction of the company's founding, is by himself in a conference room at a law firm. The depositions for the two lawsuits that provide a framing device for the film have concluded for the day, but Eisenberg remains seated, alone, with his laptop open, the only sound coming from the faint hum of the fluorescent lights. There is a window of what appears to be computer code open on his laptop, but instead of working, he goes to his browser window, which has the Facebook website loaded. He navigates to the search bar and types in "Erica Albright," the person who dumped him in the first scene of the film for being, according to her, an "asshole." This rejection begins the sequence of events that make up the action of the film, as Zuckerberg stays up working late that night creating Facemash, the eventual precursor to Facebook.[7]

Back in the conference room, Eisenberg clicks on the text hyperlinked as "Add Erica as a friend." He pauses for a second with his mouse hovering over the blue "Send Request" box. When he clicks to confirm the friend request, a groove consisting of drums, piano, and an insistent bass riff comes in on the film's soundtrack. A few seconds later, as Eisenberg refreshes his browser window, an early synthesizer with an oboe-like sound called the clavioline joins the groove. For the next minute, Eisenberg sits at the conference table staring at his laptop screen, occasionally refreshing the page to see if Albright has accepted his friend request. David Fincher, the film's director, superimposes intertitles—small bits of text—on top of the shot of Eisenberg, text which serves to tell viewers what happens to various characters after the events of the film. Eventually, a voice enters on the music track, and though he is singing in falsetto, viewers of the film would probably recognize one of the most iconic voices in the history of recorded music as he asks, in the song's opening line: "How does it feel to be one of the beautiful people?" In fact, the singer performing that line was ranked by *Rolling Stone* magazine as #5 on their list of "100 Greatest Singers of All Time" published in 2008, only two years before the release of *The Social Network*: a list typical of the remembrance and veneration of prior figures in popular music history that characterizes the historical consciousness in popular music analyzed in this book.

As the song works its way through the first verse, the intertitles tell us that the Winklevoss twins and Eduardo Saverin, former classmates of Zuckerberg's at Harvard, settled their lawsuits with Zuckerberg and that Saverin was eventually credited with being a cofounder of Facebook. Eisenberg remains seated, expressionless, refreshing his browser window to check on the status of his friend request. Two final intertitles close the film. The first reads: "Facebook has 500 million members in 207 countries. It's currently valued at 25 billion dollars."[8] Fincher switches back to a shot of the laptop. Eisenberg is looking at Albright's profile picture on her Facebook page, refreshing the browser again to see if she has accepted his friend request. The final shot of the film has Eisenberg in focus in the right part of the frame, with an out-of-focus background as white text on the left part of the screen reads: "Mark Zuckerberg is the youngest billionaire in the world." The screen fades to black for the credits, but the song on the soundtrack keeps going. As the film's credits begin to roll, the song reaches its triumphant chorus:

> Baby, you're a rich man!
> Baby, you're a rich man!
> Baby, you're a rich man, too!

The song is "Baby You're a Rich Man" by the Beatles, with lead vocals by John Lennon. I was surprised by its usage for the conclusion of *The Social Network* for several reasons. First, "Baby You're a Rich Man" is not one of the Beatles' more well-known songs. It was released as a B-side to the single "All You Need is Love" in 1967 and included on the US version of the soundtrack to their film *Magical Mystery Tour*. However, *Magical Mystery Tour* is one of the Beatles' most-overlooked albums, passed over by fans and critics in favor of the concept album *Sgt. Pepper's Lonely Hearts Club Band* (which immediately preceded it in the spring of 1967) and the sprawling experiments of *The White Album* (a double album released in 1968).[9] Of the 213 songs the Beatles recorded over the course of their career, "Baby You're a Rich Man" is not often heard on the radio, not frequently played as "background music" at grocery stores or pharmacies, rarely encountered on jukeboxes (possibly because it was not included on either *1967–1970* or *1*, two of the most widely circulated Beatles compilation albums), has been covered by comparatively few artists, and does not regularly appear on the set lists of tribute bands.[10] If there is a canon of venerated classic rock from the past that these sources, among others, have helped to construct, "Baby You're a Rich Man" is not exactly a charter member of it.

Second, the message of the song also seems to be at odds with the film and its closing scene. Various scholars have discussed the use of preexisting songs in films, as opposed to newly composed scores; Ramsey notes that such use "encourages perceivers to make external associations with the song in question, and these associations become part of the cultural transaction occurring between the film and its audience."[11] While there is no doubt that Zuckerberg is literally "a rich man"—the final intertitle before the chorus comes thundering in reminds us that Zuckerberg is a billionaire—many fans of the Beatles have interpreted the song to be more in line with "1960s" values. Richness, in this interpretation, has to do more with spiritual awareness and hipness, rather than with material wealth. This is exactly the opposite of how Zuckerberg is portrayed in the film. Zuckerberg is emphatically not "one of the beautiful people" that Lennon is singing about; the end of the film presents him as wealthy, but alone, seeking human connection by refreshing the browser on his laptop. Perhaps this itself is a commentary on the ultimately empty promises of the 1960s: that the hip, community-minded counterculturalists all end up as lonely capitalists, not so different from Zuckerberg building his incredible wealth by monetizing our need for the simulacrum of human connection that social networks provide.

Additionally, the Beatles—or, rather, the estate of the Beatles, run in a tenuous partnership by Paul McCartney, Ringo Starr, and the widows of John Lennon and George Harrison—are also notoriously reluctant to allow their songs to be licensed for usage in advertisements, television shows, or films. Director David Fincher must have somehow convinced them to allow him to include the song, almost certainly by negotiating a deal that added significantly to the budget of the film. Not only did Fincher likely pay a great deal of money to use "Baby You're a Rich Man," but he decided not to use music written by the composers of the film's score, Trent Reznor and Atticus Ross, whose music had served as nearly all of the film's music up to that point, and which would eventually earn the duo an Oscar for Best Original Score. Reznor is the leader of the industrial rock band Nine Inch Nails, which also features Ross as a member. Fincher already had two literal rock stars on his payroll, but he still chose to license a song by the Beatles.

However, what was most surprising to me was that, in a movie about youth culture in the first decade of the twenty-first century, music from forty years earlier would get the final word. The usage of "Baby You're a Rich Man" could be interpreted in any number of ways, and I will not attempt to catalogue the various meanings it could have for viewers of the film. What I will say, following the work of musicologist Susan McClary, is that interpretation depends on intelligibility.[12] "Baby You're a Rich Man" does not have one transparent meaning; instead, filmgoers have to learn the musical and cultural codes in which this song is participating in order to have any understanding of its usage at the end of Fincher's film. They also have to be aware of the social and historical matrix in which "Baby You're a Rich Man" and other popular music from the 1960s and 1970s has functioned: a matrix that includes things like popular music museums, "classic rock," "oldies," and "throwback" radio stations, sampling in hip-hop, and tribute bands. The use of "Baby You're a Rich Man" is what film music scholars would call nondiegetic music: it is not audible to the characters in the film—in this case Mark Zuckerberg, as played by Jesse Eisenberg. The bet that Fincher makes in *The Social Network* is both that audience members would understand "Baby You're a Rich Man" (from 1967) and also that audience members would place Zuckerberg himself in the same universe in which—as a former Harvard student in the first decade of the 2000s, born in 1984 to baby boomer parents and growing up in a world in which classic rock music was inescapable—he would have understood this sound. Fincher must have believed that this song from forty-three years before would still be relevant to the film's wide audience and that it would function as a meaningful commentary on the lives of the Millennial generation characters the film chronicles.

But perhaps I should not have been surprised. After all, this is the same bet on familiarity, relevance, and reverence hip-hop producers make when they continue to sample music from the 1960s and 1970s in their new songs, or when hip-hop and R&B musicians invoke the sound world of 1970s soul and funk without directly sampling music from this era (and negotiating the high fees to do so). It is why tribute bands performing faithful, note-for-note copies of rock songs from the 1960s and 1970s still find enthusiastic audiences. It is why artists like Ella Fitzgerald, Willie Nelson, and Bob Dylan recorded albums of standards from the Great American Songbook, decades after these songs were originally written and first performed. And it is why Miles Davis's decision to stop performing this material in live performances in the late 1960s was such a controversial one: because improvising on the melodies and chord structures of pop songs from ten, twenty, thirty, or even forty years earlier—and thereby constantly reminding listeners of popular music history—was a key part of jazz performance practice.

One of the reasons I talk about birthdates in this book is to clearly situate artists and listeners in terms of their relationship to popular music of various time periods. I also want to acknowledge my own position as a scholar (and consumer) of engagements with the popular music past. I was born at a time quite similar to that of many of the artists and figures that I discuss in this book. Zuckerberg and Ben Shapiro—the right-wing pundit whose criticism of Monáe we examined in the introduction—were both born in 1984, one year after me. Rapsody, born on January 21, 1983, is exactly a week younger than I am. Other artists I consider in this book like Janelle Monáe, Kendrick Lamar, Bruno Mars, and Beyoncé were all born within a few years of me in the 1980s. As of this writing, all of us are in the process of exiting the stage of life that can be credibly described as "youth": the time period that, according to the ideology of newness, is supposed to be coterminous with an interest in popular music. Yet we all retain deep personal and professional relationships with the popular music past and the popular music present. I do not want to overstate my kinship to these figures based solely on our similarities in age. I grew up in a white, middle-class household and was privileged enough to receive degrees from two Ivy League universities. I also certainly was not a child star like Beyoncé; clearly her youth and adolescence were very different from mine—and likely very different from those of anyone reading this book. Nevertheless, technology and the mass distribution of popular culture can at least partially help bridge these divides. My interest in how popular musicians and listeners engage with the past is in part inspired by my own obsession with the musical past. Some of the mid to late 1990s popular culture that Rapsody references in *Eve*—the Notorious B.I.G., the Wu-Tang Clan, Erykah Badu, the film *Sister Act*—is culture that I also consumed as an adolescent and for which I still feel a sense of warmth and nostalgia. The 1970s soul and funk constantly evoked and reused by hip-hop artists and contemporary R&B musicians is music I discovered as a relic from the past in my teens and early twenties. To me as a listener, this was a qualitatively "better" type of the music than the majority of the music that was popular at the time, around the turn of the millennium, and it remains music that I enjoy listening to far more than the most popular of contemporary pop music in the 2020s. Classic rock from the Beatles, Bob Dylan, Led Zeppelin, and Pink Floyd served a similar role in my teenage years. However, the story of my listening to and finding deep meaning in the popular music past is certainly not unique to me; it is shared by a vast community of listeners and fans, some of whom end up becoming performing musicians themselves. The very real differences between our lives and upbringings, musical or otherwise, is evidence for my main argument: that historical consciousness is a widespread characteristic of a variety of experiences with popular music culture. Often, the specific past that is referenced in popular music comes from the years around the end of the 1960s and the beginning of the 1970s. However, examples of the work of musicians like Bruno Mars and Rapsody show that we have acquired enough distance from the 1980s and 1990s for music and culture from these decades to be viewed and venerated as historical. Perhaps this suggests that a knowledge of and interest in the past—variously conceived and with different landmarks, to be sure—is likely to remain a persistent feature of popular music culture in the future.

NOTES

Introduction

1. Katherine Meizel, *Idolized: Music, Media, and Identity in American Idol* (Bloomington: Indiana University Press, 2011).
2. Elijah Wald, *How the Beatles Destroyed Rock 'n' Roll: An Alternative History of American Popular Music* (New York: Oxford University Press, 2009), 27.
3. Issy Sampson, "Hug Life: Has Rap's 'Baby' Obsession Reached Its Peak?" *The Guardian*, September 28, 2019. https://www.theguardian.com/music/2019/sep/28/rap-hip-hop-dababy-lil-uzi-vert-baby-soulja-lil-kim-bow-wow.
4. Zack Linly, "Is Today's Hip-Hop Trash or Are We Just Getting Old? Spoiler Alert: The Answer is 'Yes,'" *The Root*, February 1, 2018. https://www.theroot.com/is-today-s-hip-hop-trash-or-are-we-just-getting-old-sp-1822560290.
5. For a discussion of the frequent sampling of Nina Simone in hip-hop, see Salamishah Tillet, "Strange Sampling: Nina Simone and Her Hip-Hop Children," *American Quarterly* 66, no. 1 (2014): 119–37.
6. Sheldon Pearce's 8.4 rating (on a ten-point scale) of *4:44* on the music review site *Pitchfork* is typical of this positive response: "It only takes Jay-Z 36 minutes to create the historical artifact he's wanted to make for years, a tell-all document to be hung in the halls of rap about infidelity and outgrowing friends, the way family shapes us and the way we carry those burdens into parenthood, and about evolving into more complete versions of ourselves." For this book's discussion of the idea that popular music is viewed as appropriate for canonization and commemoration, Pearce's description of *4:44* as an "historical artifact" fit to be "hung in the halls of rap" is especially noteworthy. See Sheldon Pearce, "Jay-Z, *4:44*," *Pitchfork*, July 5, 2017. https://pitchfork.com/reviews/albums/jay-z-444/.
7. Joseph Schloss's *Making Beats: The Art of Sample-Based Hip-Hop* (Middletown, CT: Wesleyan University Press, 2004) is the classic study of this kind of hip-hop beat-making.
8. Michael Eric Dyson, *Jay-Z: Made in America* (New York: St. Martin's Press, 2019), 147. See also the extensive discussion of Black masculinity in hip-hop in Miles White, *From Jim Crow to Jay-Z: Race, Rap, and the Performance of Masculinity* (Urbana: University of Illinois Press, 2011).

9. Andy Greene, "The Who Announce Dates for 2022 North American Tour," *Rolling Stone*, February 7, 2022. https://www.rollingstone.com/music/music-news/the-who-2022-tour-pete-townshend-interview-1294697/.

10. The US Constitution, dating from 1787, enshrines copyright protection in Article 1, Section 8, Clause 8, giving Congress the power "To promote the Progress of Science and useful Arts, by securing for limited Times to Authors and Inventors the exclusive Right to their respective Writings and Discoveries." As Lawrence Lessig explains in *Free Culture: How Big Media Uses Technology and the Law to Lock Down Culture and Control Creativity* (New York: Penguin, 2004), this "limited" copyright has been greatly expanded in recent decades.

11. J. Peter Burkholder, "Borrowing," in *Grove Music Online*, accessed February 24, 2020. https://doi-org.proxy2.library.illinois.edu/10.1093/gmo/9781561592630.article.52918.

12. Roy Shuker, *Understanding Popular Music Culture* (New York: Routledge, 2016).

13. John Strausbaugh, *Rock Til You Drop: The Decline from Rebellion to Nostalgia* (New York: Verso, 2001), 11.

14. Several works of scholarship have challenged this widespread view of the blues, by placing blues musicians and audiences firmly in the modern world of power, politics, technology, and agency. See Clyde Woods, *Development Arrested: The Blues and Plantation Power in the Mississippi Delta* (London: Verso, 1998); and Elijah Wald, *Escaping the Delta: Robert Johnson and the Invention of the Blues* (New York: HarperCollins, 2004).

15. On ragtime, see Wald, *How the Beatles Destroyed Rock 'n' Roll*; on jazz, see Kathy Ogren, *The Jazz Revolution* (New York: Oxford University Press, 1992); on rock 'n' roll, see Albin Zak, *I Don't Sound Like Nobody: Remaking Music in 1950s America* (Ann Arbor: University of Michigan Press, 2010); on disco, see Alice Echols, *Hot Stuff: Disco and the Remaking of American Culture* (New York: W.W. Norton, 2010); for a firsthand look at music censorship in the 1980s, see Tipper Gore, *Raising PG Kids in an X-Rated Society* (Nashville: Parthenon Press, 1987).

16. "Shapiro RIPS Obscene Feminist Music Video," *Ben Shapiro Show*, December 12, 2018. https://www.youtube.com/watch?v=f4U3JIbqhkg.

17. Barbara Kirshenblatt-Gimblett, "Theorizing Heritage," *Ethnomusicology* 39 (1995): 369–70.

18. Michel-Rolph Trouillot, *Silencing the Past* (Boston: Beacon Press, 1995), 19.

19. George Plasketes, "Pimp My Records: The Deluxe Dilemma and Edition Condition: Bonus, Betrayal, or Download Backlash?" *Popular Music and Society* Volume 31, no. 3 (2008): 389–93.

20. Rob Drew, *Karaoke Nights: An Ethnographic Rhapsody* (Walnut Creek, CA: AltaMira Press, 2001).

21. Jason Lipshutz, "Opinion: The Problem with the Tupac Hologram," *Billboard*, April 16, 2012. https://www.billboard.com/articles/columns/the-juice/494288/opinion-the-problem-with-the-tupac-hologram.

22. For example, U2 and the Rolling Stones were the top two highest-grossing live concert acts of the 2010s, according to *Pollstar*. Other long-established artists on this list include Bon Jovi (#5), Paul McCartney (#7), Bruce Springsteen and the E Street Band (#9), Roger Waters (#10), Elton John (#11), Metallica (#12), Guns n' Roses (#13), and The Eagles (#14). Katrina Nattress, "U2 And the Rolling Stones Are the Decade's Top Touring Artists," *iHeart*, November 26, 2019. https://www.iheart.com/content/2019-11-26-u2-and-the-rolling-stones-are-the-decades-top-touring-artists/.

23. James Sullivan, "Nas Introduces Harvard Fellowship," *Rolling Stone*, October 31, 2013. https://www.rollingstone.com/music/music-news/nas-introduces-harvard-fellowship-60396/. The introductory track to Nas's first album *Illmatic*, released in 1994, samples dialogue and the opening credits music from the 1982 Charlie Ahearn film *Wild Style*, a fictionalized depiction of the early years of hip-hop culture in New York that had already gained canonical status among hip-hop aficionados by the early 1990s. Nas's interest in hip-hop's past has been a consistent theme in his career.

24. Sarah Baker, Lauren Istvandity, and Raphäel Novak, *Curating Pop: Exhibiting Popular Music in the Museum* (New York: Bloomsbury, 2019).

25. In the case of Stax Records, the original building had been largely abandoned after Stax's bankruptcy in 1976 and was torn down in 1989. In a confluence of the growing historical consciousness that characterized popular music culture around the year 2000 and a push to revitalize this Black working-class neighborhood of Memphis, a replica building was constructed on the original site and the Stax Museum of American Soul Music opened to the public in May 2003. For a discussion of the tension between the stakeholders in this revitalization project, see Zandria F. Robinson, "After Stax: Race, Sound, and Neighborhood Revitalization," in *An Unseen Light: Black Struggles for Freedom in Memphis, Tennessee*, ed. Aram Goudsouzian and Charles W. McKinney Jr. (Lexington: University Press of Kentucky, 2018).

26. Simon Reynolds, *Retromania: Pop Culture's Addiction to Its Own Past* (New York: Faber and Faber, 2011), xviii–xix.

27. Reynolds, *Retromania*, xxi–xxii.

28. Tracy McMullen, *Haunthenticity: Musical Replay and the Fear of the Real* (Middletown, CT: Wesleyan University Press, 2019), 17.

29. Slavoj Žižek, *First as Tragedy, Then as Farce* (London: Verso, 2009). The global turn toward nationalist populism, most strongly epitomized by the election of Donald Trump as president of the United States and the vote for Great Britain to exit the European Union, could be viewed as a last-gasp attempt to consolidate a stable, bounded sense of identity in uncertain times.

30. Svetlana Boym, *The Future of Nostalgia* (New York: Basic Books, 2001).

31. Reynolds, *Retromania*, 403.

32. Moran has taken his Monk "tribute" on the road; I attended a performance of "In My Mind: Monk at Town Hall, 1959" on November 14, 2017, at the Krannert Center in Urbana, Illinois.

33. These questions were (and are) central to the study of music and contemporary culture, and studying tribute bands was particularly attractive to me because they engaged all of these ideas. A complete list of citations would be unfeasibly long, but some scholarly works that have guided my thoughts on these topics include, on authenticity: Richard Taruskin, *Text and Act: Essays on Music and Performance* (New York: Oxford University Press, 1995); Timothy Taylor, *Global Pop: World Music, World Markets* (New York: Routledge, 1997); John Jackson, *Real Black: Adventures in Racial Sincerity* (Chicago: University of Chicago Press, 2005); on works, Lydia Goehr, *The Imaginary Museum of Musical Works: An Essay in the Philosophy of Music* (New York: Oxford University Press, 1994); on performance and identity, Philip Auslander, *Performing Glam Rock: Gender and Theatricality in Popular Music* (Ann Arbor: University of Michigan Press, 2006); on the global spread of popular music, E. Taylor Atkins, ed., *Jazz Planet* (Jackson: University Press of Mississippi, 2003);

Carol Muller and Sathima Bea Benjamin, *Musical Echoes: South African Women Thinking in Jazz* (Durham, NC: Duke University Press, 2011).

34. John Paul Meyers, "The World According to Marsalis: Difference and Sameness in Wynton Marsalis's *From the Plantation to the Penitentiary*," *Journal of Popular Music Studies* 22 (2010): 416–35.

35. One milestone in jazz's institutional acceptance is the 1987 congressional resolution in which "jazz is hereby designated as a rare and valuable national American treasure to which we should devote our attention, support and resources to make certain it is preserved, understood, and promulgated." *H.Con.Res. 57 (100th): A concurrent resolution expressing the sense of Congress respecting the designation of jazz as a rare and valuable national American treasure.* https://www.govtrack.us/congress/bills/100/hconres57/text.

36. Guthrie Ramsey, *Race Music: Black Cultures from Bebop to Hip-Hop* (Berkeley: University of California Press, 2003).

37. For more on how rock music functions as a tool of identity construction in Latin America (including among Latinos in the United States), see Roberto Avant-Mier, *Rock the Nation: Latin/o Identities and the Latin Rock Diaspora* (London: Continuum, 2010).

38. While rock music—and the tribute band scene as a subset of rock culture—have been viewed as white since the 1970s, rock 'n' roll's most influential pioneers and performance practices were of course African American. The "whitening" of rock and the erasure of the genre's Black beginnings are analyzed in Jack Hamilton, *Just Around Midnight: Rock and Roll and the Racial Imagination* (Cambridge, MA: Harvard University Press, 2016). After this apparent rupture between Black musicians and rock music culture, the work of Black musicians to reclaim for themselves a place in rock is best analyzed in Maureen Mahon's *Right to Rock: The Black Rock Coalition and the Cultural Politics of Race* (Durham, NC: Duke University Press, 2004).

39. Jeremy A. Smith, "'Sell It Black': Race and Marketing in Miles Davis's Early Fusion Jazz," *Jazz Perspectives* 4, no. 1 (2010): 7–33.

40. Stuart Cosgrove, *Young Soul Rebels: A Personal History of Northern Soul* (Edinburgh: Birlinn, 2017); Will Straw, "Sizing Up Record Collections: Gender and Connoisseurship in Rock Music Culture," in *Sexing the Groove: Popular Music and Gender*, ed. Sheila Whiteley (New York: Routledge, 1997).

41. Writing in the *New York Times Magazine*, Chuck Klosterman summarizes the critic and historian Ted Gioia's assessment of his profession: "Critics have almost no impact on what music is popular at any given time, but they're extraordinarily well positioned to dictate what music is reintroduced after its popularity has waned." It is worth noting that Gioia and Klosterman themselves both fit the profile of middle-class, white, male guardians of musical memory. Chuck Klosterman, "Which Rock Star Will Historians of the Future Remember?" *New York Times Magazine*, May 23, 2016.

42. Several recent works have sought to complicate our understandings of Black engagements with the past, including Mark Anthony Neal, *Black Ephemera: The Crisis and Challenge of the Musical Archive* (New York: New York University Press, 2022); and Badia Ahad-Legardy, *Afro-Nostalgia: Feeling Good in Contemporary Black Culture* (Urbana: University of Illinois Press, 2021).

Chapter 1: Twenty Years Ago Today: Tribute Bands and Historical Consciousness in Popular Music

1. This periodization can be seen in the Beatles' *Anthology* series: a set of outtakes and unreleased performances that was released in the mid-1990s part of the first wave of historical consciousness in rock that I describe in this chapter. *Anthology* was divided into three two-disc volumes matching the early, middle, and late periods ascribed to the output of the Beatles.

2. Indeed, the Gretsch company has partnered with George Harrison's son, Dhani Harrison, to produce a replica of a guitar that the elder Harrison used in the 1960s, a guitar that was featured prominently during televised performances during this time and, twenty years later, on the cover of Harrison's *Cloud Nine* album.

3. Antti-Ville Karja, "A Prescribed Alternative Mainstream: Popular Music and Canon Formation," *Popular Music* 25, no. 1 (2006): 3–19; Marion Leonard, "Constructing Histories Through Material Culture: Popular Music, Museums, and Collecting," *Popular Music History* 2, no. 2 (2007): 147–67; Tim Brooks, *Survey of Reissues of U.S. Recordings* (Washington: Council on Library and Information Resources, 2005); Kay Simpson, *Early '70s Radio: The American Format Revolution* (New York: Continuum, 2011).

4. Devon Powers, *Writing the Record: The Village Voice and the Birth of Rock Criticism* (Amherst: University of Massachusetts Press, 2013); Robert Draper, *Rolling Stone Magazine: The Uncensored History* (New York: Doubleday, 1990).

5. Jann Wenner, *Lennon Remembers* (London: Verso, [1971] 2000), 48.

6. William Mann, "What Songs the Beatles Sang," *London Times*, December 27, 1963.

7. For example, see Bob Dylan, *Chronicles Volume One* (New York: Simon and Schuster, 2004).

8. Keir Keightley, "Reconsidering Rock," in *The Cambridge Companion to Pop and Rock*, ed. Simon Frith and Will Straw (New York: Cambridge University Press, 2001), 116.

9. Clive Davis, *The Soundtrack of My Life* (New York: Simon and Schuster, 2013), 32.

10. Alan Merriam, *The Anthropology of Music* (Evanston, IL: Northwestern University Press, 1964); Mantle Hood, *The Ethnomusicologist* (New York: McGraw-Hill, 1971); Timothy Rice, "Towards a Remodeling of Ethnomusicology," *Ethnomusicology* 31, no. 3 (1987): 469–88; Bruno Nettl, *The Study of Ethnomusicology: Thirty-Three Discussions* (Urbana: University of Illinois Press, 2015).

11. Lise Waxer, *The City of Musical Memory: Salsa, Record Grooves, and Popular Culture in Cali, Colombia* (Middletown, CT: Wesleyan University Press, 2002), 88.

12. Kay Shelemay, *Let Jasmine Rain Down: Song and Remembrance Among Syrian Jews* (Chicago: University of Chicago Press, 1998), 3.

13. Gabriel Solis, *Monk's Music: Thelonious Monk and Jazz History in the Making* (Berkeley: University of California Press, 2007), 6.

14. Hayden White, *Metahistory: The Historical Imagination in the Nineteenth Century* (Baltimore: Johns Hopkins University Press, 1973), 38, 40.

15. Peter Seixas, ed., *Theorizing Historical Consciousness* (Toronto: University of Toronto Press, 2004).

16. Pierre Nora, "Between Memory and History: *Les Lieux de Mémoire*," *Representations* 26 (Spring 1989): 7–24.

17. Alan Williams, "'Pay Some Attention to the Man Behind the Curtain'—Unsung Heroes and the Canonization of Process in the *Classic Albums* Documentary Series," *Journal of Popular Music Studies* 22, no. 2 (2010): 166–79.

18. For an interesting counterexample to this rather narrow vision of the "best of the millennium," see Richard Thompson, *1000 Years of Popular Music*, Cooking Vinyl Records, 2003.

19. Reynolds, *Retromania*.

20. In addition to its production of CD box sets offered for sale and events for which purchased tickets are required, historical consciousness also produces social communities which are not so easily commoditized. A good example of this would be the community that has formed around the Abbey Road on the River Festival, described later in this chapter. Beatles fans from across the country and around the world attend this annual festival year after year, forming friendships and connections, while keeping in contact throughout the year via the festival's active Facebook page and online guestbook.

21. Jonathan Sterne, *MP3: The Meaning of a Format* (Durham, NC: Duke University Press, 2012).

22. James Miller, *Flowers in the Dustbin: The Rise of Rock 'n' Roll, 1947–1977* (New York: Simon and Schuster, 1999), 18.

23. Miller, *Flowers in the Dustbin*, 18–19.

24. Carol Muller, "American Musical Surrogacy: A View from Post–World War II South Africa," *Safundi: The Journal of South African and American Comparative Studies* 7, no. 3 (2006): 1–18.

25. Jean Baudrillard, "The System of Collecting," in John Elsner and Roger Cardinal, eds., *The Cultures of Collecting* (Cambridge, MA: Harvard University Press, 1994), 7.

26. George Plasketes, "Pimp My Records: The Deluxe Dilemma and Edition Condition: Bonus, Betrayal, or Download Backlash?" *Popular Music and Society* 31 (2008): 389–93.

27. Jesse Samba Wheeler, "'Toca Raul!' Praise Singers on Brazil's Central Plateau," in Shane Homan, ed., *Access All Eras: Tribute Bands and Global Pop Culture* (Maidenhead, UK: Open University Press, 2006), 198–212.

28. Richard Taruskin, "On Letting the Music Speak for Itself: Some Reflections on Musicology and Performance," *Journal of Musicology* 1, no. 3 (1982): 338–49.

29. McMullen, *Haunthenticity*.

30. Steven Kurutz, *Like a Rolling Stone: The Strange Life of a Tribute Band* (New York: Broadway Books, 2008), 155.

31. Much of this material is now housed at the Grateful Dead Archive at the University of California, Santa Cruz.

32. Greil Marcus, *Invisible Republic: Bob Dylan's Basement Tapes* (New York: Henry Holt, 1997), xvii.

33. Draper, *Rolling Stone Magazine: The Uncensored History*, 8.

34. For an example of this mythology, see the 2007 PBS documentary *American Experience: The Summer of Love*, directed by Gail Dolgin and Vicente Franco. The last day of the festival at AROTR is deemed Summer of Love Day, when the festival broadens its focus from exclusively playing the music of the Beatles to include other bands from the late 1960s, including the Rolling Stones, the Who, Jimi Hendrix, and the Kinks.

35. In the case of Hendrix's "All Along the Watchtower," it is literally part of the soundtrack. This song, along with the Rolling Stones' 1969 "Gimme Shelter," have collectively been used dozens of times in film, television shows, and commercials to quickly suggest the revolutionary change and violence of the late 1960s and early 1970s.

36. For an example of the retrospective myth-making that typifies much contemporary reception of the Woodstock festival, see Pete Fornatale, *Back to the Garden: The Story of Woodstock* (New York: Touchstone, 2009).

37. Gerry Bloustien, "Still Picking Children From the Trees? Re-imagining Woodstock in Twenty-first Century Australia," in *Remembering Woodstock*, ed. Andy Bennett (Aldershot, UK: Ashgate, 2004), 127–45.

38. Andy Bennett, "Even Better Than the Real Thing? Understanding the Tribute Band Phenomenon," in *Access All Eras: Tribute Bands and Global Pop Culture*, ed. Shane Homan (Maidenhead, UK: Open University Press, 2006), 23.

39. David Damrsoch, *What Is World Literature?* (Princeton, NJ: Princeton University Press, 2003), 15.

40. This is also how the critic and scholar Harold Bloom views the formation of the literary tradition: as new writers grappling with foundational works and claiming their rightful place in history by showing themselves equal to the fight. See Harold Bloom, *The Anxiety of Influence: A Theory of Poetry* (New York: Oxford University Press, 1973).

41. Parry does not use the term "classic" in the same rigorous way as Damrosch uses it. For our purposes, it is important to note that rock music is being directly compared to the canon of Western classical music. See *CBS Sunday Morning*, "A Summer Song," September 22, 2007.

42. Clifford Geertz, "Distinguished Lecture: Anti Anti-Relativism," *American Anthropologist* 86, no. 2 (1984): 263–78; Judith Becker, "Is Western Art Music Superior?" *Musical Quarterly* 72, no. 3 (1986): 341–59.

43. Allan Bloom, *The Closing of the American Mind* (New York: Simon and Schuster, 1987), 69.

44. Tony Horwitz, *Confederates in the Attic: Dispatches from the Unfinished Civil War* (New York: Vintage, 1999).

45. Jean-Francois Lyotard, *The Postmodern Condition: A Report on Knowledge* (Minneapolis: University of Minnesota Press, [1979] 1984), xxiv.

46. Jon Caramanica, "How Do You Capture Four Decades of Hip-Hop? Very Broadly," *New York Times*, August 5, 2021. https://www.nytimes.com/2021/08/05/arts/music/smithsonian-anthology-hip-hop-rap.html.

47. Daphne Brooks, *Liner Notes for the Revolution: The Intellectual Life of Black Feminist Sound* (Cambridge, MA: Belknap Press, 2021).

Chapter 2: Yesterdays: Performing the Past Through the Great American Songbook from Ella Fitzgerald to Bob Dylan

1. A note on terminology: I use the words "standard," "Songbook," and "Great American Songbook" throughout this chapter to refer to the same body of material. "Tin Pan Alley"—first a geographic location referring to the area in Manhattan where music publishing offices were clustered—is also occasionally used to refer to these songs. However, I find this term to be too broad. A small minority of songs coming out of Tin Pan Alley are canonized as historically important, whereas most musicians, listeners, and critics use the terms "standard" and "Great American Songbook" interchangeably.

2. Ben Beaumont-Thomas, "Madonna 'Madame X' Review—Her Most Bizarre Album Ever," *The Guardian*, June 4, 2019. https://www.theguardian.com/music/2019/jun/04/madonna-madame-x-review-her-most-bizarre-album-ever.

Radio 2 is the most popular radio station in the UK, playing, according to its website, "the widest selection of music on the radio—from classic and mainstream pop to a specialist portfolio including classical, country, folk, jazz, soul, rock 'n' roll, gospel, blues, organ music, big band and brass band." Since this is a government-funded radio station, there is publicly available documentation describing its intended listenership; Radio 2 is "targeted at a broad audience, appealing to all age groups over 35." For Beaumont-Thomas, these are exactly the listeners who might have been interested in purchasing a hypothetical jazz standards album by Madonna, but are not the target market for *Madame X*. See BBC, "What Is Radio 2?" https://www.bbc.co.uk/radio2/about/whatis.shtml; and BBC Trust, "BBC Radio 2," https://www.bbc.co.uk/bbctrust/our_work/services/radio/service_licences/bbc_radio_2.html.

3. Alexis Petridis, "Bob Dylan's *Shadows in the Night* review—An Unalloyed Pleasure," *The Guardian*, January 29, 2015. https://www.theguardian.com/music/2015/jan/29/bob-dylan-shadows-in-the-night-review.

4. Jesse Cataldo, "Review: Bob Dylan, *Shadows in the Night*," *Slant*, February 2, 2015. https://www.slantmagazine.com/music/bob-dylan-shadows-in-the-night/#When:21:26:52Z.

5. Timothy Taylor discusses economic precarity and an indifference to the market as a key part of authenticity in the discourse surrounding world music in the 1990s. Taylor's "authenticity of positionality" is also widespread in discussions of other popular music genres. See Timothy Taylor, *Global Pop: World Music, World Markets* (New York: Routledge, 1997).

6. Recent years have seen a flowering of scholarship on genre categorizations in popular music. See Fabian Holt, *Genre in Popular Music* (Chicago: University of Chicago Press, 2007); and David Brackett, *Categorizing Sound: Genre and Twentieth-Century Popular Music* (Oakland: University of California Press, 2016).

7. Alec Wilder, *American Popular Song* (New York: Oxford University Press, 1972).

8. Wilder, *American Popular Song*, xxxvii.

9. Wilder, *American Popular Song*, xxxvi–xxxvii.

10. Will Friedwald, *Stardust Melodies: The Biography of Twelve of America's Most Popular Songs* (New York: Pantheon, 2002); Will Friedwald, *A Biographical Guide to the Great Jazz and Pop Singers* (New York: Pantheon, 2010); Will Friedwald, *The Great Jazz and Pop Vocal Albums* (New York: Pantheon, 2017).

11. Will Friedwald, *Sinatra! The Song Is You: A Singer's Art* (New York: Scribner, 1995); Tony Bennett with Will Friedwald, *The Good Life: The Autobiography of Tony Bennett* (New York: Atria, 1998).

12. Philip Furia, *The Poets of Tin Pan Alley: A History of America's Great Lyricists* (New York: Oxford University Press, 1990).

13. Allen Forte, *The Structure of Atonal Music* (New Haven, CT: Yale University Press, 1973); Allen Forte, *The Atonal Music of Anton Webern* (New Haven, CT: Yale University Press, 1998).

14. Allen Forte, *The American Popular Ballad of the Golden Era, 1924–1950* (Princeton, NJ: Princeton University Press, 1995); Allen Forte, *Listening to Classic American Popular Songs* (New Haven, CT: Yale University Press, 2001).

15. Ben Yagoda, *The B-Side: The Death of Tin Pan Alley and the Rebirth of the Great American Song* (New York: Riverhead, 2015), 5.

16. Walter Benjamin, "The Work of Art in the Age of Mechanical Reproduction," in *Illuminations*, ed. H. Arendt (New York: Schocken, 1969 [1936]), 217–51.

17. Benedict Anderson's *Imagined Communities: Reflections on the Origins and Spread of Nationalism* (London: Verso, 1983) is the standard source on how the consumption of mass-mediated products allows individuals to think of themselves as part of a greater public.

18. Albin Zak, *I Don't Sound Like Nobody: Remaking Music in 1950s America* (Ann Arbor: University of Michigan Press, 2010).

19. Mark Katz, *Capturing Sound: How Technology Has Changed Music* (Berkeley: University of California Press, 2004).

20. Charles Hamm, *Yesterdays: Popular Song in America* (New York: W.W. Norton, 1979), 338.

21. Hamm, *Yesterdays*, 388.

22. Hamm, *Yesterdays*, 358.

23. Hamm, *Yesterdays*, 376–77. My thanks to my colleague Jeffrey Magee for pointing out that Hamm may be overstating his case here. Songs addressing political and social issues from this time period include "Brother, Can You Spare a Dime?" (1932), "Supper Time" (1933), and "Strange Fruit" (1939).

24. Stuart Nicholson, *Ella Fitzgerald: A Biography of the First Lady of Jazz* (New York: Scribner, 1994), 8. Nicholson's biography of Fitzgerald will be a key source for this section. As this book goes to press, Judith Tick's biography of Fitzgerald is forthcoming from W.W. Norton; I expect this will be an important addition to our understanding of Fitzgerald's life, career, and reception.

25. Nicholson, *Ella Fitzgerald*, 33.

26. Nicholson, *Ella Fitzgerald*, 34.

27. Christi Jay Wells [formerly Christopher Jay Wells], "'A Dreadful Bit of Silliness': Feminine Frivolity and Ella Fitzgerald's Early Career Critical Reception," *Women and Music: A Journal of Gender and Culture* 21 (2017): 44.

28. Nicholson, *Ella Fitzgerald*, 39.

29. Nicholson, *Ella Fitzgerald*, 49.

30. Nicholson, *Ella Fitzgerald*, 50.

31. Nicholson, *Ella Fitzgerald*, 65.

32. Nicholson, *Ella Fitzgerald*, 87.

33. Granz's role as a crusader for jazz musicians has not gone unnoticed by his biographers. Tad Hershorn's measured biography of Granz is subtitled "The Man Who Used Jazz for Justice." Dempsey J. Travis's biography of Granz is subtitled, even more provocatively, "The White Moses of Black Jazz." Tad Hershon, *Norman Granz: The Man Who Used Jazz for Justice* (Berkeley: University of California Press, 2011); Dempsey J. Travis, *Norman Granz: The White Moses of Black Jazz* (Chicago: Urban Research Press, 2003).

34. Nicholson, *Ella Fitzgerald*, 119.

35. Albums had existed before the late 1940s. Will Friedwald and Mike Biel trace the beginnings of the modern popular music album back to 1926, with *To Mother*, a collection of six songs on three 10-inch, two-sided 78 RPM records issued by RCA Victor. This is far earlier than most popular music scholars typically pay attention to when thinking about albums—probably our most cherished documents. According to Friedwald, even the concept of the album as "songbook," as a collection of songs by the same composer, was already in place by 1939, with albums appearing around that time devoted to the songs of composers such as Hoagy Carmichael, Irving Berlin, and Rodgers and Hart. This supports his claim: "The concept album was not invented in the wake of the long-playing format; rather, the

LP was developed as an easier means of distributing the concept albums that were already being produced." Friedwald, *The Great Jazz and Pop Vocal Albums*, xiv–xv, xix.

36. Nicholson, *Ella Fitzgerald*, 133.

37. Nicholson, *Ella Fitzgerald*, 153.

38. Hershon, *Norman Granz*, 219

39. Hershon, *Norman Granz*, 220.

40. Grammy categories have frequently been altered over the decades. Neither of the awards Fitzgerald won in 1959 is currently awarded in its previous form.

41. There are two "encores" to Fitzgerald's Songbook albums on Verve, though neither of these albums received anything approaching the critical and popular success of the albums discussed above. In 1972, Fitzgerald again collaborated with Riddle on *Ella Loves Cole*, another set of songs by Cole Porter. By this time, however, the music industry had changed drastically, as I discuss later in this chapter and in the following chapter on the work of Miles Davis in the 1960s. In 1981, Fitzgerald recorded *Ella Fitzgerald Sings the Antonio Carlos Jobim Songbook* (alternately titled *Ella Abraça Jobim*). Jobim occupies a complicated position with regard to the "Great American Songbook." He was, of course, born in Brazil and not in the United States. His career peak as a songwriter—roughly the late 1950s and early 1960s—was also toward the later end of the years that the Great American Songbook typically draws from. Still, the bossa nova style that Jobim is associated with became, in some sense, "domesticated" into the Anglophone popular music world, and Jobim's compositions are generally now viewed by North American singers, instrumentalists, and listeners as "standards." For more discussion, see K. E. Goldschmitt, *Bossa Mundo: Brazilian Music in Transnational Media Industries* (New York: Oxford University Press, 2020).

42. Robert Fink, *Repeating Ourselves: American Minimal Music as Cultural Practice* (Berkeley: University of California Press, 2005); Janet Borgerson and Jonathan Schroeder, *Designed for Hi-Fi Living: The Vinyl LP in Midcentury America* (Cambridge, MA: MIT Press, 2017).

43. Nicholson, *Ella Fitzgerald*, 164.

44. For discussion of the reception of Billie Holiday, see Farah Jasmine Griffin, *If You Can't Be Free, Be a Mystery: In Search of Billie Holiday* (New York: Free Press, 2001); and John Szwed, *Billie Holiday: The Musician and the Myth* (New York: Viking, 2015).

45. Miles Davis with Quincy Troupe, *Miles: The Autobiography* (New York: Simon and Schuster, 1991), 236. In fact, the song's lyrics are slightly different from what Davis remembers here: "Don't let him handle me with his hot hands."

46. Davis with Troupe, *Miles*, 399.

47. On this recording, "I Loves You, Porgy" is retitled as "I Wants to Stay Here," the opening phrase of one of its verses.

48. Linda Martin and Kerry Segrave, *Anti-Rock: The Opposition to Rock and Roll* (Hamden, CT: Archon Books, 1988), 8.

49. Jan Reid, *The Improbable Rise of Redneck Rock* (Austin: University of Texas Press, 2004), is a classic source originally published in 1974, released in an updated edition in 2004. Other more recent studies of Austin's iconoclastic music scene include Travis Stimeling, *Cosmic Cowboys and New Hicks: The Countercultural Sounds of Austin's Progressive Country Music Scene* (New York: Oxford University Press, 2011); and Jason Mellard, *Progressive Country: How the 1970s Transformed the Texan in Popular Culture* (Austin: University of Texas Press, 2014).

50. For further discussion of "outlaw country," see Michael Streissguth, *Outlaw: Waylon, Willie, Kris, and the Renegades of Nashville* (New York: It Books, 2013).

51. The most significant musical outcome of this dispute was Nelson's 1991 album, *The IRS Tapes: Who'll Buy My Memories?*, comprised of stripped-down performances of songs from Nelson's back catalogue, recorded and released specifically to raise money to help pay off his tax debts.

52. Rob Bowman, *Soulsville: The Story of Stax Records* (New York: Schirmer, 1997); Charles Hughes, *Country Soul: Making Music and Making Race in the American South* (Chapel Hill: University of North Carolina Press, 2015).

53. Willie Nelson with David Ritz, *It's a Long Story: My Life* (New York: Little, Brown, 2015), 266.

54. Nelson with Ritz, *It's a Long Story*, 267.

55. Willie Nelson with Bud Shrake, *Willie: An Autobiography* (New York: Simon and Schuster, 1988), 71.

56. Michael Walker, *Laurel Canyon: The Inside Story of Rock-and-Roll's Legendary Neighborhood* (New York: Faber and Faber, 2006).

57. Linda Ronstadt, *Simple Dreams: A Musical Memoir* (New York: Simon and Schuster, 2013), 142.

58. Peter J. Levinson, *September in the Rain: The Life of Nelson Riddle* (New York: Billboard, 2001), 268.

59. Evidence of Hamill's interest in the American popular song tradition can be seen in the short book eulogizing Frank Sinatra that Hamill published in 1998, the year of Sinatra's death. See Pete Hamill, *Why Sinatra Matters* (New York: Little, Brown, 1998). But Hamill's musical tastes also crossed over to the folk-rock tradition closer to Ronstadt's 1970s performing style as well; Hamill won a Grammy award for writing the liner notes to Bob Dylan's 1975 *Blood on the Tracks* album.

60. Ronstadt, *Simple Dreams*, 115.

61. Ronstadt, *Simple Dreams*, 158.

62. Ronstadt, *Simple Dreams*, 146.

63. Ronstadt, *Simple Dreams*, 152.

64. Ronstadt, *Simple Dreams*, 157. In the 1970s, Ronstadt had recorded three songs either written or performed by Holly: "It Doesn't Matter Anymore," "It's So Easy," and "That'll Be the Day."

65. Christopher Connelly, "Review of *What's New*," *Rolling Stone*, October 13, 1983. https://www.rollingstone.com/music/music-album-reviews/whats-new-182822/.

66. Indeed, Gormé was later spoofed in a *Saturday Night Live* sketch in 1991 as a hack from the clubby, insular popular culture world that had, mercifully, been made obsolete.

67. Greil Marcus, *Invisible Republic: Bob Dylan's Basement Tapes* (New York: Henry Holt, 1997); Greil Marcus, *Like a Rolling Stone: Bob Dylan at the Crossroads* (New York: PublicAffairs, 2005).

68. David Browne, "How Bob Dylan's 'Make You Feel My Love' Became a Modern Standard," *Rolling Stone*, October 28, 2019. https://www.rollingstone.com/music/music-features/bob-dylan-make-you-feel-my-love-covers-903941/.

69. Nate Sloan points out how Dylan had, at various times in his career, expressed contempt for the Great American Songbook/Tin Pan Alley tradition, perhaps most prominently in his spoken introduction to "Bob Dylan's Blues" from his 1963 album *The Freewheelin' Bob*

Dylan. See Nate Sloan, "When Rock Meets the Great American Songbook in the 21st Century," (paper presentation, Conference of the American Musicological Society, November 12, 2021).

70. Stephen M. Deusner, "Bob Dylan: Shadows in the Night," *Pitchfork*, February 3, 2015. https://pitchfork.com/reviews/albums/20190-shadows-in-the-night/.

71. Kyle Anderson, "'Shadows in the Night': EW Review," *Entertainment Weekly*, February 6, 2015. https://ew.com/article/2015/02/06/shadows-night-ew-review/.

72. See Hamill, *Why Sinatra Matters*. For discussion of some of the ways Sinatra is mythologized in contemporary culture, see John Gennari, *Flavor and Soul: Italian America at its African American Edge* (Chicago: University of Chicago Press, 2017).

73. Michael Simmone, "Bob Dylan—Shadows in the Night," *MOJO*, February 6, 2015. https://www.mojo4music.com/articles/18828/bob-dylan-shadows-night.

74. Douglas Heselgrave, "Bob Dylan: *Shadows in the Night* Review," *Paste*, February 3, 2015. https://www.pastemagazine.com/music/bob-dylan/bob-dylan-shadows-in-the-night-review/.

75. See Kelefa Sanneh, *Major Labels: A History of Popular Music in Seven Genres* (New York: Penguin, 2021), especially pages 410–19, for a discussion of "rockism" and "poptimism."

76. Heselgrave, "Bob Dylan: *Shadows in the Night* Review."

77. Jim Farber, "Album Review: Bob Dylan's 'Shadows In the Night' Features Covers of American Standards," *New York Daily News*, February 2, 2015. https://www.nydailynews.com/entertainment/bob-dylan-songs-sung-frank-sinatra-article-1.2100696.

78. Corbin Reiff, "There's Nothing Standard About Bob Dylan's Latest," *A/V Club*, February 3, 2015. https://music.avclub.com/there-s-nothing-standard-about-bob-dylan-s-latest-1798182598.

79. Petridis, "Bob Dylan's *Shadows in the Night* review."

80. Matt Melis, "Album Review: Bob Dylan—Shadows in the Night," *Consequence of Sound*, February 13, 2015. https://consequenceofsound.net/2015/02/album-review-bob-dylan-shadows-in-the-night/.

81. Steve Smith, "Bob Dylan: Shadows in the Night," *Boston Globe*, February 3, 2015.

82. Janne Oinonen, "Bob Dylan—Shadows in the Night," *The Line of Best Fit*, February 10, 2015. https://www.thelineofbestfit.com/reviews/albums/bob-dylan-shadows-in-the-night.

83. There are comparatively few Hendrix tribute bands, however, considering his stature in the rock canon. Perhaps his guitar pyrotechnics and improvisational virtuosity are not a good fit for a performance format based on the meticulous reproduction of an already-familiar song or album.

84. Badia Ahad-Legardy, *Afro-Nostalgia: Feeling Good in Contemporary Black Culture* (Urbana: University of Illinois Press, 2021), 1.

85. Ahad-Legardy, *Afro-Nostalgia*, 3.

Chapter 3: Memories and Standards: Miles Davis and "I Fall in Love Too Easily," 1963–1970

1. Nate Chinen, *Playing Changes: Jazz for the New Century* (New York: Pantheon, 2018), x.

2. Fred Kaplan, *1959: The Year Everything Changed* (Hoboken, NJ: Wiley, 2009). Additionally, the journalist Natalie Weiner produced a detailed day-by-day analysis of jazz recordings and live gigs from 1959 for the year's sixtieth anniversary in 2019; see the1959project.com.

3. Eric Nisenson, *The Making of Kind of Blue: Miles Davis and His Masterpiece* (New York: St. Martin's, 2000), 20.

4. Scott DeVeaux analyzes the idea of progress in jazz history in *The Birth of Bebop: A Musical and Social History* (Berkeley: University of California Press, 1997); see especially the chapter "Progress and the Bean," 35–71.

5. In the preface to Gillespie's autobiography, *To Be, or Not . . . To Bop*, Gillespie and his coauthor Al Fraser frame this musical consistency in a more optimistic manner: "His music, bebop, 'has stood the test of time,' and he has remained prominent in the public eye despite many changes in musical vogue that followed his own exceptionally durable pioneering efforts—the modern and Afro-Cuban styles he introduced during the 1940s." Dizzy Gillespie with Al Fraser, *To Be, or Not . . . To Bop* (New York: Da Capo, 1979), xviii.

6. Ian Carr, *Miles Davis: The Definitive Biography* (New York: Thunder's Mouth Press, 1998), 209.

7. Richard Cook, *It's About That Time: Miles Davis On and Off Record* (Oxford: Oxford University Press, 2007), 132.

8. Jack Hamilton's *Just Around Midnight: Rock and Roll and the Racial Imagination* examines the codification and hardening of racial boundaries in popular music during this time. While only ten years earlier the genre had been associated with Black musicians such as Chuck Berry and Fats Domino, by the end of the 1960s rock was viewed as almost exclusively a "white" music, leading to much confusion in the reception of Hendrix. Hendrix's music, particularly early in his career, was most popular among white rock fans. The African American poet (and later collaborator with Davis on his autobiography) Quincy Troupe confirms as much when recounting Hendrix's meeting with Troupe: "He was a shy man and was flattered that I loved his music so much and that I knew who he was, because, as he later told me, most blacks had never heard of him. That was because the kind of music he played appealed mostly to young white fans of rock and roll." See Quincy Troupe, *Miles and Me* (Berkeley: University of California Press, 2000), 137. Davis himself also seems to have preferred Hendrix's collaborations with the African American musicians Buddy Miles and Billy Cox on the *Band of Gypsies* album. As recounted in *Miles: The Autobiography*, "But when he [Hendrix] started playing with Buddy and Billy in the Band of Gypsies, I think he brought what he was doing all the way out. But the record companies and white people liked him better when he had the white guys in the band" [i.e., Mitch Mitchell and Noel Redding, who played drums and bass, respectively, in the Jimi Hendrix Experience]. See Davis with Troupe, *Miles: The Autobiography*, 293. However, since the similarity in language between these two accounts of Hendrix's music is so striking, it is worth remembering that, at minimum, Davis's autobiography is a compromised document. Davis's role as the sole or primary authorial voice behind *Miles: The Autobiography* has been questioned by several writers, as Ken Prouty has summarized. Throughout this chapter, *Miles: The Autobiography* will be treated less as an oracle than as one particularly interesting, if problematic, account of Davis's life and career. See Ken Prouty, "Plagiarizing Your Own Autobiography, and Other Strange Tales: Miles Davis, Jazz Discourse, and The Aesthetics of Silence," *Jazz Research Journal* 4, no. 1 (2010): 15–41.

9. Ned Rorem, *Knowing When to Stop* (New York: Simon and Schuster, 1994). John Litweiler's biography of Coleman suggests Bernstein even sat in on piano with Coleman's group at the Five Spot club in New York. See John Litweiler, *Ornette Coleman: A Harmolodic Life* (New York: William Morrow, 1992), 82.

10. Ned Rorem, "The Music of the Beatles," *New York Review of Books*, January 18, 1968. In the 1950s and 1960s, Leonard Bernstein served as a kind of musical public intellectual and translator of popular music styles for a presumed middlebrow audience. Compare Bernstein's explanations of jazz for curious listeners on the 1956 LP *What is Jazz?* with his explanations of songs by the Beatles, the Monkees, and the Left Banke, for CBS News, *Inside Pop: The Rock Revolution*, April 1967.

11. Keir Keightley, "Taking Popular Music (And Tin Pan Alley and Jazz) Seriously," *Journal of Popular Music Studies* 22, no. 1 (March 2010): 90–97.

12. On his status compared with that of Hancock, Davis writes: "[In 1974] we started a tour of the United States playing with Herbie Hancock's group. Herbie had a big hit album [*Head Hunters*, released in October 1973] and he was really well liked among the young black kids. We agreed to be his opening act. Deep down that pissed me off." A bit later, the book frames these same events more optimistically: "I was touring all over with Herbie and we were killing everybody. Most of the audiences were young and black and that was good. That's what I wanted, and I was finally getting there." See Davis with Troupe, *Miles: The Autobiography*, 330–31. For further discussion of Davis's desire to appeal to a young, Black audience during this time period, see Jeremy A. Smith, "'Sell It Black': Race and Marketing in Miles Davis's Early Fusion Jazz," *Jazz Perspectives* 4 (April 2010): 7–33. For a summary of the marketing and promotion of the *Head Hunters* album, see Steven F. Pond, *Head Hunters: The Making of Jazz's First Platinum Album* (Ann Arbor: University of Michigan Press, 2005), 155–86.

13. Stanley Crouch, "Play the Right Thing," *New Republic* (February 12, 1990), reprinted in *The Miles Davis Companion: Four Decades of Commentary*, ed. Gary Carner (New York: Schirmer, 1996), 34.

14. Leonard Feather, "Miles Smiles," in *The Miles Davis Companion*, 131–32.

15. Greg Tate, "The Electric Miles, Parts One and Two [1983]," reprinted in Greg Tate, *Flyboy in the Buttermilk: Essays on Contemporary America* (New York: Simon and Schuster, 1992), 74.

16. Gary Tomlinson, "Cultural Dialogics and Jazz: A White Historian Signifies," *Black Music Research Journal* 11, no. 2 (Autumn 1991): 251, 261.

17. Eric Porter, "'It's About That Time': The Response to Miles Davis's Electric Turn," in *Miles Davis and American Culture*, ed. Gerald Early (St. Louis: Missouri Historical Society Press, 2001), 130–46; Jeremy A. Smith, *Sound, Mediation, and Meaning in Miles Davis's A Tribute to Jack Johnson* (PhD diss., Duke University, 2008); Victor Svorinich, *Listen to This: Miles Davis and Bitches Brew* (Jackson: University Press of Mississippi, 2015); George Grella Jr., *Bitches Brew* (New York: Bloomsbury, 2015).

18. Chris Robinson, "Media Review," *Jazz Perspectives* 8, no. 3 (2015): 321.

19. For a general discussion of the song, see Ted Gioia, *The Jazz Standards: A Guide to the Repertoire* (New York: Oxford University Press, 2012), 163–65.

20. Don DeMichael, Review of *Seven Steps to Heaven* [1963], reprinted in *The Miles Davis Reader*, ed. Frank Alkyer, Ed Enright, and Jason Koransky (New York: Hal Leonard, 2007), 229.

21. For discussion, see John Szwed, *So What: The Life of Miles Davis* (New York: Simon and Schuster, 2002), 128, 134; Ian Carr, *Miles Davis: The Definitive Biography*, 95–104; *Miles: The Autobiography*, 200–205.

22. The main exceptions to this were his orchestral collaborations with the arranger Gil Evans, including an album that featured their versions of songs from the Gershwin opera *Porgy and Bess*. But in his studio work with small groups, Davis rarely recorded Songbook tunes during this time.

23. For example, see the July 1964 performance issued as *Miles Davis Quintet in Tokyo* (CBS-Sony 60064R) and the September 1964 concert released as *Miles Davis Quintet in Berlin* (CBS 62976).
24. Katz, *Capturing Sound*, 89.
25. Alex Ross, *Listen to This* (New York: Picador, 2011).
26. Reynolds, *Retromania*, xxxv.
27. Reynolds, *Retromania*, 404.
28. Henry Louis Gates Jr., *The Signifying Monkey: A Theory of Afro-American Literary Criticism* (New York: Oxford University Press, 1988).
29. Howard Brofsky, "Miles Davis and 'My Funny Valentine': The Evolution of a Solo," *Black Music Research Journal* 3 (1983): 35.
30. Robert Walser, "Out of Notes: Signification, Interpretation, and the Problem of Miles Davis," *Musical Quarterly* 77, no. 2 (Summer 1993): 351.
31. Two in-depth musical analyses of Davis's music during this period have been published: Jeremy Yudkin, *Miles Smiles: Miles Davis and the Invention of Post-Bop* (Bloomington: Indiana University Press, 2008); and Keith Waters, *The Studio Recordings of the Miles Davis Quintet, 1965–1968* (Oxford: Oxford University Press, 2011). Additionally, Todd Coolman's dissertation provides detailed transcriptions and analyses of several performances by the quintet. See Todd Coolman, *Miles Davis Quintet of the Mid-1960s: Synthesis of Improvisational and Compositional Elements* (PhD diss., New York University, 1997).
32. Presciently, Davis observed in his autobiography, "I made six studio dates with this group [the 'second great quintet'] in four years . . . and there were some live recordings that I guess Columbia will release when they think they can make the most money, probably after I'm dead." Davis with Troupe, *Miles: The Autobiography*, 278.
33. Michelle Mercer, *Footprints: The Life and Work of Wayne Shorter* (New York: Penguin, 2004), 104–8; Jack Chambers, *Milestones 2: The Music and Times of Miles Davis Since 1960* (New York: Beech Tree Books, 1985), 90.
34. Limited excerpts from the recordings were first released in 1976 and 1982. While all live recordings are mediated, the Plugged Nickel box set recordings are particularly important in that they preserve order and running times. This approach differs from some other live jazz recordings that either take a "best of" approach, combining performances from various nights or venues onto a single recording or editing lengthy live performances for time to fit the constraints of physical media. It is also significant that this box set was released posthumously, at a time when Davis had (and has continued to have) a dependable commercial appeal. In this context, complete, lengthy live performances are not a commercial liability but an attraction for jazz CD buyers.
35. Davis with Troupe, *Miles: The Autobiography*, 278. The reference to Davis performing "Kind of Blue" is either a misprint or a misunderstanding between Davis and Quincy Troupe, the writer who drafted *Miles: The Autobiography* based on interviews with Davis. However, "All Blues" and "So What," two compositions from the *Kind of Blue* album, were often performed by the Davis quintet during the 1960s. Confusing the matter is the fact that the titles that are listed here in quotation marks are also the titles of albums Davis released. Elsewhere in the autobiography, however, album names are italicized.
36. Lionel Olay, "Miles Davis: Winner Take All [1964]," reprinted in *Miles on Miles: Interviews and Encounters with Miles Davis*, eds. Paul Maher Jr. and Michael K. Dorr (Chicago: Lawrence Hill Books, 2009), 26.
37. Arthur Taylor, "I Don't Have to Hold the Audience's Hand [1977]," in *The Miles Davis Companion: Four Decades of Commentary*, ed. Gary Carner (New York: Schirmer, 1996), 111.

38. Herbie Hancock with Lisa Dickey, *Possibilities* (New York: Viking, 2014), 92–93.

39. The 1966 Newport performances were recently released by Columbia Recordings on *The Bootleg Series Volume 4: Miles Davis at Newport 1955–1975*.

40. Chambers, *Milestones 2*, 116.

41. Chambers, *Milestones 2*, 277.

42. Information on set lists from live performances is taken either from commercially released recordings or from Peter Losin's "Miles Ahead" website, www.plosin.com.

43. Timings are taken from the DVD of this concert included on *The Bootleg Series, Volume 1: Live in Europe 1967*.

44. Chambers, *Milestones 2*, 115–16; Nate Chinen, "Miles Davis, Live at the Apogee," *New York Times* (September 8, 2011).

45. Davis with Troupe, *Miles: The Autobiography*, 297.

46. This is a position it would also have on the *Bitches Brew* album, in which its opening melody makes a brief cameo appearance at the beginning of "Sanctuary."

47. During the performance in Berlin, DeJohnette and Holland both wipe their faces with a towel after the workout of the preceding "It's About That Time."

48. Coolman quotes the saxophonist Dave Liebman describing the band's playing in the mid-1960s: "What's great about it is that he has these young cats, especially Herbie [Hancock] and Tony [Williams] playing standards from such a different standpoint." Coolman, *Miles Davis Quintet of the Mid-1960s*, 19.

49. In a review of the album, the jazz critic Martin Williams was shocked that "a portion of the music is inadvertently repeated" on the album. Of course, this repetition was actually intentional. See Martin Williams, "Jazz: Some Old Favorites are Back," *New York Times* (January 18, 1970).

50. Davis with Troupe, *Miles: The Autobiography*, 301.

51. Tomlinson, "Cultural Dialogics and Jazz," 260.

52. Smith, "Sell It Black," 11.

53. Smith, "Sell It Black," 7.

54. Surprisingly, Davis returned to what might be broadly termed "popular songs" during his "comeback" in the 1980s: "Time After Time" by Cyndi Lauper and "Human Nature" by Michael Jackson. A detailed description of these studio recordings (and subsequent live recordings: both songs remained a part of Davis's live repertoire until his death in 1991) is beyond the scope of this book. However, Davis's versions of these tunes differ in several important respects from his versions of "I Fall in Love Too Easily" and other standards during the mid-1960s and into his electric era. Perhaps most importantly, the harmonic form of the song is clearly audible in live performances of both "Time after Time" and "Human Nature." The striking shifts in rhythmic feel and texture that Tony Williams brought to live performances of standards in the mid-1960s are also absent from these performances in the 1980s. "Time after Time" and "Human Nature" also are not considered part of the Great American Songbook, which essentially stopped admitting new entries by 1960. The flow of compositions from "popular music" to "jazz" was very different in the 1980s than it was in the 1940s and 1950s. See Ben Yagoda, *The B Side: The Death of Tin Pan Alley and the Rebirth of the Great American Song* (New York: Riverhead Books, 2015).

Chapter 4: Old School: Sampling, Re-Playing, and Re-Hearing the 1970s in Hip-Hop

1. Various sources describe this party, including Jeff Chang, *Can't Stop Won't Stop: A History of the Hip Hop Generation* (New York: Picador, 2004); and Mark Katz, *Groove Music: The Art and Culture of the Hip-Hop DJ* (New York: Oxford University Press, 2010).

2. Katz's *Groove Music* provides a concise definition and discussion of breaks in hip-hop: "A break is a brief percussion solo, typically found toward the end of a funk song.... It lays bare a stretch of unadulterated rhythm as the singer and other instrumentalists abruptly drop out.... Rhythmically speaking, they are usually anchored by a heavy downbeat emphasized by the bass (or kick) drum—'the one' as it's often called—but are dominated by forward leaning syncopations that seem to propel themselves back to 'the one.' Over the course of just a few seconds—usually two to four bars—a sense of stability is constantly being undermined, reestablished, and undermined once again" (14–15, 24).

3. See Albin Zak, *I Don't Sound Like Nobody: Remaking Music in 1950s America* (Ann Arbor: University of Michigan Press, 2010), 104.

4. The credit that Presley has received as a "groundbreaking," "revolutionary" artist whose debts to Black culture have been erased has attracted attention within hip-hop. Chuck D eviscerates Presley in Public Enemy's 1989 song "Fight the Power": "Elvis was a hero to most but he never meant shit to me / Straight up racist that sucker was simple and plain / Motherfuck him and John Wayne."

5. The story of Cindy Campbell's involvement in this mythical first hip-hop party is well-known among hip-hop scholars, but women's contributions to the hip-hop scene are often deemphasized in favor of attention given to the male figures in hip-hop culture (like DJs and MCs), who played more public roles. See Kathy Iandoli, *God Save the Queens: The Essential History of Women in Hip-Hop* (New York: Dey Street, 2019), 1–3.

6. A discography of forty-seven breakbeats often played by early hip-hop DJs is collected in Jim Fricke and Charlie Ahearn, *Yes Yes Y'All: The Experience Music Project Oral History of Hip-Hop's First Decade* (Cambridge, MA: Da Capo Press, 2002), 345.

7. Other candidates for the first hip-hop record include "Rhymin' and Rappin'" by Paulette and Tanya Winley and "King Tim III (Personality Jock)" by the Fatback Band and rapper Timothy Washington—both released 1979. However, in comparison to "Rapper's Delight," these songs made little impact at the time and are not often cited by early hip-hop listeners or artists as being influential. Perhaps most importantly, these other songs have not featured nearly as prominently in formal or informal narratives of hip-hop history as "Rapper's Delight." David Toop suggests that stylistic differences between "King Tim III (Personality Jock)" and "Rapper's Delight" may be responsible for the latter's greater influence on hip-hop: "Though Fatback's record was a success of sorts, its style harked back to the days when radio rapping jocks heated up the airwaves with rhyming jive. 'Rapper's Delight,' on the other hand, not only stole MC rapping but also appropriated the idea of using a remake of Chic's huge disco hit 'Good Times' as its backing track." That is, part of the appeal of "Rapper's Delight" may be that it reused an already-familiar disco/funk hit. See David Toop, *Rap Attack 3: African Rap to Global Hip Hop* (London: Serpent's Tail, 2000), 16.

8. Carl Bialik, "Is the Conventional Wisdom Correct in Measuring Hip-Hop Audience?" *Wall Street Journal*, May 5, 2005.

9. Among the many sources documenting these scenes, see Tony Mitchell, ed., *Global Noise: Rap and Hip-Hop Outside the USA* (Middletown, CT: Wesleyan University Press,

2002); Eric Charry, ed., *Hip Hop Africa: New African Music in a Globalizing World* (Bloomington: Indiana University Press, 2012); Ian Condry, *Hip-Hop Japan: Rap and the Paths of Cultural Globalization* (Durham, NC: Duke University Press, 2006).

10. For the sake of brevity, I typically refer to music from the 1970s in this chapter, even though not all of the examples I examine come from between the years of 1970 and 1979. In fact, one of the most reused, replayed, and sampled recordings of hip-hop is the 1969 track "Amen, Brother" by The Winstons. As I will discuss later in this chapter, Otis Redding's 1966 recording of "Try a Little Tenderness" was also sampled by Kanye West for his track "Otis." Some of the soul and R&B tracks that have been prominently and repeatedly repurposed for hip-hop also stretch into the following decade, the 1980s. Nevertheless, the majority of records that early hip-hop DJs played at parties, that producers have musicians re-create in the studio, and that are sampled digitally do indeed come from the decade of the 1970s.

11. Joanna Teresa Demers, *Sampling as Lineage in Hip Hop* (PhD diss., Princeton University, 2002), 39.

12. Henry Louis Gates Jr., *The Signifying Monkey: A Theory of Afro-American Literary Criticism* (New York: Oxford University Press, 1988); Robert Walser, "Out of Notes: Signification, Interpretation, and the Problem of Miles Davis," *Musical Quarterly* 77 (2): 343–65.

13. Jennifer Lynn Stoever draws our attention specifically to the ways that the records purchased and played by mothers were influential on early hip-hop musicians, making this intervention to counter the ignoring of these "feminine," domestic listening spaces in most hip-hop history. See Jennifer Lynn Stoever, "Crate Digging Begins at Home: Black and Latinx Women Collecting and Selecting Records in the 1960s and 1970s Bronx," in *The Oxford Handbook of Hip Hop Music*, ed. Justin D. Burton and Jason Lee Oakes (New York: Oxford University Press, 2018).

14. Chang, *Can't Stop Won't Stop*; Joseph Schloss, *Foundation: B-boys, B-girls, and Hip-Hop Culture in New York* (New York: Oxford University Press, 2009); Schloss, *Making Beats*.

15. Schloss, *Foundation*, 17–18.

16. Will Hermes, "All Rise for the National Anthem of Hip-Hop," *New York Times*, October 29, 2006.

17. Schloss, *Foundation*, 25.

18. Katz, *Groove Music*, 21.

19. Nelson George, "Hip-Hop's Founding Fathers Speak the Truth," *The Source*, November 1993.

20. Robert Fink, "The Story of ORCH5, or, The Classical Ghost in the Hip-Hop Machine," *Popular Music* 24, no. 3 (2005): 344.

21. Fink, "The Story of ORCH5," 348.

22. Katz, *Groove Music*, 29.

23. Liner notes to Jay-Z, *The Hits Collection: Volume One*, 2010.

24. Genre distinctions between "soul," "funk," and "R&B" may be more important to record store owners and industry executives than to hip hop listeners, producers, and DJs. Amanda Sewell, in her typology of hip hop sampling, notes that "nearly every producer I interviewed referred to [funk and soul] both collectively and interchangeably.... Separating 'funk' and 'soul' creates a distinction that many hip hop producers do not make themselves." See Amanda Sewell, "*Paul's Boutique* and *Fear of a Black Planet*: Digital Sampling and Musical Style in Hip Hop," *Journal of the Society for American Music* 8, no. 1 (2014): 42. Guthrie Ramsey also points to a lack of clear genre distinctions in Black popular music. Reappropriating music industry jargon, his notion of "race music" aims to draw connections

between the many kinds of music (classified variously as soul, R&B, gospel, jazz, funk, and hip-hop) listened to by working-class African Americans in the middle to late decades of the twentieth century. Ramsey's research is particularly important because it focuses on exactly the time period when many hip-hop musicians grew into musical maturity. See Guthrie Ramsey, *Race Music: Black Cultures from Bebop to Hip-Hop* (Berkeley: University of California Press, 2003).

25. Justin Williams, "Intertextuality, Sampling, and Copyright," in *The Cambridge Companion to Hip-Hop*, ed. Justin Williams (Cambridge: Cambridge University Press, 2015), 206–20.

26. Lydia Goehr, *The Imaginary Museum of Musical Works* (New York: Oxford University Press, 1994). In Goehr's influential formulation, a "work" of Western classical music is, for example, Beethoven's 7th Symphony when considered in the abstract, not any specific recording, score, or performance of that work. "Works" are venerated in Western classical music, and while this veneration can certainly be seen analogously in hip-hop and rock music traditions, the concept of "work" is typically understood to apply more directly to specific recordings. In early hip-hop, live performances are treated as fleeting—not intended to be venerated or preserved for posterity.

27. Dan Charnas, *The Big Payback: The History of the Business of Hip-Hop* (New York: New American Library, 2011), 32.

28. Toop, *Rap Attack 3*, 16.

29. Katz, *Capturing Sound*.

30. Loren Kajikawa, *Sounding Race in Rap Songs* (Berkeley: University of California Press, 2015), 74.

31. While Byrd takes lead vocals on this track and the track was released under Byrd's name, it otherwise shows heavy influence from Brown, in that he produced the recording, can be heard counting off the band at the beginning of the recording, and the instrumentalists (as well as Byrd himself) were members of Brown's band. Byrd's contributions are unfortunately forgotten in this allusion, but Stetsasonic is right to refer by name to the overall influence of Brown in the production of this track. Brown's recordings, such as "Funky Drummer" and "Give It Up or Turnit a Loose," were often played by DJ at parties in the 1970s and sampled by producers in the 1980s. While Brown's distinctive grunts, shouts, moans, and other vocalizations do get reused in hip-hop, the most important elements of these tracks for producers and DJs have been their drum parts—which were not performed by Brown but by drummers such as Clyde Stubblefield and John "Jabo" Starks.

32. Kajikawa, *Sounding Race in Rap Songs*, 95.

33. Steingo notes the (perhaps apocryphal) story of the genesis of the South African popular music style known as kwaito: "Kwaito, in fact, is often referred to as a form of *slowed-down* house: while much house in the late 1980s and early 1990s clocked in at around 120 beats per minute (bpm), early kwaito was generally around 100 bpm. There is an oft-cited anecdote, or myth, that a club DJ in the early 1990s played an LP at the wrong (slower) speed, but the crowd liked it, and so kwaito was born." Gavin Steingo, *Kwaito's Promise: Music and the Aesthetics of Freedom in South Africa* (Chicago: University of Chicago Press, 2016), 49.

34. "Manipulability" is another one of the important differences between recordings and conventional live performance that Katz analyzes in *Capturing Sound*.

35. Gates's theory of signifyin(g) and the related concept of "call-response" form a major part of Samuel Floyd's understanding of a wide variety of Black music-making. See Samuel

A. Floyd Jr., *The Power of Black Music: Interpreting Its History from Africa to the United States* (New York: Oxford University Press, 1995).

36. Gates, *The Signifying Monkey*, 123.

37. Tricia Rose, *Black Noise: Rap Music and Black Culture in Contemporary America* (Middletown, CT: Wesleyan University Press, 1994), 22.

38. William Julius Wilson, *The Declining Significance of Race: Blacks and Changing American Institutions*, 3rd ed. (Chicago: University of Chicago Press, 2012).

39. William Julius Wilson, *The Truly Disadvantaged: The Inner City, the Underclass, and Public Policy* (Chicago: University of Chicago Press, 1987); William Julius Wilson, *When Work Disappears: The World of the New Urban Poor* (Chicago: University of Chicago Press, 1996).

40. Michelle Alexander, *The New Jim Crow: Mass Incarceration in the Age of Colorblindness* (New York: New Press, 2012), 49.

41. Mitchell Duneier, *Ghetto: The Invention of a Place, The History of an Idea* (New York: FSG, 2016), xii.

42. Ned and Constance Sublette, *The American Slave Coast: A History of the Slave-Breeding Industry* (Chicago: Lawrence Hill Books, 2016).

43. Isabel Wilkerson, *The Warmth of Other Suns: The Epic Story of America's Great Migration* (New York: Vintage, 2011).

44. Mitchell Duneier provides a thorough discussion of the ideas of each of these figures in *Ghetto*.

45. Charles Murray, *Losing Ground: American Social Policy: 1950–1980* (New York: Basic Books, 1984).

46. Questlove with Ben Greenman, *Mo' Meta Blues: The World According to Questlove* (New York: Grand Central Publishing, 2013).

47. Questlove with Greenman, *Mo' Meta Blues*, 25. Questlove's description here is slightly off: he was born in 1971, but *Music of My Mind* was released in March 1972.

48. Questlove with Greenman, *Mo' Meta Blues*, 26.

49. Questlove with Greenman, *Mo' Meta Blues*, 16.

50. Questlove with Greenman, *Mo' Meta Blues*, 17.

51. Jay-Z, *Decoded* (New York: Spiegel and Grau, 2010), 254. Not incidentally, many of these artists are also name-checked by West in "Slow Jamz," discussed above.

52. Jay-Z, *Decoded*, 254–55.

53. Adam Bradley and Andrew DuBois, eds., *The Anthology of Rap* (New Haven, CT: Yale University Press, 2011).

54. Jay-Z, *Decoded*, 26.

Chapter 5: "I Just Wanna Go Back, Baby, Back to the Way it Was": The Past, Activism, and Recent Black Popular Music

1. For a reasonably successful R&B musician like Robin Thicke, performing on *The Voice* and *The Ellen DeGeneres Show* can be a way to introduce his music to a larger and wider audience. *The Ellen DeGeneres Show* was one of the highest-rated programs on daytime television, a format that has largely been targeted to middle-class white women. The episode of *The Voice* where Thicke and Williams performed "Blurred Lines" had over ten million viewers, drawing a diverse audience.

2. "The 2013 Pazz & Jop Critics' Poll," *Village Voice*, January 15, 2014. https://www.village voice.com/2014/01/15/the-village-voices-2013-pazz-jop-critics-poll/.

3. Diane Martel, the director who helmed both versions of the "Blurred Lines" video, disagrees with this assessment of who has power in the video and who does not. In an interview with the website *Grantland*, Martel described her creative vision for the video: "I wanted to deal with the misogynist, funny lyrics in a way where the girls were going to overpower the men. Look at Emily Ratajkowski's performance; it's very, very funny and subtly ridiculing. That's what is fresh to me. It also forces the men to feel playful and not at all like predators. I directed the girls to look into the camera, this is very intentional and they do it most of the time; they are in the power position. I don't think the video is sexist. The lyrics are ridiculous, the guys are silly as fuck. That said, I respect women who are watching out for negative images in pop culture and who find the nudity offensive, but I find [the video] meta and playful." Martel's artistic intent aside, the video has largely not been interpreted through the lens of female empowerment. See Eric Ducker, "Q&A: Veteran Music Video Director Diane Martel On Her Controversial Videos for Robin Thicke and Miley Cyrus," *Grantland*, June 26, 2013. https://grantland.com/hollywood-prospectus/qa-veteran-music-video-director-diane-martel-on-her-controversial-videos-for-robin-thicke-and-miley-cyrus/.

4. Tricia Romano, "'Blurred Lines,' Robin Thicke's Summer Anthem, Is Kind of Rapey," *Daily Beast*, June 17, 2013. https://www.thedailybeast.com/blurred-lines-robin-thickes-summer-anthem-is-kind-of-rapey.

5. Claire Carter, "More Universities Ban 'Blurred Lines' Over Fears It Promotes Rape," *The Telegraph*, November 6, 2013. https://www.telegraph.co.uk/culture/music/10427870/More-universities-ban-Blurred-Lines-over-fears-it-promotes-rape.html.

6. Will Welch, "Pharrell on Evolving Masculinity and 'Spiritual Warfare,'" *GQ*, October 14, 2019. https://www.gq.com/story/pharrell-new-masculinity-cover-interview.

7. Ronan Farrow, "From Aggressive Overtures to Sexual Assault: Harvey Weinstein's Accusers Tell Their Stories," *New Yorker*, October 23, 2017 (originally published online October 10, 2017).

8. Katherine M. Leo, *Forensic Musicology and the Blurred Lines of Federal Copyright History* (Lanham, MD: Lexington, 2021).

9. Eriq Gardner, "'Blurred Lines' Appeal Gets Support From More Than 200 Musicians," *Hollywood Reporter*, August 30, 2016. https://www.hollywoodreporter.com/thr-esq/blurred-lines-appeal-gets-support-924213.

10. Jody Rosen, "Questlove on Working with Elvis Costello, Miley's Twerking, and His Lunchtime D.J. Sets," *Vulture*, September 18, 2013. https://www.vulture.com/2013/09/questlove-on-his-new-album-with-elvis-costello.html.

11. Wayne Marshall has an informative discussion of The Roots' musical practices in his article "Giving up Hip-Hop's Firstborn: A Quest for the Real after the Death of Sampling," *Callaloo* 29, no. 3 (Summer 2006): 868–92.

12. The objectification of women in popular music—along with possible challenges to this objectification—has been a frequently discussed topic in popular music scholarship. For one classic consideration of these ideas, see Tricia Rose, "Never Trust a Big Butt and a Smile," *Camera Obscura* 8, no. 2 (23) (1990): 108–31.

13. Eric Lott traced this development back to blackface minstrelsy in the nineteenth century. Recent scholarship by Matthew D. Morrison has traced what he terms "blacksound"— the imitation of Black musical practices by non-Black musicians—as intimately involved

with the rise of musical scholarship as a modern discipline. See Eric Lott, *Love and Theft: Blackface Minstrelsy and the American Working Class* (New York: Oxford University Press, 1993); and Matthew D. Morrison, "Race, Blacksound, and the (Re)Making of Musicological Discourse," *Journal of the American Musicological Association* 72, no. 3 (2019): 781–823.

14. Complicating this dynamic in the "Blurred Lines" case is the participation of Pharrell Williams, an African American, as the song's producer and main songwriter. Thicke was signed to Williams's record label, Star Trak, and Williams may have been in a much stronger position to influence Thicke's recording output and, eventually, profit from the success of "Blurred Lines," even if Thicke was the ostensible "front man" for this song.

15. Kembrew McLeod and Peter DiCola, *Creative License: The Law and Culture of Digital Sampling* (Durham, NC: Duke University Press, 2011), 2.

16. Jeff Chang, *Can't Stop Won't Stop: A History of the Hip-Hop Generation* (New York: Picador, 2005), 79.

17. Colin Symes, *Setting the Record Straight: A Material History of Classical Music Recording* (Middletown, CT: Wesleyan University Press, 2004).

18. Here I am echoing ideas from Mark Katz about the social construction of technology in the production and dissemination of music. In Katz's view, technology (musical or otherwise) is not deterministic: humans still have to make choices about how, or if, they are going to adopt new technology. See Katz, *Capturing Sound*. For a discussion of composers and musicians from the Western art music world who have been more willing to incorporate new technology and new instruments into their creative practice, see Thomas Patteson, *Instruments for New Music: Sound, Technology, and Modernism* (Berkeley: University of California Press, 2015).

19. Robert Loss, *Nothing Has Been Done Before: Seeking the New in 21st Century American Popular Music* (New York: Bloomsbury, 2017).

20. Since his death in 2016, there have been several academic conferences and special issues of journals devoted to Prince.

21. See for example Robert Walser, "Prince as Queer Post-Structuralist," *Popular Music and Society* 18, no. 2 (1994): 79–89; Anne Danielsen, "His Name Was Prince: A Study of *Diamonds and Pearls*," *Popular Music* 16, no. 3 (1997): 275–91; Touré, *I Would Die 4 U: Why Prince Became an Icon* (Atria: New York, 2013).

22. Betty Houchin Winfield, "Because of the Children: Decades of Attempted Controls of Rock 'n' Rap Music," in *Bleep! Censoring Rock and Rap Music*, edited by Betty Houchin Winfield and Sandra Davidson (Westport, CT: Greenwood Press, 1999).

23. The second chapter of Griffin Woodworth's dissertation engages what he calls Prince's ambivalence toward hip-hop music. While both Prince and hip-hop as a musical style were interested in 1970s funk rhythms, as Griffin notes, Prince criticizes rap for being, in Woodworth's terms, "musically impoverished." Griffin Woodworth, "Just Another One of God's Gifts: Prince, African-American Masculinity, and the Sonic Legacy of the Eighties," PhD diss., University of California, Los Angeles, 2008, 266. Prince critiques hip-hop perhaps most directly on the 1994 song "Dead On It," in which he both parodies the technique of rapping and criticizes rap as a genre. Woodworth offers further thoughts on Prince's relationship to rap in his article, "'Rapping Done Let Us Down': Prince's Hip-Hop Ambivalence," *Popular Music and Society* 43, no. 3 (2020): 281–300.

24. A cover of this song would eventually be released by Prince as a B-side in 2001.

25. Robert Loss analyzes Prince's critique of the racial capitalism evident in the music industry in his paper "Deconstruction: Work and Racial Capitalism in *The Rainbow Children*

(And Yes, We'll Be Talking About 'Avalanche')," collected in De Angela L. Duff, Zachary Hoskins, Kamilah Cummins, and Robert Loss, "#1plus1plus1is3: Transcripts from a Virtual Symposium on Iconic Prince Albums," *Journal of Popular Music Studies* 34, no. 2 (2022): 5–27.

26. Prince, *The Beautiful Ones*, edited by Dan Piepenbring (New York: Spiegel and Grau, 2019).

27. Matthew Valnes, "Taking It Higher: The Spirituality of Sensuality in Funk Performance," *African and Black Diaspora: An International Journal* 9 (2016): 3–15.

28. Thomas Brett, "Prince's Rhythm Programming: 1980s Music Production and the Esthetics of the LM-1 Drum Machine," *Popular Music and Society* 43, no. 3 (2020): 244–61; Megan Lavengood, "What Makes it Sound '80s? The Yamaha DX7 Electric Piano Sound," *Journal of Popular Music Studies* 31, no. 3 (2019): 71–94.

29. Adilfu Nama, *I Wonder U: How Prince Went Beyond Race and Back* (New Brunswick, NJ: Rutgers University Press, 2020).

30. Griffin Woodworth, "Prince, Miles, and Maceo: Horns, Masculinity, and the Anxiety of Influence," *Black Music Research Journal* 33, no. 2 (2013): 117–50.

31. Portia K. Maultsby, "Funk," in *African American Music: An Introduction*, 2nd ed., edited by Mellonee V. Burnim and Portia K. Maultsby (New York: Routledge, 2015), 301–19.

32. Nelson George, *The Death of Rhythm and Blues* (New York: Penguin, 1988), 102.

33. There is a forty-five-second section of low-pitched voiceover to end the track, but since this shows no sonic similarity with the rest of the song, it should probably be considered a part of the album's narrative, and not part of the song proper.

34. Nelson George refers to "Cold Sweat" as an "early funk experiment" in *The Death of Rhythm and Blues*, 101. Similarly, Rickey Vincent notes that "Cold Sweat" is "often acknowledged as the closest thing to the first funk groove" in *Funk: The Music, The People, and The Rhythm of the One* (New York: St. Martin's, 1996), 123.

35. Brown's exhortations for Wesley to take a solo—"Hit Me, Fred!"—became such an important feature of Brown's performances that Wesley borrowed it for the title of his own autobiography. Fred Wesley, *Hit Me, Fred! Recollections of a Sideman* (Durham, NC: Duke University Press, 2002).

36. There is recorded precedent for this as well in the history of funk. On Isaac Hayes's title track to the soundtrack to the 1971 movie *Shaft*, Hayes is interrupted in the middle of saying, "You know, they say this cat Shaft is a bad mother . . ." by a chorus of female back-up singers admonishing him, "Shut your mouth!"

37. Since Prince's death in 2016, this live set and many other recordings have become more broadly available on streaming music services.

38. This formula comes from Parker's spoken introduction to the song "Shake Everything You've Got" on his career-rejuvenating live album *Life on Planet Groove* (1992). This became something of a catchphrase for Parker, such that he titled his later autobiography *98% Funky Stuff: My Life in Music* (Chicago: Chicago Review Press, 2016).

39. In addition to these songs, Prince actually did play "Purple Rain" frequently on this tour, despite his warning in the introduction to "Xenophobia" that those wanting to hear that song are "in the wrong place." It seems that even Prince had to indulge his audiences by the playing hits.

40. Between *The Rainbow Children* and *Musicology*, Prince had also released several instrumental albums of soundchecks and studio jams.

41. *The Tonight Show with Jay Leno*, February 26, 2004. Available at https://youtu.be/Bc48X-ehlfY.

42. A few years later, in 2009 Prince would reiterate this retro-leaning sentiment in the song "Ol' Skool Company":

> Every once in a while
> You need some old school company
> Somebody that appreciates a sexy groove
> And a old school melody

43. *Welcome 2 America* is also the name of an album and box set released posthumously by the Prince estate in 2021. This includes an album with that title that Prince recorded in the spring and summer of 2010. For unknown reasons, Prince decided to not release this music during his lifetime. While the music would stay unheard until after his death, Prince clearly decided that he liked the "Welcome 2" brand, as he also gave that name to the tour he would begin six months after these recordings. In the special edition box set released in 2021, the original 2010 studio recordings are included on both CD and vinyl, along with a DVD of the April 28, 2011, concert at the Forum in Inglewood, California, that was a stop on the Welcome 2 America tour. To make this package even more appealing to Prince fans, the box set also comes with a poster and a replica setlist, ticket, and backstage pass for the April 28 show. Such an elaborate package is typical of the kind of "celebratory commodities" produced by historical consciousness in the popular music industry, such that even the unreleased music and ephemera of an honored artist are deemed worthy of veneration and collection.

44. @JanelleMonae, December 30, 2013, 12:26 a.m.

45. *Blues People* (New York: William Morrow, 1963) by Leroi Jones/Amiri Baraka emphasized the blues as the authentic working-class expression of African American culture and key for understanding American society as a whole. Codified in two anthologies, *The Jazz Cadence of American Culture* (New York: Columbia University Press, 1998) and *Uptown Conversation: The New Jazz Studies* (New York: Columbia University Press, 2004), scholars associated with Robert G. O'Meally's Center for Jazz Studies at Columbia University privileged jazz as the central genre of African American music. Emily Lordi's book *The Meaning of Soul* (Durham, NC: Duke University Press, 2020) argues for the centrality of soul music and discourse as crucial for understanding the last sixty years of African American musical history. All of these accounts are convincing and well supported by evidence; they are also necessarily partial and incomplete.

46. Prince gives an impromptu music history lesson and critique during the song "Welcome 2 America." As discussed above, this song was recorded in the *Welcome 2 America* studio sessions, before he launched the Welcome 2 America tour but not released until after his death. A trio of female singers provide the melodic vocals on this track, but Prince delivers spoken word comments lamenting the current state of American culture, including: "Welcome to America. One of our greatest exports was a thing called jazz. You think today's music'll last?" One of his vocalists provides a brief scat solo demonstration in response to his statement, demonstrating the skill involved in earlier styles of Black popular music, which Prince contrasts with his skepticism over the aesthetic and historical worth of the contemporary music scene.

47. For a wide-ranging discussion of Obama's engagements with hip-hop (and vice versa), see Travis L. Gosa and Erik Nielson, eds., *The Hip-Hop and Obama Reader* (New York: Oxford University Press, 2015).

48. Ta-Nehisi Coates, *We Were Eight Years in Power: An American Tragedy* (New York: One World, 2017).

49. Feminista Jones, *Reclaiming Our Space: How Black Feminists Are Changing the World from the Tweets to the Streets* (Boston: Beacon Press, 2019).

50. Evan Serpick, "Prince Promotes Peace at Baltimore Show: 'The System is Broken,'" *Rolling Stone*, May 11, 2015. https://www.rollingstone.com/music/music-live-reviews/prince-promotes-peace-at-baltimore-show-the-system-is-broken-188895/.

51. Matthew Valnes, "Janelle Monáe and Afro-Sonic Feminist Funk," *Journal of Popular Music Studies* 27, no. 3 (2017).

52. To be sure, there are elements in Monáe's musical universe other than funk, including 1970s prog rock. However, it is important to remember that George Clinton's groups in the 1970s also dabbled strongly in mythological, otherworldly narratives and distorted electric guitars. As a 1978 Funkadelic song asks, "Who says a funk band can't play rock?"

53. Lordi, *The Meaning of Soul*, 154–55.

54. Lordi, *The Meaning of Soul*, 161.

55. Brittany Spanos, "Janelle Monáe Frees Herself," *Rolling Stone*, April 26, 2018. https://www.rollingstone.com/music/music-features/janelle-monae-frees-herself-629204/.

56. Though her examination of Monáe in the conclusion of her 2013 book *Sounding Like a No-No* was published five years before the release of *Dirty Computer*, Francesca T. Royster finds a similar liberatory message in Monáe's music video for "Tightrope." See Francesca T. Royster, *Sounding Like a No-No: Queer Sounds and Eccentric Acts in the Post-Soul Era* (Ann Arbor: University of Michigan Press, 2013).

57. Phillip Lamarr Cunningham, "'There's Nothing Really New under the Sun': The Fallacy of the Neo-Soul Genre," *Journal of Popular Music Studies* 22, no. 3 (2010): 241.

58. In fact, this image comes from film shot at Afropunk's annual summer concert of 2014, at a time in which audience members were asked to raise their hands in the air in protest.

59. Rob Bowman, *Soulsville, U.S.A.: The Story of Stax Records* (New York: Schirmer, 1997), 237–40.

60. Ward Churchill and Jim Vander Wall, *The COINTELPRO Papers: Documents from the FBI's Secret Wars Against Dissent in the United States* (Boston: South End Press, 1990).

61. Jeffrey Haas, *The Assassination of Fred Hampton: How the FBI and the Chicago Police Murdered a Black Panther* (Chicago: Chicago Review Press, 2011).

62. Astra Taylor, *The People's Platform: Taking Back Power and Culture in the Digital Age* (New York: Metropolitan Books, 2014).

63. Dan Hyman, "D'Angelo and Bobby Seale on the Past and Future of Political Protest," *New York Times*, June 19, 2015. https://www.nytimes.com/2015/06/21/arts/music/dangelo-and-bobby-seale-on-the-past-and-future-of-political-protest.html.

64. Melinda Mills, *Racial Mixture and Musical Mash-ups in the Life and Art of Bruno Mars* (Landham, MD: Lexington Books, 2021).

65. Kinitra D. Brooks and Kameelah L. Martin, eds., *The Lemonade Reader: Beyoncé, Black Feminism, and Spirituality* (New York: Routledge, 2019); Omise'eke Natasha Tinsley, *Beyoncé in Formation: Remixing Black Feminism* (Austin: University of Texas Press, 2018).

66. Lordi, *The Meaning of Soul*, 151.

Conclusion

1. Farah Jasmine Griffin, *If You Can't Be Free, Be a Mystery: In Search of Billie Holiday* (New York: Free Press, 2001); David Margolick, *Strange Fruit: The Biography of a Song* (New York: Ecco, 2001).

2. Eddie Fu, "For the Record: Rapsody Explains Why She's Not a 'Female MC' & Raps a Lauryn Hill Verse," *Genius*, August 23, 2019. https://genius.com/a/for-the-record-rapsody-explains-why-shes-not-a-female-mc-raps-a-lauryn-hill-verse. There is clearly a genealogy of influence and admiration between Rapsody, Lauryn Hill, and Nina Simone. Simone is a lyrical and personal touchstone for Hill. Rapsody admires both Simone and Hill; in the same interview in which she speaks about Simone's influence, she raps an entire verse from Hill's "Lost Ones" track.

3. Michael Eric Dyson discusses both Afeni Shakur and the legacy of the Panthers in Tupac's "postrevolutionary childhood" in *Holler If You Hear Me: Searching for Tupac Shakur* (New York: Basic Civitas Books, 2003).

4. Queen Latifah's contributions to Black culture have recently been recognized not just by Rapsody; Latifah was honored with a Lifetime Achievement Award from BET in 2021.

5. Steven F. Pond, *Head Hunters: The Making of Jazz's First Platinum Album* (Ann Arbor: University of Michigan Press, 2010). Coincidentally, the song is also a notorious ethnomusicological case study of cultural appropriation, in that the distinctive whistling sound produced by blowing across the top of a beer bottle was copied directly from the *hindewhu* technique of the Central African BaBenzélé Pygmies. Percussionist Bill Summers heard this on a field recording made by Simha Arom and Geneviève Taurelle and imitated the exact pitches and rhythms for use on "Watermelon Man." After the massive success of *Head Hunters*, no royalties were paid to the original musicians who came up with this melody and rhythm, though Hancock has been certain to secure payment to himself when other musicians have sampled this recording of "Watermelon Man" on their own new songs—such as Madonna's 1994 song "Sanctuary" and "Whoopi" by Rapsody. See Steven Feld, "Pygmy POP: A Genealogy of Schizophonic Mimesis," *Yearbook for Traditional Music* 28 (1996): 1–35.

6. Perhaps the most poignant documentation of 1970s and early 1980s New York can be found in the street photography of Jamel Shabazz. See Jamel Shabazz, *A Time Before Crack* (New York: Powerhouse Books, 2005).

7. While Mark Zuckerberg is a real person, "Erica Albright" is a fake name for a person who may not even have a "real-world" analog. But whether Albright actually exists is irrelevant to *The Social Network* functioning not as a documentary but as creation myth of the Millennial generation.

8. These numbers were accurate when the film was released in the fall of 2010.

9. Indeed, *Sgt. Pepper* has been perhaps the most canonized Beatles album. It is the only work of popular music with a volume devoted to it in the Cambridge Music Handbooks series, which otherwise focuses exclusively on symphonies, song cycles, oratorios, string quartets, and concertos of the Western classical tradition. See Allan Moore, *Sgt. Pepper's Lonely Hearts Club Band* (Cambridge: Cambridge University Press, 1995). As I discussed in chapter 2, *The White Album* was described by Abbey Road on the River Festival promoter Gary Jacob as the Beatles' "magnum opus" at a concert marking the fortieth anniversary of its release. Such reception is typical of the way *Sgt. Pepper* and *The White Album* have been talked about by journalists, critics, and fans, as is the relative lack of attention and acclaim bestowed on *Magical Mystery Tour*.

10. The names of all 213 songs recorded by the Beatles are printed on two large banners that frame the main lawn stage at the Beatles tribute festival Abbey Road on the River. In addition, the tribute artist Hal Bruce is known for performing a marathon-length medley of all of these songs.

11. Ramsey, *Race Music*, 171.

12. McClary has explored ideas of musical signification in *Feminine Endings: Music, Gender, and Sexuality* (Minneapolis: University of Minnesota Press, 1993) and *Conventional Wisdom: The Content of Musical Form* (Berkeley: University of California Press, 2000).

BIBLIOGRAPHY

Ahad-Legardy, Badia. *Afro-Nostalgia: Feeling Good in Contemporary Black Culture*. Urbana: University of Illinois Press, 2021.
Alexander, Michell. *The New Jim Crow: Mass Incarceration in the Age of Colorblindness*. New York: New Press, 2012.
Anderson, Benedict. *Imagined Communities: Reflections on the Origins and Spread of Nationalism*. London: Verso, 1983.
Anderson, Kyle. "Shadows in the Night: EW Review." *Entertainment Weekly*. February 6, 2015. https://ew.com/article/2015/02/06/shadows-night-ew-review/.
Atkins, E. Taylor, ed. *Jazz Planet*. Jackson: University Press of Mississippi, 2003.
Auslander, Philip. *Performing Glam Rock: Gender and Theatricality in Popular Music*. Ann Arbor: University of Michigan Press, 2006.
Avant-Mier, Roberto. *Rock the Nation: Latin/o Identities and the Latin Rock Diaspora*. London: Continuum, 2010.
Baker, Sarah, Lauren Istvandity, and Raphäel Novak. *Curating Pop: Exhibiting Popular Music in the Museum*. New York: Bloomsbury, 2019.
Baudrillard, Jean. "The System of Collecting." In *The Cultures of Collecting*, edited by John Elsner and Roger Cardinal, 7–24. Cambridge, MA: Harvard University Press, 1994.
BBC. "What is Radio 2?" https://www.bbc.co.uk/radio2/about/whatis.shtml.
BBC Trust. "BBC Radio 2." https://www.bbc.co.uk/bbctrust/our_work/services/radio/service_licenses/bbc_radio_2.html.
Beaumont-Thomas, Ben. "Madonna *Madame X* Review—Her Most Bizarre Album Ever." *The Guardian*, June 4, 2019. https://www.theguardian.com/music/2019/jun/04/madonna-madame-x-review-her-most-bizarre-album-ever.
Becker, Judith. "Is Western Art Music Superior?" *Musical Quarterly* 72, no. 3 (1986): 341–59.
Benjamin, Walter. "The Work of Art in the Age of Mechanical Reproduction." In *Illuminations*, edited by Hannah Arendt, 217–51. New York: Schocken, 1969 [1936].
Bennett, Andy. "Even Better Than the Real Thing? Understanding the Tribute Band Phenomenon." In *Access All Eras: Tribute Bands and Global Pop Culture*, edited by Shane Homan, 19–31. Maidenhead, UK: Open University Press, 2006.
Bennett, Tony, with Will Friedwald. *The Good Life: The Autobiography of Tony Bennett*. New York: Atria, 1998.

Bialik, Carl. "Is the Conventional Wisdom Correct in Measuring Hip-Hop Audience?" *Wall Street Journal*, May 5, 2005.
Bloom, Allan. *The Closing of the American Mind*. New York: Simon and Schuster, 1987.
Bloom, Harold. *The Anxiety of Influence: A Theory of Poetry*. New York: Oxford University Press, 1973.
Bloustien, Gerry. "Still Picking Children From the Trees? Re-imagining Woodstock in Twenty-first Century Australia." In *Remembering Woodstock*, edited by Andy Bennett, 127–45. Aldershot, UK: Ashgate, 2004.
Borgerson, Janet, and Jonathan Schroeder. *Designed for Hi-Fi Living: The Vinyl LP in Midcentury America*. Cambridge, MA: MIT Press, 2017.
Bowman, Rob. *Soulsville: The Story of Stax Records*. New York: Schirmer, 1997.
Boym, Svetlana. *The Future of Nostalgia*. New York: Basic Books, 2001.
Brackett, David. *Categorizing Sound: Genre and Twentieth-Century Popular Music*. Oakland: University of California Press, 2016.
Bradley, Adam, and Andrew DuBois, eds. *The Anthology of Rap*. New Haven, CT: Yale University Press, 2011.
Brett, Thomas. "Prince's Rhythm Programming: 1980s Music Production and the Esthetics of the LM-1 Drum Machine." *Popular Music and Society* 43, no. 3 (2020): 244–61.
Brofsky, Howard. "Miles Davis and 'My Funny Valentine': The Evolution of a Solo." *Black Music Research Journal* 3 (1983): 23–45.
Brooks, Daphne. *Liner Notes for the Revolution: The Intellectual Life of Black Feminist Sound*. Cambridge, MA: Belknap Press, 2021.
Brooks, Kinitra D., and Kameelah L. Martin, eds. *The Lemonade Reader: Beyoncé, Black Feminism, and Spirituality*. New York: Routledge, 2019.
Brooks, Tim. *Survey of Reissues of U.S. Recordings*. Washington: Council on Library and Information Resources, 2005.
Browne, David. "How Bob Dylan's 'Make You Feel My Love' Became a Modern Standard." *Rolling Stone*, October 28, 2019. https://www.rollingstone.com/music/music-features/bob-dylan-make-you-feel-my-love-covers-903941/.
Burkholder, J. Peter. "Borrowing." In *Grove Music Online*. https://doi-org.proxy2.library.illinois.edu/10.1093/gmo/9781561592630.article.52918.
Caramanica, Jon. "How Do You Capture Four Decades of Hip-Hop? Very Broadly." *New York Times*, August 5, 2021. https://www.nytimes.com/2021/08/05/arts/music/Smithsonian-anthology-hip-hop-rap.html.
Carner, Gary, ed. *The Miles Davis Companion: Four Decades of Commentary*. New York: Schirmer, 1996.
Carr, Ian. *Miles Davis: The Definitive Biography*. New York: Thunder's Mouth Press, 1998.
Carter, Claire. "More Universities Ban 'Blurred Lines' Over Fears It Promotes Rape." *The Telegraph*, November 6, 2013. https://www.telegraph.co.uk/culture/music/10427870/More-universities-ban-Blurred-Lines-over-fears-it-promotes-rape.html.
Cataldo, Jesse. "Review: Bob Dylan, *Shadows in the Night*." *Slant*, February 2, 2015. https://www.slantmagazine.com/music/bob-dylan-shadows-in-the-night/#When:21:26:52Z.
CBS News. *Inside Pop: The Rock Revolution*. April 1967.
CBS Sunday Morning. "A Summer Song." September 22, 2007.
Chambers, Jack. *Milestones 2: The Music and Times of Miles Davis Since 1960*. New York: Beech Tree Books, 1985.

Chang, Jeff. *Can't Stop Won't Stop: A History of the Hip Hop Generation*. New York: Picador, 2004.
Charnas, Dan. *The Big Payback: The History of the Business of Hip-Hop*. New York: New American Library, 2011.
Charry, Eric, ed. *Hip Hop Africa: New African Music in a Globalizing World*. Bloomington: Indiana University Press, 2012.
Chinen, Nate. "Miles Davis, Live at the Apogee." *New York Times*, September 8, 2011.
Chinen, Nate. *Playing Changes: Jazz for the New Century*. New York: Pantheon, 2018.
Churchill, Ward, and Jim Vander Wall. *The COINTELPRO Papers: Documents from the FBI's Secret Wars Against Dissent in the United States*. Boston: South End Press, 1990.
Condry, Ian. *Hip-Hop Japan: Rap and the Paths of Cultural Globalization*. Durham, NC: Duke University Press, 2006.
Connelly, Christopher. "Review of *What's New*." *Rolling Stone*, October 13, 1983. https://www.rollingstone.com/music/music-album-reviews/whats-new-182822.
Coates, Ta-Nehisi. *We Were Eight Years in Power: An American Tragedy*. New York: One World, 2017.
Cook, Richard. *It's About That Time: Miles Davis On and Off Record*. Oxford: Oxford University Press, 2007.
Coolman, Todd. *Miles Davis Quintet of the Mid-1960s: Synthesis of Improvisational and Compositional Elements*. PhD diss., New York University, 1997.
Cosgrove, Stuart. *Young Soul Rebels: A Personal History of Northern Soul*. Edinburgh, UK: Birlinn, 2017.
Crouch, Stanley. "Play the Right Thing." *New Republic*, February 12, 1990.
Cunningham, Philip Lamarr. "'There's Nothing Really New under the Sun': The Fallacy of the Neo-Soul Genre." *Journal of Popular Music Studies* 22, no. 3 (2010): 240–58.
Damrsoch, David. *What Is World Literature?* Princeton, NJ: Princeton University Press, 2003.
Danielsen, Anne. "His Name Was Prince: A Study of Diamonds and Pearls." *Popular Music* 16, no. 3 (1997): 275–91.
Davis, Clive. *The Soundtrack of My Life*. New York: Simon and Schuster, 2013.
Davis, Miles, with Quincy Troupe. *Miles: The Autobiography*. New York: Simon and Schuster, 1991.
Demers, Joanna Teresa. *Sampling as Lineage in Hip Hop*. PhD diss., Princeton University, 2002.
DeMichael, Don. "Review of *Seven Steps to Heaven*" [1963]. In *The Miles Davis Reader*, edited by Frank Alkyer, Ed Enright, and Jason Koransky, 228–29. New York: Hal Leonard, 2007.
Deusner, Stephen M. "Bob Dylan: *Shadows in the Night*." *Pitchfork*, February 3, 2015. https://pitchfork.com/reviews/albums/20190-shadows-in-the-night/.
DeVeaux, Scott. *The Birth of Bebop: A Musical and Social History*. Berkeley: University of California Press, 1997.
Dolgin, Gail, and Vicente Franco. *American Experience: The Summer of Love*. PBS, 2007.
Draper, Robert. *Rolling Stone Magazine: The Uncensored History*. New York: Doubleday, 1990.
Drew, Rob. *Karaoke Nights: An Ethnographic Rhapsody*. Walnut Creek, CA: AltaMira Press, 2001.
Ducker, Eric. "Q&A: Veteran Music Video Director Diane Martel On Her Controversial Videos for Robin Thicke and Miley Cyrus." *Grantland*, June 26, 2013. https://grantland.com/Hollywood-prospectus/qa-veteran-music-video-cirector-diane-martel-on-her-controversial-videos-for-robin-thicke-and-miley-cyrus/.

Duff, De Angela L., Zachary Hoskins, Kamilah Cummins, and Robert Loss. "#1plus1plus1is3: Transcripts from a Virtual Symposium on Iconic Prince Albums." *Journal of Popular Music Studies* 34, no. 2 (2022): 5–27.

Duneier, Mitchell. *Ghetto: The Invention of a Place, The History of an Idea*. New York: FSG, 2016.

Dylan, Bob. *Chronicles Volume One*. New York: Simon and Schuster, 2004.

Dyson, Michael Eric. *Holler If You Hear Me: Searching for Tupac Shakur*. New York: Basic Civitas Books, 2003.

Dyson, Michael Eric. *Jay-Z: Made in America*. New York: St. Martin's Press, 2019.

Echols, Alice. *Hot Stuff: Disco and the Remaking of American Culture*. New York: W.W. Norton, 2010.

Farber, Jim. "Album Review: Bob Dylan's *Shadows in the Night* Features Covers of American Standards." *New York Daily News*, February 2, 2015. https://www.nydailynews.com/entertainment/bob-dylan-songs-sung-frank-sinatra-article-1.2100696.

Farrow, Ronan. "From Aggressive Overtures to Sexual Assault: Harvey Weinstein's Accusers Tell Their Stories." *New Yorker*, October 23, 2017 [originally published online October 10, 2017].

Feather, Leonard. "Miles Smiles." In *The Miles Davis Companion: Four Decades of Commentary*, edited by Gary Carner, 117–47. New York: Schirmer, 1996.

Feld, Steven. "Pygmy POP: A Genealogy of Schizophonic Mimesis." *Yearbook for Traditional Music* 28 (1996): 1–35.

Fink, Robert. *Repeating Ourselves: American Minimal Music as Cultural Practice*. Berkeley: University of California Press, 2005.

Fink, Robert. "The Story of ORCH5, or, The Classical Ghost in the Hip-Hop Machine." *Popular Music* 24, no. 3 (2005): 339–56.

Floyd, Samuel A., Jr. *The Power of Black Music: Interpreting Its History from Africa to the United States*. New York: Oxford University Press, 1995.

Fornatale, Pete. *Back to the Garden: The Story of Woodstock*. New York: Touchstone, 2009.

Forte, Allen. *The Structure of Atonal Music*. New Haven, CT: Yale University Press, 1973.

Forte, Allen. *The American Popular Ballad of the Golden Era, 1924–1950*. Princeton, NJ: Princeton University Press, 1995.

Forte, Allen. *The Atonal Music of Anton Webern*. New Haven, CT: Yale University Press, 1998.

Forte, Allen. *Listening to Classic American Popular Songs*. New Haven, CT: Yale University Press, 2001.

Fricke, Jim, and Charlie Ahearn. *Yes Yes Y'All: The Experience Music Project Oral History of Hip-Hop's First Decade*. Cambridge, MA: Da Capo Press, 2002.

Friedwald, Will. *A Biographical Guide to the Great Jazz and Pop Singers*. New York: Pantheon, 2010.

Friedwald, Will. *The Great Jazz and Pop Vocal Albums*. New York: Pantheon, 2017.

Friedwald, Will. *Sinatra! The Song Is You: A Singer's Art*. New York: Scribner, 1995.

Friedwald, Will. *Stardust Melodies: The Biography of Twelve of America's Most Popular Songs*. New York: Pantheon, 2002.

Fu, Eddie. "For The Record: Rapsody Explains Why She's Not A 'Female MC' & Raps A Lauryn Hill Verse." *Genius*, August 23, 2019. https://genius.com/a/for-the-record-rapsody-explains-why-shes-not-a-female-mc-raps-a-lauryn-hill-verse.

Furia, Philip. *The Poets of Tin Pan Alley: A History of America's Great Lyricists*. New York: Oxford University Press, 1990.

Gardner, Eriq. "'Blurred Lines' Appeal Gets Support From More Than 200 Musicians." *Hollywood Reporter*, August 30, 2016. https://www.hollywoodreporter.com/thr-esq/blurred-lines-appeal-gets-support-924213.
Gates, Henry Louis, Jr. *The Signifying Monkey: A Theory of Afro-American Literary Criticism.* New York: Oxford University Press, 1988.
Geertz, Clifford. "Distinguished Lecture: Anti Anti-Relativism." *American Anthropologist* 86, no. 2 (1984): 263–78.
Gennari, John. *Flavor and Soul: Italian America at Its African American Edge.* Chicago: University of Chicago Press, 2017.
George, Nelson. *The Death of Rhythm and Blues.* New York: Penguin, 1988.
George, Nelson. "Hip-Hop's Founding Fathers Speak the Truth." *The Source*, November 1993.
Gillespie, Dizzy, with Al Fraser, *To Be, or Not . . . To Bop.* New York: Da Capo, 1979.
Gioia, Ted. *The Jazz Standards: A Guide to the Repertoire.* New York: Oxford University Press, 2012.
Goehr, Lydia. *The Imaginary Museum of Musical Works: An Essay in the Philosophy of Music.* New York: Oxford University Press, 1994.
Goldschmitt, K. E. *Bossa Mundo: Brazilian Music in Transnational Media Industries.* New York: Oxford University Press, 2020.
Gore, Tipper. *Raising PG Kids in an X-Rated Society.* Nashville: Parthenon Press, 1987.
Gosa, Travis L., and Erik Nielson, eds. *The Hip-Hop and Obama Reader.* New York: Oxford University Press, 2015.
Greene, Andy. "The Who Announce Dates for 2022 North American Tour." *Rolling Stone*, February 7, 2022. https://www.rollingstone.com/music/music-news/the-who-2022-tour-pete-townshend-interview-1294697/.
Grella, George, Jr. *Bitches Brew.* New York: Bloomsbury, 2015.
Griffin, Farah Jasmine. *If You Can't Be Free, Be a Mystery: In Search of Billie Holiday.* New York: Free Press, 2001.
Haas, Jeffrey. *The Assassination of Fred Hampton: How the FBI and the Chicago Police Murdered a Black Panther.* Chicago: Chicago Review Press, 2011.
Hamilton, Jack. *Just Around Midnight: Rock and Roll and the Racial Imagination.* Cambridge: Harvard University Press, 2016.
Hamm, Charles. *Yesterdays: Popular Song in America.* New York: W.W. Norton, 1979.
Hamill, Pete. *Why Sinatra Matters.* New York: Little, Brown, 1998.
Hancock, Herbie, with Lisa Dickey. *Possibilities.* New York: Viking, 2014.
Hermes, Will. "All Rise for the National Anthem of Hip-Hop." *New York Times*, October 29, 2006.
Hershon, Tad. *Norman Granz: The Man Who Used Jazz for Justice.* Berkeley: University of California Press, 2011.
Heselgrave, Douglas. "Bob Dylan: Shadows in the Night Review." *Paste*, February 3, 2015. https://www.pastemagazine.com/music/bob-dylan/bob-dylan-shadows-in-the-night-review/.
Holt, Fabian. *Genre in Popular Music.* Chicago: University of Chicago Press, 2007.
Hood, Mantle. *The Ethnomusicologist.* New York: McGraw-Hill, 1971.
Horwitz, Tony. *Confederates in the Attic: Dispatches from the Unfinished Civil War.* New York: Vintage, 1999.
Hughes, Charles. *Country Soul: Making Music and Making Race in the American South.* Chapel Hill: University of North Carolina Press, 2015.

Hyman, Dan. "D'Angelo and Bobby Seale on the Past and Future of Political Protest." *New York Times*, June 19, 2015. https://www.nytimes.com/2015/06/21/arts/music/dangelo-and-bobby-seale-on-the-past-and-future-of-political-protest.html.

Iandoli, Kathy. *God Save the Queens: The Essential History of Women in Hip-Hop*. New York: Dey Street, 2019.

Jackson, John. *Real Black: Adventures in Racial Sincerity*. Chicago: University of Chicago Press, 2005.

Jay-Z. *Decoded*. New York: Spiegel and Grau, 2010.

Jones, Feminista. *Reclaiming Our Space: How Black Feminists Are Changing the World from the Tweets to the Streets*. Boston: Beacon Press, 2019.

Jones, Leroi. *Blues People*. New York: William Morrow, 1963.

Kajikawa, Loren. *Sounding Race in Rap Songs*. Berkeley: University of California Press, 2015.

Kaplan, Fred. *1959: The Year Everything Changed*. Hoboken, NJ: Wiley, 2009.

Katz, Mark. *Capturing Sound: How Technology Has Changed Music*. Berkeley: University of California Press, 2004.

Katz, Mark. *Groove Music: The Art and Culture of the Hip-Hop DJ*. New York: Oxford University Press, 2010.

Karja, Antti-Ville. "A Prescribed Alternative Mainstream: Popular Music and Canon Formation." *Popular Music* 25, no. 1 (2006): 3–19.

Keightley, Keir. "Reconsidering Rock." In *The Cambridge Companion to Pop and Rock*, edited by Simon Frith and Will Straw. New York: Cambridge University Press, 2001.

Keightley, Keir. "Taking Popular Music (and Tin Pan Alley and Jazz) Seriously." *Journal of Popular Music Studies* 22, no. 1 (March 2010): 90–97.

Kirshenblatt-Gimblett, Barbara. "Theorizing Heritage." *Ethnomusicology* 39 (1995): 367–80.

Klosterman, Chuck. "Which Rock Star Will Historians of the Future Remember?" *New York Times Magazine*, May 23, 2016. https://www.nytimes.com/2016/05/29/magazine/which-rock-star-will-historians-of-the-future-remember.html.

Kurutz, Steven. *Like a Rolling Stone: The Strange Life of a Tribute Band*. New York: Broadway Books, 2008.

Lavengood, Megan. "What Makes It Sound '80s? The Yamaha DX7 Electric Piano Sound." *Journal of Popular Music Studies* 31, no. 3 (2019): 71–94.

Leo, Katherine M. *Forensic Musicology and the Blurred Lines of Federal Copyright History*. Lanham, MD: Lexington, 2021.

Leonard, Marion. "Constructing Histories Through Material Culture: Popular Music, Museums, and Collecting." *Popular Music History* 2, no. 2 (2007): 147–67.

Lessig, Lawrence. *Free Culture: How Big Media Uses Technology and the Law to Lock Down Culture and Control Creativity*. New York: Penguin, 2004.

Levinson, Peter J. *September in the Rain: The Life of Nelson Riddle*. New York: Billboard, 2001.

Linly, Zack. "Is Today's Hip-Hop Trash or Are We Just Getting Old? Spoiler Alert: The Answer is 'Yes.'" *The Root*, February 1, 2018. https://www.theroot.com/is-today-s-hip-hop-trash-or-are-we-just-getting-old-sp-1822560290.

Lipshutz, Jason. "Opinion: The Problem with the Tupac Hologram." *Billboard*, April 16, 2012. https://www.billboard.com/articles/columns/the-juice/494288/opinion-the-problem-with-the-tupac-hologram.

Litweiler, John. *Ornette Coleman: A Harmolodic Life*. New York: William Morrow, 1992.

Lordi, Emily. *The Meaning of Soul*. Durham, NC: Duke University Press, 2020.

Loss, Robert. *Nothing Has Been Done Before: Seeking the New in 21st Century American Popular Music*. New York: Bloomsbury, 2017.
Lott, Eric. *Love and Theft: Blackface Minstrelsy and the American Working Class*. New York: Oxford University Press, 1993.
Lyotard, Jean-Francois. *The Postmodern Condition: A Report on Knowledge*. Minneapolis: University of Minnesota Press, [1979] 1984.
Mahon, Maureen. *Right to Rock: The Black Rock Coalition and the Cultural Politics of Race*. Durham, NC: Duke University Press, 2004.
Mann, William. "What Songs the Beatles Sang." *London Times*, December 27, 1963.
Marcus, Greil. *Invisible Republic: Bob Dylan's Basement Tapes*. New York: Henry Holt, 1997.
Marcus, Greil. *Like a Rolling Stone: Bob Dylan at the Crossroads*. New York: PublicAffairs, 2005.
Margolick, David. *Strange Fruit: The Biography of a Song*. New York: Ecco, 2001.
Marshall, Wayne. "Giving up Hip-Hop's Firstborn: A Quest for the Real after the Death of Sampling." *Callaloo* 29, no. 3 (Summer 2006): 868–92.
Martin, Linda, and Kerry Segrave. *Anti-Rock: The Opposition to Rock and Roll*. Hamden, CT: Archon Books, 1988.
Maultsby, Portia K. "Funk." In *African American Music: An Introduction*, 2nd ed., edited by Mellonee V. Burnim and Portia K. Maultsby, 301–19. New York: Routledge, 2015.
McClary, Susan. *Conventional Wisdom: The Content of Musical Form*. Berkeley: University of California Press, 2000.
McClary, Susan. *Feminine Endings: Music, Gender, and Sexuality*. Minneapolis: University of Minnesota Press, 1993.
McLeod, Kembrew, and Peter DiCola. *Creative License: The Law and Culture of Digital Sampling*. Durham, NC: Duke University Press, 2011.
McMullen, Tracy. *Haunthenticity: Musical Replay and the Fear of the Real*. Middletown, CT: Wesleyan University Press, 2019.
Meizel, Katherine. *Idolized: Music, Media, and Identity in American Idol*. Bloomington: Indiana University Press, 2011.
Melis, Matt. "Album Review: Bob Dylan—*Shadows in the Night*." *Consequence of Sound*, February 13, 2015. https://consequenceofsound.net/2015/02/album-review-bob-dylan-shadows-in-the-night/.
Mellard, Jason. *Progressive Country: How the 1970s Transformed the Texan in Popular Culture*. Austin: University of Texas Press, 2014.
Mercer, Michell. *Footprints: The Life and Work of Wayne Shorter*. New York: Penguin, 2004.
Merriam, Alan. *The Anthropology of Music*. Evanston, IL: Northwestern University Press, 1964.
Meyers, John Paul. "The World According to Marsalis: Difference and Sameness in Wynton Marsalis's *From the Plantation to the Penitentiary*." *Journal of Popular Music Studies* 22 (2010): 416–35.
Miller, James. *Flowers in the Dustbin: The Rise of Rock 'n' Roll, 1947–1977*. New York: Simon and Schuster, 1999.
Mitchell, Tony, ed. *Global Noise: Rap and Hip-Hop Outside the USA*. Middletown, CT: Wesleyan University Press, 2002.
Moore, Allan. *Sgt. Pepper's Lonely Hearts Club Band*. Cambridge: Cambridge University Press, 1995.
Morrison, Matthew D. "Race, Blacksound, and the (Re)Making of Musicological Discourse." *Journal of the American Musicological Association* 72, no. 3 (2019): 781–823.

Muller, Carol. "American Musical Surrogacy: A View from Post–World War II South Africa." *Safundi: The Journal of South African and American Comparative Studies* 7, no. 3 (2006): 1–18.

Muller, Carol, and Sathima Bea Benjamin. *Musical Echoes: South African Women Thinking in Jazz*. Durham, NC: Duke University Press, 2011.

Murray, Charles. *Losing Ground: American Social Policy, 1950–1980*. New York: Basic Books, 1984.

Nama, Adilfu. *I Wonder U: How Prince Went Beyond Race and Back*. New Brunswick, NJ: Rutgers University Press, 2020.

Nattress, Katrina. "U2 and the Rolling Stones Are the Decade's Top Touring Artists." *iHeart*, November 26, 2019. https://www.iheart.com/content/2019-11-26-u2-and-the-rolling-stones-are-the-decades-top-touring-artists/.

Neal, Mark Anthony. *Black Ephemera: The Crisis and Challenge of the Musical Archive*. New York: New York University Press, 2022.

Nelson, Willie, with Bud Shrake. *Willie: An Autobiography*. New York: Simon and Schuster, 1988.

Nelson, Willie, with David Ritz. *It's a Long Story: My Life*. New York: Little, Brown, 2015.

Nettl, Bruno. *The Study of Ethnomusicology: Thirty-Three Discussions*. Urbana: University of Illinois Press, 2015.

Nicholson, Stuart. *Ella Fitzgerald: A Biography of the First Lady of Jazz*. New York: Scribner, 1994.

Nisenson, Eric. *The Making of Kind of Blue: Miles Davis and His Masterpiece*. New York: St. Martin's, 2000.

Nora, Pierre. "Between Memory and History: Les Lieux de Mémoire." *Representations* 26 (Spring 1989): 7–24.

Oinonen, Janne. "Bob Dylan—*Shadows in the Night*." *The Line of Best Fit*, February 10, 2015. https://www.thelineofbestfit.com/reviews/albums/bob-dylan-shadows-in-the-night.

Ogren, Kathy. *The Jazz Revolution*. New York: Oxford University Press, 1992.

Olay, Lionel. "Miles Davis: Winner Take All" [1964]. In *Miles on Miles: Interviews and Encounters with Miles Davis*, edited by Paul Maher Jr. and Michael K. Dorr, 21–34. Chicago: Lawrence Hill Books, 2009.

O'Meally, Robert G., ed. *The Jazz Cadence of American Culture*. New York: Columbia University Press, 1998.

O'Meally, Robert G., Brent Hayes Edwards, and Farah Jasmine Griffin, eds. *Uptown Conversation: The New Jazz Studies*. New York: Columbia University Press, 2004.

Parker, Maceo. *98% Funky Stuff: My Life in Music*. Chicago: Chicago Review Press, 2016.

Patteson, Thomas. *Instruments for New Music: Sound, Technology, and Modernism*. Berkeley: University of California Press, 2015.

Pearce, Sheldon. "Jay-Z, 4:44" [review]. *Pitchfork*, July 5, 2017. www.pitchfork.com/reviews/albums/jay-z-444.

Petridis, Alex. "Bob Dylan's *Shadows in the Night* review—An Unalloyed Pleasure." *The Guardian*, January 29, 2015. https://www.theguardian.com/music/2015/jan/29/bob-dylan-shadows-in-the-night-review.

Plasketes, George. "Pimp My Records: The Deluxe Dilemma and Edition Condition: Bonus, Betrayal, or Download Backlash?" *Popular Music and Society* 31, no. 3 (2008): 389–93.

Pond, Steven F. *Head Hunters: The Making of Jazz's First Platinum Album*. Ann Arbor: University of Michigan Press, 2005.

Porter, Eric. "'It's About That Time': The Response to Miles Davis's Electric Turn." In *Miles Davis and American Culture*, edited by Gerald Early, 130–46. St. Louis: Missouri Historical Society Press, 2001.
Powers, Devon. *Writing the Record: The Village Voice and the Birth of Rock Criticism*. Amherst: University of Massachusetts Press, 2013.
Prince. *The Beautiful Ones*. Edited by Dan Piepenbring. New York: Spiegel and Grau, 2019.
Prouty, Ken. "Plagiarizing Your Own Autobiography, and Other Strange Tales: Miles Davis, Jazz Discourse, and the Aesthetics of Silence." *Jazz Research Journal* 4, no. 1 (2010): 15–41.
Questlove with Ben Greenman. *Mo' Meta Blues: The World According to Questlove*. New York: Grand Central Publishing, 2013.
Ramsey, Guthrie. *Race Music: Black Cultures from Bebop to Hip-Hop*. Berkeley: University of California Press, 2003.
Reid, Jan. *The Improbable Rise of Redneck Rock*. Austin: University of Texas Press, 2004.
Reiff, Corbin. "There's Nothing Standard About Bob Dylan's Latest." *A/V Club*, February 3, 2015. https://music.avclub.com/there-s-nothing-standard-about-bob-dylan-s-latest-1798182598.
Reynolds, Simon. *Retromania: Pop Culture's Addiction to Its Own Past*. New York: Faber and Faber, 2011.
Rice, Timothy. "Towards a Remodeling of Ethnomusicology." *Ethnomusicology* 31, no. 3 (1987): 469–88.
Robinson, Chris. "Media Review." *Jazz Perspectives* 8, no. 3 (2014): 321–26.
Robinson, Zandria F. "After Stax: Race, Sound, and Neighborhood Revitalization." In *An Unseen Light: Black Struggles for Freedom in Memphis, Tennessee*, edited by Aram Goudsouzian and Charles W. McKinney Jr. Lexington: University Press of Kentucky, 2018.
Romano, Tricia. "'Blurred Lines,' Robin Thicke's Summer Anthem, Is Kind of Rapey." *Daily Beast*, June 17, 2013. https://www.thedailybeast.com/blurred-lines-robin-thickes-summer-anthem-is-kind-of-rapey.
Ronstadt, Linda. *Simple Dreams: A Musical Memoir*. New York: Simon and Schuster, 2013.
Rorem, Ned. *Knowing When to Stop*. New York: Simon and Schuster, 1994.
Rorem, Ned. "The Music of the Beatles." *New York Review of Books*, January 18, 1968.
Rose, Tricia. *Black Noise: Rap Music and Black Culture in Contemporary America*. Middletown, CT: Wesleyan University Press, 1994.
Rose, Tricia. "Never Trust a Big Butt and a Smile." *Camera Obscura* 8, no. 2 (23) (1990): 108–31.
Rosen, Jody. "Questlove on Working with Elvis Costello, Miley's Twerking, and His Lunchtime D.J. Sets." *Vulture*, September 18, 2013. https://www.vulture.com/2013/09/questlove-on-his-new-album-with-elvis-costello.html.
Ross, Alex. *Listen to This*. New York: Picador, 2011.
Sanneh, Kelefa. *Major Labels: A History of Popular Music in Seven Genres*. New York: Penguin, 2021.
Sampson, Issy. "Hug Life: Has Rap's 'Baby' Obsession Reached Its Peak?" *The Guardian*, September 28, 2019. https://www.theguardian.com/music/2019/sep/28/rap-hip-hop-dababy-lil-uzi-vert-baby-soulja-lil-kim-bow-wow.
Shapiro, Ben. "Shapiro RIPS Obscene Feminist Music Video." *The Ben Shapiro Show*, December 12, 2018. https://www.youtube.com/watch?v=f4U3JIbqhkg.
Schloss, Joseph. *Foundation: B-boys, B-girls, and Hip-Hop Culture in New York*. New York: Oxford University Press, 2009.

Schloss, Joseph. *Making Beats: The Art of Sample-Based Hip-Hop*. Middletown, CT: Wesleyan University Press, 2004.

Seixas, Peter, ed. *Theorizing Historical Consciousness*. Toronto: University of Toronto Press, 2004.

Serpick, Evan. "Prince Promotes Peace at Baltimore Show: 'The System is Broken.'" *Rolling Stone*, May 11, 2015. https://www.rollingstone.com/music/music-live-reviews/prince-promotes-peace-at-baltimore-show-the-system-is-broken-188895/.

Sewell, Amanda. "*Paul's Boutique* and *Fear of a Black Planet*: Digital Sampling and Musical Style in Hip Hop." *Journal of the Society for American Music* 8, no. 1 (2014): 28–48.

Shabazz, Jamel. *A Time Before Crack*. New York: Powerhouse Books, 2005.

Shelemay, Kay. *Let Jasmine Rain Down: Song and Remembrance Among Syrian Jews*. Chicago: University of Chicago Press, 1998.

Shuker, Roy. *Understanding Popular Music Culture*. New York: Routledge, 2016.

Simmone, Michael. "Bob Dylan—Shadows in the Night." *MOJO*, February 6, 2015. https://www.mojo4music.com/articles/18828/bob-dylan-shadows-night.

Simpson, Kay. *Early '70s Radio: The American Format Revolution*. New York: Continuum, 2011.

Sloan, Nate. "When Rock Meets the Great American Songbook in the 21st Century." Paper presented at the Conference of the American Musicological Society, November 12, 2021.

Smith, Jeremy A. "'Sell It Black': Race and Marketing in Miles Davis's Early Fusion Jazz." *Jazz Perspectives* 4, no. 1 (2010): 7–33.

Smith, Jeremy A. *Sound, Mediation, and Meaning in Miles Davis's* A Tribute to Jack Johnson. PhD diss., Duke University, 2008.

Smith, Steve. "Bob Dylan: Shadows in the Night." *Boston Globe*, February 3, 2015.

Solis, Gabriel. *Monk's Music: Thelonious Monk and Jazz History in the Making*. Berkeley: University of California Press, 2007.

Spanos, Brittany. "Janelle Monáe Frees Herself." *Rolling Stone*, April 26, 2018. https://www.rollingstone.com/music/music-features/Janelle-monae-frees-herself-629204/.

Steingo, Gavin. *Kwaito's Promise: Music and the Aesthetics of Freedom in South Africa*. Chicago: University of Chicago Press, 2016.

Sterne, Jonathan. *MP3: The Meaning of a Format*. Durham, NC: Duke University Press, 2012.

Stimeling, Travis. *Cosmic Cowboys and New Hicks: The Countercultural Sounds of Austin's Progressive Country Music Scene*. New York: Oxford University Press, 2011.

Stoever, Jennifer Lynn. "Crate Digging Begins at Home: Black and Latinx Women Collecting and Selecting Records in the 1960s and 1970s Bronx." In *The Oxford Handbook of Hip Hop Music*, edited by Justin D. Burton and Jason Lee Oakes. New York: Oxford University Press, 2018.

Strausbaugh, John. *Rock Til You Drop: The Decline from Rebellion to Nostalgia*. New York: Verso, 2001.

Straw, Will. "Sizing Up Record Collections: Gender and Connoisseurship in Rock Music Culture." In *Sexing the Groove: Popular Music and Gender*, edited by Sheila Whiteley, 3–16. New York: Routledge, 1997.

Streissguth, Michael. *Outlaw: Waylon, Willie, Kris, and the Renegades of Nashville*. New York: It Books, 2013.

Sublette, Ned, and Constance Sublette. *The American Slave Coast: A History of the Slave-Breeding Industry*. Chicago: Lawrence Hill Books, 2016.

Sullivan, James. "Nas Introduces Harvard Fellowship." *Rolling Stone*, October 31, 2013. www.rollingstone.com/music/music-news/nas-introduces-harvard-fellowship-60396/.

Svorinich, Victor. *Listen to This: Miles Davis and Bitches Brew*. Jackson: University Press of Mississippi, 2015.

Symes, Colin. *Setting the Record Straight: A Material History of Classical Music Recording*. Middletown, CT: Wesleyan University Press, 2004.

Szwed, John. *Billie Holiday: The Musician and the Myth*. New York: Viking, 2015.

Szwed, John. *So What: The Life of Miles Davis*. New York: Simon and Schuster, 2002.

Taruskin, Richard. "On Letting the Music Speak for Itself: Some Reflections on Musicology and Performance." *Journal of Musicology* 1, no. 3 (1982): 338–49.

Taruskin, Richard. *Text and Act: Essays on Music and Performance*. New York: Oxford University Press, 1995.

Tate, Greg. *Flyboy in the Buttermilk: Essays on Contemporary America*. New York: Simon and Schuster, 1992.

Taylor, Arthur. "'I Don't Have to Hold the Audience's Hand'" [1977]. In *The Miles Davis Companion: Four Decades of Commentary*, edited by Gary Carner, 103–11. New York: Schirmer, 1996.

Taylor, Astra. *The People's Platform: Taking Back Power and Culture in the Digital Age*. New York: Metropolitan Books, 2014.

Taylor, Timothy. *Global Pop: World Music, World Markets*. New York: Routledge, 1997.

Thompson, Richard. *1000 Years of Popular Music*. New York: Cooking Vinyl Records, 2003.

Tillet, Salamishah. "Strange Sampling: Nina Simone and Her Hip-Hop Children." *American Quarterly* 66, no. 1 (2014): 119–37.

Tinsley, Omise'eke Natasha. *Beyoncé in Formation: Remixing Black Feminism*. Austin: University of Texas Press, 2018.

Tomlinson, Gary. "Cultural Dialogics and Jazz: A White Historian Signifies." *Black Music Research Journal* 11, no. 2 (Autumn 1991): 229–64.

Toop, David. *Rap Attack 3: African Rap to Global Hip Hop*. London: Serpent's Tail, 2000.

Touré. *I Would Die 4 U: Why Prince Became an Icon*. Atria: New York, 2013.

Travis, Dempsey J. *Norman Granz: The White Moses of Black Jazz*. Chicago: Urban Research Press, 2003.

Troupe, Quincy. *Miles and Me*. Berkeley: University of California Press, 2000.

Trouillot, Michel-Rolph. *Silencing the Past*. Boston: Beacon Press, 1995.

"2013 Pazz & Jop Critics' Poll." *Village Voice*, January 15, 2014. https://www.villagevoice.com/2014/01/15/the-village-voices-2013-pazz-jop-critics-poll/.

Valnes, Matthew. "Janelle Monáe and Afro-Sonic Feminist Funk." *Journal of Popular Music Studies* 27, no. 3 (2017).

Valnes, Matthew. "Taking It Higher: The Spirituality of Sensuality in Funk Performance." *African and Black Diaspora: An International Journal* 9 (2016): 3–15.

Vincent, Rickey. *Funk: The Music, The People, and The Rhythm of the One*. New York: St. Martin's, 1996.

Wald, Elijah. *Escaping the Delta: Robert Johnson and the Invention of the Blues*. New York: HarperCollins, 2004.

Wald, Elijah. *How the Beatles Destroyed Rock 'n' Roll: An Alternative History of American Popular Music*. New York: Oxford University Press, 2009.

Walker, Michael. *Laurel Canyon: The Inside Story of Rock-and-Roll's Legendary Neighborhood*. New York: Faber and Faber, 2006.

Walser, Robert. "Out of Notes: Signification, Interpretation, and the Problem of Miles Davis." *Musical Quarterly* 77, no. 2 (Summer 1993): 343–65.

Walser, Robert. "Prince as Queer Post-Structuralist." *Popular Music and Society* 18, no. 2 (1994): 79–89.

Waters, Keith. *The Studio Recordings of the Miles Davis Quintet, 1965–1968*. Oxford: Oxford University Press, 2011.

Waxer, Lise. *The City of Musical Memory: Salsa, Record Grooves, and Popular Culture in Cali, Colombia*. Middletown, CT: Wesleyan University Press, 2002.

Weiner, Natalie. *The 1959 Project*. the1959project.com, 2019.

Welch, Will. "Pharrell on Evolving Masculinity and 'Spiritual Warfare.'" *GQ*, October 14, 2019. https://www.gq.com/story/pharrell-new-masculinity-cover-interview.

Wells, Christi Jay [formerly Christopher Jay Wells]. "'A Dreadful Bit of Silliness': Feminine Frivolity and Ella Fitzgerald's Early Career Critical Reception." *Women and Music: A Journal of Gender and Culture* 21 (2017): 43–65.

Wenner, Jann. *Lennon Remembers*. London: Verso, [1971] 2000.

Wesley, Fred. *Hit Me, Fred! Recollections of a Sideman*. Durham, NC: Duke University Press, 2002.

Wheeler, Jesse Samba. "'*Toca Raul!*' Praise Singers on Brazil's Central Plateau." In *Access All Eras: Tribute Bands and Global Pop Culture*, edited by Shane Homan, 198–212. Maidenhead, UK: Open University Press, 2006.

White, Hayden. *Metahistory: The Historical Imagination in the Nineteenth Century*. Baltimore: Johns Hopkins University Press, 1973.

White, Miles. *From Jim Crow to Jay-Z: Race, Rap, and the Performance of Masculinity*. Urbana: University of Illinois Press, 2011.

Wilder, Alec. *American Popular Song: The Great Innovators, 1900–1950*. New York: Oxford University Press, 1972.

Wilkerson, Isabel. *The Warmth of Other Suns: The Epic Story of America's Great Migration*. New York: Vintage, 2011.

Williams, Alan. "'Pay Some Attention to the Man Behind the Curtain'—Unsung Heroes and the Canonization of Process in the *Classic Albums* Documentary Series." *Journal of Popular Music Studies* 22, no. 2 (2010): 166–79.

Williams, Justin. "Intertextuality, Sampling, and Copyright." In *The Cambridge Companion to Hip-Hop*, edited by Justin Williams, 206–20. Cambridge: Cambridge University Press, 2015.

Williams, Martin. "Jazz: Some Old Favorites Are Back." *New York Times*, January 18, 1970.

Wilson, William Julius. *The Declining Significance of Race: Blacks and Changing American Institutions*, 3rd ed. Chicago: University of Chicago Press, 2012.

Wilson, William Julius. *The Truly Disadvantaged: The Inner City, the Underclass, and Public Policy*. Chicago: University of Chicago Press, 1987.

Wilson, William Julius. *When Work Disappears: The World of the New Urban Poor*. Chicago: University of Chicago Press, 1996.

Winfield, Betty Houchin. "Because of the Children: Decades of Attempted Controls of Rock 'n' Rap Music." In *Bleep! Censoring Rock and Rap Music*, edited by Betty Houchin Winfield and Sandra Davidson, 9–20. Westport, CT: Greenwood Press, 1999.

Woods, Clyde. *Development Arrested: The Blues and Plantation Power in the Mississippi Delta*. London: Verso, 1998.

Woodworth, Griffin. "Just Another One of God's Gifts: Prince, African-American Masculinity, and the Sonic Legacy of the Eighties." PhD diss., University of California, Los Angeles, 2008.

Woodworth, Griffin. "Prince, Miles, and Maceo: Horns, Masculinity, and the Anxiety of Influence." *Black Music Research Journal* 33, no. 2 (2013): 117–50.

Woodworth, Griffin. "'Rapping Done Let Us Down': Prince's Hip-Hop Ambivalence." *Popular Music and Society* 43, no. 3 (2020): 281–300.

Yagoda, Ben. *The B-Side: The Death of Tin Pan Alley and the Rebirth of the Great American Song.* New York: Riverhead, 2015.

Yudkin, Jeremy. *Miles Smiles: Miles Davis and the Invention of Post-Bop.* Bloomington: Indiana University Press, 2008.

Zak, Albin. *I Don't Sound Like Nobody: Remaking Music in 1950s America.* Ann Arbor: University of Michigan Press, 2010.

Žižek, Slavoj. *First as Tragedy, Then as Farce.* London: Verso, 2009.

INDEX

"1000 Deaths" (D'Angelo), 174
24K Magic (Mars), 177
4:44 (Jay-Z), 4, 189n6
45 King, 122
9th Wonder, 181

Abbey Road (Beatles), 22, 23, 37, 44, 45
Abbey Road on the River, 37, 38, 39, 194n20
Academy Awards. *See* Oscar Awards
activism, 20
"Adam's Apple" (Shorter), 106
Adderley, Cannonball, 95, 174
Adele, 80
"Afeni" (Rapsody), 180
Afrofuturism, 128, 165, 167, 168
Afropresentism, 167, 168, 178
"Agitation" (Davis), 106
Ahad-Legardy, Badia, 87
"Ain't No Love in the Heart of the City" (Bland), 143
"All Blues" (Davis), 98
"All of Me" (Nelson), 69
"All of You" (Davis), 107, 109
All Platinum Records, 125
All Seeing Eye, The (Shorter), 102
"All You Need is Love" (Beatles), 183
"Amen, Brother" (Winstons), 128
American Classic (Nelson), 72
American Popular Ballad of the Golden Era (Forte), 53
American Popular Song (Wilder), 52
"Americans" (Monáe), 170
Anchors Aweigh (film), 95

Andrews Sisters, 81
Annie (musical), 122
anniversaries, 30–31, 36–38, 46
Anthology (Beatles), 26
Anthology (documentary), 26
Anthology of Rap (book), 141
anti-music, 104, 105, 108
"Apache" (Incredible Bongo Band), 118, 121
Apollo Theater, 57, 162
ARC Gospel Choir, 132
ArchAndroid, The (Monáe), 165
Arista Records, 27
Armstrong, Louis, 56, 57, 64, 65, 74, 86
arrangements, 69, 72, 76, 77, 79, 81, 82, 84, 94–96, 103, 104, 107, 108, 110, 111, 114, 115, 145, 153–57, 159, 160, 164–66, 168, 170, 176
art music, 15
Ashford & Simpson, 130
Asylum Records, 76
Atlantic Records, 68, 75
audiences, 43, 54, 102, 103, 107, 114, 150, 151, 154, 155; Black, 41, 113, 115, 202n12; middle-aged, 18, 45, 64, 69, 70, 72, 73, 74, 76, 83, 84, 125, 195–96n2; middle-class, 18, 19, 45, 64, 67, 69, 70, 72, 92; white, 58, 59, 64, 67, 68, 113, 115; young, 18, 25, 74, 91, 92, 113, 120, 125, 142, 152, 202n12
aura, 53
Australian Pink Floyd Show, 35
authenticity, 14, 24, 38, 59, 81, 83, 119, 151
Autry, Gene, 71
"Autumn Leaves" (Davis), 107, 109, 114
"Autumn Leaves" (Dylan), 81

Average White Band, 139
Ayler, Albert, 102

Babe Ruth (band), 118
baby boomer generation, 5, 7, 16, 25, 26, 33, 40, 42, 67, 73, 91, 141, 184
"Baby Won't You Please Come Home," 96
"Baby You're a Rich Man" (Beatles), 182–85
Badu, Erykah, 86, 167, 171, 173, 186
Baker, Anita, 86
Baker, Chet, 95, 100
"Baltimore" (Prince), 164–65
Bambaataa, Afrika, 121, 122, 134, 140
Basement Tapes, The (Dylan), 79
"Basin Street Blues," 96
Baudrillard, Jean, 33
b-boys and b-girls, 120–23
Beatles, 21, 22, 23, 26, 30, 34, 35, 38–41, 44, 47, 66, 76, 91, 117, 125, 182–86; first appearance on The Ed Sullivan Show, 21, 22, 23, 34, 36, 40, 42, 67, 117; reception of, 22
Beatles, The (album), 22. See White Album, The
Beats, the (Beatles tribute band), 36, 38, 39
Beaumont-Thomas, Ben, 50
Beautiful Ones, The (Prince), 153
"Beautiful Ones, The" (Prince), 161
bebop, 98
Beck, Joe, 109
Benjamin, Walter, 53
Bennett, Andy, 43–46
Bennett, Tony, 52, 69, 100
Benson, George, 109
Berlin, Irving, 55, 62, 66
Berry, Chuck, 40
Best, Pete, 39, 40
"Between the Sheets" (Isley Brothers), 128, 133
Beyoncé, 86, 149, 155, 165, 177, 178, 186
Bieber, Justin, 161
Big Bank Hank, 124, 125
"Big Poppa" (Notorious B.I.G.), 128, 133, 134
Billboard, 63, 67, 73, 78, 85, 129, 146, 153, 165
Biographical Guide to the Great Jazz and Pop Singers, A (Friedwald), 52
Birth of the Cool (Davis), 90

Bitches Brew (Davis), 90, 92, 94, 110, 113
"Bitches Brew" (Davis), 111
Björn Again, 36
Blacc, Aloe, 147
Black Beauty: Miles Davis at Fillmore West, 112
Black capitalism, 98
Black Coffee (Lee), 75
Black Lives Matter, 20, 163–67, 174–78
Black Messiah (D'Angelo), 173–76
Black Messiah, The (Adderley), 174
Black Moses (Hayes), 173
Black Music Research Journal, 99
Black Panther Party, 174, 175, 177, 178, 180
Blackbyrds, 139
Blackness, 18, 58, 86, 87, 120, 154, 179, 192n38, 201n8
Blakey, Art, 93
Bland, Bobby "Blue," 143
Bland, Sandra, 164, 166, 167
Blige, Mary J., 86
Blonde on Blonde (Dylan), 79
Blood on the Tracks (Dylan), 79, 199n59
Bloom, Harold, 45, 46
Blue Magic, 139
"Blue 'n' Boogie" (Gillespie), 93
Blue Note Records, 101, 102
"Blue Skies" (Nelson), 69
Blueprint, The (Jay-Z), 129
blues, 7, 74, 81, 84, 94, 190n14
Blumenthal, Bob, 114
"Blurred Lines" (Thicke), 145–49
"Bongo Rock" (Incredible Bongo Band), 118
Boone, Pat, 59
bootleg cassettes, 124
Borgerson, Janet, 64
Bossa Nova, 198n41
Boston Marathon bombing, 142, 143
box sets, 10, 27, 30, 31, 33, 47, 66, 86, 94, 101, 105, 109, 114, 157, 203n34
Boym, Svetlana, 11
Brandy, 86
Braxton, Toni, 86
breaks, 117, 205n2
Bregman, Buddy, 62, 63
BritBeat (Beatles tribute band), 36
British invasion, 67

Brofsky, Howard, 99
Bronx, 117, 118, 122, 123
Brooks, Daphne, 47
Brooks, Garth, 80
Brown Sugar (D'Angelo), 171–72
"Brown Sugar" (D'Angelo), 172
Brown, Clifford, 89
Brown, James, 91, 94, 128, 139, 153–56, 158–62, 165–66
Brown, Michael, 164, 175
Brubeck, Dave, 91
Bublé, Michael, 72
Buchanan, Charlie, 57
Buenos Aires, 14, 16, 34, 38
Burkholder, J. Peter, 5, 6
Butler, Frank, 96
Byrd, Bobby, 127, 128

Cahn, Sammy, 95
Campbell, Cindy, 30, 118
Campbell, Clive. *See* Kool Herc
Canada, Geoffrey, 137
canonization, 14, 15, 25, 58–62, 66, 67, 70, 71, 79, 120, 129, 130, 133, 183, 192n41, 195n40; of hip-hop, 47, 189n6, 191n23; of jazz, 192n35; of rock music, 184, 214n9
Can't Slow Down (Richie), 78
capitalism, 50, 51, 184
Capitol Records, 63
Caramanica, Jon, 47
Carey, Mariah, 86
Carter, Ron, 95, 96, 101–5, 109
censorship, 152
Chambers, Jack, 105, 106
Chambers, Paul, 95
Chang, Jeff, 120
"Charade, The" (D'Angelo), 176
Charles, Ray, 129
Chase, Charlie, 122, 124
Chauvin, Derek, 164
Chet Baker Sings (Baker), 95
Chic, 139
"Children Get Together" (Hawkins), 132
Christgau, Robert, 25
Christianity, 131, 132, 163, 174
Christmas in the Heart (Dylan), 81
Christy, June, 74

Chronic, The (Dre), 128
Chronicles Volume One (Dylan), 80
Chuck D, 47, 162
"Circle" (Davis), 105
civil rights movement, 20, 40, 65, 135, 138, 152–55, 162, 164, 165, 167, 173–76, 179, 180
Civil War reenactors, 46
Clapton, Eric, 40
Clark, Kenneth, 137
classic (idea of), 44
classic rock, 15, 23, 28, 83, 184–86; radio, 25; and rock imperialism, 32
"Cleo" (Rapsody), 181
Cleveland, James, 132
Cline, Patsy, 68
Clinton, George, 128, 153. *See also* Funkadelic; Parliament-Funkadelic
Closing of the American Mind, The (Bloom), 45
Coates, Ta-Nehisi, 163
Cobb, Jimmy, 95
COINTELPRO, 174
Cold Crush Brothers, 122, 124
"Cold Sweat" (Brown), 156
Coldplay, 177
Coleman, George, 101
Coleman, Ornette, 92
collecting, 33
College Dropout, The (West), 129, 130
Collins, Bootsy, 177
Coltrane, John, 44, 89, 95
Columbia Records, 27, 68, 69, 74, 76, 78, 80, 91, 96, 97, 105, 107, 113
commercialism, 58, 93
commodity fetishism, 33
Commodores, 139
Common, 163
"Common Man" (Ruffin), 129
competition TV shows, 3, 145
Con Funk Shun, 139
Connelly, Christopher, 78–79
Connor, Chris, 74
Cook, Richard, 91
Cooke, Sam, 171
Cookin' (Davis), 96
Copeland, Misty, 161, 162
copyright, 5, 98, 146–50, 190n10

Corea, Chick, 109–12
country music, 68, 71, 73
Country Music Hall of Fame and Museum, 30
crack cocaine, 136, 181
"Crazy" (Nelson), 68
"Crazy Blues" (Smith), 48
"Crazy Classic Life" (Monáe), 169
Crosby, Stills, and Nash, 73
Crouch, Stanley, 92–93, 102, 109, 110, 113
Crudup, Arthur "Big Boy," 118
Cullors, Patrisse, 164
cultural relativism, 45, 46
culture of poverty, 137
Cunningham, Phillip Lamarr, 171
Curatolo, Joey, 22

Daft Punk, 119
Daily Beast, The, 146
Damrosch, David, 44
"Dance or Die" (Monáe), 166
"Dancing Machine" (Jackson 5), 139
D'Angelo, 19, 119, 149, 155, 171–76, 178, 181, 182
Dark Ghetto (Clark), 137
Dark Side of the Moon (Pink Floyd), 44
Dark Star Orchestra (Grateful Dead), 35, 36
Davis, Clive, 27, 33, 84
Davis, Miles, 17–19, 49, 56, 65, 69, 90–115, 119, 125, 185; criticism of, 92–93
Day, Morris and the Time, 160, 177
"Day in the Life, A" (Beatles), 35
Decca Records, 62, 66
Declining Significance of Race, The (Wilson), 135
Decoded (Jay-Z), 138–40, 143
deindustrialization, 135, 136
DeJohnette, Jack, 110, 112
Demers, Joanna, 119
DeMichael, Don, 96
Deusner, Stephen M., 82
DiCola, Peter, 149
"Different Drum" (Stone Poneys), 73
"Directions" (Zawinul), 110, 111, 113
Dirty Computer (Monáe), 168–71
disco, 125, 145, 146
DJs, 117, 118, 120, 122–24, 130, 149, 150, 154

"Dolores" (Shorter), 105
Doors, 34, 35, 91, 113
doo-wop, 126
DownBeat, 58, 60, 96
Dr. Dre, 123, 128
Draper, Robert, 40
drum machines, 121, 127, 130, 153, 154, 160
Duneier, Mitchell, 136
Dylan, Bob, 17, 26, 40, 50, 71, 76, 77, 79–85, 185, 186, 199n59

Eagles, 7
Earth, Wind & Fire, 130, 147, 154, 159, 162
Eisenberg, Jesse, 182, 185
Electric Lady, The (Monáe), 165, 168
electric pianos, 153, 172. *See also* Fender Rhodes
electronic keyboards, 160. *See also* synthesizers
Ellen DeGeneres Show, The, 145
Ellington, Duke, 44, 57, 63, 75, 86
emotional expression, 76, 78, 80, 83, 84
Emotions, 139
"Enjoy Yourself" (Jackson 5), 139
Eric B and Rakim, 127, 128
E.S.P. (Davis), 101, 106
Esquire, 63
Estefan, Gloria, 50
Etcetera (Shorter), 102
ethnomusicology, engagements with the past, 28–29
Evans, Bill, 95
Evans, Dale, 71
Evans, Elle, 146
Evans, Gil, 91
Eve (Rapsody), 179–82, 186
Evening with Silk Sonic, An (Mars and .Paak), 177
"Everlasting Now, The" (Prince), 156, 157
Evers, Medgar, assassination of, 174, 180
Evers, Myrlie, 180

Facebook, 182, 184, 185
Fallen Angels (Dylan), 81
family, 74, 119, 137–41, 181
"Family Name" (Prince), 156
Farber, Jim, 83

Feather, Leonard, 93
feedback loop, 97
Feldman, Victor, 96
"Felon Brun" (Davis), 109
Fender Rhodes, 109, 145, 147, 153
Ferry, Bryan, 50
Filles de Kilimanjaro (Davis), 109
Fillmore East and Fillmore West, 112–14
film music, 182–85
Fincher, David, 184
Fink, Robert, 64, 121
Fitzgerald, Ella, 17, 18, 49, 56–67, 74, 76, 86, 185
Flowers in the Dustbin: The Rise of Rock and Roll, 1947–1997 (Miller), 32
"Fly Me to the Moon" (Nelson), 72
Fly Me to the Moon (Stewart), 85
"Foggy Day, A" (Nelson), 72
folk music, 73, 81
"Footprints" (Shorter), 105, 111
For Sentimental Reasons (Ronstadt), 77–79
For You (Prince), 152, 154
Forensic Musicology and the Blurred Lines of Federal Copyright History, 146
"Formation" (Beyoncé), 177
Forte, Allen, 53
Foundation (Schloss), 120
Four Tops, 139
Foxx, Jamie, 130
Franklin, Aretha, 78, 129, 171
free jazz, 105
"Freedom Jazz Dance" (Harris), 96, 105
freedom songs, 167
Friedwald, Will, 52
funk, 91, 94, 118–20, 123, 125–28, 138, 142, 152, 153, 154, 158, 165, 166, 185, 186
Funkadelic, 127–28. *See also* Clinton, George; Parliament-Funkadelic
Furia, Philip, 52
fusion, 18, 69, 92, 94, 97, 102, 109, 110, 113–15; criticism of, 92, 93
Future of Nostalgia, The (Boym), 11

Gabler, Milt, 62, 64
Gap Band, 177
Gardner, Eric, 164
Garfunkel, Art, 50, 77
Garnier, Tony, 82

Garza, Alicia, 164
Gates, Henry Louis, Jr., 98, 100, 111, 114, 115, 119, 133, 134
Gaye, Marvin, 44, 146, 147, 172
Geffen, David, 76
gender, 58, 93
genius, 5, 6, 27, 39, 40, 137
Genius (website), 133, 175
gentrification, 191n25
George, Nelson, 156
"Georgia on My Mind" (Nelson), 69, 71
Gershwin, George, 56, 61–63, 65, 66, 69, 72, 78
Gershwin, Ira, 63, 65, 66, 69, 72, 78
Get Back (documentary), 30
"Get Up, Get Into It, Get Involved" (Brown), 156
"Get Up Offa That Thing" (Brown), 156
"Gett Off" (Prince), 152
G-funk, 128
"Ghetto Woman" (Monáe), 166
Gibson, Mel, 158–59
Gillespie, Dizzy, 90, 93
"Gingerbread Boy" (Heath), 105, 106, 108
Girl at Her Volcano (Jones), 79
girl singers, 58, 73
"Giving 'Em What They Love" (Monáe), 168
"God Is" (Cleveland), 132, 133
"God Is" (West), 132, 133
Goehr, Lydia, 123
Goldberg, Whoopi, 181
Golden age, 1960s and 1970s as, 179
"Golden Slumbers" / "Carry That Weight" / "The End" (Beatles), 23
Goldstein, Richard, 25
Good as I Been to You (Dylan), 81
"Good Times" (Chic), 125, 140
Gordy, Berry, 129
Gore, Tipper, 152, 153
Gormé, Eydie, 79
gospel, 132
"Got to Give It Up" (Gaye), 146–48
GQ, 146
Graham, Larry, 153, 156, 161
Graham Central Station, 161
Grammy Awards, 3, 31, 63, 71, 78, 80, 161, 177, 198n40

Grandmaster Caz, 124
Grandmaster Flash, 121, 140
Grandmixer D.ST, 121, 134
Granz, Norman, 59–67, 75
Grateful Dead, 35, 36, 44, 112
Gray, Freddie, 164
Great American Songbook, 17, 18, 48–85, 94, 95, 126–27, 141, 151, 185; bias in, 86–87; formal characteristics, 55–56, 62; genre crossing, 68–85; lyrical subjects, 56; resistance to, 78; sources of, 53. *See also* standards; Tin Pan Alley
Great American Songbook, The (McCrae), 68
Great Jazz and Pop Vocal Albums, The (Friedwald), 52
Great Migration, 137
Green, Al, 86, 130, 162
Green, Cee-Lo, 161
Greenwich Village, 81
Grella, George, 94
"Groovin'" (Mitchell), 181
Grossman, Steve, 112
Guardian, The, 50
Guthrie, Woody, 81
GZA, 181

Hal Leonard (publisher), 52
Haley, Bill, 64
Hamill, Pete, 199n59
Hamilton, Jack, 201n8
Hamm, Charles, 55, 67
Hammond, John, 58–60
hampton, dream, 139
Hampton, Fred, 174
Hancock, Herbie, 92, 95, 100–105, 109, 181, 202n12, 214n5
"Hard Knock Life" (Jay-Z), 122
Hargrove, Roy, 172
Harlem, 57
Harlem Cultural Festival, 41, 42
Harris, Eddie, 105
Harrison, George, 40, 43, 184
Hartman, Johnny, 95, 100
Hathaway, Donny, 160
"Hatsheput" (Rapsody), 181
Haunthenticity (McMullen), 11
Hawkins, Edwin, 132

Hayes, Isaac, 130, 139, 173, 211n36
Haynes, Roy, 102
Head Hunters (Hancock), 181
Healing Hands of Time (Nelson), 72
Heart Like a Wheel (Ronstadt), 73
"Heart of the City" (Jay-Z), 143
Heath, Jimmy, 96, 105, 106
Heatwave, 139
Hefner, Hugh, 65
"Hell You Talmbout" (Monáe), 166, 167
Hendrix, Jimi, 41, 42, 86, 91, 94, 112, 113, 201n8
"Here" (Prince), 160
heritage, 9, 30
Herron, Donnie, 82
Hershorn, Tad, 62, 63
Heselgrave, Douglas, 83
heteropatriarchy, 148, 154
hierarchies in popular music, 6, 51, 58
High Fidelity (magazine), 63
hip-hop, 87, 117–44, 150, 152, 154, 162, 179–82, 185, 186; canonization of, 15, 28, 141; masculinity in, 4; older musicians, 4; younger musicians, 4, 5; youth, 3–5
hippies, 113. *See also* rednecks and hippies
historical consciousness, 8–10, 13, 14, 15, 24, 25–34, 36, 38, 44, 46, 53, 55, 62, 63, 66, 68, 80, 85, 120, 141, 151, 154, 155, 158, 159, 171, 178, 183, 186; among Black Americans, 19; criticism of, 10; in hip-hop, 10, 47, 123; in jazz, 89, 90, 101; 187; in Prince, 152; in the future, 179
historical narratives, production of, 9, 22, 23, 31, 40–43, 46, 47, 52, 53, 66, 74, 82, 83, 86, 121, 155, 160–62, 171
Holiday, Billie, 56, 65, 66, 74, 75, 86, 89, 92, 180
Holland, Dave, 109
Holly, Buddy, 78
Hollywood, 71
Honeycomb, 139
"Hot Pants" (Brown), 159
"House Is Not a Home, A" (Bacharach and David), 130
Houston, Whitney, 86
"How High the Moon" (Hamilton and Lewis), 98
"How Much a Dollar Cost?" (Lamar), 163
Hudson, Jennifer, 147

Index

"Hustle, The" (McCoy), 139
Hyman, Dan, 175

"i" (Lamar), 163
"I Fall in Love Too Easily" (Styne and Cahn), 17, 18, 94–97, 100–105
"I Got the Juice" (Monáe), 169
"I Know You Got Soul" (Byrd), 127
"I Know You Got Soul" (Eric B and Rakim), 127
"I Love Kanye" (West), 131, 132
"I Loves You, Porgy" (Gershwin), 65
"I Need a Beat" (LL Cool J), 127
"I Thought About You" (Davis), 107, 109
"Ibithaj" (Rapsody), 181
ideology of newness, 3–8, 11, 14, 18, 19, 24, 26, 31, 51, 52, 70, 79, 90, 117, 118, 143, 151, 154, 186
"If I Were a Bell" (Davis), 107, 109, 114
impersonators, 10
importance of hip-hop in the 1970s, 119; mythology, 19, 20, 135–37, 139, 140
importance of rock music in the 1960s, 25
improvisation, 96, 97, 99, 107, 110
In a Silent Way (Davis), 90, 94, 109, 110, 112, 113
Incredible Bongo Band, 118, 121
influence, across racial lines, 148–50
innovation, 18, 90, 91, 117, 147, 150
inspiration, 147–50
instrumentation, 153–57, 159, 160, 164–66, 168, 170, 176, 182
intellectual property, 150. *See also* copyright
Isle of Wight, 113
Isley, Ronald, 163
Isley Brothers, 128, 130, 133, 134, 163
It Had to Be You (Stewart), 85
"It Only Takes a Minute" (Tavares), 139
"It's About That Time" (Davis), 111
"It's Just Begun" (Jimmy Castor Bunch), 118, 121
"Izzo (H.O.V.A.)" (Jay-Z), 129

J Records, 84
Jackson, Freddie, 130
Jackson, Janet, 86
Jackson, Michael, 78, 86

Jackson, Peter, 30
Jackson 5, 129, 139
Jacob, Gary, 37
Jagger, Mick, 7, 40, 74, 75
Jam Master Jay, 162
Jam Session (Verve), 75
James, Mark. *See* 45 King
Jarrett, Keith, 112
Jay-Z, 4, 122, 129, 131, 138–43, 148, 153, 174, 189n6
jazz, 32, 49, 56, 84, 89–115, 119, 127, 151; arrangement, 100; canonization of, 93; creation of, 56–57; formal structure of, 92–96, 100–105, 107, 108, 110, 111, 114, 115, 185
Jazz at the Philharmonic, 60, 61, 75
JBs, 158
Jehovah's Witnesses, Prince's membership in, 153, 155, 157, 158
Jesus Is King (West), 132
"Jesus Walks" (West), 132
Jimmy Castor Bunch, 118, 121, 154
Jodeci, 130
Joel, Billy, 80
Jones, Booker T., 69, 72
Jones, Quincy, 72
Jones, Ricki Lee, 79
Jones, Sharon, 161, 162
Joplin, Janis, 40, 78

Kajikawa, Loren, 127–28
karaoke, 10
Kashmir (Led Zeppelin tribute), 35
Katz, Mark, 54, 97, 121, 126
Keightley, Keir, 26, 92
Kelly, Wynton, 95
Kennedy, John F., assassination of, 40
Kern, Jerome, 56, 62
Keys, Alicia, 86
Khan, Chaka, 129, 162
Kids See Ghosts (West and Cudi), 132
Kind of Blue (Davis), 90, 102
King, Martin Luther, Jr., assassination of, 41, 135, 174, 180
King, Coretta Scott, 180
King, Evelyn "Champagne," 130, 139
Kirshenblatt-Gimblett, Barbara, 9, 30

"Kiss" (Prince), 152, 168
Knight, Gladys, 130
Kool Herc, 31, 117, 118, 120–22, 140
Kraftwerk, 121, 122
Kurutz, Steven, 35
kwaito, 207n33

Lacan, Jacques, 11, 13
Lady in Satin (Holiday), 75
Lamar, Kendrick, 119, 149, 163, 175, 186
Lanois, Daniel, 176
Larkins, Ellis, 61
Late Registration (West), 129, 131
Latifah, Queen, 50, 181
Latin America, 17
Lauper, Cyndi, 50
Led Zeppelin, 66, 141, 186
Led Zeppelin II (album), 44
Lee, Peggy, 74, 75
Legend, John, 171
Lennon, John, 25, 26, 39, 40, 43, 183, 184
Lennox, Annie, 50
Leo, Katherine M., 146
Let It Be (Beatles), 36
Let Jasmine Rain Down (Shelemay), 29
"Let Me Ride" (Dre), 128
"Let's Go Crazy" (Prince), 170
"Let's Groove" (Earth, Wind & Fire), 159
"Let's Stay Together" (Green), 162
Levinson, Peter J., 75
Lewis, Oscar, 137
Liberty Records, 68
Lil Wayne, 148
Linton, Charles, 57
"Liquid Swords" (GZA), 181
Listening to Classic American Popular Song (Forte), 53
"Little Bird Told Me, A" (Fitzgerald), 60
live performance, 16, 176
live performances, compared to recordings, 54, 55, 126, 127
live recordings, 94, 97, 101, 102, 105, 106, 109, 110, 112, 114, 157, 203n34
LL Cool J, 127
Lloyd, Charles, 102
Lordi, Emily J., 167, 178
Lost Quintet, 109–12, 114

"Love and Kisses" (Webb), 58
Love and Theft (Dylan), 79–81, 84
"Love Rollercoaster" (Ohio Players), 158
Love Unlimited Orchestra, 139
Lovebug Starski, 124
"Love's Theme" (Love Unlimited Orchestra), 139
LP format, 60–64, 67, 68, 74, 75, 91, 138, 139, 141, 197n35, 207n33
Lush Life (Ronstadt), 77–79
Lyotard, Jean François, 46

Mabry, Betty, 112
Macero, Teo, 91
Madame X (Madonna), 50
"Mademoiselle Mabry" (Davis), 109
Madonna, 50
Magical Mystery Tour (Beatles), 183
Maher, James T., 52
Maiden Voyage (Hancock), 101
Main Ingredient, 139
"Make Me Feel" (Monáe), 168
"Make You Feel My Love" (Dylan), 80
Mancini, Henry, 63
manipulability, 132
Marcus, Greil, 79
Mars, Bruno, 149, 155, 163, 177, 178, 186
Martin, Dean, 69, 82
Martin, Linda, 67
Martin, Trayvon, 163
masculinity, 154
"Masqualero" (Shorter), 106
mass incarceration, 136
Massenburg, Kedar, 171
masterpiece (idea), 44
Mayfield, Curtis, 129, 131, 139
Maze, 130
M'Bengue, Jessi, 146
McCartney, Paul, 7, 25, 26, 40, 50, 77, 184
McClary, Susan, 185
McCoy, Van, 139
McDaniels, Darryl, 181
McKnight, Brian, 86
McLaughlin, John, 109
McLeod, Kembrew, 149
McMullen, Tracy, 11, 13, 16
McPhee, Katharine, 147

Index

McRae, Carmen, 68
Meaning of Soul, The (Lordi), 167
Meeropol, Abel, 65, 180
Melis, Matt, 84
Mercury, Freddie, 43
Metahistory (White), 29
"Metal on Metal" (Kraftwerk), 122
#MeToo movement, 146
"Mexican, The" (Babe Ruth), 118
Mexico City, 14, 16, 34
MFSB, 139
middle-class status, 44. *See also* audiences: middle-class
Miguel, 165
"Miles Runs the Voodoo Down" (Davis), 111
Miles Smiles (Davis), 90, 105, 106
"Milestones" (Davis), 98, 102, 110, 111
Millennial generation, 180, 182, 185, 186
Miller, Glenn, 1944 concert reenactment, 12
Miller, James, 32
Miller, Mitch, 76
Miller, Steve, 112
Mingus, Charles, 98
Minneapolis, 151, 160, 161, 164, 170
Mint Condition, 160, 161
Mitchell, Joni, 73, 78
Mitchell, Willie, 181
Mo' Meta Blues (Questlove), 138
Modern Times (Dylan), 81, 84
modernism, 12, 13, 98. *See also* ideology of newness; progress
MOJO, 83
Monáe, Janelle, 8, 19, 119, 149, 155, 160–62, 165–71, 173, 177, 178, 186
Monk, Thelonious, 13, 29, 93, 96, 98, 105, 106
Moran, Jason, 12
Moreira, Airto, 112
Morrison, Jim, 26, 35, 43
"Mothership Connection (Starchild)" (Parliament), 128
Motown, 91, 129
"Move on Up" (Mayfield), 131
Moynihan, Daniel Patrick, 137
MPLSoUND (Prince), 160
"Mr. Paganini" (Fitzgerald), 60
MTV Video Music Awards, 152

"Murder to Excellence" (West and Jay-Z), 174
Murray, Charles, 137
Museum of Pop Culture, 30, 86
museums, 10, 20, 25, 26, 30, 86
music criticism, 25
Music of My Mind (Wonder), 138
music videos, 146
Musical Box (Genesis tribute), 12, 35
musical surrogacy, 24, 33, 34
musical works, 14, 124, 207n26
Musicology (Prince), 158–59
"Musicology" (Prince), 158, 159, 162
"My Funny Valentine" (Davis), 99, 100, 102, 107
"My Generation" (Who), 5
My Way (Nelson), 50, 72
"My Wubba Dolly" (Fitzgerald), 59

Nacogdoches (Nelson), 72
Nas, 132
National Book Critics Circle Award, 80
Navarro, Fats, 89
Nefertiti (Davis), 105
Negro Family, The (Moynihan report), 137
Nelson, Willie, 17, 50, 68–72, 77, 78, 82, 185
neo-soul, 171, 173
"Never Change" (Jay-Z), 129
Never Mind the Bollocks (Sex Pistols), 32
New York Times, 175
New Yorker, 63
Newport Jazz Festival, 60, 105
Nicholson, Stuart, 57–60
"Nina" (Rapsody), 180
Nine Inch Nails, 184
Nisenson, Eric, 90
"No Blues" (Davis), 107, 110, 111
No I.D., 4
"No Mistakes" (West), 132
Nobel Prize, 89
Nora, Pierre, 30, 32
North, Alex, 71
nostalgia, 7, 11, 18, 19, 51, 67, 79, 84–87, 89, 140, 181
Notes and Tones (Taylor), 102
Notorious B.I.G., 133, 181, 186
"Numbers" (Kraftwerk), 121
"Nuthin' But a 'G' Thang" (Dre), 128

Index

N.W.A, 128
Nyro, Laura, 112

Oakland, 175
Oates, John, 147
Obama, Barack, 162, 163
"Oh Happy Day" (Hawkins), 132
Ohio Players, 139, 158
Oinonen, Janne, 85
O'Jays, 139
OK Computer (Radiohead), 80
"Ol' Skool Company" (Prince), 212n42
Olay, Lionel, 102
"Old Mother Hubbard" (Fitzgerald), 60
"On Green Dolphin Street" (Davis), 107
On the Corner (Davis), 90, 92
"On the Sunny Side of the Street" (Nelson), 69
One Nite Alone . . . Live! (Prince), 157–59
"Orbits" (Shorter), 105, 106
originality, 5, 6. *See also* ideology of newness
"Ornithology" (Parker), 98
Oscar Awards, 80, 184
"Otis" (West and Jay-Z), 131
outlaw country, 68–70, 74

.Paak, Anderson, 177
Paisley Park vault, 155
Palladino, Pino, 172
Parents Music Resource Center, 152, 153
Parker, Charlie, 89, 98
Parker, Maceo, 153, 158, 159, 161
Parliament, 128. *See also* Clinton, George; Funkadelic; Parliament-Funkadelic
Parliament-Funkadelic, 158, 172
Parry, Jeff, 45
"Pass the Peas" (JBs), 158
"Pastures of Plenty" (Guthrie), 81
patriarchy, 70, 84, 119, 152
Paul, Billy, 139
Pazz and Jop Poll, 80, 145
Pendergrass, Teddy, 130
performance venues: auditoriums and arenas, 71, 73, 75, 76, 81, 159, 160; ballrooms and dancehalls, 60–61, 64; baseball stadiums, 71; dance clubs, 118, 124, 125, 136; festivals, 60–61, 71; formal auditoriums, 60–61, 100, 101, 107, 115; parks, 118; rock clubs, 94, 112–14; small clubs, 60–61, 94, 172, 176; Super Bowl, 177–78
Peter Gunn (Mancini), 63
Peterson, Oscar, 62
Petridis, Alex, 50, 51, 84
Phases and Stages (Nelson), 68
"Pick up the Pieces" (Average White Band), 139
Pines of Rome (Respighi), 150
Pink Floyd, 44, 66, 186
Pirates of Penzance, The (Gilbert and Sullivan), 73
Pitchfork, 82
Pizzarelli, Bucky, 109
"Planet Rock" (Bambaataa), 121, 122
Plant, Robert, 78
Playboy's Penthouse (TV show), 65
Plugged Nickel, 102–5, 107, 114
Poets of Tin Pan Alley (Furia), 52
politics of respectability, 163
popular music: African American roots of, 8; conservative critiques of, 8; seriousness in, 26–28; spread across distance and time, 14, 33, 42, 119, 127, 182; television, 3, 145; youth, 3, 10
Porgy and Bess (Davis), 90
Porgy and Bess (Gershwin), 65, 75
portability, 127
Porter, Cole, 62, 63, 66
Porter, Eric, 94
postmodernism, 12, 46, 47; and tribute bands, 43
Presley, Elvis, 32, 47, 64, 74, 117, 118
Prestige Records, 96
Prince, 19, 130, 149, 151–65, 168, 170, 171, 173, 177, 178; attitude towards hip-hop, 210n23; dispute with Warner Bros., 152; Rally 4 Peace concert, 164–65; sexualized performances, 152, 153, 154
Prince (Prince), 154
"Prince, Miles, and Maceo: Horns, Masculinity and the Anxiety of Influence," 154

progress, 98, 190n14
progressive ideology, 12. *See also* ideology of newness
Prouty, Ken, 201n8
Pulitzer Prize, 80
Purple Rain (album), 152, 170
Purple Rain (film), 152, 170
"Purple Rain" (song), 152, 157, 158
Pusha T, 132

"Q.U.E.E.N." (Monáe), 166
Questlove, 31, 42, 138, 143, 147, 148, 172

Ra, Sun, 102
radio, 54, 57
Radio 2 (radio station), 50
Radiohead, 80
ragtime, 56
Rain (Beatles tribute band), 21, 22, 23, 24, 35, 36
Rainbow Children, The (Prince), 155–58
Ramsey, Guthrie, 16, 184
R&B, 15, 16, 87, 94, 119, 123, 145, 146, 180; canon of, 4. *See also* funk; soul
Raphael, Mickey, 69
"Rapper's Delight" (Sugar Hill Gang), 118, 124–27, 140, 162
Rapsody, 179–82, 186
"Raspberry Beret" (Prince), 152
Ratajkowski, Emily, 146
Rave Un2 the Joy Fantastic (Prince), 162
RCA Victor, 68
Read Dead Redemption 2 (video game), 176
Reagan, Ronald, 135–37
Real, 11
Recording Industry Association of America, 33
Redding, Otis, 131
Red-Headed Stranger (Nelson), 68
rednecks and hippies, 68–70, 72. *See also* hippies
Reiff, Corbin, 84
reissues, 10, 20, 25, 30, 33, 34, 66, 71, 86, 101
Relaxin' (Davis), 96
repeatability, 54, 55, 97, 98, 126, 127
respectability, 12
Respighi, Ottorino, 150

Retromania (Reynolds), 10, 30
"Revolution Number 9" (Beatles), 37
Reynolds, Simon, 10–13, 16, 30, 46, 98
Reznor, Trent, 184
Richard, Keith, 7, 74
Richie, Lionel, 78, 86
Riddle, Nelson, 50, 63, 64, 76, 77, 79, 82
Rihanna, 86, 165
"Riot" (Hancock), 106, 108
Robinson, Smokey, 130, 171
Robinson, Sylvia, 124, 125
Roc-a-Fella Records, 140
Rock and Roll Hall of Fame and Museum, 26, 30
"Rock and Roll Music" (Berry), 40
rock music, 7, 15, 17, 26, 27, 47, 64, 73, 74, 84, 91, 94, 117, 158; canonization, 92; historical consciousness in, 10; youth, 5
Rodgers, Richard, 56
Rogers, Roy, 71
Rolling Stone (magazine), 25, 30, 40, 41, 78, 79, 183
Romano, Tricia, 146
Ronson, Mark, 177
Ronstadt, Linda, 17, 50, 66, 73–79, 141
Roots, 138, 147, 148
Rorem, Ned, 92
Ross, Alex, 98
Ross, Atticus, 184
'Round About Midnight (Davis), 96
"'Round Midnight" (Monk), 93, 96, 102, 106, 107, 110, 111
Royce, Rose, 139
Ruffin, David, 129
Rufus, 139
Run-DMC, 127, 162, 181
Russo, Joe, 34

Sade, 86
salsa, 29, 122
sampling, 4, 16, 19, 20, 119–23, 126–34, 136, 139, 143, 144, 148–51, 162, 179–82, 185
"Sanctuary" (Davis), 111, 112
"Satisfaction" (Rolling Stones), 7
Savoy Ballroom, 57, 58
"Say It Loud (I'm Black and I'm Proud)" (Brown), 156

Schloss, Joseph, 120, 121
Schroeder, Jonathan, 64
Scott, Jill, 171
Scott-Heron, Gil, 129
Seal, 50
Seale, Bobby, 175, 176
Second Great Quintet, 95, 97, 100–110; attitude towards Plugged Nickel performances, 104
Segrave, Kerry, 67
Seixas, Peter, 29
"September" (Earth, Wind & Fire), 159
seriousness, 57, 66, 79, 92
Set It Off (film), 181
Seven Steps to Heaven (Davis), 95, 96
Sex Pistols, 32, 47
sexism, 146, 148, 152
Sgt. Pepper's Lonely Hearts Club Band (Beatles), 22, 35, 36, 41, 45, 183
Shabazz, Betty, 180
Shadows in the Night (Dylan), 81
Shakur, Afeni, 180
Shakur, Tupac, 10, 180
Shapiro, Ben, 8, 186
Shavers, Charlie, 75
sheet music, 54
Shelemay, Kay, 29
Shepp, Archie, 105
Shorter, Wayne, 91, 95, 100–105
Shouts (Beatles tribute band), 36
Shuker, Roy, 6, 7
signifyin(g), 17, 98–101, 111, 114, 115, 119, 133, 134
Simmons, Michael, 83
Simon, Carly, 50
Simon, Paul, 26
Simone, Nina, 65, 66, 180
Simple Dreams (Ronstadt), 73
Sinatra, Frank, 50, 52, 56, 63, 69, 72, 76, 81–83, 95, 115, 199n59
"Sing a Simple Song" (Sly and the Family Stone), 158
Sister Act (film), 181, 186
sites of memory, 30, 32
Sketches of Spain (Davis), 90
Slave, 139
"Slippery When Wet" (Commodores), 139

"Slow Jamz" (West), 129, 130
Sly and the Family Stone, 91, 94, 113, 127, 138, 153–56, 158–60, 162, 172
Smith, Bessie, 57, 74
Smith, Jeremy A., 94, 113
Smith, Lonnie Liston, 127, 128
Smith, Mamie, 48
Smith, Ralston, 164
Smith, Steve, 85
"So What" (Davis), 98
Social Network, The (film), 182–85
Soft Parade (Doors tribute band), 34
Solis, Gabriel, 29
Someday My Prince Will Come (Davis), 91
"Someone to Watch Over Me" (Gershwin), 69, 75
Somewhere Over the Rainbow (Nelson), 72
"Song for You, A" (Hathaway), 160
Sons of the Pioneers, 71
Soothsayer, The (Shorter), 102
Sorcerer (Davis), 105
soul, 118–23, 126–31 138, 142, 171, 174, 185, 186. *See also* funk; R&B
Soul Train (TV show), 139
Spalding, Esperanza, 161
"Spanish Key" (Davis), 111
Spinners, 130
spirituals, 128
Spring (Williams), 102
standards, 17–19, 49, 50, 95–98. *See also* Great American Songbook; Tin Pan Alley
Staple Singers, 139, 152, 165
Staples, Mavis, 162
Stardust (Nelson), 50, 68–72, 74, 78
"Stardust" (Nelson), 69
Stardust Melodies (Friedwald), 52
Starr, Ringo, 39, 40, 184
Staton, Candi, 139
Stax Records, 69, 131
Steamin' (Davis), 96
"Stella by Starlight" (Davis), 109
Stetsasonic, 127
Stewart, Rod, 50, 77; comparison to Bob Dylan, 84–85
Stitt, Sonny, 93
Stone, Angie, 171
Stone Poneys, 73

Stone the Crows, 112
"Straight, No Chaser" (Monk), 93
"Straight Outta Compton" (N.W.A), 128
"Strange Fruit" (Meeropol), 65, 180
Strausbaugh, John, 7, 74
Stylistics, 139
Styne, Jule, 95
"Sucker M.C.'s" (Run-DMC), 127
Sugar Hill Gang, 118, 124, 125, 140, 162
Summer of Soul (Questlove), 42
Summertime: Willie Nelson Sings Gershwin (Nelson), 72
Sun Kings (Beatles tribute), 35
Sun Records, 117
Superfly (Mayfield), 139
Svorinich, Victor, 94
Sweat, Keith, 130
"Swing Low Sweet Chariot," 128
Sylvers, 139
synthesizers, 154

"Talkin' All That Jazz" (Stetsasonic), 128
Taste of Honey, 139
Tate, Greg, 93, 94, 115
Tavares, 139
Taylor, Arthur, 102
Taylor, James, 50, 71, 73, 77
Taylor, Teyana, 132
"Tell Me Something Good" (Rufus), 139
Tempest (Dylan), 81
Temptations, 129
Terry, Clark, 93, 113
"That Lady" (Isley Brothers), 163
"That's Alright Mama" (Crudup), 118
That's Life (Nelson), 50, 72
"Theme, The" (Davis), 103, 107
Theorizing Historical Consciousness (Seixas), 29
There's a Riot Goin' On (Sly and the Family Stone), 138
Thicke, Robin, 145-49
"Things Done Changed" (Notorious B.I.G.), 181
"Things Have Changed" (Dylan), 80
Thompson, Ahmir. *See* Questlove
Thompson, Chucky, 128, 134
Thompson, Tessa, 169

Thriller (Jackson), 78
T.I., 145, 146, 148
Tidal, 153
"Tightrope" (Monáe), 165-66
Time Out of Mind (Dylan), 79-81
Tin Pan Alley, 55, 71, 98
Together Through Life (Dylan), 81
Tometi, Opal, 164
Tomlinson, Gary, 93, 94, 113, 115
Tommy (Who), 37
Tonight Show with Jay Leno, 158-59
Toop, David, 125, 126
"Touch the Sky" (West), 131
Tower of Power, 154
Townshend, Pete, 40
Trans-Europe Express (Kraftwerk), 122
"Trans-Europe Express" (Kraftwerk), 121, 122
tribute bands, 5, 6, 11-14, 16, 17, 20, 21-48, 49, 66, 141, 151, 158, 184
Triplicate (Dylan), 81
Trouillot, Michel-Rolph, 9, 46
Troupe, Quincy, 201n8
Truly Disadvantaged, The (Wilson), 135
Trump, Donald, 168
"Try a Little Tenderness" (Redding), 131
Tsarnaevs, Johar and Tamerlan, 142, 143
"TSOP (The Sound of Philadelphia)" (MFSB), 139
Tutu (Davis), 90
Twitter, 175

"Unchained Melody" (Nelson), 71
"Undisputed" (Prince), 162
"Uptown Funk" (Ronson and Mars), 177
Usher, 86

Vandross, Luther, 130
Vaughan, Sarah, 86, 105
Verve Records, 60, 62, 65, 74, 76
Vietnam War, 41
Village Voice, 25, 80, 145
Vincent, Rickey, 156
vintage instruments, 22, 24, 172
Voice, The (TV show), 145
Voodoo (D'Angelo), 172, 175

Wald, Elijah, 3
"Walk With Me" (ARC Gospel Choir), 132

Walkin' (Davis), 90
"Walkin'" (Davis), 107
"Walking in Rhythm" (Blackbyrds), 139
Walser, Robert, 100
War on Drugs, 136
Warner Bros., 152, 155
Warwick, Dionne, 130
Watch the Throne (West and Jay-Z), 131
"Watermelon Man" (Hancock), 181, 214n5
Waters, Roger, 7
Waxer, Lise, 29
"We Shall Not Be Moved," 167
"We Shall Overcome," 167
Webb, Chick, 57, 59, 66
Webster, Ben, 75
Wein, George, 60
Weinstein, Harvey, 146
Welcome 2 America tour, 160–64
Wells, Christi Jay, 57–58
Wenner, Jann, 25, 40
Wesley, Fred, 156
West, Kanye, 129–33, 143, 148, 174
Western classical music, 5, 6, 15, 24, 44, 53, 98, 150; compared to jazz, 91, 92; compared to rock, 25, 26, 45, 91, 92
Wexler, Jerry, 68, 69, 75
What a Wonderful World (Nelson), 72
What Happened, Miss Simone? (documentary), 65
What's New (Ronstadt), 75–79
"What's New" (Songbook standard), 75
"When I Fall in Love" (Davis), 109
"When Will We Be Paid?" (Staple Singers), 152, 153, 165
When Work Disappears (Wilson), 135
Whispers, 130
White, Hayden, 29
White Album, The (Beatles), 22, 36, 37, 41, 183
Whiteman, Paul, 59
whiteness, 15, 16, 17, 18, 27, 42, 58, 83, 84, 86, 87, 120, 142, 192n38, 201n8
Who, 5, 7, 37, 113
"Whoopi" (Rapsody), 181
WhoSampled, 133
Wikipedia, 175
Wilder, Alec, 52
Williams, Hank, 74

Williams, Pharrell, 19, 119, 145–49, 169
Williams, Tony, 95, 101–5
Williams, Vanessa, 86
Willis, Ellen, 25
Wilson, Darren, 164, 175
Wilson, William Julius, 135, 137
Without a Song (Nelson), 72
Wonder, Stevie, 78, 86, 138, 162, 163, 168, 171
Wonder Boys (film), 80
Woodstock, 41, 42, 86, 112, 113
Woodworth, Griffin, 154
"Work, Pt. 1, The" (Prince), 155–56
Workin' (Davis), 96
World Gone Wrong (Dylan), 81
Wright, Jaguar, 171
Wu-Tang Clan, 181, 186

X, Malcolm, 122; assassination of, 135, 174, 180

Yagoda, Ben, 53, 95
ye (West), 132
"You'll Like It Too" (Funkadelic), 127
Young, Neil, 112
Young Jeezy, 175
Young Thug, 175
Your Hit Parade (radio show), 54
You're Under Arrest (Davis), 90
youth, 70, 73, 118, 143, 186
YouTube, 164, 177

Zapp, 177
Zaret, Hy, 71
Zawinul, Joe, 109
Zimmerman, George, 163
Žižek, Slavoj, 11
Zuckerberg, Mark, 182, 184, 185, 186

ABOUT THE AUTHOR

John Paul Meyers is assistant professor of African American Studies at the University of Illinois at Urbana-Champaign. He won the Richard Waterman Prize from the Popular Music Section of the Society for Ethnomusicology and the Lincoln Excellence for Assistant Professors award from the University of Illinois. His work has been published in journals including *Ethnomusicology*, *Ethnomusicology Forum*, *Journal of Popular Music Studies*, *Jazz Perspectives*, and *CLA Journal*.

www.ingramcontent.com/pod-product-compliance
Lightning Source LLC
Chambersburg PA
CBHW022005220426
43663CB00007B/969